COAL
IN AMERICA

AN ENCYCLOPEDIA OF
RESERVES, PRODUCTION
☆ ☆ ☆ AND USE ☆ ☆ ☆

COAL IN AMERICA

AN ENCYCLOPEDIA OF RESERVES, PRODUCTION ☆ ☆ ☆ AND USE ☆ ☆ ☆

by Richard A. Schmidt

Published by COAL WEEK
McGraw-Hill Publications Company

BOOK DESIGN: Richard P. Kluga
EDITING: Alice S. Goehring, Earle Resnick
PRODUCTION: William Baker, Kathy Kopf
GENERAL MANAGER: Morrie Helitzer
PUBLISHER: George P. Lutjen
COMPOSITION: DMS Information Processing Systems, West Point, Pa.

COAL IN AMERICA:
An Encyclopedia of Reserves, Production and Use

1234567890WCWC7865432109

Library of Congress Cataloging in Publication Data

Schmidt, Richard A.
    Coal in America.

    Includes index.
    1. Coal—United States.   I.   Title.
TN805.A5S35   333.8'2   78-11372
ISBN 07-606576-6

Acknowledgements

This book originated in a series of lectures prepared as part of a course at Stanford University on the geology of energy, at the invitation of Dr. Kenneth Crandall and Professors Frederick Kruger and Evan Just. Their continued interest, advice, and support, especially that of Evan Just who also reviewed an early draft of the manuscript and offered many helpful suggestions that materially improved the final text, is gratefully acknowledged.

A participant in the first lecture series at Stanford was Mike Morrison of McGraw-Hill's *Coal Week,* who was kind enough to look over a rough version of the manuscript and call it to the attention of Morrie Helitzer of the McGraw-Hill Publications Company. Since I had not attempted a book before, the experience and know-how that Morrie Helitzer patiently provided were invaluable.

The manuscript was edited with painstaking care by Mrs. Alice Goehring, a lady of good humor and charm whose logical mind and attention to detail are highly admired.

Preface

Coal deposits of the United States are receiving much attention as the nation seeks solutions to its energy dilemma. Coal has been part of the American scene for so long that it has been largely taken for granted. Yet, although simple in concept, coal development is actually quite complex in detail. Furthermore, while much is known about coal, a great deal remains to be learned about the nature of this substance and how to use it in an efficient and effective manner. In many respects, essential data are incomplete or lacking entirely.

Major research programs are searching for answers to the pressing questions influencing potentials for coal use. Still, it is important to remember that the present stage of coal development represents a long history of evolutionary progress. Therefore, a knowledge of basic facts about coal is an undeniable first step in evaluating the emerging patterns of coal production and use. The intent of this work is to contribute to the process of resolving fundamental issues controlling coal development by a review of such facts.

Information on coal reserves, production and use in the United States is presented in this book, which is divided into three parts.

Part One covers the origin of coal and a description of its properties, together with an analysis of resources and recoverable reserves.

Part Two evaluates coal production. Industry components are identified, and mining methods are summarized. Trends in coal production technology are investigated as a guide to assessing the role of existing technology in future production, and the interaction of technology upon operating productivity. Methods for coal preparation and transportation are described, and water requirements for coal development are outlined.

Part Three considers coal use. Trends in coal utilization are reviewed as a basis for presenting an overview of power generation capacity in the remaining years of the twentieth century. Estimates of the numbers of potential gasification and liquefaction plants are presented, and the technology for underground coal gasification is evaluated. Economic trends in coal utilization are examined, and future conditions of coal supply and demand are assessed. Finally, factors which influence coal development are summarized.

Each of these topics, and the sum of their interactions, is critical if coal is again to become the "keystone" of American energy supply.

Richard A. Schmidt

TABLE OF CONTENTS

INTRODUCTION

Coal is being rediscovered by Americans after decades of indifference or neglect. This rediscovery may be illustrated by the many articles appearing over the last few years in the popular and technical press. A sampling of some recent articles provides a useful indication of the amount of attention that is presently being devoted to coal.[1] More importantly, they reveal the level of general knowledge about coal and the need for comprehensive information about coal reserves, production and use in the United States to guide public and private activities.

Historically, coal provided the resource base for the industrialization of the U.S. economy, and it is only natural for Americans to regard coal as an old reliable energy source which can be called on once more to help meet the nation's needs of the future.[2] Although this expectation for a re-emphasis on coal can probably be realized, coal development and utilization are influenced by many factors requiring careful assessment if objectives are to be attained. A firm understanding of the reasons why growth in coal development is important to the national energy scene is required, so that the implications of factors influencing coal growth upon the industry's ability to realize national energy objectives may be determined.

THE IMPORTANCE OF COAL

Coal is America's "most abundant domestic fossil fuel resource and reserve."[3] The magnitude of the coal resources and reserves of the United States is typi-

---

[1]See, for example, The Coal Industry Makes a Dramatic Comeback, *Bus. Week,* pp. 50−58, Nov. 4, 1972; Our National Security is Coal, *Min. Congr. J.,* pp. 58−76, July 1973; John Papamarcos, King Coal's Last Chance, *Power Eng.,* pp. 39−45, March 1974; Freeman Bishop, Energy Pendulum Must Swing to Coal, *Min. Congr. J.,* pp. 48−49, August 1973; Sen. R. C. Byrd, Coal Will Rise Like the Phoenix, *Min. Congr. J.,* pp. 22−25, September 1973; Carl Bagge, Coal—An Overlooked Energy Source, presented at Colby College, Waterville, Maine, Mar. 2, 1972; R. P. Ovelette, Coal—The Black Magic, *MITRE Corp. Rep.,* pp. 72−170, September 1972.

[2]See, for example, J. P. Henry, Jr., and R.A. Schmidt, Coal—Still Old Reliable? *Ann. Am. Acad. Political Soc. Sci.,* vol. 410, pp. 35−51, November, 1973.

[3]"Energy Research Program of the U.S. Department of the Interior," Office of Research and Development, March 1974.

cally described as enormous, measured in many billions of tons. In 1976, more than 665 million tons of coal were produced in the United States. Locally, coal production was a major economic factor in several states or smaller regional areas; these states were concentrated in the Appalachian and Midwestern regions of the nation—as used in this book, these regions would be considered "eastern" as compared to those areas lying west of the Mississippi River (primarily in the northern Great Plains).

Once coal has been extracted, it can be utilized as a raw solid, processed to improve its qualities as a solid fuel, or converted into either gas or oil.[1] Regardless of the technology employed in coal utilization, the fact remains that coal production is the essential first step in deriving energy or chemical products from coal. Any influences upon coal production, therefore, exert considerable effect on the amounts of coal which can be available for subsequent processing or use.

COAL AND ELECTRIC UTILITIES

The electric utility industry is the largest single consumer of U.S. coal, accounting for roughly two-thirds of total annual production. In the future, coal will continue to be an essential fuel in existing utility facilities, those converted from fluid hydrocarbon fuels, and new power plants.

For the most part, particularly for the remainder of the twentieth century, coal will be burned to raise steam for power generation. Accordingly, the electric utility industry's objectives for coal research can be stated with confidence; these concern the array of interlocking factors pertaining to the entire system of coal utilization (Figure 1).

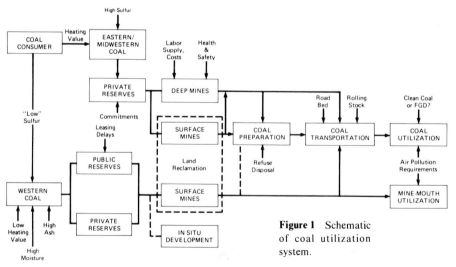

Figure 1 Schematic of coal utilization system.

---

[1] For a concise summary of coal technology, see I. L. White et al., "The Coal and Oil Shale Resource Development System," manuscript, University of Oklahoma, July 27, 1974.

As the principal consumer, electric utilities are concerned with the quantity of recoverable coal reserves, their quality in various utilization systems, and environmental effects of production and consumption. Historically, it was possible for utilities to concentrate on the engineering aspects of individual coals in specific facilities for optimum power generation, and a wealth of empirical data was acquired. The present situation, in which concern over environmental pollutants influences coal selection and utilization, suggests the need for a framework for analysis of coal reserves, production, and use in the future.

A FRAMEWORK FOR ANALYSIS

Present approaches to coal development and utilization are distinguished mainly by their similarity to those in use in the early part of the twentieth century.[1] To be sure, there have been important improvements to components and systems employed in coal operations during this century, but these mainly reflect the normal evolutionary refinements which every technology experiences through continued use in serving commercial operations. While not without innovation, compared with other activities over the same time interval, coal production and use is relatively lacking in basic and wide-ranging changes in technologies known as *breakthroughs*. Is this historical pattern inherent in the nature of coal utilization, or can the pattern be altered by pursuing new or underexplored avenues that may, in time, permit breakthroughs to be achieved?

In attempting to address this question, it is suggested that there is a hierarchy of coal production and utilization technologies (Table 1). Each level of technology may have many alternative approaches or methods. Any of them may be combined to yield coals differing in character, quality, or ease of use. Development begins with the extraction of coal from nature's deposits; the technologies employed for this purpose may be classed as *primary*. Primary technologies exert considerable influence upon the final physical characteristics of coal, especially on size distribu-

Table 1 Hierarchy of coal development technologies

Class*	Description
1. Primary	*Extraction* from natural deposits: Determination of size consist and noncombustible content
2. Secondary	*Preparation:* Use of physical properties to beneficiate extracted coal and separate noncombustibles
3. Tertiary	*Blending:* Mixing of coals with different properties to achieve a desired product in terms of heating value, ash and sulfur content
4. Quaternary	*Utilization:* Actual use of coals in plant or process applications (with or without final treatment or additives)

*Classes reading down indicate decreasing opportunity to alter coal characteristics but increasing importance of chemical properties as compared to physical properties.

[1]See, for example, W. S. Boulton, (ed.), "Practical Coal Mining," Gresham, London, 1913 (6 volumes).

tion, populations in each size interval, and particularly on the content of noncombustible admixed with the coal. Care in coal extraction offers the greatest opportunity for securing a high-quality product upon which higher-order technologies may operate. While selective extraction was once practiced using hand methods, the advent of mechanized mining led to a dramatic influence upon coal character that had a great impact on subsequent coal preparation and use.

Years ago, when coal was mined by pick and shovel, the quality was generally satisfactory because the impurities were not loaded, but productivity per miner was low. Mechanization improved the productivity but impurities increased to the extent that some form of cleaning became necessary at many mines. The transformation from hand loading to mechanical loading was quite radical during the mid-thirties. Tipples and earlier type cleaning units became inadequate almost overnight. Coal quality was jeopardized, until adequate cleaning could be installed, by the adoption of full-seam mining throughout the industry. Cleaning units were installed on coarse coal sizes to eliminate labor used for hand picking. Finer sizes then had to be cleaned to upgrade the slack coal.[1]

Secondary technologies operate on the products of primary technologies. For example, coal preparation has lesser opportunity than extraction to alter the characteristics of the final product as received by the consumer because it is limited by the nature of the raw coal received from the mine. As practiced at present, coal preparation employs physical properties in separating desired from undesired materials (especially hardness, size, specific gravity). Because the physical properties of coals and associated rocks may vary widely within any given coal seam throughout a mine, it has been difficult to derive quantitative technical information about these properties to guide refinement of preparation technologies. There are, simply, so many special cases that it has been quite difficult to derive meaningful generalizations. In consequence, coal preparation engineers have been forced to rely on empirical information stemming from numerous individual situations which can be related to one another (if at all) only with difficulty. Further, at present, the technical base upon which secondary technologies are based is limited to physical properties, and chemical characteristics are considered in gross terms (if at all) and then rarely on a routine basis; this has important impacts on coal utilization.

Although used in the steel industry for many years, the widespread practice of coal preparation with respect to electric utility applications is a relatively new undertaking but may increase in future years. "Traditionally . . . power coals generally have been prepared at specific gravities higher than those of metallurgical coals, thus generally simplifying design."[2] Preparation was practiced mainly in an attempt to reduce costs. "Coals destined for distant markets are intensively prepared to increase carbon content [metallurgical coals] or energy content [power coals], and thus make the product more attractive, decrease cost of transportation per unit of value, and make the increased cost more tolerable."[3]

[1] R. L. Llewellyn, Coal Preparation, in S. M. Cassidy (ed.), "Elements of Practical Coal Mining," AIME, New York, 1973.

[2] J. W. Leonard, Special Section—Coal, in A. B. Cummins and I. A. Given (eds.), "SME Mining Engineering Handbook," sec. 28 (Mill Design), AIME, New York, 1973.

[3] *Ibid.*

Despite these apparent advantages in quality and lower transport cost, coal preparation has been employed in a rather random fashion by the electric utility industry, dealing with particular coals under specific utilization conditions. Moreover, the principal beneficiary of coal preparation historically was the coal producer. "The coal industry utilizes mechanical coal preparation methods and equipment for two reasons: (1) to increase its net income per ton of product, and (2) to provide a steady outlet for its products."[1] In particular, it is noteworthy that:

> It might be said that a coal operator generally does not get paid for the direct cost of producing a better product, but rather that *he enjoys economic benefits from coal preparation efforts by being able to decrease face production costs and by turning out a more salable product in sufficient volume to justify investments in mine and plant.* It is primarily through these indirect economic benefits that most operators profit from their preparation efforts.[2] [Emphasis added.]

Clearly coal producers recognize the close interdependence of extraction and preparation and are able to employ each technology to complement the other (at least to a limited degree). Still, the tendency is to suboptimize on individual classes of coal utilization technology rather than on overall system performance. In the future, it would be reasonable to expect even more detailed and systematic "matching" of extraction and preparation technologies so as to approach an overall operational optimum oriented toward meeting consumer product specifications.

To move toward improvement of coal utilization technologies, it will be essential to place the empirical engineering data for physical properties on a quantitative basis relative to detailed chemical parameters for coal components and associated mineral matter. This will require the development, perfection, and dissemination of instruments and apparatus for rapid, nondestructive coal analysis not presently available.

Tertiary technologies or practices may be employed on the products from secondary technologies. In many cases, secondary processing will result in a product adequate for most uses, and tertiary processing will be unnecessary. In other cases, however, tertiary processing may prove to be essential in enabling the use of a particular coal because of coal properties, utilization conditions, or regulations pertaining to coal consumption. For example, a coal produced by a preparation plant may still require blending to meet emission control requirements at a given power plant.

Tertiary methods of coal processing commonly attempt to achieve a measure of control over the chemical properties of coal (such as sulfur content, ash content) as well as the physicochemical properties (such as heating value, ash-fusion temperature, critical viscosity, etc.) that influence its utilization. In particular, these methods are related to an array of empirical engineering data on coals and their behavior in various systems. Often tertiary methods are employed through trial and error in seeking to achieve products having values of "standard engineering parameters" that fall within "typical" limits. The degree of success in the application of tertiary methods is limited by the character of the material it is to deal with,

---

[1] *Ibid.*

[2] F. R. Zacher and A. G. Gilbert, Economics of Coal Preparation, in J. W. Leonard and D. R. Mitchell (eds.), "Coal Preparation," AIME, New York, 1968.

and this could have been strongly influenced by prior primary and secondary processing. Moreover, since the chemistry of the coal (and the influence of processing upon it) is imperfectly known, the outcome of tertiary processing upon final coal quality is not predictable with much accuracy. The uncertainty in the effects of processing coal by tertiary (and secondary) methods has probably deterred their widespread application; faced with production operations already replete with uncertainties, many coal producers may have concluded that attempting to resolve such further uncertainties did not yield benefits to them commensurate with their costs. Few consumers are sufficiently knowledgeable about the potentials or practices of lower-order coal technologies, and therefore are in a poor position to specify their use or monitor performance in their application unless they engage in trial-and-error testing. Consumers, therefore, have been forced to rely upon adjustments in coal utilization equipment to cope with the characteristics of coals supplied to them.

Coal utilization technology is classified as *quaternary* in this book. It is the furthest removed from nature's coal deposits (often geographically as well as figuratively). Although it is possible for some utilization processes to accept coal essentially as it comes from the mine, it is becoming more common for coals to be processed by secondary (and even tertiary) means. While physical properties of coals fed to utilization systems are of great importance in terms of phenomena associated with combustion and heat transfer (much of which is, at best, semiquantitative and empirical), chemical properties of ashes and other combustion products often prove to be the actual determinants of the viability and acceptability of such systems. For example, concerns over the magnitudes of oxides of sulfur and nitrogen released from coal combustion in power plants have resulted in a host of impacts upon the plants, their operations, and the character of the coals they employ. This has led to increasing interest in various segments of the coal utilization system; however, much of recent attention has been piecemeal and limited rather than the system-level approach that addresses the actual operations of principal consumers, particularly the electric utility industry. In view of the foregoing, it is apparent that a piecemeal approach will not be sufficient in achieving effective solutions to systemic problems.

With the above conceptual framework as background, it is now possible to consider the question posed at the outset of this section about the prospects for change and innovation in coal development. Dependent upon the nature of coal deposits, primary extraction technologies may or may not produce coal that is amenable to subsequent processing or utilization in an acceptable manner. Higher-order technologies exert little, if any, influence on primary technologies although the converse appears to be the rule (e.g., coal extraction strongly influences preparation, blending, and utilization whereas the reverse is rarely true). Each technological level is distinguished mainly by its reliance upon empiricism, and the analytical base upon which to establish a quantitative accounting of technological performance is, at best, incomplete. The present approach to operations in each element of the technical hierarchy is carried on separately, by groups of engineering (largely) personnel whose attention is devoted to "making things work" within the confines of natural bounds and regulatory requirements rather than to seeking a more complete understanding of these activities. In fact, the output of many academicians is frequently difficult to apply in response to operating situations.

The hierarchy of coal development technologies evolved at an arms-length relationship with one another. Each set of technologies concentrated on its own problems, independent of the others (except for the fact that advances in higher-order technologies take precedence over lower-order technologies). There has been notably poor communication among practitioners of different segments of the fuel sequence, and knowledge gained about one aspect has not necessarily been shared with others at different levels, even though each may benefit as a result.

As a result of this historical pattern, there is no substitute for experience in coal production and utilization. As practiced today, it remains a set of activities dominated by a few master technicians who have worked on the subject for years but whose know-how is difficult to transfer to a new generation of personnel through anything but an apprenticelike exposure to actual operation experiences. It does not seem likely that this pattern can be changed significantly in a short time; this would appear to place limits to the scale of future coal development activities, as well as exerting control over the pace of its expansion during the latter part of the twentieth century. The future of coal development, in short, will probably be much like its past, and the process of information exchange will be facilitated by compiling basic facts on coal reserves, production and utilization.

ONE

COAL PROPERTIES
AND RESERVES

What is coal? A simple-enough question. After all, if the United States is to expand its use of coal, it seems only logical that we comprehend the primary nature of this fuel. But there are no simple answers to this question. Coal is a very complex substance.

Partial answers to the question may be obtained by reviewing existing information on coal. Conditions of coal formation were investigated by geologists, and hypotheses of coal evolution are available for consideration. Various properties of coal were studied by chemists, physicists, and engineers searching for explanations of coal phenomena. Familiarity with the known characteristics of coal is the root from which more complete understanding may emerge. At least, this should permit more pointed questions to be posed, leading to new insights about coal that may facilitate its production and use.

Of particular importance for future coal development is a firm appreciation of the magnitude of remaining resources and reserves. Although the apparent coal resources in place are large, the presently estimated recoverable reserves represent less than one-tenth of the total resources. The amount of recoverable reserves may be increased through new discoveries to augment known deposits as well as by advances in the technology of mining and processing. Still, these potentials, while great, are yet to be demonstrated. Both are areas of extensive government- and industry-sponsored programs, especially in surveys to better define the deposits themselves.

In short, while the apparent body of knowledge about coal is great, there is much to learn about why coal behaves as it does in specific conditions. Similarly, the exact dimensions of the recoverable reserves of coal are not precisely known. It is valuable to bear in mind these uncertainties so as to maintain perspective regarding the outlook for coal production and use.

CHAPTER TWO

ORIGIN AND PROPERTIES OF COAL

BACKGROUND

Investigation of the properties and occurrence of coal occupied the attention of scientists and engineers over many centuries. As a result of previous work, much is known about particular characteristics of individual coals under specific circumstances of processing and use. In large measure, the available information results from an array of trial-and-error attempts to solve some individual problem. In so doing, a bewildering variety of separate measurements of most of the conceivable properties of coal have been performed and compiled.[1]

Despite the depth and breadth of previous investigations, the essence of coal remains an enigma. Conditions of its formation and evolution are not well-understood, notwithstanding numerous theories and hypotheses put forward and earnestly defended by serious workers. The imperfectly understood processes of nature that created coal deposits influence production operations to the extent that they are known in the profession as *winning*.[2] Following extraction, the variability in coal character and properties is such that its utilization is essentially controlled by a set of empirical factors derived from practical experience in a particular process or plant. Many of these factors are quite specific to a given facility, making their more general application difficult if not impossible and greatly complicating the task of coal utilization.

In view of this situation, it would be presumptuous indeed for this chapter to attempt more than to place in perspective several of the key parameters of coal as a guide to those pursuing further developments. Toward this end, a review and assessment of facts pertaining to the nature and origin of coal is presented. The physical and chemical properties of coal are then described, followed by a discussion of engineering properties in relation to utilization and process design.

[1]See, for example, T. A. Hendricks, "Chemistry of Coal Utilization," Wiley, New York, 1945, and H. H. Lowry (ed.), "Chemistry of Coal Utilization, Supplementary Volume," Wiley, New York, 1963.
[2]U.S. Bureau of Mines, "Dictionary of Mining, Mineral, and Related Terms," 1968.

ORIGIN OF COAL

Coal is a "solid, brittle, more or less distinctly stratified, combustible, carbonaceous rock."[1] The heterogeneous nature of coal constituents and their variable chemical composition identify coal as a rock rather than a mineral.

The elementary microscopic constituents of coal are known as *macerals*, which are analogous to the minerals of other rocks.[2] Macerals occur in three distinct groups, recognized according to their properties. These groups are (1) vitrinite, representing plant-matter remains, (2) exinite, representing waxy-resinous components, and (3) inertinite, representing a group of several distinct organic remains, particularly fusinite. The macerals may be associated in varying proportions in different coals, and their difference in properties leads to recognition of distinct coal lithotypes, synonymous with rock types of inorganic sediments. Originally, four major lithotypes were identified:

Class	Subclass	Lithotypes
Humic coal	Bright coal	Vitrain
		Clarain
		Fusain
	Dull coal	Durain

Vitrain is largely composed of the maceral vitrinite, clarain is a mixture of all three maceral groups, and fusain is largely composed of inertinite. Durain has a high content of inorganic mineral matter deposited together with the coal.

Coal deposits occur as distinct strata or "seams" interbedded with inorganic sedimentary rocks, and it is inferred that coal represents the accumulation of organic materials through normal sedimentary processes.[3] The presence in coal seams of extensive, recognizable remains of plants and trees is interpreted as indicative that the coal "is formed from plant substances preserved from complete decay in a favorable environment and later altered by various chemical and physical agencies . . . ."[4]

The starting material for coal formation is commonly considered to be peat, defined as "a caustobiolith of low diagenetic degree."[5] Peat is believed to have accumulated in a near-shore, nonmarine environment of low topographic relief which was exceptionally favorable for plant growth and for preservation of plant remains against destruction by biochemical agencies.[6] The sedimentary basins were continuous across large areas and in many instances were characterized by remarkably uniform sedimentary conditions throughout.[7] It is commonly

[1] *Ibid*, p. 222.

[2] I. A. Williamson, "Coal Mining Geology," p. 222, Oxford University Press, London, 1967.

[3] *Ibid*.

[4] B. C. Parks, Origin, Petrography, and Classification of Coal, in H. H. Lowry (ed.), *op. cit.*, pp. 1–34.

[5] U.S. Bureau of Mines, *op. cit.*, p. 799. A caustobiolith is a rock with a "fairly high content of organic carbon compounds."

[6] Parks, *op. cit.*

[7] Williamson, *op. cit.*, pp. 219–235.

hypothesized that accumulation of floriclastic sediments was slow and in a relatively quiet and stable environment.[1]

A favorable growth environment for plant material is presumed, in which there were ample nutrients. A tropical climate of high humidity is postulated for most of the major coal seams formed during the Carboniferous period (300 million years ago), based on the analogy of the absence of tree rings in coal remains and a similar lack of rings in trees found in modern tropical areas.[2] However, peat may form in a variety of conditions, and a warm climate appears not to be a necessity.

The cause of peat accumulation is attributed to the normal life cycle of plants existing in extensive swampy areas and the accumulation of the remains of plants completing that cycle.[3] The life cycle of plants in near-sea-level swamps may be influenced by changes in relative sea level, resulting in elevation or inundation that could arrest the normal life cycle.[4]

A relatively stable environment of accumulation is hypothesized, characterized by a succession of plant communities.

> The sequence of plants is interpreted as a response by the vegetation to changing ground-water conditions [associated with the availability of plant food], proceeding in the direction of removal of free-surface water as the deposits increased in thickness . . . . The succession is not considered due to climatic changes, although the climate must favor the formation of peat above the ground water level. Generally, the time required to deposit peat equivalent to a moderately thick coal seam was probably too short for major climatic changes to have taken place.[5]

A further factor contributing to the accumulation of coal may be the influence of dissolved or colloidal organic matter occurring in the oceans, as well as the microscopic and semimicroscopic organisms occurring there.[6] Photosynthesis in the oceans have been estimated to produce 12 million tons of hydrocarbon material annually. Over geological time, a minute fraction of this amount would account for all the fossil fuel deposits.

Levorsen noted that coastal waters produce rich organic material, especially off the mouths of rivers (which are typically deltaic or swampy areas). A metastable equilibrium exists between marine water and the various organic fractions. Conditions occasionally favor one particular organism, which then multiplies rapidly or "blooms." This can result in either extensive development of a particular organism or in a toxic substance that kills organisms it encounters. Dead organic tissue can accumulate as a sapropel (organic debris) in an oxygen-deficient environment. Levorsen suggests that this mechanism could produce large quantities of material with a high carbon and hydrogen content over a widespread area.

[1] J. W. Hemingway, Sedimentology of Coal-Bearing Strata, in D. Murchinson and T. S. Westoll (eds.), "Coal and Coal-Bearing Strata," American Elsevier, New York, 1968.

[2] Williamson, *op. cit.*

[3] L. R. Moore, Some Sediments Closely Associated with Coal Seams, in D. Murchison and T. S. Westoll (eds.), "Coals and Coal-Bearing Strata," pp. 105–123, American Elsevier, New York, 1968; Parks, *op. cit.*

[4] Williamson, *op. cit.*, Moore, *loc. cit.*; Parks, *op. cit.*

[5] A. H. V. Smith, Seam Profiles and Seam Characters, in D. Murchison and T. S. Westoll (eds.), "Coal and Coal-Bearing Strata," pp. 31–40, American Elsevier, New York, 1968.

[6] A. I. Levorsen, "Geology of Petroleum," 2d ed., Freeman, San Francisco, 1967.

In the context of coal formation, it could be significant, as Levorsen suggests, that "vast quantities of humic acid are forming constantly in swampy regions and, especially in the tropics, are carried into the oceans, either in solution or in colloidal suspension. Mingling of fresh and salt water might cause the precipitation of the organic material. Temperature changes alone would be sufficient cause for extensive precipitation of some of the organic matter . . . ."[1]

A somewhat similar mechanism was suggested by Moore.[2] "Salt water invaded the peat swamps, either in the water table or by marine incursions across the peat swamps at frequent intervals. From this water, by a process of reduction involving the partially decayed vegetation, mineral solutions with high calcium and magnesium content were produced and caused petrification of tissues."

The postulated mingling of fresh and salt water and its contained humic acids and organic matter would be enhanced by relative subsidence of the land near the shoreline. This would shift the position of shallow water and result in precipitation of ocean-borne organic matter, possibly as a colloid, in the same area where plant remains were accumulating. Colloidal deposition would completely cover the plant remains that had accumulated in the swamps and would enclose them in a shroud of organic matter. The fact that such deposition would be a colloid would mean that it could develop even the most delicate plant remains (and living plants trapped by the inundation/deposition) without disrupting their features; this could explain the presence of many of the extensive, fine plant fossils found in coal seams. Additionally, this mechanism would be consistent with the occurrence of "tree trunks, many feet in length . . . in the upright position, apparently in the original position of growth, with their roots in the underclay of a coal seam, and the trunk passing through the seam into the overlying structure."[3] The deposition of colloidal material would surround a growing tree but not otherwise affect its position or characteristic. It was even noted that "tree growth may have continued throughout part of the deposition of the surrounding sediment."[4] There are numerous accounts of such trees as Boulton describes, and it is difficult to account for their undisturbed character by a dynamic process.[5] Under the conventional coal formation hypothesis, vegetal matter would need to be compressed to form peat, and this would in turn require further compaction and volume reduction to form coal. As a result, there would be substantial changes in size and volume of deposits. If it takes 20 feet of vegetal matter to form 1 foot of coal,[6] then the amount of compression and structural change involved must surely have had an effect on associated trees; yet, no distortion or change in condition is apparent. Additionally, with the enormous changes in volume that would be required under such a hypothesis, then disruptions in overlying strata might be expected also; yet none are evident. A further factor to consider with regard to the origin of coal from peat

[1] *Ibid.*

[2] Moore, *loc. cit.*

[3] W. S. Boulton (ed.), "Practical Coal Mining," Vol. 1, pp. 7, 63, Gresham, London, 1913.

[4] Hemingway, *loc. cit.*

[5] See, for example, G. Young, Will Coal Be Tomorrow's 'Black Gold'?, *National Geographic Magazine,* vol. 148, no. 2, p. 245, August 1975.

[6] E. S. Moore, "Coal," p. 159, Wiley, New York, 1940.

is the length of time required for peat deposition; Moore states that "under the most favorable conditions, 1 foot of peat may form in 5 years, and that 1 foot in 10 years is a fair average maximum."[1] It was estimated that 1 foot of peat at the surface shrinks to ⅛ foot at depth. Thus, if 20 feet of vegetal matter are required to form 1 foot of coal, then this will require on the order of three centuries. During all this time, conditions would have to be such as to permit trees extending through coal seams to persist unchanged; for a 6-foot-thick coal seam, this would be 1800 years. The amount of time over which no essential change in conditions is required under this hypothesis is not long in the geological sense but is rather excessive for ordinary vegetation such as trees. It seems more likely that a shorter period of time was involved in the accumulation of vegetal matter. This would be more consistent with an alternative view of the formation of the seams such as the colloidal deposition hypothesis described above.

Preservation of accumulated organic material requires relatively rapid burial to protect against decomposition. In this regard, it is noted that "the dominantly inorganic sedimentation of the great volume of coal-bearing strata was relatively rapid, turbulent, and variable."[2] The inorganic sedimentary strata demonstrate "a low degree of packing or high interstitial water content, with subsequent adjustment phenomena . . . ."[3]

"One of the more remarkable features of a coal seam is its extraordinary extensiveness compared with its slight thickness. It is certainly an astonishing fact that a stratum with a thickness of several feet, sometimes extends over areas of hundreds of square miles."[4]

It would be truly remarkable to expect relatively uniform conditions to extend over very wide areas and to persist for the estimated long periods of time required for the accumulation of vegetable matter as indicated in the peat hypothesis discussed above. The data of the coal seams and the vegetation which they apparently represent thus could be interpreted as representing a relatively short period of accumulation.

The question of time required for the accumulation of vegetal materials and their transformation into coals is central to an understanding of the coal-forming process, the character of the coals, and the reasons behind the wide variability in coal properties. It was noted that "perhaps the greatest possibility of error is in the estimation of the number of years between the geological periods during which coals were laid down and the duration of the process of coal formation . . . ."[5] A more detailed discussion of the influence of time on the evolution of coal is given in a later part of this section.

Variability in organic matter and in environmental conditions of its accumulation and preservation by burial are hypothesized as the principal cause of the formation of different types of coals.[6] Two elements of a concept were offered by

[1] *Ibid.*

[2] Hemingway, *loc. cit.*

[3] *Ibid.*

[4] D. W. Van Krevelen, "Coal," p. 55, American Elsevier, New York, 1961.

[5] W. Francis, "Coal—Its Formation and Composition," p. 453, E. Arnold, London, 1954.

[6] See, for example, Parks, *op. cit.*, E. S. Moore, *op. cit.*

Parks to explain the lateral changes in a given coal horizon and vertical changes in a sequence of coal-bearing strata.

Lateral variability. Varied types of organic material accumulated in greatly different environments existing contemporaneously and related to each other.

Sequential variability. Varied types of organic material accumulated essentially at the same locality but under successively changing environmental conditions.

Actually, it appears that the origin of coal in a given locality is influenced by the complex interaction of each of these elements of environmental variability.

The coal deposits originated from masses of vegetable matter that accumulated in sedimentary deposits which formed in a shallow or brackish water environment in coastal swamps. The area of deposition was flat and just above or below sea level, so that a slight relative change of sea level was sufficient to produce vast inundations or equally large emergence. The dominant character of sedimentation was cyclic accumulation of varied clastic and calcareous deposits which can be differentiated and traced with confidence for hundreds of miles. The phases of each cyclic succession are records of environments which prevailed in areas of deposition as seas advanced and retreated.[1]

A "remarkable succession of cyclical deposits" occur in the Pennsylvanian coal measures of the Eastern and Midwestern United States.[2] These cyclical deposits are known as *cyclothems*.[3] The ideal cyclothem consists of 10 members, one of which is coal (Table 1). Cyclothems are commonly believed to be associated with unstable shelf or intracratonic basic conditions in which alternate marine submergence and emergence occur.

The cycles of sedimentation are "represented by multiple repetition of packets of sedimentary strata, each packet being recognizably similar in its internal sequence."[4] Each sequence is characterized by "rapid marine transgressions followed by regression."[5] Well-developed rhythmic sequences "may include several tens [sometimes over a hundred] of rhythms. Many such successions have wide lateral extents, and nearly all of them are composed very largely of essentially deltaic deposits."[6]

Strakhov[7] noted that "the accumulation of coal was not a continuous process, but, on the contrary, was characterized by interruptions . . . ." He went on to state

[1]R. C. Moore, Late Paleozoic Cyclic Sedimentation in Central United States, in Cloud (ed.), "Adventure in Earth History," pp. 541–552, Freeman, San Francisco, 1970; see also W. H. Twenhofel, "Principles of Sedimentation," 2d ed., pp. 550–554, McGraw-Hill, New York, 1950.

[2]W. C. Krumbein and L. L. Sloss, "Stratigraphy and Sedimentation," pp. 375–381, Freeman, San Francisco, 1955.

[3]J. M. Weller, Cyclical Sedimentation of the Pennsylvanian Period and its Significance, *J. Geol.*, vol. 38, pp. 97–135, 1930.

[4]T. S. Westoll, Sedimentary Rhythms in Coal-Bearing Strata, in D. Murchison and T. S. Westoll (eds.), "Coal and Coal-Bearing Strata," pp. 71–103, American Elsevier, New York, 1968.

[5] *Ibid.*

[6] *Ibid.*

[7]N. M. Strakhov, "Principles of Lithogenesis," vol. 2, Consultants Bureau, Plenum, New York, 1969.

Table 1 Members of an idealized cyclothem

Member	Description
Transgressing sea:	
1. Sandstone	Continental
2. Gray sandy shale	Continental
3. Limestone	Fresh water
4. Underclay	Continental
5. Coal	Coastal
6. Gray shale	Marine
7. Limestone	Marine
8. Black shale	Marine
9. Limestone	Marine
10. Gray shale	Marine
Regressing sea:	

Source: Adapted from W. C. Krumbein and L. L. Sloss, "Stratigraphy and Sedimentation," pp. 375–381, Freeman, San Francisco, 1955.

that "coal accumulation was confined to times of less intense tectonic movements, and the barren deposits formed during times of accentuated tectonic movements."

Coal makes up an extremely small proportion of the total thickness of coal-bearing formations, usually less than 4 percent; this amount includes many seams too thin to be economically workable. In places there are a large number of coal seams distributed through the sedimentary sequence; for example, there are 117 named coal seams in the Pennsylvanian and Permian strata of West Virginia alone.[1] Coals represent rather specialized conditions of deposition at or near sea level. Therefore, if the coals of North America were formed in place through cyclic sedimentary processes, it seems reasonable to conclude that a sizable portion of the continent must have bobbed up and down like a cork throughout much of the latter part of the Paleozoic era. "A very complicated oscillatory relationship between subsiding basement and changing sea-level is necessary . . . ."[2] to account for the rhythmic succession. Some fundamental force operated repeatedly over extensive areas for a substantial time.[3] What was this force? How did it influence the process of coal formation?

In examining these questions, it is important to cite the work of Westoll.[4] Limestones occurring in the cyclic sedimentary sequences containing coal are presently. interpreted as having formed in shallow waters (up to 200 feet) in

[1] C. W. Lotz, "Probable Original Minable Extent of the Bituminous Coal Seams in West Virginia," West Virginia Geological Survey, Morgantown, 1970, (Map.)

[2] Westoll, *loc. cit.*

[3] Note that cyclic sedimentation is also observed in the more recent coal deposits of the Western United States (see Williamson, *op. cit.,* and Parks, *op. cit.*). "An examination of the conditions in the Western part of the continent at a later period shows that the conditions found in the East during the Carboniferous were practically duplicated in the West during the Jurassic and Cretaceous periods." E. S. Moore, *op. cit.,* p. 1630.

[4] Westoll, *loc. cit.*

contrast to the deeper water environment previously considered. Westoll stated that "the importance of these supposed (shallow) depths is that, in order to accommodate the depth-fluctuations during formation of (a cycle) . . . a very long complicated oscillatory relationship between subsiding basement and changing sea-level is necessary." [1]

The nature of this oscillatory relationship was considered by Westoll to be "repeated periods of relative subsidence, rapid enough to inundate vast delta complexes by the sea without the supply of sediments to the delta being able to keep pace" [2] (with subsidence and maintain the original depth conditions). It was suggested that "the earth's crust in an area of widespread cyclic sedimentation was more or less continually under stress, which could be accommodated in part by gradual adjustment, but . . . [which] could well have been released from time to time in very much more rapid movements . . . ." [3]

It is speculated by the writer that the force responsible for the changes in sea level recorded in cyclic sedimentation (including coal deposits) may stem from sea floor spreading. There is evidence to suggest that rapid increases in the rate of sea-floor spreading coincided with times when the oceans spread over the land in huge, shallow inland seas. [4] In fact, Rona [5] suggested that:

> Major eustatic changes in sea level, other than glacio-eustatic, result from changes in the cubic capacity of ocean basins primarily caused by changes in the volume of the worldwide mid-oceanic ridge system and by orogenic compression of continental crust. These two factors are related in a cycle manifested in the stratigraphic record of epicontinental marine transgression and regression:
>
> 1. Rapid upwelling along the worldwide mid-oceanic ridge system associated with relatively fast sea-floor spreading and *net* orogenic quiescence of continents results in transgression of the seas because of relative reduction in volume of the oceans.
> 2. Relative quiescence along the worldwide mid-oceanic ridge system associated with relatively slow sea-floor spreading and *net* orogenic activity of continents results in regression of the seas because of a relative increase in volume of the oceans.

Rona concluded that, "to a first approximation, the average rates of sediment accumulation on the continental shelves are directly proportional to the rates of spreading of the . . . sea floor." [6]

As indicated above, progressive transgression by seas would result in a gradual change in the character of sedimentary environments that would be recorded in a regular sequence of deposits. Is it not possible, therefore, that patterns of rhythmic sedimentation represented by coal-bearing strata in cyclothems in general may be interpreted as lithologic records of seafloor-spreading episodes during the geologic

---

[1] *Ibid.*

[2] *Ibid.*

[3] *Ibid.*

[4] R. L. Larson, and W. C. Pitman, III, World-wide Correlation of Mesozoic Magnetic Anomalies, and its Implications, *Geol. Soc. Am. Bull.*, vol. 83, no. 12, pp. 3645–3661, 1972.

[5] P. A. Rona, Relations between Rates of Sediment Accumulation on Continental Shelves, Sea-Floor Spreading, and Eustacy Inferred from the Central North Atlantic, *Geol. Soc. Am. Bull.*, vol. 84, pp. 251–287, 1973.

[6] *Ibid.*

past? Further, is it not possible that individual units composing cyclothems may be employed to aid in deciphering fossil-spreading characteristics just as magnetic anomalies are used to evaluate more recent spreading events?

Conceivably, to follow this speculation further, any of the units composing cyclothems could be used as marker horizons. As noted, most common rocks can be differentiated and traced for large distances. However, coal is much more readily distinguishable than its surrounding rocks. Additionally, coal represents a special place in the cyclothem sequence, occurring at the approximate boundary between nonmarine and marine conditions. Finally, the relatively small amount of coal present in the sedimentary sequence accentuates its occurrence and facilitates its recognition, all of which should aid in identifying successive cycles (except perhaps where erosion has removed part of the stratigraphic section).

The potential significance of coal-bearing strata may extend beyond the identification of spreading episodes; the record in the rocks may provide data on actual spreading rates. As noted above, Rona[1] found that sedimentation rates are proportional to spreading rates. Is it not possible that this relationship is recorded in the coal-bearing strata? To carry the question further, is it possible that the thickness of rhythmic sedimentary strata and their coal seams provide indicators of spreading rate during at least part of the sedimentation cycle? For example, do thick seams represent relatively slow and uniform sedimentation (spreading) rates that maintained particular horizons in position to support extensive vegetation growth for some time, allowing this matter to collect in great quantity and ultimately to be transformed to coal? Do thin seams represent periods of rapid spreading where the deposition sites are quickly buried by sediments of later stages in the cycle? Can similar arguments be formulated about other units of the sedimentary cycle? In short, can the character and thickness of coal-bearing strata be employed to determine (at least semiquantitatively) the timing and manner of past major geological events such as spreading of the seafloor? Can these data be used, together with physicochemical data on the coals, to obtain a better understanding of the process(es) of coal formation and the coal itself?

Process of Coal Formation

The series of deposits of organic material experience progressive changes in physical and chemical properties subsequent to burial in the sedimentary environment. These changes are known as the *process of coalification*, defined as a gradual increase in carbon content of fossil organic material in the course of a natural process.[2] Because of known transitions from peat into lignite and from lignite into coal, and because peat beds have never been found to occur beneath lignite deposits nor lignite beneath coal, it is hypothesized that the genesis of coal occurred in the sequence peat to lignite to coal. This hypothesis is supported by two empirical rules.

---

[1] *Ibid.*
[2] Van Krevelen, *op. cit.*

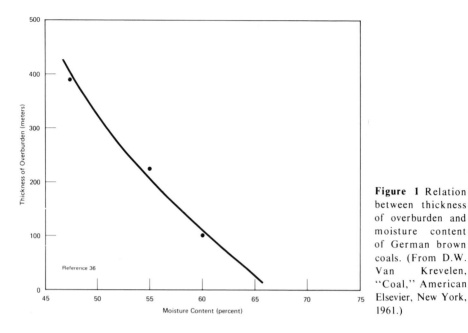

Figure 1 Relation between thickness of overburden and moisture content of German brown coals. (From D.W. Van Krevelen, "Coal," American Elsevier, New York, 1961.)

Schurman's rule. The water content of lignite decreases with increasing depth (see Figure 1).

Hilt's rule. Volatile matter content decreases with increasing depth (see Figure 2).

Although these empirical rules account for observed variations in coal character in a simple, straightforward fashion, the transformation of accumulated organic material into coal is a complex chemical and physical process that varies at different times. Two main phases in coal formation are recognized, the biochemical phase and the dynamochemical or geochemical phase; each will be discussed separately below.

Biochemical phase. The biochemical phase of coal formation includes the chemical changes in organic material that occur following accumulation and/or burial of organic material in the sedimentary environment. The original organic material loses oxygen and hydrogen, resulting in an increase in carbon content.[1] During degradation of plant material, cellulose and proteins are decomposed much more rapidly than lignin and the action of microorganisms on plant remains is a significant factor in decomposition; particularly important are bacteria and other low organisms.[2] Koyawa found that the organic matter in sediments in which microorganisms are active:

[1]W. Flaig, Biochemical Factors in Coal Formation, in D. Murchison and T. S. Westoll (eds.), "Coal and Coal-Bearing Strata," p. 197, American Elsevier, New York, 1968.

[2]E. S. Moore, *op. cit.,* p. 168.

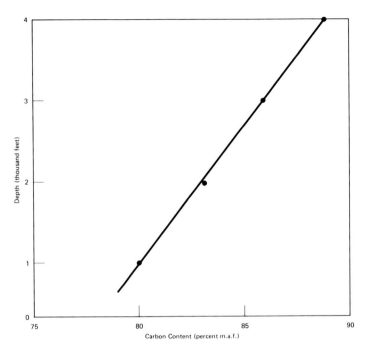

Figure 2. Variation in coal rank with depth (Hilt's rule). (From D.W. Van Krevelen, "Coal," American Elsevier, New York, 1961.)

... generally will decompose according to the following steps:

Solid state ⟶ colloidal state ⟶ soluble, gaseous

The degree to which the decomposition process proceeds will be determined by the original starting material and environmental conditions [such as temperature, time, solutions, and competing reactions].[1]

It was pointed out by Taylor[2] that base-exchange properties of sediments overlying coals have much to do with the rank of the resulting deposit.

Acid conditions without a roof result in *peat*.

Acid conditions under a roof containing a calcium aluminosilicate complex result in *lignite*.

Anaerobic conditions under a roof containing a sodium aluminosilicate complex result in *bituminous* or *anthracite coal*.

Hemingway pointed out that:

Much of the sediment must have passed at least once through conditions of oxidation before reduction was ultimately attained. During this phase some fraction of organic matter in the sediment, both animal and vegetable, must have been destroyed with the evolution of carbon dioxide, methane, and water, with the degree of destruction varying with the rate of superposition and burial. There is, however, no clear evidence of the amount of vegetable matter in the original sediment.[3,]

[1] T. Koyawa, Ratios of Organic Carbon, Nitrogen, and Hydrogen in Recent Sediments, "Coal Science," *Adv. Chem. Ser.,* no. 55, pp. 43–57, 1966.

[2] E. M. K. Taylor, *Fuel Sci. Pract.,* vol. 7, pp. 127–128, 130–134, 227–229, 234–235, 1928.

[3] Hemingway, *loc. cit.*

Hemingway described three main aspects of a "highly variable sedimentary . . . physicochemical system which was . . . essentially unstable, with substantial reactions between the detrital minerals, the abundant organic matter, and the interstitial waters."[1] These aspects are:

1. Oxidation, occurring in the top few centimeters, providing iron oxides and destruction of some organic constituents.

2. Reduction, occurring in the top several meters, forming iron sulfides, carbonates, and silicates during early diagenesis. This was favored by the great abundance of organic material which acted as a reducing agent. In the upper part of this same zone, anaerobic bacterial action contributed further to the reducing tendencies.

3. Redistribution, occurring throughout the deposit over a relatively lengthy period of time, involving the selective solution, removal, and reprecipitation of various constituents.

These aspects were not uniform in effect but varied both horizontally and vertically. Migration of saturated interstitial waters from one lithological type to another would make the process even more complex. It is hypothesized that the conclusion of this phase resulted in the transformation of original organic material into peat.

Three paths of subsequent coal development are believed to be initiated in the biochemical phase: (1) the formation of fusain (coal material having the appearance and structure of charcoal), which progresses very rapidly in the biochemical phase, (2) the formation of vitrain (coal material derived from the lignic and cellulosic substances in plant remains), which progresses much more slowly in the biochemical stage, and (3) the waxy and resinous remains, which undergo very small change during the biochemical stage.[2]

Geochemical (or dynamochemical) phase. The processes that act upon plant remains following completion of the biochemical stage to continue the alteration and produce different ranks of coal are less well-understood. Dependent upon the starting organic material and upon the nature of changes experienced during the biochemical stage, the operation of geochemical or dynamic processes can result in markedly different coals. As indicated earlier, the geochemical stage is characterized as the period when chemical changes are caused mainly by temperature increases, and to a lesser extent, by the time that the higher temperature persists.

Earlier it was postulated that a short period of accumulation for vegetal matter is not inconsistent with observed phenomena, with a more lengthy period of time during which such material was transformed into what we now recognize as coal. However, it was noted that an extremely short time could account for production of high-carbon-content coals under appropriate temperature conditions.[3] For

[1] *Ibid.*

[2] U.S. Bureau of Mines, "Dictionary of Mining, Mineral, and Related Terms," p. 471, 1968.

[3] Francis, *loc. cit.*

example, anthracite could be produced in half a million years at temperatures between 120 and 150°C.[1] As a result, it was concluded that "both the temperatures tures and times necessary to convert peat into high rank coals are much smaller than have generally been agreed in the past."[2] It appears that time alone may be sufficient to produce the changes observed in coals, although moderate heat and pressure may accelerate such changes.

Support for the above is also found in the work of Levorsen,[3] who noted that low temperatures apparently prevailed for other organic accumulations in petroleum reservoirs: "most oil-producing reservoirs have temperatures less than 200°F [93° C] *and in many reservoirs this temperature has probably never been exceeded.*" Further support is found in the work of Teichmuller and Teichmuller,[4] who noted that "maximum temperatures of 100 to 200°C are sufficient for the formation of bituminous coals and even of anthracites, provided that the heat acted over a sufficiently long period."

Pressure does not promote chemical processes, and even retards reactions. Pressure may, however, lead to structural development of coals through orientation of particular units.[5] Pressures exerted upon beds of organic material by the weight of overlying sediments (lithostatic pressures) appear to be adequate to account for the changes observable in coal seams. It does not appear to be necessary to have severe orogenic pressures to accomplish the progressive changes in organic material; indeed, there are only relatively rare instances where mountain-building or intrusive pressures appear to have exerted significant influences on coal development.[6]

The hypothesized low-temperature, low-pressure environment of coalification suggests that the exposure time of biologically altered organic remains to these conditions may determine the ultimate character of resulting coals. "These findings may explain why coals of Tertiary age [30 million years] are still mainly in the brown-coal stage, whereas coals of the Carboniferous [300 million years] have commonly reached the stage of bituminous coals or anthracites, even if the degree of subsidence was the same in each case."[7]

The relationship between carbon content of coals to geologic age is shown for a small sampling in Figure 3. The figure illustrates the above statement and suggests that there is a relatively rapid increase in carbon content with age. Tertiary lignites have 10 to 15 percent more carbon than do recent peats. The rate of change becomes slower with time, however, as Cretaceous bituminous coals are within about 10 percent of the carbon content of Carboniferous bituminous coals.

The result of these biochemical and geochemical changes upon organic deposits is to produce coals of different *rank*. Rank is defined as a classification of coals ac-

[1] *Ibid.*

[2] *Ibid.*

[3] A. I. Levorsen, "Geology of Petroleum," 2d ed., Freeman, San Francisco, 1967.

[4] M. Teichmuller and R. Teichmuller, Geological Aspects of Coal Metamorphism, in D. Murchinson and T. S. Westoll (eds.), "Coal and Coal-Bearing Strata," p. 233, American Elsevier, New York, 1968.

[5] *Ibid.*

[6] See, for example, E. S. Moore, *op. cit.*

[7] Teichmuller and Teichmuller, *op. cit.*

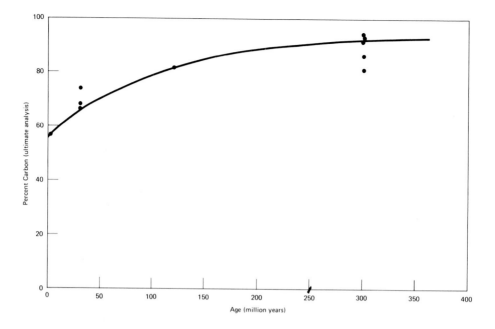

Figure 3. Relationship of carbon content of coals to geologic age. (From I. A. Williamson. "Coal Mining Geology," Oxford University Press, London, 1967.)

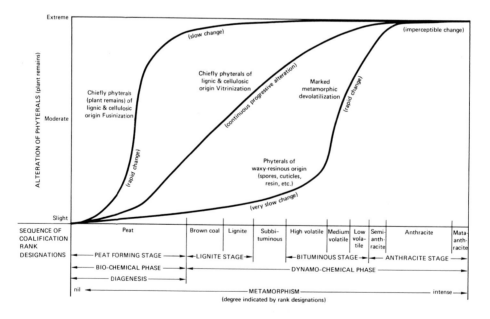

Figure 4. Metamorphic alteration of phyteral constituents. (From J.M. Schopf, *Econ. Geol.,* vol. 43, pp. 207-225, 1948.)

cording to their physical and chemical properties, especially their heating value, moisture content, carbon content, ash characteristics, and presence of associated minerals. Figure 4 illustrates the stages of coal formation and the several ranks of coal that result. In the following sections, the physical and chemical properties of coals of each rank are presented and examined.

PHYSICAL PROPERTIES

Numerous physical properties of coal have been studied by large numbers of investigators. Among the properties determined are x-ray diffraction, ultraviolet and visible absorption, reflectance, refractive index, infrared absorption, electron-spin resonance, proton-spin resonance, electrical conductivity, diamagnetic susceptibility, dielectric constant, sound velocity, density, porosity, strength, reflectance, caking properties, and heating value.[1] No attempt will be made here to repeat previous comprehensive discussions of these properties. Instead, this section will be limited to a brief review of these inherent physical properties that are of principal apparent importance to processing: density, physical constitution, and heating value. A description of derived physical or mechanical properties of coal is presented in a later section.

Density

The density of coal measures its weight per unit volume. Because coal is a porous substance, it is difficult to determine its volume accurately. Accordingly, most measurements of coal density are *apparent* rather than true densities. The apparent density curve passes through a minimum at about 85 percent carbon; thus, bituminous coals are the least dense of any of the other members of the coal series (Figure 5).

There is a general correlation between density and ash content in coals,[2] although the relation differs for various ranks. For bituminous coals, the ash contents for various densities are as follows:

Density	Ash content, %
1.3 – 1.4	1 – 5
1.4 – 1.5	5 – 10
1.5 – 1.6	10 – 35
1.6 – 1.8	35 – 60
1.8 – 1.9	60 – 75
1.9 and greater	75 – 90

Source: "Steam: Its Generation and Use," p. 8-5, Babcock & Wilcox Company, New York, 1972.

[1] See extensive description by H. Tschamler and E. deRuiter, Physical Properties of Coals, in H. H. Lowry (ed.), "Chemistry of Coal Utilization, Supplementary Volume," pp. 35 – 118, Wiley, New York, 1968.
[2] *Ibid.*

These data are empirically determined for each coal rank and are used to guide the design of coal preparation methods; the various mechanical properties of coals associated with their use will be described in a later section.

In assessing coal reserves, a convenient way to express coal density for various ranks is as tons per acre-foot of coal (Figure 6). Then, with knowledge of the thickness of seams from mapping or drill core data and of the areas covered by the seam, it is possible to calculate rapidly the amount of coal present.

Physical Constitution

The several ranks of coal are characterized by variation in a number of physical properties.

Color. A general darkening of color is evidenced by increasing rank from peat to subbituminous coal.[1]

Luster. Lower-rank coals (peat, lignite) have a dull and earthy luster, while higher-rank coals (subbituminous and bituminous) have a progressively brighter luster, reaching a uniformly brilliant appearance in anthracite.

Constituent changes. Essentially unaltered plant debris can be recognized in peat and lignite, but it becomes progressively more difficult to readily distinguish among constituents in higher-rank coals.

Porosity. The porosity of coals passes through a minimum at around 89 percent carbon; lower-rank coals exhibit a wide variation in porosity. While the porosity of high-rank coals increases somewhat from the minimum, the increase is small and varies over a narrow range (Figure 7).

Strength. The strength of coal is related to its hardness and friability. A maximum in microhardness occurs at around 83 percent carbon (bituminous coals), with a minimum at around 90 percent carbon. Anthracites behave as elastic materials (Figure 8).

Reflectance. Reflectance is the percentage of incident light reflected from a polished coal surface. Figure 9 shows that reflectance increases progressively with rank and is used as a rapid method of assessing carbon content.

Each of these properties of coal is employed in classifying coals and in guiding the conduct of specific tests to determine its behavior under conditions of utilization (these derived properties are discussed in a later section).

Heating Value

The heating value of coals is typically expressed in British thermal units (Btu).[2] Heating value increases progressively with rank (expressed as carbon content) from peat through bituminous coals; a slight decrease in heating value occurs with anthracite (Figure 10). Heating value is a function of many physical coal parameters as well as its chemical properties.

[1] Williamson, *op. cit.*

[2] A British thermal unit is the quantity of heat required to raise the temperature of one pound of water one degree Fahrenheit.

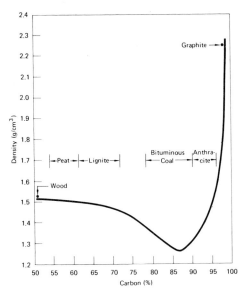

Figure 5. Relationship between apparent density and the rank of coal (as indicated by carbon content). (From I. A. Williamson, "Coal Mining Geology," Oxford University Press, London, 1967.)

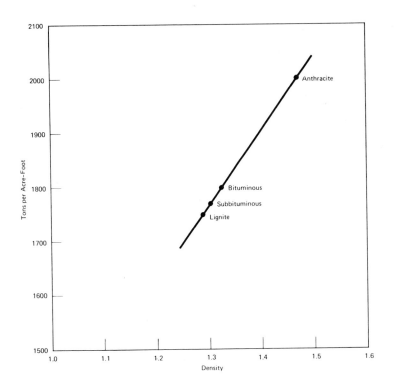

Figure 6. Density and weight of coal by rank. (After P. Averitt, *US Geol. Surv. Bull.* 1412, 1975.)

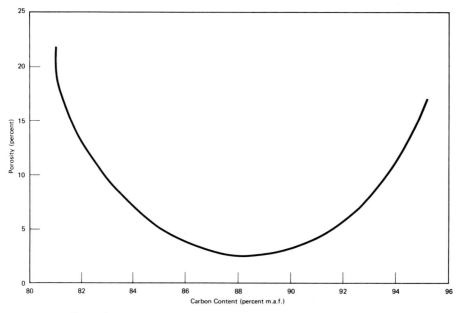

Figure 7. Variation in coal porosity with rank. (From J.G. King, and E.T. Wilkins, The Internal Structure of Coal, *Proc. Conf. Ultra-Fine Structure of Coals and Cokes, BCURA*, p. 46-56, 1944.

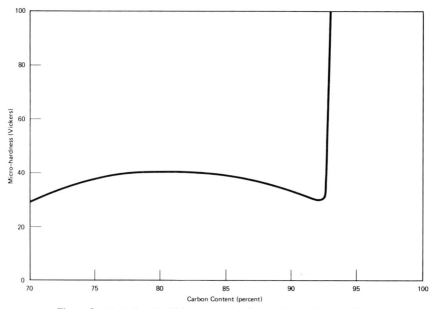

Figure 8. Variation in Vickers microhardness with coal rank. (From D.W. Van Krevelen, "Coal," American Elsevier, New York, 1961.)

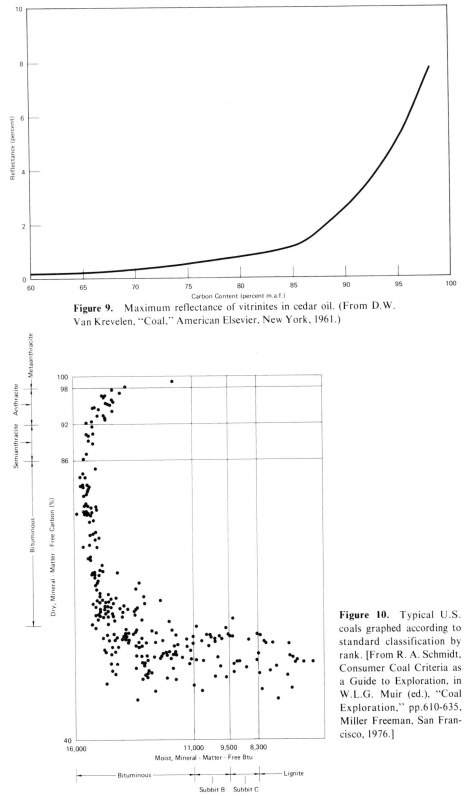

Figure 9. Maximum reflectance of vitrinites in cedar oil. (From D.W. Van Krevelen, "Coal," American Elsevier, New York, 1961.)

Figure 10. Typical U.S. coals graphed according to standard classification by rank. [From R. A. Schmidt, Consumer Coal Criteria as a Guide to Exploration, in W.L.G. Muir (ed.), "Coal Exploration," pp.610-635, Miller Freeman, San Francisco, 1976.]

The principal physical properties of coal have been discussed in terms of their relationship to rank, expressed as carbon content. To complete the description of coals, it is necessary next to examine the main chemical properties and their variations among different members of the coal types.

CHEMICAL PROPERTIES

The chemical analysis of coals has been a challenge to chemists for centuries. As a result of previous work, analytical techniques have been developed and standardized so that results may be correlated between different laboratories. Numerous accounts of this previous work have been prepared.[1] This section cannot attempt to supplant such thorough and comprehensive compilations; rather, the presentation will be limited to a brief review of the principal chemical properties of coals that appear to be of primary importance in processing and utilization. The discussion covers classes of coal analysis, relations of principal constituents to rank, content and occurrence of mineral matter and three elements, and representative analyses of principal U.S. coal seams.

Classes of Coal Analyses

Two main classes of coal analyses are employed:[2] (1) *Ultimate analysis* determines the elemental composition of the coal (particularly the carbon, hydrogen, sulfur, nitrogen and ash content; oxygen is estimated by difference). The ultimate analysis may be supplemented by measurements of trace elements present in either the organic or inorganic constituents of coal. (2) *Proximate analysis* determines the presence of certain coal compounds (namely, moisture, volatile matter, and ash; fixed carbon content is estimated by difference). The proximate analysis is often supplemented by determination of sulfur content and estimation of heating value.

Ultimate analysis. Ultimate analysis expresses coal composition in weight percentages of carbon, hydrogen, nitrogen, sulfur, oxygen, and ash. Carbon content includes that present in organic material, and hydrogen content includes water of mineral constitution in addition to that present in organic matter. Sulfur may occur as part of the organic matter, sulfide minerals, or as sulfates. All nitrogen is present in the organic material.

As indicated in the previous section, there is a continuous variation in physical properties with rank; similar variations occur in ultimate analysis. These variations are illustrated in Figure 11, which shows the progressive increase in carbon content and decrease in oxygen content with increasing rank. This direct relationship suggests that slight changes in composition have an important influence on the

---

[1] See, for example, the comprehensive syntheses of data prepared by W. H. Ode, Coal Analysis and Mineral Matter, and I. G. C. Dryden, Chemical Constitution and Reactions in Coal, both in H. H. Lowry (ed.), "Chemistry of Coal Utilization: Supplementary Volume, pp. 202–231 and 232–295, respectively, Wiley, New York, 1963.

[2] U.S. Bureau of Mines, *op. cit.*, p. 872.

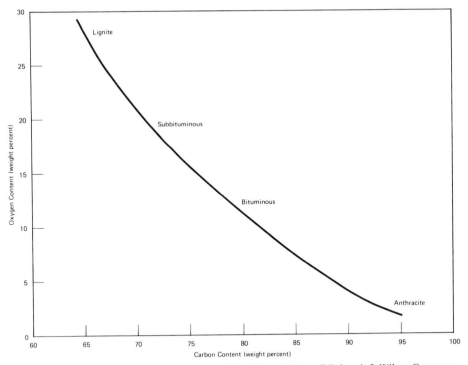

Figure 11. Continuous variation in coal composition. (From "Steam," Babcock & Wilcox Company, New York, 1972.)

resulting character of coal, emphasizing the sensitivity of coal evolution to the interplay among many relatively independent variables and conditions.

The individual constituents of coals appear to be affected differently during coal evolution. Figure 12 shows variations in carbon and oxygen content among coal lithotypes and related organic materials. The data suggest that an individual coal's composition and related proterties will be strongly influenced by the proportions of different macerals present and in turn by the specific composition of each constituent.

In addition to investigating carbon-oxygen relationships, it is also essential to examine carbon-hydrogen variations (Figure 13). In contrast to the progressive and direct increase in carbon content with increasing rank, hydrogen content remains relatively constant at about 5 percent for lignites and most bituminous coals but decreases to 3 to 4 percent for higher-rank bituminous coals and anthracites. The extent of conversion of original carbohydrates to hydrocarbons appears to be the principal factor influencing the changes in hydrogen content with rank. The decreases in hydrogen content with increasing rank is related to the decrease in volatile matter content. As will be shown in the following discussion of proximate analysis, the change in total hydrogen content is also related to the amount and character of volatiles.

Figure 14 shows the relationship of nitrogen content to carbon content for a representative sampling of coals of varying rank. Maximum nitrogen contents are

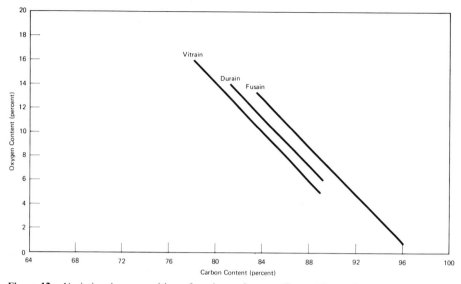

Figure 12. Variation in composition of coal constituents. (From "Steam," Babcock & Wilcox Company, New York, 1972.)

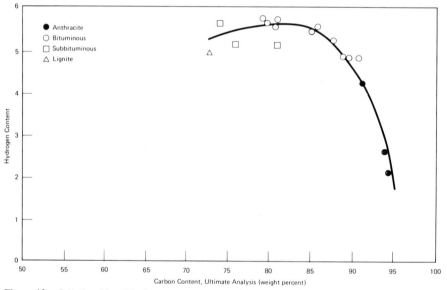

Figure 13. Relationship of hydrogen content to carbon content for coals of varying rank. (From "Steam," Babcock & Wilcox Company, New York, 1972.)

about 1.7 percent for bituminous coals and less for coals of lower and higher rank. There is considerable variability in nitrogen content among lower-rank coals, and although the data are limited, there is a suggestion that such variability is less for higher-rank coals.

Figure 15 shows the relationship of sulfur content to carbon content for a

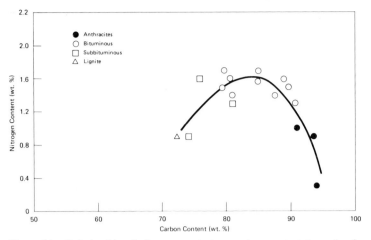

Figure 14. Relationship of nitrogen content to carbon content in coals of varying rank. (From "Steam," Babcock & Wilcox Company, New York, 1972.)

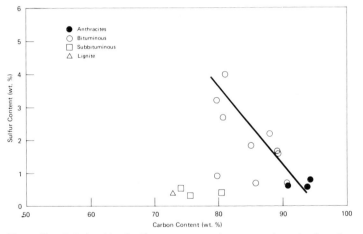

Figure 15. Relationship of sulfur content to carbon content in coals of varying rank. (From "Steam," Babcock & Wilcox Company, New York, 1972.)

representative sampling of coals of varying rank. Lignites, subbituminous coals, certain bituminous coals, and anthracites show low sulfur contents (less than 1 percent by weight). Highest sulfur contents are found in bituminous coals; a progressive decrease in sulfur content with increased carbon content is indicated for these coals (shown by the heavy line in Figure 15).

Minor or trace elements. In addition to the major elements determined by ultimate analysis as described above, a number of minor or trace elements are found in coals. For example, it was found that at least some chlorine probably occurred in organic combination and that part of the sodium in Illinois coals could be attributed to clay minerals.[1]

Analyses of trace elements present in low-temperature ash resulted in the recognition of four groups of potentially volatile trace elements.[2]

1. Elements of greatest organic affinity that are concentrated in clean-coal fractions: Ge, Be, B
2. Elements of least organic affinity that are concentrated in the mineral matter of coal: Hg, Zr, Zn, Cd, As, Pb, Mn, and Mo
3. Elements associated with both organic and inorganic matter but which tend to be more closely allied with the organic fractions: P, Ga, Ti, Sb, and V
4. Elements found in both organic and inorganic matter but which tend to be more closely associated with inorganic fractions: Co, Ni, Cr, Se, and Cu

These associations appear to be controlled by the physicochemical properties of the trace elements, especially the ionic potential (species with the largest ionic potential have the largest organic affinity).[3] These elements are also concentrated near the source areas of a coal basin.[4]

It was suggested that "considerable portions of the trace-element contents . . . [of coal-bearing rocks] were already present in the lattices of the detrital minerals when these were delivered to the site of deposition."[5] Organic matter appears to have been an effective sorbant in determining final trace-element contents and associations.

Ultimate analysis, however necessary to provide data on the total elemental composition of coals of varying type, is time-consuming and costly. As a result, ultimate analyses are not performed regularly on most coals produced and used in the United States; out of 255 coal samples for which analyses were reported, ultimate analyses were reported for only 39.* All samples reported indicated proximate analyses, a more rapid and simpler procedure which provides information about coals according to their response to heating under controlled conditions.

Proximate analysis. Proximate analysis characterizes coals in connection with conditions of utilization by determining the distribution of products obtained by incremental applications of heat in a controlled atmosphere. Proximate analysis separates coal compounds into four groups: (1) water or moisture, (2) volatile mat-

[1]H. J. Gluskoter and R. R. Ruch, Chlorine and Sodium in Illinois Coals as Determined by Neutron Activation Analysis, *Fuel,* pp. 65−76, January 1971.

[2]R. R. Ruch, H. J. Gluskoter, and N. F. Shimp, Occurrence and Distribution of Potentially Volatile Trace Elements in Coal, *Ill. State Geol. Surv., Environ. Geol. Notes,* no. 72, August 1974.

[3]P. Zubrovic, Physicochemical Properties of Certain Minor Elements as Controlling Factors in their Distribution in Coal, "Coal Science," *Adv. Chem. Ser.,* no. 55, pp. 221−231, 1966.

[4]P. Zubrovic, Minor Element Distribution in Coal Samples of the Interior Coal Province, "Coal Science," *Adv. Chem. Ser.,* no. 55, pp. 232−247, 1966.

[5]G. D. Nicholls, The Geochemistry of Coal-Bearing Strata, in D. Murchison and T. S. Westoll (eds.), "Coal and Coal-Bearing Strata," p. 209, American Elsevier, New York, 1968.

*See Analyses of Tipple and Delivered Samples of Coal Collected During Fiscal Year 1971, *US Bur. Mines, Rep. Invest.,* no. 7588, 1972. (20 pages.)

ter consisting of gases and vapors driven off during pyrolysis, (3) mineral impurities as ash, and (4) fixed carbon,[1] the remaining nonvolatile fraction of the pyrolyzed coal, obtained by difference following determination of the above groups.

The variation in proximate analyses with rank are given in Table 2. The data show that with higher-coal rank there is a progressive increase in fixed carbon, a progressive decrease in moisture, and an overall decrease in volatile matter (except for maxima with high-volatile bituminous coals).

The composition of the fixed carbon in all types of coal is "substantially all carbon,"[2] and "the variable constituents of coals can, therefore, be considered as concentrated in the volatile matter."[3] The heating value of the volatile matter is "perhaps the most important property as far as combustion is concerned."[4]

Figure 16 shows the relationship of volatile matter to organic sulfur content for coals of varying rank. Organic sulfur varies widely among coals of different rank; the range of organic sulfur content is greatest for coals of lowest rank and least for those of higher rank. For the majority of bituminous coals included in this limited sample, the data suggest that higher volatile contents are accompanied by larger ranges of organic sulfur contents.

Figure 17 shows the relationship of ash content with carbon content for coals of different rank. No district trend is indicated, and considerable variation is present. Ash content appears to be relatively independent of fixed carbon content, perhaps reflecting variations in initial deposition of mineral matter in coals as well as subsequent alterations in such minerals or formation of new mineral species subsequent to deposition.

Mineral matter. In addition to various organic constituents, coals contain a variety of inorganic mineral compounds. Present in mineral matter may be (1) silicates of alkalis, calcium, magnesium, iron, and titanium; (2) oxides of iron and silica; (3) carbonates of iron, calcium, and magnesium (which may change to oxides on heating); and (4) sulfides of iron and minor amounts of sulfates, phosphates, arsenides and others.[5]

The mineral matter or ash in coal has often been classified as *inherent* [stemming from the plant material in the coal swamp] and *adventitious* [added in the swamp] after the deposition of the plant material. This classification is misleading, especially in the use of the term "adventitious," a synonym of which is "accidental." The detrital and antrigenic minerals associated with coal are definitely not there by accident. They are the necessary results of a definite set of biological, chemical, and

[1]Actually, "the fact that coal on distillation gives a residue of impure carbon [coke] and volatile products [tar and gas] suggested the idea that coal contained free carbon, associated in some way with bituminous matter. The terms, 'bituminous coal' and 'fixed carbon' [for ash-free coke] are survivals of this idea, which is, however, entirely incorrect. The process of distillation results in an entire destruction of the original coal and the rearrangement of its elements—neither the coke nor gas are contained in the coal as such." W. S. Boultòn (ed.), "Practical Coal Mining," vol. 1, pp. 7, 63, Gresham, London, 1913.

[2]"Steam: Its Generation and Use," p. 5-14, Babcock & Wilcox Company, New York, 1972.

[3]*Ibid.*

[4]*Ibid.*

[5]L. R. Moore, *op. cit.*

Table 2 Classification* of coals by rank

Class, group	Fixed carbon limits (dry, mineral-matter-free basis), %		Volatile matter limits (dry, mineral-matter-free basis), %		Calorific value limits (moist, mineral-matter-free basis), †Btu/lb		Agglomerating character
	Equal or greater than	Less than	Equal or greater than	Less than	Equal or greater than	Less than	
I. Anthracitic:							
1. Meta-anthracite	98			2			
2. Anthracite	92	98	2	8			Nonagglomerating†
3. Semianthracite	86	92	8	14			
II. Bituminous:							
1. Low-volatile bituminous coal	78	86	14	22			
2. Medium-volatile bituminous coal	69	78	22	31			Commonly, agglomerating¶
3. High-volatile A bituminous coal		69	31		14,000§		
4. High-volatile B bituminous coal					13,000§	14,000	
5. High-volatile C bituminous coal					11,500	13,000	
					10,500	11,500	Agglomerating
III. Subbituminous:							
1. Subbituminous A coal					10,500	11,500	
2. Subbituminous B coal					9,500	10,500	Nonagglomerating
3. Subbituminous C coal‡					8,300	9,500	
IV. Lignitic:							
1. Lignite A					6,300	8,300	
2. Lignite B						6,300	

*This classification does not include a few coals, principally nonbanded varieties, which have unusual physical and chemical properties and which come within the limits of fixed carbon or calorific value of the high-volatile bituminous and subbituminous ranks. All these coals either contain less than 48 percent dry, mineral-matter-free fixed carbon or have more than 15,500 Btu per pound, calculated on the moist, mineral-matter-free basis.

†Moist refers to coal containing its natural inherent moisture but not including visible water on the surface of the coal.

‡If agglomerating, classify in low-volatile group of the bituminous class.

§Coals having 69 percent or more fixed carbon on the dry, mineral-matter-free basis shall be classified according to fixed carbon, regardless of calorific value.

¶It is recognized that there may be nonagglomerating varieties in these groups of the bituminous class, and there are notable exceptions in the high-volatile C bituminous group.

Source: US Geol. Surv. Bull. 1412.

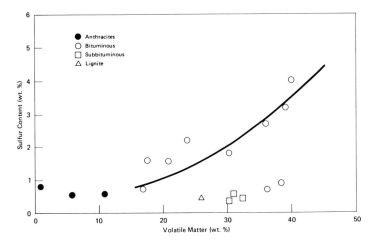

Figure 16. Relationship of sulfur content to volatile matter content in coals of varying rank (proximate analysis). "Steam," Babcock & Wilcox Company, New York, 1972.)

physical conditions, all of which combined to provide an environment in which the minerals could be deposited or in which they could form.[1]

For Illinois coals, the presence of typical mineral species in low-temperature ash is as follows:[2]

Mineral	Weight percent
1. Illite, kaolinite, and mixed-layer clays	52
2. Sulfides (mainly pyrite)	23
3. Quartz	15
4. Carbonates (calcite)	9
5. All others	1
	100

The dominant clay minerals in coal and other silicates appear to have developed from clastic material deposited during accumulation of organic matter. Sulfides and carbonates are interpreted to be largely of secondary origin, having formed at some time subsequent to accumulation to fill voids along cleats or joints.[3]

The character and distribution of mineral matter in coal can be used in interpreting the origin of the deposits. For example, Rao and Gluskoter suggested that for the Illinois basin the high quartz content of younger coals indicated a greater detrital contribution to mineral matter and an association with fresh waters. Nicholls pointed out that "precipitated inorganic components of [coal and] the strata associated with coal seams can be used to deduce the pH and Eh conditions

[1]C. P. Rao and H. J. Gluskoter, Occurrence and Distribution of Minerals in Illinois Coals, *Ill. State Geol. Surv., Circ.* 476, 1973.
[2]*Ibid.*
[3]Williamson, *op. cit.*

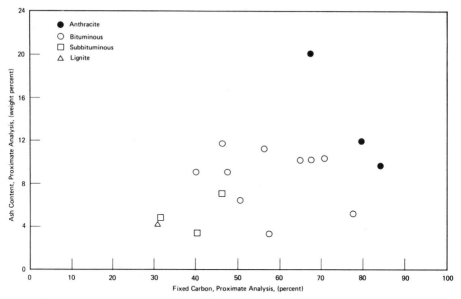

Figure 17. Relationship of ash content to fixed carbon content for coals of varying rank. (From "Steam," Babcock & Wilcox Company, New York, 1972.)

of the newly formed sediment."[1] Consequently, the study of mineral matter can be considerably important to a better understanding of coal development. Such an understanding is essential to establishing an effective means of coal utilization. However, it is necessary to have in mind the magnitude and occurrence of coals of varying rank before consideration of coal use, and this topic is covered next.

The relationship between heating value of pure coal and volatile matter is shown for coals of varying rank in Figure 18. For low-rank coals, the organic matter in the coal has a higher heating value than the volatile matter. The coal and volatile matter have approximately equal heating values for subbituminous coals. The heating value of volatile matter exceeds that of coal for most bituminous coals. The heating value of volatile matter continues to increase for low-volatile bituminous coals and anthracites, while the heating value of the coal itself remains essentially constant. This suggests that the character of volatile matter is strongly related to the evolution of coals and that the process of change continues even upon reaching high rank.

ENGINEERING PROPERTIES OF COAL

The physical and chemical properties of coal described earlier serve to distinguish among various coals and aid in establishing preliminary criteria in connection with design and performance parameters for coal utilization equipment and facilities. It is noteworthy that standard coal properties are typically determined on rather

[1]Nicholls, *op. cit.*

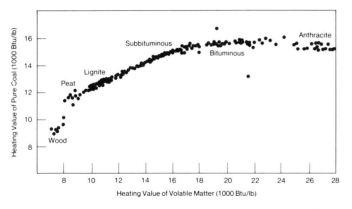

Figure 18. A suggested coal classification using the relationship of the respective heating values of "pure coal" and the volatile matter. (From "Steam," Babcock & Wilcox Company, New York, 1972.)

small samples of coal in contrast to the large volumes consumed by a commercial facility. Additionally, test conditions rarely duplicate those of actual operations, and the applicability of coal data obtained through such measurements to full-scale operation may be incomplete. Although the basic coal properties are useful, it is also essential to know more detailed data on coals under conditions of use. It is the engineering data for actual operations (largely empirical information for particular coals in well-defined utilization conditions on standardized equipment and is derived from a history of trial-and-error iterations) that are of primary importance in assessing potentials for coal utilization. This section will present an overview of selected information on coal production factors, an introduction to sampling methods, engineering properties, effects of preparation on properties, and the effect of coal properties on utilization conditions.

Production Factors

As indicated in Chapter 3, the bulk of U.S. coal reserves occurs at sufficient depth to require underground mining. Also, historically, coal production from underground mining has predominated. Much of our knowledge of coal seams stems directly from the integrated experience of these previous operations and, more recently, from surface mines. The details of coal extraction will be covered in Chapter 5 (see also Cassidy).[1] This section will emphasize selected aspects of coal properties and occurrence that influence production and utilization factors.

Coal seams display a natural vertical fracture system known as *cleat*, formed as a result of tectonic forces. Coal breaks along cleats into relatively regular, cubic pieces. "Coal has been mined parallel to the directions of the cleat almost since the start of coal mining. . . . It is easier to mine parallel to cleat directions than at an angle to the cleats."[2] As a result, coal mines are planned to take advantage of

[1]S. M. Cassidy, "Elements of Practical Coal Mining," AIME, New York, 1974.

[2]C. M. McCullough, M. Deul, P. W. Jeran, Cleat in Bituminous Coal Beds, *US Bur. Mines, Rep. Invest. No.* 7910, 1974.

natural breakages along the cleat. This practice persists despite the development of mechanized mining equipment that is capable of breaking coal irrespective of cleat directions. It is important to note that "some manufacturers of coal cutters design these tools primarily for cutting the impurities in coal; these manufacturers have found that coal cutting forces are so low that they design the cutters primarily for the iron pyrites."[1]

The trend in coal mining machinery is toward more highly powered equipment that is capable of cutting any materials encountered (Figure 19). This would appear to offer a degree of flexibility in mine planning and development that was not possible previously.

However, the more highly mechanized equipment produces a product that is both smaller in size and diluted by admixture of noncombustible material.[2] Conventionally mined coal contains less total fines and less dust of aerofloat size than that produced by continuous mining equipment.

The manner of coal cutting is related to the rate of methane release. Generally speaking, higher rates of methane emission are found with finer coal particles.[3] The methane emission ratio varies among coal seams, and in the same seam, with methods of mining.[4] From the standpoint of utilization, therefore, finer coal produced by continuous mining methods has lost more of its methane content than coal from the same seam mined by conventional methods.

Generally speaking, the end result of modern coal production, therefore, is a product that is small in size, an intimate mixture of combustible and noncombustible material, and from which much of the inherent volatile matter has been lost. Coal utilization processes, accordingly, are presented with a material whose natural variability in essential properties has been accentuated and compounded in a relatively random manner as a consequence of its extraction from the earth.

Sampling

The importance of coal sampling is well-stated as follows:

> Although the character, quantity, and distribution of minerals may vary considerable within the coal seam, much of this diversity is masked in the as-fired fuel as a result of cutting, transporting, size reduction, washing, classifying, storing, and pulverizing—operations which tend to distribute the mineral matter content more uniformly throughout the coal.

> Nevertheless, the fuel is by far the greatest source of the contaminating materials that are responsible for some of the most complex, obscure, and variable problems encountered in design and operation of [coal utilization] equipment.[5]

[1]P. F. Rad, Mechanical Properties and Cutting Characteristics of Coal, *US Bur. Mines, Inf. Cir. No.* 8584, 1973.

[2]R. L. Schmidt, W. H. Engelman, and R. R. Fumanti, A Comparison of Borer, Ripper, and Conventional Mining Products in Illinois No. 6 Coal, *US Bur. Mines, Rep. Invest. No.* 7687, 1972. See also O. Stutzer, "Geology of Coal," p. 261, University of Chicago Press, Chicago, 1940.

[3]F. N. Kissell, J. L. Banfield, R. W. Dalzell, and M. G. Zabetakis, Peak Methane Concentrations During Coal Mining, *US Bur. Mines, Inf. Cir. No.* 7885, 1974.

[4]Methane Control in Eastern U.S. Coal Mines, *US Bur. Mines, Inf. Cir. No.* 8621, 1973.

[5]F. G. Ely and D. H. Barnhart, Coal Ash—Its Effect on Boiler Availability, in H. H. Lowry (ed.), "Chemistry of Coal Utilization, Supplementary Volume," p. 820, Wiley, New York, 1963.

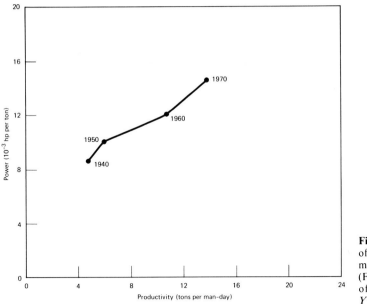

Figure 19. Relation of power to deep-mine productivity. (From U.S. Bureau of Mines, *Miner. Yearb.*, 1940-1974.)

Each coal has its distinctive sampling characteristics, and these change with production conditions. In an attempt to systematize sampling operations, two basic procedures of coal sampling are used to aid in addressing these problems. First, a *Special-purpose-sampling Procedure* of high accuracy is used to classify coals and to establish equipment design and performance specifications. This procedure characterizes coals from new deposits or guides the development of new utilization facilities. Second, a *Commercial-sampling Procedure* is used in monitoring the routine production quality of coal to determine its compliance with the operating conditions previously specified. The latter procedure is much more commonly used than is the former. Many consumers lack the technical and economic wherewithal to establish the sampling characteristics of a given coal through the Special-purpose Procedure. Instead, a set of sampling standards for testing coal maintained by the American Society for Testing Materials (ASTM) is employed in ordinary commercial operations; these are summarized in Table 3.

Unfortunately, even when these standard sampling methods are employed, differences in sampling results can occur among analyses taken by producers and consumers. These differences may stem from the inherent variability in coal properties and from the fact that measurements of a variable substance are only estimates of average values. To approach a "true" value, it is necessary to have a series of analyses on the same coal to observe the patterns of variability in inherent properties and in sampling itself.

Collection of samples requires great care to avoid introducing errors. Coal at rest in storage piles or in rail cars has experienced an unknown degree of size segregation or influence by moisture, and samples from these sources will possess an unknown basis. Sampling of coal in motion along conveyors or through chutes

Table 3 ASTM standards for testing coal, specifications and definitions of terms

ASTM standards for testing coal			
*D 1756	Carbon Dioxide in Coal	D 2639	Plastic Properties of Coal by the Automatic Gieseler Plastometer
*D 2361	Chlorine in Coal		
*D 291	Cubic Foot Weight of Crushed Bituminous Coal	D 197	Sampling and Fineness Test of Powdered Coal
*D 440	Drop Shatter Test for Coal	*D 271	Sampling and Analysis, Laboratory, of Coal and Coke
*D 547	Dustiness, Index of, of Coal and Coke	D 492	Sampling Coals Classified According to Ash Content
*D 1857	Fusibility of Coal Ash		
*D 1412	Equilibrium Moisture of Coal at 96 to 97% Relative Humidity and 30C	*D 2234	Sampling, Mechanical, of Coal
		*D 2013	Samples, Coal, Preparing of Analysis
*D 2014	Expansion or Contraction of Coal by the Sole-Heated Oven	*D 410	Screen, Analysis of Coal
*D 720	Free-Swelling Index of Coal	D 311	Sieve Analysis of Crushed Bituminous Coal
D 409	Grindability of Coal by the Hardgrove-Machine Method	D 310	Size of Anthracite
*D 2015	Gross Calorific Value of Solid Fuel by the Adiabatic Bomb Calorimeter	*D 431	Size of Coal, Designating from its Screen Analysis
		*D 1757	Sulfur in Coal Ash
		*D 2492	Sulfur, Forms of, in Coal
D 1812	Plastic Properties of Coal by the Gieseler Plastometer	*D 441	Tumbler Test for Coal

Specifications			
*D 388	Classification of Coals by Rank	D 323	Perforated-Plate Sieves for Testing Purposes
*D 11	Wire-Cloth Sieves for Testing Purposes		

Definitions of terms			
*D 121	Coal and Coke	*D 407	Gross Calorific Value and Net Calorific Value of Solid and Liquid Fuels
D 2796	Lithological Classes and Physical Components of Coal		

*Approved as American National Standard by the American National Standards Institute.

gives a better opportunity for more representative results from the several testing methods.[1]

In summary, a number of sampling procedures are used to determine coal characteristics. The procedures seek especially to identify deleterious constituents which are inherent in particular coals or which become introduced through extraction. This information is indispensible for the design and operation of facilities that use naturally occurring coals, as well as for establishing coal treatment practices

[1]"Keystone Coal Industry Manual," p. 246, McGraw Hill, New York, 1974.

that seek to remove all or most of the undesirable constituents (or, failing that, to surpress them to a tolerable level).

The targets in coal sampling and analysis are to determine its primary characteristics under utilization conditions. Experience to date with various combustion systems indicates that coal grindability, moisture, and ash properties are controlling parameters (Table 4). The following discussion deals with these factors in greater detail as they affect coal grindability, separation of impurities, and ash characteristics.

Size Reduction

The main approach to treatment of raw coal[1] is comminution, with the objective of liberating noncombustible constituents for greater ease in separation and segregation. This subject is discussed in Chapter 9; also, the principles of coal breaking and crushing are well-described, together with a practical description of typical equipment.[2] The performance of this equipment is affected by the size and nature of the feed coal. As noted above, this will vary for different coals, different mining methods, and different end uses for which the coal is intended.

The hardness or softness of the coals is an important parameter which determines the relative ease of reduction of particle size. These characteristics are measured through a standard procedure that determines the relative ease of pulverizing coals in comparison to a standard coal having a *Hardgrove grindability index* of 100. Typical values of this index are:

Rank	Hardgrove grindability index
Anthracite	21−61
Low-volatile bituminous	85−115
High-volatile bituminous	40−75
West Kentucky	50−70
Ohio	45−65
Indiana	55−68
Illinois	40−75
Subbituminous and lignite	30−65

Figure 20 shows the relationship of the grindability index with the carbon content of coals. Although the sample is small, the data suggest that the grindability index is greatest for most bituminous coals and least for lignites and anthracites (bituminous coals are softer). Figure 21, again for a small sample, suggests that the grindability index increases progressively with rank ash content

---

[1] *Raw coal* refers to coal that has experienced initial, rough segregation of mining-induced wastes; coal that has not been so handled is termed *run-of-mine,* and may contain a variety of unwanted materials (e.g., wires, bits, tubing, cardboard, wood chips, etc.).

[2] See J. W. Leonard and D. R. Mitchell (eds.), "Coal Preparation," chap. 7, AIME, New York, 1968. 1968.

Table 4 Primary coal characteristics for firing

	Pulverized coal firing	Stoker firing	Cyclone Furnace firing
Grindability	X		
Rank	X	X	X
Moisture, maximum percent	15	15−20	20
Volatiles, minimum percent	15	15	15
Ash, maximum percent	20	20	25
Ash-softening temperature		X	X

Source: "Steam," Babcock & Wilcox Company, New York, 1972.

(coals become softer), with the exception of softer bituminous coals and certain harder anthracites.

Figure 22 shows that the Hardgrove grindability index correlates with volatile matter in an inverted U-shaped curve. It was noted earlier that volatile matter is directly related to rank. Therefore, low- and high-rank coals have low grindability indices (i.e., they are hard to grind), while medium-rank coals are easier to grind.

The grindability index varies greatly from seam to seam (and among samples from the same seam) because of the variations in impurities that are commonly present. Also, because impurities tend to segregate in certain size fractions, the grindability index of any given coal can vary from size to size. Fruthermore, any segregation of coal from mineral matter during handling or other processing will result in changes to the grindability index.

Further, the grindability index for lower-rank coals is influenced by moisture

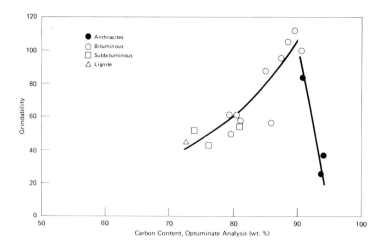

Figure 20.   Relationship of grindability of coal to carbon contents for coals of varying rank. (From "Steam," Babcock & Wilcox Company, New York, 1972.)

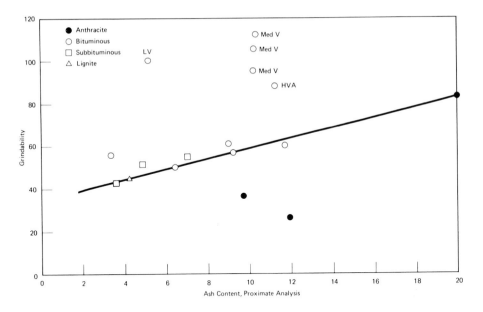

Figure 21. Relationship of grindability of coal to ash content for coals of varying rank. (From "Steam," Babcock & Wilcox Company, New York, 1972.)

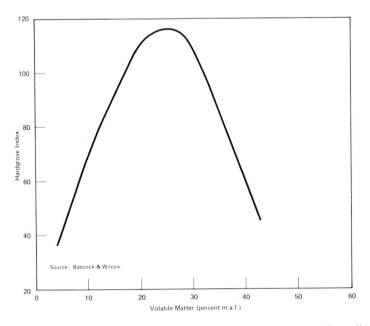

Figure 22. Influence of volatile matter on Hardgrove index. (From "Steam," Babcock & Wilcox Company, New York, 1972.)

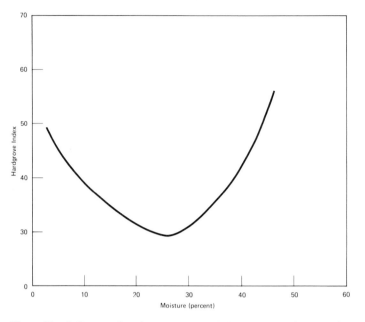

Figure 23. Influence of moisture content of lignite on Hardgrove index.
(From "Steam," Babcock & Wilcox Company, New York, 1972.)

content (Figure 23). The index passes through a minimum at intermediate-range moisture contents (i.e., these are harder to grind). Thus, partial drying of a high-moisture coals may result in a product which is more difficult to grind. While it may be intuitively desirable to dry such coals, such efforts could result in even further utilization problems and costs by increasing the difficulty of grinding.

Clearly, the Hardgrove grindability index is merely an empirical tool that represents only those coals (or fractions) that are sampled. It is subject to significant variability and if misinterpreted could result in serious operating impacts. While research is in progress to perfect hypotheses of coal breakage and distribution of particles, there seems to be no practical alternative to continued use of the index for at least the immediate future. One reason for this statement is that equipment manufacturers publish Hardgrove grindability indices for their equipment.[1] The performance of each piece of equipment is thus reflected in empirical terms as well, and it would appear to be most difficult to translate into quantitative terms (assuming that a comprehensive expression could be developed). There seems no escape, therefore from the continued use of empirical data on coal grindability. In fact, the present impetus toward rapid acceleration in coal utilization will place a premium on such knowledge and encourage others to develop expertise in such practices for the simple reason that they are known to be effective.

The effect of grinding on coal quality cannot be generalized because of the differences in coal characteristics. For example, the ash content and ash-fusion

[1]"Keystone Coal Industry Manual," *op. cit.,* p. 199.

temperatures of one coal may be lowered by grinding and separations, while those of another may be increased. The principal benefit of grinding coal is to separate ash or mineral matter to realize reduced handling and shipping costs as well as to achieve higher boiler efficiencies.

Separation

Removal of impurities liberated from coal through grinding and size reduction is typically accomplished by mechanical methods employing gravity concentration. Most common impurities are heavier than coal and will sink in an appropriate medium, while the lighter (principally coal) fractions will float. Representative densities of coal and impurities are:

Material	Density, g/cm³
Bituminous coal	1.12−1.35
Bone coal	1.35−1.7
Carbonaceous shale	1.6−2.2
Shale	2.0−2.6
Clay	1.8−2.2
Pyrite	4.8−52.

The degree of separation by density fraction is reflected in the ash content of the resulting coal. For example, the ash contents of various fractions of a typical bituminous coal are:

Density fraction	Ash content, %
1.3−1.4	1−5
1.4−1.5	5−10
1.5−1.6	10−35
1.6−1.8	35−60
1.8−1.9	60−75
1.9	75−90

The above data are generalized and have to be determined specifically for each coal.

In addition to the removal of ash, separation processes also are concerned with the removal of sulfur-bearing minerals. The potentials for sulfur reduction through mechanical methods have been investigated for several coals by the U.S. Bureau of Mines.[1] It was found less than 30 percent of the samples tested could be reduced to 1 percent or less total sulfur, although reductions of 50 percent were found in more than half the samples (Figure 24).

[1]A. Deurbrouck, Sulfur Reduction Potential of the Coals of the United States, *US Bur. Mines, Rep. Invest. No.* 7633, 1972.

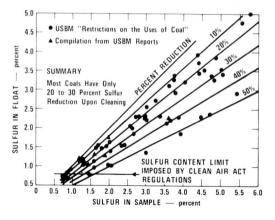

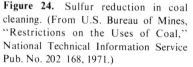

Figure 24. Sulfur reduction in coal cleaning. (From U.S. Bureau of Mines, "Restrictions on the Uses of Coal," National Technical Information Service Pub. No. 202 168, 1971.)

Table 6 shows sulfur data for principal U.S. coal seams having large reserves. Because of the organic sulfur present, and because mechanical cleaning is unable to removal all pyritic sulfur (especially at a tolerable yield), there are few coals which can be cleaned to less than 1 percent sulfur by normal preparation methods.

However, present regulations permit use of some coals having higher sulfur content in existing facilities; it was reported that some coals having a sulfur content greater than 5 percent "conformed" to air quality regulations for certain facilities.[1] This is significant for coal cleaning, because it suggests that not every coal will need to be cleaned to less than 1 percent sulfur. It was found that the total coal estimated to conform to regulations or to be otherwise legally acceptable (regardless of sulfur content) was about 70 percent of the total utility burn in 1974 (Table 5). Assuming that this percentage holds true for the future, then the coal not

Table 5 Status of coal delivered to power plants
Nov. 1973 through Oct. 1974

Status	% of total
a. Conforming with regulations	48.0
b. Nonconforming:	
(1) With plans for compliance	11.7
(2) Without plans for compliance	21.0
c. Legal disputes	19.3
d. Total estimated conforming and/or legally acceptable: (a) + (b1) + ½ (c)	69.4

Note: Nearly three-fourths of all electric utility coal is in conformance with regulations; only about one-fourth is not.

Source: Gakner et al., "The Effect of Environmental Legislation on Fuels Availability for Electric Power Generation," presented at 37th American Power Conference, Chicago, Ill., Apr. 21-23, 1975.

[1]A. Gakner, C. F. Reusch, J. Dotter, and H. Stewart, "The Effect of Environmental Legislation on Fuels Availability for Electric Power Generation," presented at 37th American Power Conference, Chicago, Ill., Apr. 21−23, 1975.

Table 6 Representative sulfur contents, cleaning potentials for principal coal seams

Seam	Heating value	Recoverable reserves, × 10⁶ tons	Sulfur content			Pyritic sulfur after mechanical cleaning yield				Total sulfur at 80% yield
			Pyritic	Organic	Total	90%	80%	70%	60%	
N. Appalachian:										
Lower Kittanning	13,500	2,480	2.31	0.94	3.25	0.40	0.52	0.42	0.36	1.46
Upper Freeport	13,900	1,430	1.72	0.70	2.42	0.41	0.35	0.28	0.22	1.05
Upper Kittanning	13,700	745	0.97	0.48	1.45	0.17	0.15	0.12	0.06	0.63
Pittsburgh	14,070	4,600	2.16	1.45	3.61	1.0	0.85	0.75	0.75	2.30
S. Appalachian:										
America	13,400	310	0.93	0.78	1.71		0.37	0.28	0.20	1.06
Clements	13,000	210	2.83	0.94	3.77		1.42	1.02	0.71	2.36
Midwestern:										
Illinois No. 6	11,000	13,650	2.11	1.66	3.77	0.75	0.80	0.60	0.50	2.46
Kentucky No. 9	12,900	5,811	2.09	1.91	4.00	0.90	0.75	0.50	0.50	2.66
Western:										
Lower Cherokee	10,900	950	1.66	0.79	2.45	0.18	0.13	0.09	0.06	0.93

Source: U.S. Bur. Mines Rep. of Invest. R18118, April 1976.

Table 7 Projected electric utility coal requirements (million tons)

	1975	1976	1977	1978	1979	1880	1981	1982	1983	1984
Total utility coal*	419.6	453.7	487.8	540.7	590.8	641.0	674.4	710.9	740.6	780.8
Total utility coal conforming with regulations or legally, acceptable at 70%†	293.7	317.6	341.5	378.5	413.6	448.7	472.1	459.6	518.4	546.6
Remaining coal not conforming with regulations	125.9	136.1	146.3	162.2	177.2	192.3	202.3	251.3	222.2	234.2

*National Electric Reliability Council, 1975
†A. Gakner et al, "The Effect of Environmental Legislation on Fuels Availability for Electric Power Generation," presented at 37th American Power Conference, Chicago, Ill., Apr. 21-23, 1975.

conforming to regulations is only about one-third of the total used by utilities (Table 7). This suggests that coal-processing activities (and especially R&D on improved processes) can be concentrated on those coals that are nonconforming; as Figure 25 shows, these are mainly coals with 3 percent sulfur and greater.

Finally, it is important to recognize that coal preparation to separate unwanted materials evolved mainly as a method to reduce transportation costs, only secondarily being concerned with quality factors.[1] Thus, the applicability of available preparation technologies to the separation of sulfur and ash needs to be reassessed to accomplish a new objective that is different from the original purpose. While reduction in coal transportation costs remains of obvious importance, the use of separation methods to gain better control over coal behavior under utilization conditions is likely to become of even greater impact. This point is illustrated by the following discussion of the characteristics of coal ash.

Ash Characteristics

Considerable attention has been given to the problems created by ash in coal-fired combustion systems. It was noted that "most of the routine coal analyses, such as proximate, calorific value, etc., are of little value in estimating the severity of ash deposition."[2]

As a result, the nature and amount of ash in coal is of major concern to the design and operation of utility facilities, and because it strongly influences efficiency and could cause outages, a number of engineering procedures have been developed to determine various empirical parameters relative to ash behavior.[3] Many of these parameters are oriented toward specific types of coal-fired units. A given coal may behave differently in different units because of inherent design conditions. As a result, the parameters must be used in connection with a particular coal under stated utilization conditions or the results will not be reliable or meaningful.

Perhaps the most common method to determine ash properties is to measure ash-fusion temperatures. The purpose of this test is to provide an indication of how coal ash will behave in the furnace. This test is strictly empirical, employing loosely defined softening and fluid points which are observed during deformation of a standard cone-shaped coal sample under heating. The following four temperatures are reported:

Initial deformation temperature, at which the first rounding of the cone apex appears

[1] D. F. Symonds, G. Norton, and G. B. Bogdanow, "Some Aspects of the Economics of Coal Preparation for Coal Conversion Processes," presented at the Engineering Foundation Conference on Coal Preparation, Rindge, N.H., Aug. 15, 1975.

[2] R. C. Attig and A. F. Duzy, Coal Ash Deposition Studies and Application to Boiler Design, *Proc. Am. Power Conf.,* Apr. 22, 1969.

[3] E. C. Winegartner, "Source Book of Procedures and Definitions of Fouling and Slagging Parameters for Coal Fired Boilers," ASME Research Committee on Corrosion and Deposits from Combustion Gases, 1974.

Softening temperature, at which the cone has been reduced in height so that height equals width of the base

Hemispherical temperature, at which the height is reduced to half the width of the base

Fluid temperature, at which the fused mass has spread out in a nearly flat layer

Table 8 shows ash-fusion temperatures of representative coals for both reducing and oxidizing conditions. Generally speaking, the ash-fusion temperatures are less for lower-rank coals. However, the variability in coal and ash content and character precludes generalization and dictates individual analyses on individual coals.

Most of the parameters compiled by the ASME are expressed in terms of ash composition (Table 9). The table shows that each of the 17 parameters listed can be determined from a knowledge of ash analysis. Representative analyses of ash from selected seams are shown in Table 10. Coals may be treated as two broad groups based on ash analysis.

Coals with *bituminous-type ash:*

$$Fe_1O_2 > CaO + MgO$$

Coals with *lignite-type ash:*

$$Fe_2O_3 < CaO + MgO$$

These criteria apply to all ranks of coal regardless of source; generally speaking, however, eastern coals have bituminous-type ash while western coals have lignite-type ash. Because eastern coals have been used more extensively than western coals, many (if not most) of the empirical parameters have been developed for utilization of these resources. It is not clear that these parameters will be applicable to western coals; indeed, the *slagging factor* and *fouling factor* are not applica-

Table 8 Ash fusion temperatures (°F) for representative coals

	Pittsburgh, W. V.	Illinois No.6	Wyoming subbituminous	Texas lignite
Initial deformation:				
Reducing	2030	2000	1990	1975
Oxidizing	2265	2300	2190	2070
Softening:				
Reducing	2175	2160	2180	2130
Oxidizing	2385	2430	2220	2190
Hemispherical:				
Reducing	2225	2180	2250	2150
Oxidizing	2450	2450	2240	2210
Fluid:				
Reducing	2370	2320	2290	2240
Oxidizing	2540	2610	2300	2290

Source: "Steam," Babcock & Wilcox Company, New York, 1972.

Table 9 Derivation of fouling and slagging parameters for coal fired boilers

Parameter	Equation
1. Total coal alkali	$\% \ Na_2O + 0.6589 \ (\% \ K_2O \times \% \ ash$
2. Total ash alkali	$\% \ Na_2O + 0.6589 \ (\% \ K_2O)$
3. Total acid	$SiO_2 + TiO_2 + Al_2O_3$
4. Total base	$Fe_2O_3 + CaO + MgO + K_2O + Na_2O$
5. Base/acid ratio	$\dfrac{Fe_2O_3 + CaO + MgO + K_2O + Na_2O}{SiO_2 + TiO_2 + Al_2O_3}$
6. Ferric/lime ratio	$\dfrac{Fe_2O_3}{CaO}$
7. Dolomite percent	$\dfrac{CaO + MgO}{Fe_2O_3 + CaO + MgO + Na_2O + K_2O} \times 100$
8. Ferric/dolomite ratio	$\dfrac{Fe_2O_3}{CaO + MgO}$
9. Silica/alumina ratio	$\dfrac{SiO_2}{Al_2O_3}$
10. Silica ratio	$\dfrac{SiO_2}{SiO_2 + Fe_2O_3 + CaO + MgO}$
11. Slagging factor	Base/acid ratio $\times$ S
12. Fouling factor	Base/acid ratio $\times$ Na_2O

ble to western coals. Probably, it will be necessary to develop a set of new empirical parameters to deal with western coals in combustion facilities. It seems likely, moreover, that a new set of parameters will probably be developed for coal conversion processes using coals from each region.

Typical data for selected parameters are shown by type of fouling and slagging

Table 10 Analyses of ash from representative coals

Parameter	Pittsburgh, Va.	Illinois No. 6	Wyoming subbituminous	Texas lignite
Ash content, %	10.87	17.36	6.6	12.8
Sulfur, %	3.53	4.17	1.0	1.1
Ash analysis, wt. %:				
SiO_2	37.64	47.52	24.0	41.8
Al_2O_3	20.11	17.87	20.0	13.6
TiO_2	0.81	0.78	0.7	1.5
Fe_2O_3	29.28	20.13	11.0	6.6
CaO	4.25	5.75	26.0	17.6
MgO	1.25	1.02	4.0	2.5
Na_2O	0.80	0.36	0.2	0.6
K_2O	1.00	1.77	0.5	0.1

Source: "Steam," Babcock & Wilcox Company, New York, 1972.

Table 11 Summary of parameters regarding fouling and slagging

Parameter	Low	Medium	High	Severe
		Fouling Type		
$Rf = \dfrac{base}{acid} \times \%Na_2O$				
	<0.2	0.2 −0.5	0.5 −1.0	>1.0
Na₂O content %	<0.5	0.5 −1.0	1.0 −2.5	>2.5
Total alkali on coal, %	<0.3	0.3 −0.45	0.45 −0.6	>0.6
Chlorine on coal, %	<0.2	0.2 −0.3	0.3 −0.5	>0.5
Ash sintering strength:				
At 925°C = mPa	6.89	6.89 −34.47	34.47 −110.32	>110.32
At 1700°F = psi	1000	1000 −5000	5000 −16,000	>16,000
		Slagging type		
T_{250}:				
°C	>1275	1400 −1150	1245 −1120	<1200
°F	>2325	2550 −2100	2275 −2050	<2200
$R_s = base$ acid $\times \%S$				
	<0.6	0.6 −2.0	2.0 −2.6	>2.6

Source: ASME Research Committee on Corrosion and Deposits from Combustion Gases.

behavior in Table 11. While it may be possible to obtain a rough idea of the behavior of individual coals by reference to such data, careful determinations are required to properly ascertain the likely performance of a particular coal.

These engineering parameters are of concern to both designers and operators of utility plants, as noted above. However, the present state of knowledge is such that it is impossible to estimate values for the parameters in terms of capital or operating and maintenance costs. Instead, these parameters generally are expressed in coal contracts or equipment specifications as limits for acceptable delivery or performance. Each manufacturer has its own set of approaches to these parameters, based on its practices for collection, organization, and utilization of basic and applied data on coals and their utilization, contributing to the proliferation of parameters as new equipment is designed. "Parameters used to judge the fouling and slagging potential of coal ash are confusing because they are numerous and because their theoretical significance has not yet been thoroughly established."[1]

A further problem is that the interrelationships between the several parameters are investigated infrequently, and potentially valuable information about coal behavior remains obscure. In an attempt to arrive at a better understanding of coal-ash behavior, it was suggested by Weingartner and Ubbens that a two-component phase diagram could be constructed for acid and basic constituents in coal as a

[1]E. C. and Winegartner and A. A. Ubbens, "Understanding Coal Ash Quality Parameters," presented at 1975 AIME Annual Meeting, New York, Feb. 16−20, 1975. Preprint no. 75-F-32.

function of T_{250} temperature (temperature at which the ash viscosity curves reaches about 250 poise). Figure 25 shows an example phase diagram constructed in this manner. While it is recognized that the actual system involved is much more complex than the simple two-component system depicted, this approach nevertheless has the promise of integrating information that is seemingly unrelated and moves in the direction of a more quantitative evaluation of the processes acting upon coal ash. It is clear that much work remains to be done to test this approach through further observation and through specifically designed experiments. It may be expected that revisions may be necessary as further data are obtained (through the same process of trial and error that led to our present set of parameters). Still, this is an encouraging start that appears quite promising in beginning to place engineering data on coal utilization on a sound theoretical basis. With such information, it may be possible to establish more effective separation and preparaton methods to achieve coals of desired properties.

The physical and chemical properties of coal described above were determined over the years as a result of practical experiences in combustion and/or coking. Much of this information is empirical and is transferrable to other applications only with difficulty.

Increasing attention is being given to various processes for coal gasification and liquefaction, which have the promise of converting coal into more easily used gases or liquids that are free from pollutants such as sulfur. However, most candidate processes are at a very early stage of development, and insufficient information exists to permit comparisons with more conventional coal uses. This and the empirical nature of available coal data make it difficult to take advantage of the vast

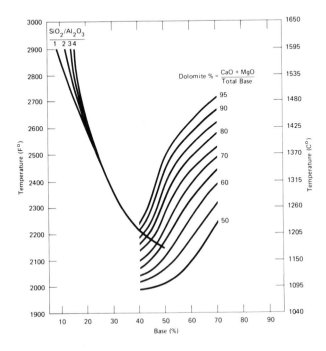

Figure 25. T_{250} temperature versus ash composition. (After E.C. Winegartner and A.A. Ubbens, "Understanding Coal Ash Quality Parameters," AIME Preprint no. 75-F-32, February 1975.)

Table 12 Summary of Coal Requirements for Coal Conversion Process

Process	Coal rank limitations	Size	Moisture
ATGAS	None	Crushed ($<\frac{1}{8}$ in)	Dried (4%)
BIGAS	None	Crushed & pulverized (70% $<$200 mesh)	Dried
CO$_2$ acceptor	Lignite, sub bituminous	Crushed	Dried
COED (L)	None	Crushed ($<\frac{1}{8}$ in)	Dried
Fischer-Tropsch	Noncaking	Crushed ($\frac{3}{8}$ — 1½ in)	Dried
CONSOL (L)	None	Crushed ($<$14 mesh)	Dried
Garrett (L)	None	Crushed	Dried
H-coal (L)	None	Pulverized ($+$40 mesh)	Dried
Hydrane	None	Pulverized	?
Lurgi	Noncaking	Crushed	Dried
Koppers-Totzek	None	Pulverized (70% $<$200 mesh	Dried
HYGAS	None	Crushed	Dried, pretreated
Molten salt	None	Crushed (12 mesh)	Dried
SRC (S, L)	None	Pulverized ($<$200 mesh)	Dried, solvent added
SYNTHANE	None	Crushed	Dried
SYNTHOIL (L)	None	Crushed	Dried
TOSCOAL (L)	None	Crushed	Dried
U-gas	None	Crushed	Dried
Union carbide	None	Crushed ($<$35 mesh)	Dried
Westinghouse	None	Crushed ($\frac{1}{8}$:¼ X 0)	Dried
Wellman-Galusha	None	Crushed (3/16 −5/16 in)	Dried
Winkler	None	Crushed (0−$\frac{3}{8}$ in)	Dried

Source: W. W. Bodle, and K. C. Vygas, Clean Fuels from Coal, *Oil Gas J.*, pp. 73-88, Aug. 26, 1974.

amount of previous work on coal in guiding process development.

Table 12 presents a summary of principal coal requirements for various clean-fuels-from-coal processes. The table shows that some processes are rather limited to certain types of coal; even if these processes can be shown as economic, their application would appear to be limited by the availability of sufficient reserves of suitable quality.

The table also shows that each process requires size reduction of coal through crushing and/or pulverizing. Most processes require drying of the finely divided coal. Following such preparatory treatment, the processes variously subject the coal to elevated temperatures, pressures, and reagents to derive the desired product. Although there may be exceptions for specific processes designed for specific coals, it appears to be generally true that the most important aspects of the processes are the process components, rather than the coal which is being treated. In other words, the processes are intended to produce such drastic changes in the coal that it is not really necessary to characterize the starting material in quantitative terms. This is in contrast to more conventional combustion or coking, where thorough knowledge of the physical and chemical aspects of individual coals is essential to their successful utilization. The study of coal properties has not been pursued extensively over the last 20 years with the advent of other fuels, and as a result, our understanding of coal itself remains incomplete. It is a matter of concern that programs on process development could be pursued with a perpetuation of the present low level of activity in the study of coal itself. This could produce another body of empirical information but would add little to the basic knowledge about coal that would enhance its utilization in various applications.

THREE

RESOURCES AND RESERVES

BACKGROUND

Assessments of the coal supply in the ground have been published by the dozens in the last few years. These assessments come in all shapes and varieties, reporting dire shortages within a few years to no likely shortage within a few million years. When one analyzes these forecasts, one can come to the conclusion that each may be correct. The variations depend entirely on the different assessments of the coal availability measured with geologic, technological, economic, and political parameters.

To most of us, a *resource* is a thing or action we can turn to in time of need or emergency. To a geologist the word indicates a concentration of raw in-place coal in such form that economic extraction is currently or potentially feasible. But the ordinary person's concept of resource, when it comes to coal, includes only *reserves*. Reserves are assumed to be ready for extraction and consumption and can be drawn upon to take care of a need or an emergency. Undiscovered seams of coal included in the total resource are not available for use; they are only presumed to be present in the earth's surface.

QUANTITY

The most serious problem in determining both coal resources and recoverable resources is that much of the basic technical fieldwork in the public domain was performed many years ago. Many estimates were founded on work done in the early part of this century without the advantage of modern techniques and instrumentation and thus are often lacking the degree of refinement and specificity necessary in assessment of potentials for the large-scale, costly developments of the present. An intensive effort in this regard is to be carried out by the present programs of the U.S. Geological Survey and the U.S. Bureau of Mines. The Geological Survey is primarily responsible for determining the nation's resources, while the Bureau of Mines provides estimates of recoverable reserves. The data on coal resources and reserves resulting from the work of the Geological Survey and the Bureau of Mines represent the only authoritative accounting of the nation's coal deposits, and these data will be used to describe the situation apparent at present.

The Geological Survey estimates the total remaining coal resource in the United States with certain specifications, namely, beds of bituminous coal and anthracite 14 inches or more thick and beds of subbituminous coal and lignite 2½ feet or more thick with overburden depths of 3000 and 6000 feet.

The resulting estimate of the amount of coal resources— 3968 billion tons —is a theoretical number; some of this coal is minable under economic conditions, but most of the coal cannot be extracted with present or prospective mining techniques.

The total remaining coal resources of the United States to a depth of 3000 feet as determined by mapping and exploration is about 1760 billion tons.[1] The total comprises, in rough terms, the following:

747 billion tons bituminous coal
485 billion tons subbituminous coal
478 billion tons lignite

Clearly this is a substantial amount. However, as will be shown in this section, not all the coal resource can be recovered, thereby reducing the quantity of usable reserves. Additionally, as will be shown in the next section, the different heating values and quality of coals further qualify the magnitude of the available coal reserves.

To be considered targets for development, coal seams must be of relatively high quality (ideally, at a minimum, high heating value and low sulfur content) occurring in relatively thick, uniform, and extensive beds that are located near enough to the earth's surface to permit application of economic mining technology. Thickness of coal seams is a most important parameter, because it controls the lateral extent of operations and strongly influences operating costs. Figure 1 shows the relationship of coal-seam thickness to area required to account for 1 million tons of reserves. It may be seen that a 4-foot coal seam (common in certain eastern coalfields) requires 140 acres for 1 million tons, whereas a 12-foot seam (common in certain western coalfields) requires only 50 acres. Clearly, other things such as coal character and quality being equal, it would be preferable to work in the more concentrated deposit. This is not always possible, however, because of consumer requirements for coal properties and quality.

As a part of planning for Project Independence, a new evaluation of the nation's coal deposits were made by the Bureau of Mines and Geological Survey. A new term was coined; the *reserve base,* defined as "the quantity of [remaining] in-place coals calculated under specified depth and thickness criteria." This new term is

---

[1]This estimate includes coals to a depth of about 3000 feet. Additional coals are known to occur down to about 6000 feet, but these are not considered further in this chapter because their extraction prospects are regarded as speculative with known technology.

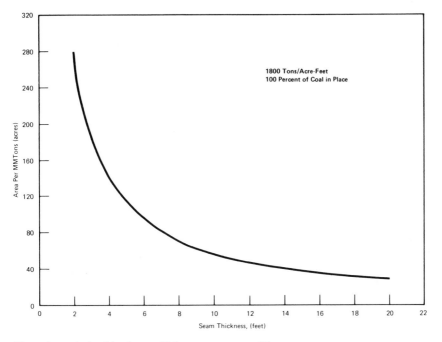

Figure 1. Relationship of seam thickness to area per million tons.

intended to be intermediate between resources (the total stock of coal in the ground) and reserves (the quantity of coal actually recoverable). (Figure 2).

The coal reserve base uses more realistic criteria for estimating. It includes only coal reserves in the measured and indicated resource category: in beds 28 inches or more thick for bituminous and anthracite and 60 inches or more for subbituminous and lignite; in the 0- to 120-foot overburden category for lignite, which is considered suitable only for strip mining; and in the 0- to 1000-foot overburden

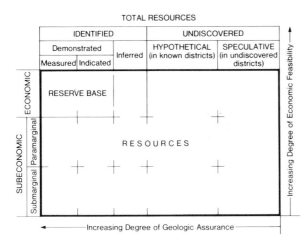

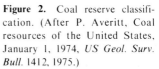

Figure 2. Coal reserve classification. (After P. Averitt, Coal resources of the United States, January 1, 1974, *US Geol. Surv. Bull.* 1412, 1975.)

category, which is deemed to be suitable for strip, auger, and underground methods.

The *demonstrated coal reserve base* includes the measured and indicated reserve categories, as in the coal reserve base, but is based on a high degree of identification and engineering evaluation with emphasis given to a high degree of certainty that the coal is technically and economically minable at some time. No consideration was given the marketability or competitiveness of one seam of coal against another. In effect it is assumed that all the coal can eventually be mined if the mining technology is perfected to extract it and there is a customer demand great enough that it is willing to pay the price. (In other words, the coal reserve magnitude is likely to increase with higher prices.)

The demonstrated reserve base contains a "vast amount of coal," which "has been used to justify assumptions of perfect elasticity for long-run coal supply . . . [and] the assumption of no increase in cost due to depletion over time."[1]

Zimmerman pointed out that the magnitude of the coal reserve base does not eliminate the need for making difficult choices associated with coal development. The importance of such choices requires thorough understanding of not just the reserve base but the portion which can actually be recovered for use. Table 1 presents the derivation of estimates of coal that can actually be recovered through underground and surface mining.

Detailed data are contained in Tables 2 to 5, which show for each of the four principal coal ranks the following information by state:

1. Total estimated identified resources
2. Indicated reserve base by mining method
3. Recoverable reserves by mining method, and total
4. Recoverable reserves as percent of identified resoures

The tables are, with one exception, compiled from available information. The exception is that an estimate of recoverable reserves by underground mining was

Table 1 Summary of recoverable coal reserves by rank (million tons)

Rank	Strippable	Deep	Total	% of total resources
Anthracite	68	2,166	2,334	10
Bituminous	13,597	54,596	68,340	10
Subbituminous	24,318	32,320	56,227	13
Lignite	8,895		8,895	2
Total	46,878	89,082	135,696	8

Source: Strippable Reserves of Bituminous Coal and Lignite in the United States, *US Bur. Mines, Inf. Cir.* 8531, 1971.

[1]M. B. Zimmerman, Modeling Depletion in a Mineral Industry: The Case of Coal, *Bell J. Econ.*, pp. 41−65, vol. 8, no. 1, Spring 1977.

Table 2 Derivation of recoverable reserves of anthracite coal in the United States* (million tons)

	(1) Total estimated identified resources Jan. 1, 1974 0–3000 ft	(2) Total measured and indicated reserve base Jan. 1, 1976 0–1000 ft	(3) Total strippable reserve base 0–150 ft	(4) Total underground reserve base (2)−(3)	(5) Projected recoverable strippable reserves (3) × 45%	(6) Projected recoverable underground reserves (4) × 30%	(7) Total projected recoverable reserves (5) + (6)	(8) Recoverable resources as % of identified resources (7)÷(1)
Ark.	428	96	8	89	4	27	31	7
Colo.	78	26		26		8	8	10
N. M.	4	2		2		neg	neg	
Pa.	18,812	7,109	143	6,967	64	2,090	2,154	11
Va.	335	138		138		41	41	12
Wash.	5							
Total	19,662	7,371	151	7,220	68	2,166	2,234	11

*The maximum depth for all ranks of coal except lignite is 1000 feet. Only the lignite beds that can be mined by surface methods are included; depths are less than about 120 feet. Seams greater than the following thicknesses are included: bituminous coal and anthracite, 28 inches or more; subbituminous coal and lignite, 60 inches or more.

These data include 100 percent of the coal in place, and no recoverability factor has been included.

Sources: Column 1: U.S. Bureau of Mines, Demonstrated Coal Reserve Base of the United States on January 1, 1974, *Min. Ind. Surv.*, June 1974. Column 2: Electric Power Research Institute, using data from the U.S. Bureau of Mines and U.S. Geological Survey. Column 3: Strippable Reserves of Coal and Lignite in the United States, *US Bur. Mines, Inf. Circ.* 8531, 1971 (referred to in Tables 3 to 5 as "IC 8531").

Table 3 Derivation of recoverable reserves of bituminous coal in the United States* (million tons)

	(1) Total estimated identified resources Jan. 1, 1974 0–3000 ft	(2) Total measured and indicated reserve base Jan. 1, 1976 0–1000 ft	(3) Total strippable reserve base 0–150 ft	(4) Total underground reserve base (2) – (3)	(5) Estimated strippable reserves	(6) Projected recoverable reserves (4) x 30%	(7) Total projected recoverable reserves (5) + (6)	(8) Recoverable resources as % of identified resources (7) ÷ (1)
Ala.	13,262	2,009	284	1,724	134	517	651	5
Alaska	19,413	698	81	617	480	185	665	3
Ariz.	21,234	326	326		147		147	1
Ark.	1,638	270	107	163	149	49	198	12
Colo.	109,117	9,144	676	8,468	500	2,540	3,040	3
Ga.	24	1						
Ill.	146,001	67,969	14,841	53,128	3,247	15,938	19,185	13
Ind.	32,868	10,714	1,775	8,939	1,096	2,681	3,777	11
Iowa	6,505	2,202	465+	1,737	180	521	701	11
Kan.	18,668	998	998		375		375	2
Ky.	64,346	26,001	8,417	17,583	1,758	5,274	7,032	11
Md.	1,152	1,048	135	914	21	274	295	26
Mich.	205	126	1	125	1	38	39	19
Mo.	31,184	5,014	3,596	1,418	1,160	425	1,585	5
Mont.	2,299	1,385		1,385		415	415	18
N. M.	10,748	1,859	601	1,258		377	377	4
N. C.	110	31		31		9	9	8
Ohio	41,166	19,230	6,140	13,090	1,033	3,927	4,960	12
Okla.	7,117	1,618	425	1,193	111	357	468	7
Oreg.	50							
Pa.	63,940	23,727	1,392	22,335	752	6,700	7,452	12
Tenn.	2,530	965	338	627	74	188	262	10
Tex.	6,048							
Utah	23,186	6,552	268	6,284	150	1,885	2,035	9
Va.	9,216	4,166	888	3,277	258	983	1,241	13
Wash.	1,867	255		255		76	76	4
W. Va.	100,150	38,606	5,149+	33,457	2,118	10,037	12,155	12
Wyo.	12,703	4,003		4,003		1,200	1,200	9
Total	747,357	228,925	46,905	182,020	13,597	54,596	68,340	9

*See footnote to Table 2.

+No coal shown in strippable reserve base for Iowa in Project Independence. Value from IC 8531 used here.

+Value shown in strippable reserve base for West Virginia in Project Independence is less than IC 8531 recoverable reserves. IC 8531 value of "recoverable strippable resource" (roughly equivalent to reserve base) used here instead.

Sources: Columns 1 to 3, see Table 2. Column 5: same as col. 3.

Table 4 Derivation of recoverable reserves of subbituminous coal in the United States* (million tons)

	(1) Total estimated identified resources Jan. 1, 1974 0–3000 ft	(2) Total measured and indicated reserve base Jan. 1, 1976 0–1000 ft	(3) Total strippable reserve base 0–150 ft	(4) Total underground reserve base (2)–(3)	(5) Estimated strippable reserves	(6) Projected recoverable reserves (4) × 30%	(7) Total projected recoverable reserves (5) + (6)	(8) Recoverable resources as % of identified resources (7)÷(1)
Alaska	110,666	5,447	641	4,806	3,926	1,442	5,368	5
Colo.	19,733	4,121	149	3,972		1,191	1,191	6
Mont.	176,819	103,417	33,843	69,574	3,400	20,872	24,272	14
M. M.	50,639	2,736	1,847	889	2,474†	266	2,740	4
Oreg.	284	18	3	15	1	5	6	2
Utah	173	1	3	15	1	5	6	2
Wash.	4,180	1,317	482	835	135	250	385	9
Wyo.	123,240	51,369	23,724	27,645	13,971	8,294	22,265	18
Others†	32							
Total	485,766	168,425	60,689	107,736	24,318	32,320	56,227	12

*See footnote to Table 2.
†IC 8531 data used here.
†OTHERS = California, Idaho
Sources: Columns 1 to 3, see Table 2. Column 5: same as col. 3.

Table 5 Derivation of recoverable reserves of lignite coal in the United States* (million tons)

	(1) Total estimated identified resources Jan. 1, 1974 0–3000 ft	(2) Total measured and indicated reserve base Jan. 1, 1976 ft 0–1000 ft	(3) Total strippable reserve base 0–150 ft	(4) Total underground reserve base (2)–(3)	(5) Estimated strippable reserves	(6) Projected recoverable reserves (4) × 30%	(7) Total projected recoverable reserves (5) + (6)	(8) Recoverable resources as % of identified resources (7)÷(1)
Ala.	2,000	1,083	1,083		488		488	24
Alaska	(?)	14	14		6		6	(?)
Ark.	350	26	26		25		25	96
Colo.	20	2,966	2,966		1,335		1,335	(?)
Mont.	112,521	15,767	15,767		3,497		3,497	3
N. D.	350,602	10,145	10,145		2,075		2,075	1
S. D.	2,185	426	426		160		160	7
Texas	10,293	3,182	3,182		1,309		1,309	13
Wash.	117	8	8					
Others†	46							
Total	478,134	33,617	33,608	0	8,895	0	8,895	2

*See footnote to Table 2.

†Others: California, Idaho, Louisiana, Mississippi.

Sources: Columns 1 to 3, see Table 2. Column 5: same as col. 3.

prepared for each rank of coal. Note that the reserve base represents 100 percent of the coal in place; no allowance for incomplete recovery has been made. Actually, the amount of coal that can be recovered from a given deposit varies from about 25 to 90 percent of the coal in place. Therefore, to arrive at a reasonable estimate of the amount of recoverable coal, the reserve base must be reduced by an appropriate amount to allow for incomplete recovery.

In general terms, the Bureau of Mines uses a round recoverability factor of 50 percent. The recoverability factor is defined as the percentage in the reserve base that can be recovered by established mining practices. The 50 percent recovery factor was established from past mining records for underground mines in the Eastern states. In the East, most of the mining to date has been accomplished in areas where multiple seams of coal are present. For economical reasons, it can be conceded that the prime seam of coal was or is being mined first. Ideally, this procedure leaves the seams above and below undisturbed. The Bureau of Mines counts undisturbed seams as minable, which may not be necessarily true. The seams above a mined-out seam, if the interval between the two is not sufficiently thick, may be fractured and subsided to such an extent that the seam is not minable under any conditions. A similar situation may develop with coal seams below the mined-out seam. Water may seep through fractures in the internal cover material to such an extent that the roof is not supportable; again the seam is lost for mining but still considered as a coal reserve.

Seams of coal under populated areas, federal- and state-owned forests, parks, reservations, navigable rivers and streams, etc., are not legally minable areas, but these areas are considered in the coal reserve count. Neither is the land around oil and gas wells minable—large blocks of coal have to be left standing to prevent oil and gas seepage.

Because of limited funds the various geological surveys that have worked many years in compiling geological data have had to use limited data, coal-seam outcrop information, water-well drilling records, and any other available data to make their judgment on the continuity of a seam of coal. Usually, this type of available data is very sparse and has to be extrapolated for very large areas. Such data, many times, does not show the thinning out of a seam of coal, seam splitting, geological faults and voids, and many other conditions, but the factors are not considered when appraising an area.

Very large tracts of land were assembled in the past for a mining operation which may have been successful in mining all the available recoverable prime seam coal, leaving the remaining seams in place. In many cases, these large tracts were later subdivided and sold off as farms, building lots, etc., making the reassembling of these lands into a minable tract impossible; again this coal is lost as a minable reserve. In the West, where very thick seams of coal are found, federal and state laws restricted the mining of coal that might disturb dry river beds, alluvial plains, ceremonial grounds, etc., which eliminates many more tons of coal reserves. The following analysis represents an initial attempt to take these factors into account in arriving at estimated actual recoverable coal reserves (e.g., the amount of coal actually extracted from deposits by mining operations.)

Recoverable reserves for underground mining were estimated by applying a recovery factor to the reserve base. Although the recovery of coal reserves *in a given deep mine* may be about 50 percent, there are substantial areas between mines, under cities, in pockets too small for economic recovery, too badly faulted, etc., where mining is either impossible or otherwise precluded. The effect of these and other conditions is to lower the recoverable reserves. To allow for the influence of the above factors, it is assumed in this analysis that coal recovery by underground mining from the reserve base will be, at a maximum, only about 30 percent of the total coal in place. Clearly, this recoverability factor is uncertain; it could go as low as about 20 percent or as high as about 35 percent of the total coal in place. It is considered unlikely, however, as suggested by the U.S. Bureau of Mines, that recoverability from the reserve base would be as high as 50 percent. Table 1 shows that the total estimated recoverable coal through underground mining is nearly 90 billion tons, with about two-thirds of the total composed of eastern and midwestern bituminous coal, about one-third subbituminous coal, and minor amounts of anthracite. This estimate, recognized to be conservative, could be increased slightly by applying a different recoverability factor. In view of the several uncertainties regarding estimating coal reserves, it is believed prudent to be conservative at present so that developments of finite resources of coal can be carefully planned and evaluated in advance.

For surface-minable reserves, the estimates of the U.S. Bureau of Mines have been adopted. These data show that the estimated recoverable coal through surface mining is roughly 47 billion tons. More than half the total is subbituminous coal, with nearly one-third bituminous coal and the remainder lignite.

The recovery of coal from reserves through surface mining may also be less than the commonly quoted estimates of 85 or 90 percent or more.[1] While these magnitudes may apply to a given mine, they may not apply to an entire coalfield. Assuming that the strippable reserve base includes all coals that may be extracted through surface mining, and assuming further that the separately estimated recoverable strippable reserves represent the portion of the reserve base that can be actually produced, then it is possible to calculate an indicated recovery percentage for surface mining for each rank of coal, by state.[2] Bearing in mind the shortcomings of the approach used, the data have been employed to calculate an "indicated recovery percentage" for strippable reserves of different rank coals, by state (Table 6). The table shows that there are few states where the indicated recovery percentage is even close to the commonly stated "norm" of 85 to 90 percent or greater recovery. In most major coal-producing states, only about one-quarter of the reserve base is estimated to be recoverable (West Virginia, Illinois, Kentucky). Stated another way, if the reserve base figure had been employed together with the "normal" 85 to 90 percent recovery factor to derive recoverable strippable reserves, values would have resulted which would be much larger than those de-

[1] See, for example, E.R. Phelps, Modern Mining Methods-Surface, in S.M. Cassidy (ed.), "Elements of Practical Coal Mining," p.377, AIME, New York, 1973.

[2] It is recognized that the reserve base estimates and the recoverable strippable reserves data were prepared at different times and used similar but somewhat different criteria. Nevertheless, the data are not significantly different, lending a measure of confidence that they could be employed together. This approach is intended to provide a rough approximation only.

Table 6 Indicated recovery percentage for strippable deposits reserve base ÷ recoverable reserves

State	Anthracite	Bituminous	Subbituminous	Lignite
Ala.		85		
Alaska		40	67	
Ariz.			97	
Ark.		65		78
Colo.		57		
Ill.		27		
Ind.		65		
Iowa		18		
Kan.		27		
Ky.		24		
Md.		14		
Mich.		100		
Mo.		34		
Mont.			10	49
N. M.			93	
N. D.				13
Ohio		28		
Okla.		26		
Pa.	76	69		
S. D.				37
Tenn.		23		
Texas				40
Utah		57		
Va.		38		
Wash.			27	
W. V.		24		
Wyo.			59	
Mean		41	49	43

termined by Bureau of Mines measurements. The actual recoverable strippable reserves, which largely are estimated here at about 45 percent of the reserve base, will clearly require careful management and conservation if they are to satisfy projected demands.

The foregoing suggests that the coal reserves recoverable from the reserve base are:

Mining method	Commonly estimated recoverable reserves, % of reserve base	Indicated recovery percentage, % of reserve base
Underground	50	30
Surface	90	45

In addition, it will be essential to extend the reserve base by more complete geological knowledge and through the perfection of new and improved technology.

The total estimated recoverable coal resources as indicated by the above data is about 136 billion tons, or about 8 percent of the total U.S. coal resources. Clearly, the quantity of recoverable reserves is still substantial. However, as will be discussed next, the coal-quality factors limit the potential use of recoverable coal reserves.

QUALITY

To an electric utility coal consumer, the heating value of coal (expressed as the number of Btu per pound or per ton) is an important parameter, not merely tonnage alone. In producing a given amount of heat for production of electricity, a utility would have to use significantly larger amounts of low-Btu coal than of high-Btu coal. Unfortunately, in consuming the additional tonnage of low-Btu coal to make up the Btu difference, the sulfur content of the additional tonnage is also emitted, and consequently the effective sulfur content of the coals is increased. Employing a standardized heating value for coals used by electric utilities, Rieber found that "conventional estimates of both known resources and recoverable reserves of low sulfur coal are grossly overstated."[1] In particular, Rieber's analysis shows a small increase in the estimates of bituminous coal resources/reserves, and to a large reduction in the estimates of subbituminous coal and lignite. A significant portion of U.S. coal resources and reserves normally considered to be low in sulfur content are reclassified to higher sulfur categories. For example, known recoverable reserves in the lowest sulfur category (less than or equal to 0.7 weight percent sulfur) are reduced from a conventional estimate of 68.2 billion tons to 16.4 billion tons on a consistent Btu-sulfur adjusted basis (Table 7). Should coal demand be such as to require a doubling over present levels by the mid-1980's, the cumulative production would be on the order of 20 million tons. With conventional reserve estimates there would be close to 50 billion tons of coal remaining, even after such expanded production. However, under the revised, standardized reserve estimates, known recoverable reserves of lowest-sulfur coal might be inadequate to satisfy the projected demands.

The effect of recalculation by heating value upon conventional reserve estimates is concentrated in the Western states (Table 7), where nearly 85 percent of these reserves is shifted to higher sulfur categories through the standardization procedures. The reserves most affected are the lower-heating-value coals (subbituminous and lignite) which are present in the largest tonnages.

These data are of exceptional significance for long-range policy planning. There seems to be no practical alternative to the use of bituminous coals of high heating value and high sulfur content, simply because of the scarcity of low-sulfur coal of equivalent heating value. Revision of air quality standards would be the most immediate way to achieve continued use of certain high-sulfur cooals and expanded use of others, with or without flue-gas desulfurization devices. Alternatively, high-sulfur coals could be gasified or liquefied to produce "clean fuels"; it remains to be seen whether such substitute fuels would be restricted to markets other than

---

[1] M. Rieber, "Low Sulfur Coal: A Revision of Reserve and Supply Estimates," University of Illinois, Center for Advanced Computation, CAC Document no. 88, Nov. 30, 1973.

**Table 7 Summary comparison of estimates of coal resources and reserves (<0.7%
sulfur), January 1, 1965 (million short tons)**

	Conventional estimates (tonnage only)		Standardized estimates (normalized for Btu/sulfur)	
	Resources	Reserves	Resources	Reserves
Appalachian:				
Bituminous	37,320	4,105	44,784	4,926
Anthracite	12,550	1,630	14,056	1,826
Interior:				
Bituminous	445	70	472	74
Rockies:				
Bituminous	45,215	4,585	48,581	4,925
Subbituminous	181,670	19,470	46,329	4,632
Lignite	344,620	37,905	0	0
West Coast:				
Bituminous	900	80	855	76
Subbituminous	3,780	340	0	0
Total	626,500	68,185	155,077	16,459

electric utilities because of the inherent properties of the converted fuels and
shortages of natural fluid hydrocarbons.

Table 8 summarizes the potential recoverable reserves for each rank by sulfur
content per million Btu. Roughly half the total recoverable reserves are bituminous coal, and roughly two-thirds of this has more than 1.5 pounds sulfur per
million Btu. The next largest amount is subbituminous coal, all of which is less
than 1.5 pounds sulfur per million Btu. The relatively smaller recoverable reserves
of anthracite and lignite are all less than 1.5 pounds sulfur per million Btu.

While about one-third of the total potential recoverable reserves has less than
0.7 pound sulfur per million Btu, nearly three-quarters of this lowest-sulfur coal
occurs in the Western states. The relatively remote location of these reserves and
the uncertainty about their development resulting from pending litigation could
delay the pace of their development. About one-quarter of the total potential
recoverable reserves are in the next lower-sulfur category; again roughly three-

Table 8 Summary of potential recoverable reserves (million tons)
Pounds sulfur per million Btu

Rank	Less than 0.7	0.7–1.5	1.5–2.1	Greater than 2.1	Total
Anthracite	2,234				2,234
Bituminous	8,884	9,568	17,085	32,803	68,340
Subbituminous	27,146	26,081			53,227
Lignite	7,204	1,691			8,895
Total	45,468	37,610	17,085	32,803	135,696

Table 9 Estimated 1985 production (million tons)

Pounds sulfur per million Btu

Region	Less than 0.7	0.7−1.5	Greater than 1.5	Total
East	39.2	135.9	487.8	622.9
West	209.8	94.6	9.5	313.9
Total	249.0	230.5	497.3	976.8

Source: National Coal Association, "New Coal Mines and Major Expansions of Existing Mines Planned, Announced, or Under Construction in the United States; 1975-1985," manuscript, June 1975.

quarters of these reserves occur in the West and their early development is not at all assured. The remaining reserves, while occurring in the East, are greater than 1.5 pounds sulfur per million Btu. Although many of these reserves have been developed, it is not at all apparent that the coal could be used without treatment of some sort of electric utility plants under present environmental control requirements.[1]

The estimated 1985 production of bituminous and subbituminous coal is distributed among broad geographic regions as shown in Table 9. The data indicate that two-thirds of total 1985 production is expected to come from east of the Mississippi River; about three-quarters of this eastern coal has greater than 1.5 pounds sulfur per million Btu, and some sort of treatment will be required to achieve environmental quality standards at coal-fired power plants.

The remaining third of total 1985 production is estimated to come from the West. About two-thirds of this western coal has less than 0.7 pound sulfur per million Btu and could be used directly in power plants. Note, however, that the development outlook for this lowest-sulfur coal is clouded by the prospect of litigation in the name of environmental protection, and there is real doubt whether the amounts estimated here can be realized in the next decade. Should there be shortfalls in production from western deposits, then it seems likely that expanded eastern production (and treatment of the higher-sulfur coal involved) would be necessary to meet electric utility industry requirements.

REMAINING RECOVERABLE RESERVES

Coal is a finite commodity; its development must lead, ultimately, to exhaustion of deposits. It is known that extensive coal production has occurred in America since colonial days and that some of the nation's accessible deposits were mined out long ago. But what portion of original reserves does this prior production represent, and how much remains? This section attempts to investigate that critical question.

Coal production statistics, it is suggested, merely represent recoverable reserves

[1]National Electric Reliability Council, "Estimated Fossil Fuel Requirements, Projected Generating Capacity, and Electric Energy Production for the Electric Utility Industry (Contiguous U.S.) 1975-1984," manuscript, July 1975.

that have already been recovered. Therefore, together with estimated remaining recoverable reserves (see Tables 2 to 5), cumulative production defines the total original recoverable reserves. When expressed as a percentage of the total original recoverable reserves, cumulative production indicates the stage of reserve exhaustion (or, in complementary fashion, the portion of remaining reserves).

Two estimates of the stage of reserve extraction are presented in this section.

1. Table 10 employs the recoverable reserves derived in the previous section. It may be recalled that these estimates were derived from the reserve base, which is equivalent to measured and indicated reserves (those that are well-known through mapping and observation). Therefore, Table 10 presents the stage of extraction of the best-known American coal deposits of all ranks.

    The table shows that extensive development has occurred in the best-defined coals of the several states, with the following results (see also Figure 3):

    a. Only one-third of original measured and indicated recoverable reserves of Alabama and Tennessee remain.
    b. Less than two-thirds of original measured and indicated recoverable reserves of Kentucky, Maryland, Kansas, Oklahoma, Pennsylvania, Virginia, and West Virginia remain.
    c. Four-fifths or less of the original recoverable reserves of Arkansas, Illinois, Indiana, Iowa, Utah, and Washington remain.
    d. Other states are at very early stages of development, and the original measured and indicated recoverable reserves are essentially intact.

2. Table 11 extends the estimated recoverable reserves of the previous section by including inferred reserves in addition to those measured and indicated. The effect of including these less-well-known deposits is to make production a smaller portion of original recoverable reserves, suggesting that, in general, coal development is at a much earlier stage than in the above discussion.

    Table 11 shows that production to date has consumer a lesser portion of total estimated recoverable reserves from this larger total (see also Figure 4):

    a. Half or less of the original measured, indicated, and inferred recoverable reserves of Maryland and Tennessee remain.
    b. More than two-thirds of the original measured, indicated, and inferred recoverable reserves of Alabama, Pennsylvania, Virginia, and West Virginia remain.
    c. Roughly nine-tenths of the original measured, indicated, and inferred recoverable reserves of Arkansas, Illinois, Indiana, Iowa, Kentucky, Oklahoma, and Washington remain.
    d. Other states are at very early stages of development and the total original measured, indicated, and inferred recoverable reserves are essentially intact.

A summary comparison of the above estimates of remaining recoverable coal as a percentage of original recoverable reserves for the categories (1) measured and

Table 10 Evaluation of remaining recoverable coal reserves, measured and indicated (billion tons)

State	(1) Cumulative production through 1974	(2) Anthracite	(3) Bituminous	(4) Sub-bituminous	(5) Lignite	(6) Total	(7) Original recoverable reserves (1) + (6)	(8) Cumulative production as percent total recoverable (1)/(7) × 100	(9) Remaining recoverable reserves as percent 100−(8)
			Estimated remaining recoverable reserves						
Ala.	1.19		0.65		0.49	1.14	2.33	51	49
Alaska	0.004		0.67	5.37		6.04	6.04	neg.	100
Ariz.	0.014		0.15			0.15	0.16	9	91
Ark.	0.10	0.03	0.20		0.03	0.26	0.36	28	72
Colo.	0.58	0.01	3.04	1.91	1.34	6.30	6.88	8	91
Ga.	neg.						neg.		
Ill.	4.48		19.19			19.19	23.67	19	81
Ind.	1.43		3.78			3.78	5.21	27	73
Iowa	0.37		0.70			0.70	1.07	35	65
Kan.	0.30		0.38			0.38	0.68	44	56
Ky.	4.12		7.03			7.03	11.15	37	63
Md.	0.29		0.29			0.29	0.58	50	50
Mich.	neg.		0.04			0.04	0.04	neg.	100
Mo.	0.34		1.59			1.59	1.93	18	88
Mont.	0.22		0.42	24.27	3.50	28.19	28.41	1	99
N. Mex.	0.19	neg.	0.38	2.74		3.12	3.31	6	94
N.C.	neg.					neg.	neg.		
N. Dak.	0.16				2.08	2.08	2.24	7	93
Ohio	2.71		4.96			4.96	7.67	35	65
Okla.	0.20		0.47			0.47	0.67	30	70
Oreg.	neg.								
Pa.	9.35	2.15	7.45			9.60	18.95	49	51
S. Dak.	neg.				0.16	0.16	0.16		
Tenn.	0.50		0.27			0.27	0.77	65	35
Texas	0.02				1.31	1.31	1.33	2	98
Utah	0.33		2.04			2.04	2.37	14	86
Va.	1.28	0.04	1.24			1.28	2.56	50	50
Wash.	0.16		0.08	0.39		0.47	0.63	25	75
W. Va.	8.32		12.16			12.16	20.48	41	59
Wyo.	0.50		1.20	22.27		23.47	23.47	2	98
Other*	0.22					neg.			
	37.38	2.23	68.34	56.23	8.90	135.7	173.46	27	73

*Other: California, Idaho, Nebraska, Nevada, Rhode Island, Massachusetts.

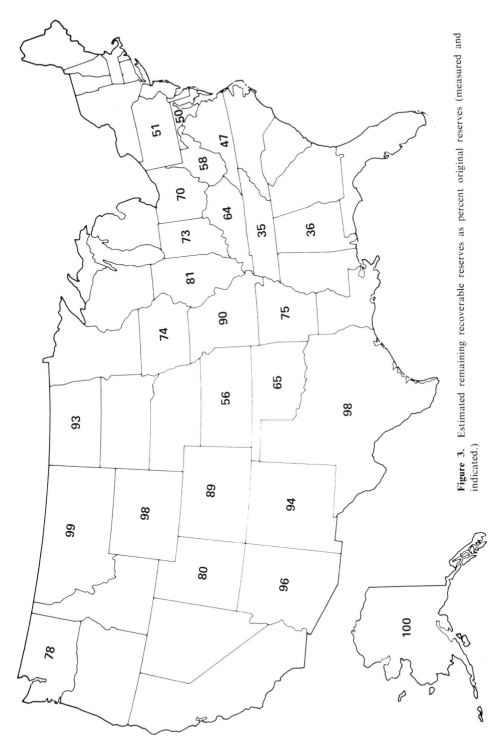

Figure 3. Estimated remaining recoverable reserves as percent original reserves (measured and indicated.)

Table 11 Evaluation of inferred recoverable reserves (million tons)

State	(1) Cumulative production through 1974	(2) Measured & indicated recoverable reserves	(3) Total original measured & indicated recoverable reserves (1) + (2)	(4) Cumulative production as percent original recoverable reserves (1)/(3)×100	(5) Inferred recoverable reserves	(6) Grand total original measured & indicated & inferred recoverable reserves (3) + (5)	(7) Cumulative production as percent grand total recoverable reserves (1)/(6)×100	(8) Remaining recoverable reserves as percent original 100-(7)
Ala.	1.19	1.14	2.23	51	3.5	5.73	21	79
Alaska	0.004	6.04	6.04	neg.	35.3	41.34	0	100
Ariz.	0.014	0.15	0.16	9	6.4	6.56	0.2	99.8
Ark.	0.10	0.26	0.36	28	0.2	0.56	18	82
Colo.	0.58	6.30	6.88	8	34.2	41.08	1	99
Ga.	neg.		neg.					
Ill.	4.48	19.19	23.67	19	25.1	48.77	9	91
Ind.	1.43	3.78	5.21	27	6.8	12.0	12	88
Iowa	0.37	0.70	1.07	35	1.2	2.27	16	84
Kan.	0.30	0.38	0.68	44	4.8	5.48	5	95
Ky.	4.12	7.03	11.15	37	11.8	22.95	18	82
Md.	0.29	0.29	0.58	50		0.58	50	50
Mich.	neg.	0.04	0.04	neg.		0.04	neg	100
Mo.	0.34	1.59	1.93	18	6.5	8.43	4	96
Mont.	0.22	28.19	28.41	1	53.1	81.51	neg.	100
N. Mex.	0.19	3.12	3.31	6	17.3	20.61	1	99
N. C.	neg.							
N. Dak.	0.16	2.08	2.24	7	95.6	97.84	0.1	99.9
Ohio	2.71	4.96	7.67	35	6.3	13.97	19	81
Okla.	0.20	0.47	0.67	30	1.8	2.47	8	92
Oreg.	neg.							
Pa.	9.35	9.60	18.95	49	12.2	31.15	30	70
S. Dak.	neg.	0.16			0.4	0.4		
Tenn.	0.50	0.27	0.77	65	0.5	1.27	39	61
Texas	0.02	1.31	1.33	2	2.9	4.23	0.5	99.5
Utah	0.33	2.04	2.37	14	5.7	8.07	4	96
Va.	1.28	1.28	2.56	50	1.9	4.46	29	71
Wash.	0.16	0.47	0.63	25	1.9	1.83	9	91
W. Ve.	8.32	12.16	20.48	41	19.1	39.58	21	79
Wyo.	0.50	23.47	23.97	2	25.5	49.47	1	99
Other	0.22	neg.						
	37.38	135.7	173.46	27	379.3	552.76	14	86

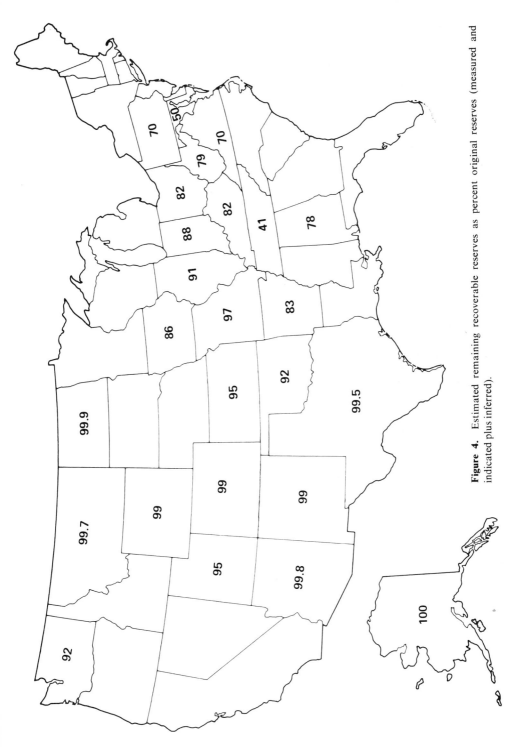

Figure 4. Estimated remaining recoverable reserves as percent original reserves (measured and indicated plus inferred).

indicated only and (2) measured and indicated plus inferred is given in Table 12. The table shows that inclusion of the inferred recoverable reserves increases the remaining recoverable reserves in most states by about one-fifth (particularly in states with large reserves such as Kentucky, Pennsylvania, and West Virginia). Such an increase in estimated recoverable reserves is of importance with respect to prospective magnitudes of coal development.

Table 13 presents estimates of the lifetime of remaining recoverable reserves for the categories (1) measured and indicated and (2) measured and indicated plus inferred. Two production rates are analyzed: 1974 production levels and new 1985 production capacity as reported by *Coal Age*. Summary data presented in Table 14 show that (using 100 years as an arbitrary yardstick for comparison):

The lifetime of recoverable reserves from measured and indicated deposits at either production rate is less than 100 years for Alabama, Arizona, Kentucky, Tennessee, and Virginia.

The lifetime of recoverable reserves from measured and indicated deposits is

Table 12 Summary comparison of estimated remaining recoverable coal reserves
Original recoverable reserves less cumulative production

State	(1) Measured and indicated only, %	(2) Measured and indicated plus inferred, %	(3) Difference, % (2) − (1)
Ala.	49	79	30
Alaska	100	100	
Ariz.	91	99.8	8.8
Ark.	72	82	10
Colo.	91	99	8
Ill.	81	91	10
Ind.	73	88	15
Iowa	65	84	19
Kan.	56	95	39
Ky.	63	82	17
Md.	50	50	0
Mo.	88	96	8
Mont.	99	100	1
N. Mex.	94	99	5
N. Dak.	93	99.9	6.9
Ohio	65	81	16
Okla.	70	92	22
Pa.	51	70	19
Tenn.	35	41	6
Texas	98	99.5	1.5
Utah	86	96	10
Va.	50	71	21
Wash.	75	91	16
W. Va.	59	79	20
Wyo.	98	99	1
Average	73	86	13

Table 13 Estimated lifetime of remaining recoverable reserves

State	(1) Measured & indicated recoverable reserves	(2) 1974 production rate, billion tons/yr	(3) Reserve lifetime at 1874 rate, years (1)/(2)	(4) Measured indicated plus inferred recoverable reserves	(5)* New mine production rate at full capacity, billion tons/yr	(6) 1974 capacity less depletion at 75% col. 2	(7) Total 1985 production capacity (5) + (6)	(8) Measured & indicated reserves lifetime at 1985 capacity, years (1)/(7)	(9) Total reserve lifetime at 1985 capacity, years (4)/(7)
Ala.	1.14	0.02	57	5.73	0.02	0.015	0.035	33	164
Alaska	6.04	0.0007	8630	41.34	neg	0.0005	0.0005	6080	82,680
Ariz.	0.15	0.007	21	6.56	0.008	0.005	0.013	12	504
Ark.	0.26	0.0005	520	0.56		0.0004	0.0004	650	1400
Col.	6.30	0.007	900	41.08	0.024	0.005	0.029	217	1417
Ill.	19.19	0.06	320	48.77	0.033	0.045	0.078	246	625
Ind.	3.78	0.02	189	12.0	0.010	0.015	0.025	151	480
Iowa	0.70	0.0006	1167	2.27		0.0005	0.0005	1400	4540
Kan.	0.38	0.0007	542	5.48	0.001	0.0005	0.0015	253	3653
Ky.	7.03	0.14	50	22.95	0.047	0.110	0.157	45	146
Md.	0.29	0.002	145	0.58	0.002	0.0015	0.0035	83	166
Mich.	0.04			0.04					
Mo.	1.59	0.005	318	8.43	0.001	0.004	0.005	318	1686
Mont.	28.19	0.014	2,014	81.51	0.056	0.011	0.067	421	1217
N. Mex.	3.12	0.01	310	20.61	0.018	0.008	0.026	120	793
N. Dak.	2.08	0.008	260	97.84	0.030	0.006	0.036	58	2718
Ohio	4.96	0.005	992	13.97	0.012	0.004	0.016	310	873
Okla.	0.47	0.002	235	2.47					
Pa.	9.60	0.08	120	31.15	0.032	0.06	0.098	98	318
S. Dak.	0.16			0.4					
Tenn.	0.27	0.007	39	1.27	0.005	0.005	0.010	27	127
Texas	1.31	0.008	160	4.23	0.020	0.006	0.206	50	21
Utah	2.04	0.006	340	8.07	0.030	0.005	0.035	58	231
Va.	1.28	0.03	43	4.46	0.009	0.023	0.032	40	139
Wash.	0.47	0.004	118	1.83	0.003	0.003	0.006	78	305
W. Va.	12.16	0.10	132	39.58	0.056	0.075	0.131	93	226
Wyo.	23.47	0.02	1174	49.47	0.124	0.015	0.139	168	355
Other	neg.								
	135.7	0.56	242	552.76	0.056	0.42	0.98	139	564

*G. F. Nielsen, Coal Mine Development Survey Shows 492.6 Million Tons of New Capacity by 1985. *Coal Age*, pp. 106-111, table 3, February 1976.

Table 14 Lifetime of measured and indicated recoverable reserves at different production levels (years)

State	1974 production capacity	Projected 1985 production capacity
Alabama	57	33
Alaska	8,630	6080
Arizona	21	12
Arkansas	520	650
Colorado	900	217
Illinois	320	246
Indiana	189	151
Iowa	1167	1400
Kansas	542	253
Kentucky	50	45
Maryland	145	83
Missouri	318	318
Montana	2014	421
New Mexico	310	120
North Dakota	260	58
Ohio	992	310
Pennsylvania	120	98
Tennessee	39	27
Texas	160	50
Utah	340	58
Virginia	43	40
Washington	118	78
West Virginia	132	93
Wyoming	1174	168

greater than 100 years at the 1974 production level but less than 100 years at the 1985 level for Maryland, North Dakota, Texas, Utah, Washington, and West Virginia.

Other states have recoverable reserve lifetimes greater than 100 years at either production level.

The addition of inferred deposits to those which are measured and indicated increases the lifetime of recoverable reserves, even at the larger production level projected for 1985, summarized in Table 15, which shows:

The lifetime of recoverable reserves is increased by inclusion of inferred deposits from less than 100 years to more than 100 years for Alabama, Arizona, Kentucky, North Dakota, Pennsylvania, Utah, Washington, and West Virginia.

The lifetime of recoverable reserves is greater than 100 years but is at least doubled by inclusion of inferred deposits for Alaska, Colorado, Illinois, Indiana, Iowa, Kansas, Missouri, Montana, New Mexico, Ohio, and Wyoming.

The lifetime of recoverable reserves remains less than 100 years even after inclusion of inferred deposits in Maryland, Tennessee, and Virginia.

Table 15 Lifetime of recoverable reserves at projected 1985 production capacity (years)

State	Measured and indicated only*	Measured and indicated plus inferred†
Alabama	33	164
Alaska	6080	82,080
Arizona	12	504
Arkansas	650	1400
Colorado	217	1417
Illinois	246	625
Indiana	151	480
Iowa	1400	4540
Kansas	253	3653
Kentucky	45	146
Maryland	83	166
Missouri	318	1686
Montana	421	1217
New Mexico	120	793
North Dakota	58	2718
Ohio	310	873
Pennsylvania	98	318
Tennessee	27	127
Texas	50	21
Utah	58	231
Virginia	40	139
Washington	78	305
West Virginia	93	226
Wyoming	168	355

*From Table 13, col. 8.
†From Table 13, col. 9.

The examples cited give indications of the reserve lifetimes at two different production rates. It is also instructive to examine the cumulative reserves depletion over an interval of time. Assuming that coal consumption were to grow at an annual rate of 5 percent, the total coal consumption in the remainder of the twentieth century would be between 15 and 20 billion tons. This is on the order of one-tenth of the estimated remaining recoverable reserves occurring in measured and indicated deposits. Continued growth of coal consumption in the next century, perhaps at greater rates, could accelerate the depletion of the best-known coal reserves.

The above data illustrate the importance of accurate knowledge of the magnitude of recoverable coal reserves, and especially the impact of the inclusion of less-well-known deposits upon reserve lifetime.

Identified coal resources also include deposits which are subeconomic under present market and technical conditions. While it may be possible to recover portions of those deposits at some future time, it is not possible to make a definitive estimate of the magnitude of potentially recoverable reserves from these deposits on the basis of present information.

Finally, it is believed that additional coal deposits remain to be discovered; these are designated *hypothetical* and *speculative* resources. Again, it is not possible to estimate potentially recoverable reserves from these deposits because of the lack of information.

Summary

The above analysis of remaining recoverable coal reserves leads to the following findings:

1. The best-known (measured and indicated) coal reserves have been extensively depleted in several key Appalachian states which are heavily dependent on coal as a mainstay of the economy. Inclusion of the estimated amounts of less-well-known (inferred) coal reserves in these states reduce the apparent depletion, but this still remains high (between one-fifth and one-third of the original recoverable reserves).

2. Unplanned or uncoordinated development of coal reserves in these states could lead to rapid depletion of remaining reserves (refer to Tables 14 and 15). Unless alternative activities are established to assume the economic role now portrayed by coal, reserve depletion (or its prospect) would have an adverse effect on state and regional economies. Such economic impacts would spill over into social, political, and environmental sectors with potentially adverse consequences in each.

3. More detailed information about the coal deposits and their amenability for development is essential to resource conservation.

4. Research and development aimed at improving production and/or productivity from deposits similar to those being worked will accelerate reserve depletion and lead to experiencing impacts sooner (unless R&D success is incomplete or its products are implemented on a delayed schedule).

5. R&D might, instead, be focused on opportunities to add to the recovery reserves, thereby deferring ultimate depletion. Work is needed in identifying remaining reserves with precision, improving recoverability from known reserves, and improved evaluation of coal quality with respect to optimum use.

RESERVES OF COAL BY END USE

As emphasized above, in evaluating coal's potential over a range of possible uses, it is essential to consider both the *quantity* and the *quality* of coals as plans are made and evaluated. Although the nation possesses large coal resources, only a portion of these can be developed for use (reserves). Even so, not all reserves can be actually recovered. It is the quantity of recoverable reserves that is critical to planning for coal developments, as production can be reasonably anticipated only through known methods. The characteristics of coal vary greatly, and in complex and subtle ways. Properties critical for a given utilization application may occur in certain coals but not in others, limiting the degree of interchangeability of coal among different end uses. Thus, the amount of recoverable reserves of identified quality is the vital parameter in determining the feasibility of coal-based projects or enterprises.

Analysis of recoverable coal reserves by quality factors is not an easy task. Much-needed data are incomplete or lacking entirely. Other available information was prepared at different times by several investigators, contributing to heightened uncertainty in any integrated analysis. Although present efforts may largely alleviate these problems, it will take considerable time for them to be completed. In the meantime, there remains a need for better understanding of the amounts of coal that can be employed in major end-use applications.

This section attempts to use existing data in estimating the recoverable reserves to bituminous coal (the most abundant domestic deposits) in terms of quality required for two end uses—coking and steam production.[1] Coking coals are essential for steelmaking, while steam coals are employed in a variety of uses, mainly in power generation. For each end use, resources, reserve base, and recoverable reserves (by mining method) are calculated on a state-by-state basis. Clearly, the analysis given here is limited by available data and by assumptions employed. Nevertheless, it is offered as at least an interim evaluation of the quantity and quality of coal by major end use to aid in planning for greater use of coal.

Data Employed

This section uses statistical data on coal resources and reserve base developed by personnel of the U.S. Department of the Interior—in particular, two members of the Geological Survey and the Bureau of Mines. The most authoritative recent compilation of the total estimated remaining *identified coal resources* of all ranks in the several states is that of Averitt;[2] these data are employed as the foundation for the present analysis. That is, in the event of uncertainty or apparent conflict with information from any other source, Averitt's data are assumed to be correct.

Data developed by Sheridan[3] for coking-coal resources are employed because they present a comprehensive and detailed account of these coals, even if somewhat older than Averitt's compilation. It is mainly for this reason that Averitt's data are used to resolve any apparent conflicts, and not any lack of confidence in Sheridan's work, which is excellent. Indeed, the present study would have been impossible without Sheridan's compilation of data on coking-coal resources.

A review of the above-cited data for total remaining bituminous coal resources (Averitt) is given in column 1 of Table 16; data on total coking-coal resources and quantities in three different grades (Sheridan) are given in columns 2 through 5,

---

[1] Coking coals, upon heating to drive off volatile matter, swell, fuse, and run together into porous masses having considerable physical strength. Steam coals generally lack this capability. U.S. Bureau of Mines, "Dictionary of Mining, Mineral and Related Terms," p. 233, 1968.

[2] P. Averitt, Coal Resources of the United States, January 1, 1974, *U.S. Geol. Surv. Bull.* 1412, 1975. (131 pages).

[3] E. T. Sheridan, "United States Coals for Coke Production," presented at Economic Commission for Europe Symposium on Developments in European World Markets for Coking Coal and Coke, Rome, Italy, Mar. 26–30, 1973. (Manuscript, 21 pages.)

Table 16 Review of data for coking-coal resources (million tons)

State	(1) Remaining identified resources (Averitt) Jan. 1, 74	(2) Total estimated coking-coal resources (Sheridan) Jan. 1, 1969	(3) Premium	(4) Marginal	(5) Latent	(6) Remarks	(7) Total	(8) Premium	(9) Marginal	(10) Latent
			Coking-coal resources by grade				Provisional values for coking-coals resources (modified from Sheridan)			
Ala.	13,262	13,000	2,000	4,000	7,000	Unlikely all resources would be coking coals	6,000	2,000	4,000	
Alaska	19,413									
Ariz.	21,234									
Ark.	1,638	2,000	1,000			Impossible: coking resources exceed totals	1,000	1,000		
Colo.	109,117	13,000	2,000	11,000		Data accepted	13,000	2,000	11,000	
Ga.	24									
Ill.	146,001	3,000	1,000	1,000	2,000	Impossible: total does not reflect components	4,000	1,000	1,000	2,000
Ind.	32,868	9,000			9,000	Possible, but unlikely	6,000			6,000
Iowa	6,505									
Kan.	18,668									
Ky.	64,346	28,000	20,000	3,000	5,000	Data accepted	28,000	20,000	3,000	5,000
Md.	1,152	1,000	4,500	< 500	< 500	Data uncertain, probably a small total	52	52		
Mich.	205									
Mo.	31,184									
Mont.	2,299									

State						Remarks				
N. Mex.	10,748	5,000		3,000	1,000	Data accepted	5,000		3,000	1,000
N. C.	110									
Ohio	41,166	13,000	1,000	3,000	9,000	Data accepted	13,000	1,000	3,000	9,000
Okla.	7,117	3,000	2,000	1,000		Data accepted	3,000	2,000	1,000	
Oreg.	50									
Pa.	63,940	57,000	5,000	35,000	17,000	Unlikely that all total resource could be coking coals	40,000	5,000	35,000	
Tenn.	2,530	2,000	1,000	1,000		Unlikely that nearly all total resource could be coking coals	1,000	1,000		
Tex.	6,048									
Utah	23,186	1,000	1,000			Data accepted	1,000	1,000		
Va.	9,216	10,000	8,000	2,000		Impossible: coking	5,000	4,000	1,000	
Wash.	1,867	1,000	< 500		< 500	Unlikely that so much of total resource could be coking coal	< 500	< 500		
W. Va.	100,150	91,000	57,000	19,000	15,000	Unlikely that nearly all total resource could be coking coal	57,000	57,000		
Wyo.	12,703									
Other	610									
Total	747,357	250,000	101,000	82,000	67,000		183,552	97,552	62,000	23,000

Sources: column 1: P. Averitt, Coal Resources of the United States, January 1, 1974, *US Geol. Surv. Bull.* 1412, column 2: E. T. Sheridan, "United States Coals for Coke Production," presented at Economic Commission for Europe Symposium on Developments in European and World Markets for Coking Coal and Coke, Rome, Italy, Mar. 26-30, 1973.

respectively, of the same table. Also included in the table are remarks addressed to Sheridan's coking-coal resource estimates. In some cases (Arkansas, Virginia), estimated coking-coal resources exceed the total estimated coal resources. This is impossible—one outcome of attempting to integrate two separate sets of statistics compiled by different investigators at different times. In an attempt to reconcile these and other apparent conflicts in the data, the writer has applied his judgment in estimating provisional values for coking-coal resources for the purposes of this analysis; these values are given in columns 7 through 10 of Table 16.

In addition to eliminating clearly impossible situations, the writer has tried to refine statistics that appear to him as unlikely. For example, it does not appear probable that essentially *all* the coal resources of Alabama, Pennsylvania, Tennessee, Washington, or West Virginia would be of coking quality. The estimated coking-coal resources in each grade were adjusted downward, somewhat arbitrarily, to reflect a more likely case. In part, this exercise of judgment was guided by Sheridan's comment that "latent" grade coking coals include "coals for which exact analytical data are not available but which are presumed to meet [stated] ash and sulfur limitations." Therefore, the provisional values are less than those suggested by Sheridan, principally by reduction in the latent-grade amount (although premium and marginal grades are lesser as well). A comparison of the total coking-coal resource data presented by Sheridan and the provisional values employed in this section is shown in Table 17. The data show that provisional values for premium and marginal grades are largely consistent with those given by Sheridan (refer also to Table 16). These provisional values are employed in further analysis (to be described later).

Two additional sources of data were used in this analysis. Again, these were prepared by personnel of the Department of the Interior. A portion of total remaining identified coal resources occurs as thick seams at shallow depth in deposits whose dimensions are measured and indicated; these deposits are known as the *reserve base*. The most recent and authoritative estimate of the total bituminous-coal reserve base is that of the U.S. Bureau of Mines;[1] these data are also employed as a basis for analysis in the present study. As with Averitt's resource estimates, these data are assumed to be correct.

Data developed by Sheridan[2] for the reserve base of premium-grade coking

Table 17 Comparison of data for coking-coal resources (million tons)

Grade	Sheridan	Provisional value this section
Premium	101,000	97,552
Marginal	82,000	62,000
Latent	67,000	23,000
Total	250,000	183,552

[1]U.S. Bureau of Mines, Demonstrated Coal Reserve Base of the United States on January 1, 1976, *Miner. Ind. Surv.*, p. 8, August 1977.

[2]E. T. Sheridan, Supply and Demand for United States Coking Coals and Metallurgical Coke, *US Bur. Mines, Spec. Pub.*, p. 23, 1976.

coals are employed to represent this class of coals. These data are also used as a yardstick for calculating the reserve base of marginal and latent grades of coking coal (as described later).

Having described the data employed in this analysis, it is important to recognize its limitations, discussed next.

Limitations

The analysis, as mentioned, is based on publicly available information compiled and published by agencies of the federal government. Although performed at different times by different investigators, it was assumed that the data from several separate studies (as adjusted) could be employed together in one analysis. Clearly, this assumption could be challenged, because the separate studies used varying criteria and approaches in examination of coal resources or reserves. Yet, in the absence of further information, it is taken as an act of faith that inconsistencies among the data employed will be relatively insignificant, or that they can be reconciled by applying professional judgment, or that such errors as may be introduced will be small. This ground rule is of overriding importance to the analysis and requires rigorous testing through future intensive work employing detailed data.

The analysis is further limited in that it is aggregated at the state level. Actually, coal occurrence in each state are in several seams, and a more meaningful analysis should be disaggregated to at least that level. Perhaps this may be possible with new data and systems being developed by several public and private organizations. Still, at present there appears to be no substitute for the state-level analysis because of insufficient data.

A further limitation is in the rather broad definition of end-use categories employed in analysis. Ideally, there should be several additional categories that reflect the particular requirements of each principal coal-consuming industry. Again, however, the character of available data does not permit a more disaggregated analysis of coal quality by end use.

It is important to bear the above limitations of the analysis in mind in reviewing the analytical procedure and the results.

Procedure

A simple analytical procedure was employed. It was assumed that coking coals and steam coals are mutually exclusive. Thus, the principal calculation was subtraction of data for coking coals from data representing all bituminous coals, the remainder being steam coal. Strictly speaking, this assumption is not entirely consistent with the real world, as some coking-quality coals may find their way into steam production, and some steam-quality coals may be blended with coking coals in metallurgical uses. With present information, it is not possible to specify the magnitude of coals used in these ways. For convenience in this analysis, it was assumed that such effects would be small and that they would be in balance (e.g., as much coking coal would be used in steam generation as steam coal blended for metallurgical coke production). Clearly, this represents a very important topic for future research to confirm or refute the above assumption.

Under the above procedure, the analysis is critically dependent on the precision of data for coking coals (because its subtraction from the total is used to derive steam coals). Here we have relied on work by Eugene T. Sheridan, mineral specialist, U.S. Bureau of Mines, who has analyzed the coking-coal sector for many years and reported his results in several publications. These data are considered in this analysis to be authoritative. Again, of course, the desirability of further refinements in the data through additional research is recognized.

The analytical procedure may be illustrated best through presentation of data and discussion of the derivation of results.

Results

Results of the analysis are given in a family of eight tables of statistics, subdivided by state. Each table will be described separately.

1. Derivation of remaining steam-coal resources (Table 18). Subtracting provisional values for coking-coal resources from the total coal resources yields steam-coal resources. A range of steam-coal resources is given, based on two different assumptions: (*a*) All coking coal would be dedicated to metallurgical uses and thereby be unavailable for steam, or (*b*) only premium-grade coking coals would be dedicated to steelmaking, and marginal- or latent-grade coking coals could be used for steam raising.[1] The total amount of steam coal calculated for these cases ranges from nearly 564 billion tons to 644 billion tons, respectively. West Virginia possesses the greatest amount of coking-coal resources, while Illinois has the largest steam-coal resources.

2. Derivation of steam-coal reserve base (Table 19). As mentioned in the discussion of data employed, the reserve base of only premium-grade coking coals was estimated by Sheridan. To be consistent with resource data given in Table 16, it was necessary to estimate the reserve base for marginal- and latent-grade coking coals. This was done by assuming that the reserve base for these grades of coking coals for each state bears the same percentage relation to total resources as does premium-grade coking coals occurring in that state. Clearly, this assumption must be tested by further analysis. However, in the absence of available information, it is employed for convenience in this analysis.

As in Table 18, subtracting coking-coal reserve base from the total bituminous coal reserve base yields the steam-coal reserve base. The amount of steam-coal reserve base ranges from 186 to nearly 209 billion tons, assuming that all coking coal goes to metallurgical use or only premium coking coal is committed to steelmaking, respectively. Comparing these data with Table 18 indicates that the

---

[1] *Premium grade* coking coals have a sulfur content of less than 1.3 percent and an ash content of less than 8.1 percent. *Marginal grade* coking coals have from 1.3 to 1.8 percent sulfur and from 8.1 to 12.0 percent ash.

Table 18 Derivation of remaining bituminous steam-coal resources (million tons)

State	(1) Remaining identified resources Jan. 1, 1974	(2) Provisional estimate of coking-coal resources Jan. 1, 1969	(3) Total premium coking-coal resources	(4) Total marginal coking-coal resources	Estimated remaining steam-coal resources		
					(5) Total latent coking coal resource	(6) Total coking coals to met. uses (1) − (2)	(7) Only premium coking coals to met. uses (1) − (3)
Ala.	13,262	6,000	2,000	4,000		7,262	11,262
Alaska	19,413					19,413	19,413
Ariz.	21,234					21,234	21,234
Ark.	1,638	1,000	1,000			638	638
Colo.	109,117	13,000	2,000	11,000		96,117	107,117
Ga.	24					24	24
Ill.	146,001	4,000	1,000	1,000	2,000	142,001	145,001
Ind.	32,868	6,000			6,000	26,868	32,868
Iowa	6,505					6,505	6,505
Kan.	18,668					18,668	18,668
Ky.	64,346	28,000	20,000	3,000	5,000	36,346	44,346
Md.	1,152	52	52			1,100	1,100
Mich.	205					205	205
Mo.	31,184					31,184	31,184
Mont.	2,299					2,299	2,299
N. Mex.	10,748	5,000		3,000	1,000	5,748	5,748
N. C.	110					110	110
Ohio	41,166	13,000	1,000	3,000	9,000	28,166	40,166
Okla.	7,117	3,000	2,000	1,000		4,117	5,117
Oreg.	50					50	50
Pa.	63,940	40,000	5,000	35,000		23,940	58,940
Tenn.	2,530	1,000	1,000			1,530	1,530
Tex.	6,048					6,048	6,048
Utah	23,186	1,000	1,000			22,186	22,186
Va.	9,216	15,000	4,000	1,000		4,216	5,216
Wash.	1,867	1,000	1,000			867	867
W. Va.	100,150	57,000	57,000			43,150	43,150
Wyo.	12,703					12,703	12,703
Other	610					610	610
Total	747,357	183,552	97,552	62,000	23,000	563,805	644,305

Sources: Column 1: P. Averitt, Coal Resources of the United States, January 1, 1974, *US Geol. Surv. Bull.* 1412, 1975. Column 2: E. T. Sheridan, United States Coals for Coke Production," presented at Economic Commission for Europe Symposium on Developments in European and World Markets for Coking Coal and Coke, Rome, Italy, Mar. 26–30, 1973.

Table 19 Derivation of reserve base of bituminous steam coals (million tons)

State	(1) Reserve base Jan. 1, 1976	(2) Reserve base of premium coking coals Jan. 1, 1974	(3) Reserve base of premium coking coals as % of resources	(4) Estimated reserve base of marginal coking coals	(5) Estimated reserve base of latent coking coals	(6) Reserve base of coking coals (2)+(4)+(5)	(7) Estimated reserve base of steam coal — Total coking coal to met. use (1)−(6)	(8) Estimated reserve base of steam coal — Only premium coal to met. use (1)−(2)
Ala.	2,009	195	10	400		595	1,414	1,814
Alaska	698						698	698
Ariz.	326						326	326
Ark.	270	20	2			20	250	250
Colo.	9,144	612	31	3,410		4,022	5,122	8,532
Ga.	1	0.3	neg			neg	1	1
Idaho	4						4	4
Ill.	67,969	n.d.		n.d	n.d	n.d	67,969	67,969
Ind.	10,714						10,714	10,714
Iowa	2,202						2,202	2,202
Kan.	998						998	998
Ky.	26,001	4,977	25	750	1,250	6,977	19,024	21,024
Md.	1,048	10				10	1,038	1,038
Mich.	127						127	127
Mo.	5,014						5,014	5,014
Mont.	1,385						1,385	1,385
N. Mex.	1,860						1,860	1,860
N. C.	32						32	32
Ohio	19,230			990	2,970	3,960	15,270	19,230
Okla.	1,618	169	8	80		249	1,369	1,449
Pa.	23,728	1,218†	24	8,523		9,741	13,987	22,510
Tenn.	965	204	20	200		404	561	761
Utah	6,552	782	78			782	5,770	5,770
Va.	4,166	1,629	20	400		2,029	2,137	2,537
Wash.	255	7	1			7	248	248
W. Va.	38,607	10,461	18	3,420		13,881	24,726	28,146
Wyo.	4,003						4,003	4,003
Total*	228,925	20,284	19	18,173	4,220	42,677	186,249	208,642

*Totals may not add due to rounding.

n.d. = not determined by Sheridan

†Sheridan's estimate covers only high-volatile coking coals of premium grade. Figure used here is for all premium-grade coking coals, derived from Sheridan's 1973 paper (cited in Table 16).

Sources: Column 1: U.S. Bureau of Mines, Demonstrated Coal Reserve Base of the United States on January 1, 1976, *Miner. Ind. Surv.*, August 1977. Column 2: E. T. Sheridan, Supply and Demand for United States Coking Coals and Metallurgical Coke, *US Bur. Mines, Spec. Pub.*, 1976. Column 3: Reserve base of marginal and latent coals calculated based on the assumption that their reserve base for each state bears the same percentage relation to total resources as does the reserve base for premium-grade coking coals in that state.

reserve base represents roughly one-third of the total identified resource of bituminous coal. The largest reserve base of coking coal is in West Virginia, consistent with Table 18, while the largest reserve base of steam coal is Illinois.

3. Comparison of steam-coal resources and reserve base (Table 20). The derived steam-coal resources (Table 18) and reserve base (Table 19) are compared in Table 20. This is done partly for convenience, by displaying steam-coal data in one place, and to provide a check on the assumptions employed in the analysis. The table, in two parts, presents steam-coal data for cases where only premium coking coal goes to metallurgical uses and where all coking coal is so used. The data show that steam-coal resources are consistent with the analytical assumptions, all being greater than estimated reserve base. At a minimum, this lends confidence that Averitt's and Sheridan's data can indeed be combined for analysis, and that the provisional values adopted for some of Sheridan's data are consistent with the analytical procedures employed.

Clearly, knowledge of the magnitude of the steam-coal reserve base is quite important, for it represents the thickest, shallowest, and best-known bituminous coal deposits—those that are most likely to experience development in the future. Still, not all the reserve base can be recovered and used. Factors influencing the recoverability of coal from the reserve base were discussed in an earlier section.[1] To complete this analysis of steam coal, it is necessary to estimate the total amount of recoverable reserves and derive the recoverable coking-coal reserves so that recoverable steam-coal reserves may be calculated.

4. Remaining recoverable reserves of coking coal (Table 21). The reserve base of each grade of coking coals, as given by Sheridan or derived in Table 19, was employed as the starting point in estimating remaining recoverable reserves of these coals. In its earlier-cited publication presenting data on coal reserve base, the U.S. Bureau of Mines also provided a breakdown of the bituminous reserve base by mining method.[2] To derive the coking-coal reserve base by mining method, it was assumed that recovery methods for these coals would be in the same proportion as for the total bituminous reserve for each state. For example, 86 percent of the total bituminous reserve base in Alabama is projected by the Bureau of Mines to require underground (or "deep") mining: it was assumed that the same percentage of the coking-coal reserve base would require deep mining as well, etc. (columns 2 and 3 of Table 21). Applying these percentages to the total coking-coal reserve base gave the coking-coal reserve base by deep mining (column 4) and surface mining (column 6).

All that remains is to apply a recoverability factor to the reserve base to arrive at estimates of recoverable reserves by each mining method. The recoverability fac-

---

[1] R. A. Schmidt, Electric Utility Industry Strategy for Research in Coal Geology, presented at "Coal Geology and the Future," a symposium organized by the U.S. Geological Survey, Reston, Va., Sept. 27-28, 1976. (Manuscript, 62 pages.)

[2] U.S. Bureau of Mines, August 1977, *op. cit.*

Table 20 Comparison of steam coal resources and reserve base (million tons)

	Only premium coking coal to metallurgical use			Total coking coals to metallurgical uses		
	Steam-coal resources	Steam-coal reserve base	Steam-coal reserve base as % of resources $(2)\div(1)\times100$	Steam-coal resources	Steam-coal reserve base	Steam-coal reserve base as % of resources $(2)\div(1)\times100$
Ala.	11,262	1,814	16	7,262	1,414	19
Alaska	19,413	698	4	19,413	698	4
Ariz.	21,234	326	2	21,234	326	2
Ark.	638	250	39	638	250	39
Colo.	107,117	8,532	8	96,117	5,122	5
Ga.	24	1	4	24	1	4
Ill.	145,001	67,969	47	142,001	67,969	47
Ind.	32,868	10,714	45	26,868	10,714	45
Iowa	6,505	2,202	34	6,505	2,202	34
Kan.	18,668	998	5	18,668	998	5
Ky.	44,346	21,024	47	36,346	19,024	52
Md.	1,100	1,038	94	1,100	1,034	94
Mich.	205	127	62	205	127	62
Mo.	31,184	5,014	16	31,184	5,014	16
Mont.	2,299	1,385	60	2,299	1,385	60
N. Mex.	5,748	1,860	32	5,748	1,860	32
N.C.	110	32	29	110	32	29
Ohio	40,166	19,230	48	28,166	15,270	51
Okla.	5,117	1,449	28	4,117	1,369	33
Oreg.	50		0	50		0
Pa.	58,940	22,510	38	23,940	13,987	58
Tenn.	1,530	761	50	1,530	561	37
Tex.	6,048	0	0	6,048	0	0
Utah	22,186	5,770	26	22,186	5,770	26
Va.	5,216	2,537	49	4,216	2,137	51
Wash.	867	248	29	867	248	29
W. Va.	43,150	18,146	65	43,150	24,726	57
Wyo.	12,703	4,003	35	12,703	4,003	32
Total	644,305	208,642	32	563,305	186,249	33

tors employed are those derived earlier in this chapter as follows:

Mining method	Indicated recoverability, % of reserve base
Underground ("deep")	30
Surface	45

These recoverability factors are less than those suggested by the U.S. Bureau of Mines, which states that "at least one-half of the inplace coals (of the reserve base) may be recovered." The reason for using lower recoverability factors is that legal restrictions, effects of past mining, or basic geological conditions will probably restrict or preclude development of some coal deposits nominally included in the reserve base, with recovery of lesser amounts of coal as the result.

The derivation of estimated recoverable reserves of coking coal for each grade is given in the three parts of Table 21. These data are summarized in Table 22.

5. Summary of recoverable reserves of coking coal by mining method (Table 22). Data derived in the three parts of Table 21 are organized by mining method and summarized in this table. Total recoverable reserves of coking coal are estimated at slightly less than 14 billion tons, of which nearly four-fifths would be from deep mines. The largest recoverable reserves of coking coal, about one-third of the total, occur in West Virginia. Pennsylvania and Kentucky each contain roughly one-fifth of the total recoverable coking coals, with Colorado and Ohio each having about one-tenth of the total. The remainder is scattered among several other states.

The largest recoverable coking-coal reserves are of premium grade, followed closely by marginal grade. This reflects Sheridan's original data, as well as the adjustments to these data discussed above. Clearly, these data are sensitive to all the assumptions employed in this analysis, but it is not possible to determine the potential range of uncertainty introduced into the analysis with available information. It is hoped that future work will be directed toward this and other limitations to the present analysis.

6. Derivation of recoverable reserves of steam coal (Table 23). Bearing in mind the limitations in deriving the recoverable reserves of coking coal, the data are taken to be indicative of at least the relative proportions of recoverable coking coal. Therefore, they can be used in deriving the estimated recoverable reserves of steam coal. The starting point for this analysis is an estimate of the total recoverable reserves of bituminous coals through deep and surface mining presented earlier. The procedure used in that earlier analysis is the same one employed here. Recoverable reserves of steam coal were estimated by subtracting recoverable reserves of coking coal from the total. Two cases were considered, as in the resource and reserve base estimates described above: (*a*) total coking coals dedi-

Table 21 Remaining recoverable reserves of bituminous coking coal (million tons)

State	(1) Reserve base of premium coking coals Jan. 1, 1976	(2) % of total reserve base for deep mining	(3) % of total reserve base for strip mining	(4) Reserve base of premium coking coals—deepcoal (1) × (2)	(5) Recoverable reserves of premium coking deepcoal—deep (4) × 30%	(6) Reserve base of premium coking coals—strip (1) × (3)	(7) Recoverable reserves of premium coking coal—strip (6) × 45%	(8) Total recoverable reserves of premium coking coal (5) + (7)
				Premium grade				
Ala.	195	86	14	168	50	27	12	62
Ark.	20	60	40	12	4	8	4	8
Colo.	612	93	7	569	171	43	19	190
Ga.	.3	56	44	neg.	neg.	neg.	neg.	neg.
Ky.	4,977	68	32	3,384	1,015	1,593	717	1,732
Md.	10	87	3	9	3	1	neg	3
Oh.		68	32					
Okla.	109	74	26	125	38	44	20	58
Pa.	1,218	94	6	1,144	343	73	33	375
Tenn.	204	65	35	133	40	71	32	72
Utah	782	96	4	751	225	31	14	239
Va.	1,629	79	21	1,287	386	342	154	540
Wash.	7	100	0	7	2	0	0	2
W. Va.	10,461	87	13	9,101	2,730	1,360	612	3,342
Total	20,284	80	20	16,690	5,007	3,593	1,617	6,623
				Marginal grade				
Ala.	400	86	14	344	103	56	25	128
Ark.		60	40					
Colo.	3,410	93	7	3,171	951	239	107	1,058
Ga.		56	44					
Ky.	750	68	32	510	153	240	108	261
Md.		87	13					
Ohio	990	68	32	673	202	317	143	345
Okla.	80	74	26	59	18	21	9	26
Pa.	8,523	94	6	8,011	2,403	511	230	2,633
Tenn.	200	65	35	130	39	70	32	71
Utah		96	4					
Va.	400	79	21	316	95	84	38	133
Wash.		100	0					
W. Va.	3,420	87	13	2,975	893	445	200	1,093
Total	18,173	80	20	16,189	4,857	1,983	892	5,748

Latent grade

State								
Ala.		86	14					
Ark.		60	40					
Colo.		93	7					
Ga.		56	44					
Ky.	1,250	68	32	850	255	400	180	435
Md.		87	13					
Ohio	2,970	68	32	2,020	606	950	428	1,034
Okla.		74	26					
Pa.		94	6					
Tenn.		65	35					
Utah		96	4					
Va.		79	21					
Wash.		100	0					
W. Va.		87	13					
Total	4,220	80	20	2,870	861	1,350	608	1,469

Notes: Columns 2 and 3. Percentages of total reserve base for each mining method calculated from U.S. Bureau of Mines *Miner. Ind. Surv.* data, August 1977. It is assumed that recovery methods for coking coals of all grades will be in the same proportion as the total reserve base of bituminous coal for each state.

Table 22 Summary of remaining recoverable reserves of bituminous coking coal by mining method (million tons)

	(1)	(2)	(3)	(4)	(5)	(6)	(7)	(8)	(9)	(10)	(11)	(12)
	Recoverable reserves, deep mining				Recoverable reserves, strip mining				Total recoverable reserves of coking coal			
State	Premium	Marginal	Latent	Total	Premium	Marginal	Latent	Total	Premium	Marginal	Latent	Total
Ala.	50	103		153	12	25		37	62	128		190
Ark.	4			4	4			4	8			8
Colo.	171	951		1,122	19	107		126	190	1,058		1,248
Ky.	1,015	153	255	1,425	717	108	180	1,005	1,732	261	435	2,428
Md.	3			3					3			3
Ohio	38	202	606	808	20	143		571	58	345	1,034	1,379
Okla.		18		56	33	9		20	375	26		84
Pa.	343	2,403		2,746	32	230		263	72	2,633		3,008
Tenn.	40	39		79	32	32		64	239	71		143
Utah	225			225	14			14	540			239
Va.	386	95		481	154	38		192	2	133		673
Wash.	2			2	0			0				2
W. Va.	2,730	893		3,623	612	200		812	3,342	1,093		4,435
Total	5,007	4,857	861	10,825	1,617	892	180	3,117	6,623	5,748	1,469	13,840

Table 23 Derivation of recoverable reserves of bituminous steam coal (million tons)

State	(1) Total projected recoverable reserves	(2)–(5) Recoverable reserves of coking coals				(6)–(7) Estimated recoverable reserves of steam coal	
		Premium (2)	Marginal (3)	Latent (4)	Total (5)	Total coking coal to met. use (1)–(5) (6)	Only premium coking coal to met. use (1)–(2) (7)
			Deep Mining				
Ala.	517	50	103		153	364	467
Alaska	185					185	185
Ark.	49	4			4	45	45
Colo.	2,540	171	951		1,222	1,418	2,369
Ill.	15,938					15,938	15,938
Ind.	2,681					2,681	2,681
Iowa	521					521	521
Ky.	5,274	1,015	153	255	1,423	3,851	4,259
Md.	274	3			3	271	271
Mich.	38					38	38
Mo.	425					425	425
Mont.	415					415	415
N. Mex.	377					377	377
N.C.	9					9	9
Ohio	3,927		202	606	808	3,119	3,927
Okla.	357	38	18		56	301	319
Pa.	6,700	343	2,403		2,746	3,954	6,357
Tenn.	188	40	39		79	109	148
Utah	1,885	225			225	1,660	1,660
Va.	983	386	95		481	502	597
Wash.	76	2			2	74	74
W. Va.	10,037	2,730	893		3,623	6,414	7,307
Wyo.	1,200						
Total	54,596	5,007	4,857	861	10,825	42,671	48,389

	Column 1			Surface Mining			
Ala.	134	12	25		37	97	122
Alaska	480					480	480
Ariz.	147					147	147
Ark.	149	4			4	145	145
Colo.	500	19	107		126	374	481
Ill.	3,247					3,247	3,247
Ind.	1,096					1,096	1,096
Iowa	180					180	180
Kan.	375					375	375
Ky.	1,758	717	108	180	1,005	753	1,041
Md.	21					21	21
Mich.	1					1	1
Mo.	1,160					1,160	1,160
Ohio	1,033		143	428	571	462	889
Okla.	111	20	9		29	82	91
Pa.	752	33	230		263	489	719
Tenn.	74	32	32		64	10	42
Utah	150	14			14	136	136
Va.	258	154	38		192	66	104
W. Va.	2,118	612	200		812	1,306	1,506
Total	13,597	1,617	892	608	3,117	10,627	11,983

Source: Column 1: R. A. Schmidt, Electric Utility Industry Strategy for Research in Coal Geology, presented at "Coal Geology and the Future," a symposium organized by the U.S. Geological Survey, Reston, Va., Sept. 27-28, 1976.

cated to metallurgical use or (*b*) only premium coking coals restricted to metallurgical use. Table 23 presents data in two parts, for deep and surface mining. The data are summarized in Table 24.

7. Summary of recoverable reserves of steam coal by mining method (Table 24). Data derived in the two parts of Table 23 are organized by mining method and summarized in this table. Total recoverable reserves of steam coal are estimated to range from about 53 billion tons (if all coking coal is used for metallurgical purposes) to about 60 billion tons (if only premium coking coal is so committed). Roughly four-fifths of all bituminous steam coal would require deep mining, in either case. The largest recoverable reserves of steam coal (about one-third of the total) occur in Illinois. The next largest recoverable reserves of steam coal are found in West Virginia, Pennsylvania, Kentucky, and Ohio (in that order). The remainder is present in lesser amounts in the other states. Again, the need for additional work on the amounts of steam coal is emphasized to refine and/or revise these estimates as may be necessary.

Table 24 Summary of remaining recoverable reserves of bituminous steam coal (million tons)

State	Total coking coal to metallurgical uses			Only premium coking coal to metallurgical uses		
	Deep	Surface	Total	Deep	Surface	Total
Ala.	364	97	461	467	122	589
Alaska	185	480	665	185	480	665
Ariz.		147	147		147	147
Ark.	45	145	190	45	145	190
Colo.	1,418	374	1,792	2,369	481	2,850
Ill.	15,938	3,247	19,185	15,938	3,247	19,185
Ind.	2,681	1,096	3,777	2,681	1,096	3,777
Iowa	521	180	701	521	180	701
Kan.		375	375		375	375
Ky.	3,851	753	4,604	4,259	1,041	5,300
Md.	271	21	292	271	21	292
Mich.	38	1	39	38	1	39
Mo.	425	1,160	1,585	425	1,160	1,585
Mont.	415		415	415		415
N. Mex.	377		377	377		377
N.C.	9		9	9		9
Ohio	3,199	462	3,581	3,927	889	4,612
Okla.	301	82	383	319	91	410
Pa.	3,954	489	4,443	6,357	719	7,076
Tenn.	109	10	119	148	42	190
Utah	1,660	136	1,796	1,660	136	1,796
Va.	502	66	568	597	104	701
Wash.	74		74	74		74
W.Va.	6,414	1,306	7,720	7,307	1,506	8,813
Total	42,671	10,627	53,298	48,389	11,983	60,372

8. Comparison of bituminous coal resources and recoverable reserves by end use (Table 25). Totals from the several preceding tables are compiled and compared in Table 25 to illustrate the relationships between remaining resources, reserve base, and recoverable reserves for all bituminous coals and for coking and steam coals. The table is in two parts, presenting separately data in tons and as a percentage. Two cases are shown, with varying amounts of coking coals dedicated to metallurgical uses.

The table shows that estimated recoverable reserves are only 9 percent of the total bituminous coal resources. Of this, nearly all is steam coal, with only 1 or 2 percent recoverable coking coal. Most bituminous coal will require deep mining for its recovery, with surface reserves including less than one-quarter of the recoverable reserves.

RESOURCES FOR UNDERGROUND GASIFICATION

Introduction

Locked in a centuries-old struggle with nature to win extraction of her coal deposits and their contained energy, humanity has longed for a means to accomplish this task with greater ease, economy, and safety. Although there have been notable improvements in technology for physical recovery of coal reserves, its practice leaves much to be desired in terms of efficient resource recovery, acceptable effects on the adjacent environment, and in posing tolerable risks to members of the work force and society in general. Thus, there appear to be strong and deeply rooted incentives for investigating approaches that offer the prospect of recovering the energy or chemical values of coal without mining.

With such impetus, it is not surprising that underground coal gasification (UCG) was explored periodically since first suggested by Siemens over a hundred years ago[1]. While interest in underground coal gasification existed principally in the scientific and technical community, its potential for relieving burdens from labor and the larger implications for society attracted the attention of politicians, notably V. I. Lenin of the Soviet Union[2]. Lenin's recommendation for experimentation in underground coal gasification ultimately led to an extensive program of work carried out in various places in the Soviet Union over a period of some three decades. Much of our present knowledge of underground coal gasification stems from the empirical engineering data collected during that continuing program.

Despite all the work on underground coal gasification carried out in the Soviet Union (and to a lesser extent in the United Kingdom, Poland, Czechoslovakia, and the United States), the basis for an economical, reliable technique for routine operations remains unperfected. Recently, major R&D efforts have been initiated

[1] W. Siemens, *Trans. Chem. Soc.* (*London*), vol. 21, p. 279, 1868.

[2] Cited by J. L. Elder, The Underground Gasification of Coal, in H. H. Lowry (ed.), "Chemistry of Coal Utilization," pp. 1023–1040, Wiley, New York, 1963.

Table 25 Comparison of bituminous coal resources and recoverable reserves by end use

		Coking coals			Steam Coals
Item	Total bituminous coal	Total	Premium grade	Total coking coal to met. use	Only premium coking coal to met. use
		Million tons			
1. Remaining identified resources	747,357	183,552	97,552	563,805	644,305
2. Demonstrated reserve base	228,925	42,677	20,284	186,249	208,642
3. Estimated recoverable reserves	68,240	13,840	6,623	54,400	60,372
4. Estimated recoverable reserves (deep mining)	54,496	10,825	5,007	43,670	48,389
5. Estimated recoverable reserves (surface mining)	13,744	3,117	1,617	10,627	11,983
		Percentage of total resources			
1. Remaining identified resources	100	33	14	67	86
2. Demonstrated reserve base	31	6	3	25	28
3. Estimated recoverable reserves	9	2	1	7	8
4. Estimated recoverable reserves (deep mining)	7	1	1	6	-
5. Estimated recoverable reserves (surface mining)	2	neg	neg	2	2

Totals may not agree exactly with Table 1 because of subsequent independent rounding.

in the United States in attempts to secure the necessary information for design and implementation of a commercial UCG system. One principal consumer prominently mentioned in regard to use of product gases is the electric utility industry. This section attempts to place underground coal gasification in perspective. Included is a brief overview of coal reserves and development approaches, a summary of the status of research and development, and an assessment of the outlook for underground coal gasification with an evaluation of implications for the electric utility industry.

Underground coal gasification technology is at an early stage of development (Chapter 14). As a result, there is considerable uncertainty regarding the magnitude of coal resources that may be amenable for development by this means. Some published estimates of the amount of coal which could be reached by underground gasification are (as will be seen later in this section) truly enormous. In an attempt to derive a realistic estimate of the potential resource for underground gasification, logic similar to that presented in the preceding section was applied, starting with basic data on the total identified coal resource.

Seam Thickness

Underground coal gasification requires relatively thick coal seams, with uniform geometry over sizable areas. Thickness is a most important parameter, because it controls the lateral extent of operations and strongly influences overall costs (through the number of drill holes that are required). For example, a 4-foot coal seam (common in eastern coalfields) requires 140 acres for 1 million tons, whereas a 12-foot seam (common in certain western coalfields) requires only 50 acres for the same quantity. Clearly, other things being equal, it would be preferable to employ gasification in the thicker, more localized deposit. Evaluation of coal resource potential for underground gasification, therefore, should logically begin with consideration of the magnitudes of coal occurring in thick seams, for which there is no presently available method for underground mining at high recoverability.

In evaluating resources, the following thickness categories are used by the Geological Survey:

Category	Bituminous and anthracite, inches	Subbituminous and lignite, feet
Thin	14−28	2.5−5
Intermediate	28−42	5−10
Thick	>42	>10

Table 26 shows the thickness of identified coal resources at depths less than 1000 feet according to the level of confidence in information about the deposits.[1] The table shows that the reserve base comprises thick and intermediate coals whose presence is measured or indicated; these coals amount to 29 percent of the total identified coal resources. Thin seams include only a small part of the measured and

[1] "Measured" resources are better defined than "indicated," which are better known than "inferred."

Table 26 Identified coal resources by seam thickness (percent)

Less than 1000-foot-depth

Thickness	Confidence level		
	Measured[1]	Indicated	Inferred
Thick	11	7 "Reserve	12
Intermediate	3	8 base"	11
Thin	1	6	32
Total	15	21	55

[1]"Measured" resources are better defined than "indicated," which are better known than "inferred."
Source: US Geol. Surv. Bull. 1412, 1975.

indicated deposits. The table also shows that the largest part of identified resources are imperfectly known, their presence being only inferred; most of these coals are in thin seams. Table 27 shows comparable data for identified coal resources occurring between 1000- and 2000-foot depths. Less than one-tenth of the total identified resources occurs at these depths, although the coal appears to be found in relatively thick seams.

Table 28 summarizes the preceding data on the thick and intermediately thick coal seams at less than 2000-foot depth. The table shows that the reserve base accounts for 29 percent of the total resource. All other thick coals (those outside the reserve base at shallow depth or at greater depth) compose another 14.2 percent of the total identified resource. The total coal present in thickest seams thus represents nearly half (43.2 percent) of the total identified resources. It seems reasonable to conclude that UCG developments in the foreseeable future (by whatever method) will be concentrated in these thicker seams. Depending on the local conditions, developments in thick seams could effectively preclude later recovery of thin seams as well. In view of the fact that existing technology and present R&D is oriented toward thick seams, there seems to be value in examining the potential for future recovery of even a portion of the thin coal seams so as to make most effective use of this sizable, known resource. However, for the present

Table 27 Identified coal resources by seam thickness (percent)

1000- to 2000-foot depth

Thickness	Confidence level		
	Measured[1]	Indicated	Inferred
Thick		1.2	1.0
Intermediate		1.0	2.2
Thin	0.1	0.5	1.7
Total	0.1	2.7	4.9

[1]"Measured" resources are better defined than "indicated," which are better known than "inferred."
Source: US Geol. Surv. Bull. 1412, 1975.

Table 28 Summary of data on thicker seams at shallow depth (percent)

Less than 2000-foot depth

1.	Reserve base, thick and intermediate seams, measured and indicated, <1000 ft	29
2.	Nonreserve base, thick seams: a. Inferred, <1000 ft	12
	b. Indicated and inferred, 1–2000 ft	2.2
	Total	14.2
3.	Grand total	43.2

there seems to be no alternative but to concentrate upon the thicker seams for the purpose of analysis.

Estimated Resource Magnitude

The foregoing suggests that thick coal seams found at modest depths are likely to be targets for development, regardless of technology. However, to assess the potential for development of underground coal gasification, it is essential to have an estimate of the magnitude of coal resources which could be processed by such techniques. It is possible to arrive at such an estimate by reasoning from basic resource data, according to coal-deposit criteria for underground gasification processes. Ideally, each candidate process for underground coal gasification would have established its own set of criteria, but this is not generally the case because many programs are at early experimental stages and details are lacking. For the purposes of this analysis, a set of criteria has been established; the criteria are as identified in Table 29.

Table 29 Preliminary coal deposit criteria for underground gasification

1. The minimum cumulative thickness of combustible coal shall be 10 feet. If shale, bone coal, or other incombustible stringers exist, the individual combustible coal beds shall be separated by no more than 5 feet of noncombustibles.

2. The depth of overburden shall be more than 500 feet but less than 3000 feet; preferably, however, the overburden shall not exceed 2000 feet (selected as the maximum depth of Soviet experiments).

3. Overburden permeability should be substantially less than the natural permeability of the coal.

4. There shall be no prolific acquifers in the roof rock directly above the coals, and the coal seam should not be a prolific acquifer.

5. Roof and floor rock material preferably shall be composed of shale or clay or other relatively plastic rocks.

6. The terrain in the immediate area of the project site should be suitable for drilling holes and for the installation of surface facilities.

7. The proposed site should be sufficiently remote to avoid interference with neighboring operators. Furthermore, the site should be sufficiently large so that the effects of applying the technology will not transcend the site boundaries (particularly for subsidence effects).

Use of these criteria is justifiable in that the UCG processes undergoing the most active testing in the United States today are aimed at thick seams greater than or equal to 10 feet. To the extent that it may ultimately be possible to gasify thinner seams underground, the resource magnitudes resulting from use of these criteria may be too conservative. Still, at the present early stage of technology development, it is probably preferable to employ conservative estimates and refrain from raising expectations that may be unrealizable.

Based on the above criteria, resource magnitudes for underground gasification were estimated. Details of these estimates, by rank, are given in Tables 30 to 34. The following procedure was used to obtain these estimates (the numbers refer to the columns in Tables 30 to 34):

1. Total estimated identified coal resources for all ranks except anthracite[1] and all depths down to 3000 feet were compiled for each state from *US Geol. Surv. Bull.* 1412, 1975 (representing the situation as of Jan. 1, 1974).

2. Because the preferred overburden depth for underground coal gasification by known methods is less than 2000 feet, resources occurring at such depths were calculated from the total. The U.S. Geological Survey reported that 98.7 percent of the total identified resources were found at less than 2000-foot depth; this average value was used in lieu of detailed state data for the purposes of this preliminary analysis.

3. The total reserve base of thickest and best-defined coals was compiled from the Geological Survey report. By definition, the reserve base is considered to be "suitable for mining by 1974 methods." *It is assumed that coals of the reserve base will be developed largely by conventional mining methods and that they still will be unavailable to underground coal gasification* (except as indicated in item 6 below). This assumption may prove to be overly conservative, and it is entirely possible that some part of the reserve base may experience development through underground gasification; however, data upon which to perform such a refined analysis are not presently available. When sufficient data are obtained, it may be determined that only a small part of the total reserve base would experience other than conventional mining.

Note, moreover, that the above assumption appears to be consistent with present U.S. thinking about the potential for underground coal gasification. The ERDA Laramie Energy Research Center stated that "if UCG can be successfully developed, it could *supplement* current coal mining technology and lead to increased utilization of coal for the intermediate term until energy supplies from other than fossil fuels can be developed. *UCG is not being developed to replace present coal mining.*"[2] [Emphasis added.] In view of the original intent for underground coal gasification as an alternative to mining, the quote clearly represents a change in basic concept.

---

[1] Anthracite was excluded from this analysis because of limited resources and because the largest resources occur in populated areas.

[2] Energy Research and Development Administration, "The Laramie Energy Research Center's Underground Coal Gasification Program," manuscript, 1976.

4. Coal resources occurring at depths less than 2000 feet but outside the reserve base and therefore, by definition, "not suitable for mining," were calculated by subtracting the reserve base (column 3) from resources at less than 2000 feet (column 2). It is assumed that this derived resource category would be prime targets for underground coal gasification, because they do not appear to be recoverable in the foreseeable future by any other means. Included in this category are resources in (*a*) thin seams at less than 1000-foot depth and (*b*) all seam thicknesses down to 2000 feet.

5. Only thick seams are assumed to be satisfactory targets for underground coal gasification (refer to Table 28). Thus, the not-suitable-for-mining resources down to 2000 feet of column 4 must be reduced to reflect their thick seam portion. It was shown earlier that only 14.2 percent of these nonreserve-base coals were in thick seams. This average value was used to calculate column 5 in the absence of detailed state-level data.

6. It is possible that advances in coal mining technology may be secured from present R&D that would permit mining to be practiced on a portion of the thicker seams calculated in column 5. Such coals would therefore be added to the reserve base and would no longer be candidates for underground coal gasification, according to the assumption stated in the above discussion of column 3. For purposes of analysis, it is assumed that as much as 30 percent of presently unminable thick seams could be added to the reserve base in this fashion; column 6 presents these estimates.

Alternatively, it is possible that pressing needs for gas supplies may require dedication of a portion of the reserve base to underground coal gasification. Such coals would no longer be available for mining. For purposes of analysis, it is assumed that as much as 30 percent of presently minable thick seams of subbituminous coal could be deleted from the reserve base in this fashion; two tables are presented for subbituminous coal to show these minimum and maximum figures. A maximum estimate of UCG potentials was not prepared for bituminous coal because of its tendency to swell upon heating and because most seams are less than about 5 to 6 feet thick. Two lignite estimates were prepared, differing only in the magnitude of coal assumed to be added to the reserve base as a result of improvements in mining methods.

7. Unminable coals in thick seams that are targets for underground gasification were calculated by subtracting column 6 from column 5.

8. Based on the seam thicknesses employed in the present processes, the estimated annual amounts of gas production, and a total project lifetime of 20 years, a total of 180 million tons of coal resources would need to be committed to a single project. The maximum number of possible UCG projects possible for each state were calculated by dividing the total project resource requirements into the apparent target resources of column 7.

9. The results of columns 7 and 8 were compared against three of the principal criteria: (*a*) coal thickness, (*b*) suitable terrain, and (*c*) remote location.

The results of this analysis, while recognized to be crude, are summarized on page 110:

Table 30 Bituminous coal resources for underground coal gasification (million tons)

	(1)a Total estimated identified resources 0–3000 ft (1/1/74)	(2)b Resources 2000 ft (1) x 98.7%	(3)c Total reserve base 0–1000 ft (1/1/76)	(4)d Resources < 2000 ft not suitable for mining (2) − (3)	(5)e Resources not suitable for mining in thick beds (4) x 14.2%	(6)f Potential additions to reserve base (5) x 30%	(7)g Remaining unminable thick seams (5) − (6)	(8)h Maximum number in situ developments (7) − 180x10⁶ tons resources	#1 (thickness 10 ft)	#7 (suitable terrain)	#8 (remote location)
Ala.	13,262	13,089	2,009	11,080	1,573	472	1,101	6	No		No
Alaska	19,413	19,160	698	18,462	2,622	786	1,836	10	?	?	
Ariz.	21,234	20,958	326	20,632	2,930	878	2,052	11	No		No
Ark.	1,638	1,617	270	1,347	191	57	134	0			
Colo.	109,117	107,699	9,144	98,555	13,995	4,198	9,797	54	?		
Ga.	24	24	1	23	3	1	2	0			
Ill.	146,001	144,103	67,969	76,134	10,811	3,243	7,568	42	No		No
Ind.	32,868	32,441	10,714	21,727	3,085	925	2,160	12	No		No
Iowa	6,505	6,420	2,202	4,208	598	179	419	2	No		No
Kan.	18,668	18,425	998	17,427	2,474	742	1,732	9	No		No
Ky.	64,346	63,510	26,001	37,509	5,326	1,598	3,728	20	No		No
Md.	1,152	1,137	1,048	89	13	4	9	0			
Mich.	205	202	126	76	11	3	8	0			
Mo.	31,184	30,779	5,014	25,765	3,658	1,097	2,561	14	No		No
Mont.	2,299	2,269	1,385	884	125	38	87	0			
N. Mex.	10,748	10,608	1,859	8,749	1,242	372	870	4	?		
N.C.	110	109	31	78	11	3	8	0			
Ohio	41,166	40,631	19,230	22,998	3,266	979	2,287	12	No		No
Okla.	7,117	7,024	1,618	6,148	873	261	612	3			
Oreg.	50	49	49	49	7	2	5	0			
Pa.	63,940	63,109	23,727	40,134	5,699	1,709	3,990	22	No		No
Tenn.	2,540	2,497	965	1,532	217	65	152	0	?		
Tex.	6,048	5,969		5,969	848	254	594	3	?		
Utah	23,186	22,885	6,552	16,333	2,319	695	1,624	9	No	?	
Va.	9,216	9,096	4,166	5,472	805	241	564	3	No		
Wash.	1,867	1,842	255	1,587	225	68	157	0	No	No	
W. Va.	100,150	98,848	38,606	60,242	8,554	2,566	5,988	32	No	No	No
Wyo.	12,703	12,538	4,003	8,535	1,211	363	848	4	?	?	

| Other | 610 | 602 | 228,925 | 512,546 | 602 | 86 | 26 | 60 | 0 |
| Total | 747,357 | 737,641 | | | | 72,778 | 21,825 | 50,953 | 273 |

a P. Averitt, Coal Resources of the United States, January 1, 1974, *US Geol. Surv. Bull.* 1412, 1975.

b *Ibid.*, p. 38. (Preferred overburden depth for in situ processing is less than 2000 ft. per Lawrence Livermore Laboratory report TID-27008, Feb. 24, 1976.) Average value used in lieu of detailed state data.

c *Ibid.*, p. 33. The reserve base is a selected portion of the identified resources deemed to be suitable for mining by 1974 methods.

d Resources at depths less than 2000 ft. which are not suitable for mining could be prime targets for in situ processing, because they do not appear to be recoverable by any other means. Includes (1) thin seams at depths greater than 1000 ft.

e Average values used in lieu of detailed state data.

f Advancements in mining technology assured to permit mining of about a third the presently unminable thick seams.

g Self-explanatory.

h Resource requirements for in situ gasification for 20-year operation estimated as follows: Lawrence Livermore Laboratory process, 180 million tons; Laramie Energy Research Center process, 168 million tons. The 180 million ton figure is used in this analysis. (See Chapter 14, "Present U.S. Underground Gasification Concepts," for discussions of these processes.)

Table 31 Minimum subbituminous coal resources for underground coal gasification (million tons)

	(1) Total estimated identified resources 0–3000 ft (1/1/74)	(2) Resources 2000 ft (1) x 98.7%	(3) Total reserve base 0–1000 ft (1/1/76)	(4) Resources < 2000 ft not suitable for mining (2) – (3)	(5) Resources not suitable for mining in thick beds (4) x 14.2%	(6) Potential additions to reserve base (5) x 30%	(7) Remaining unminable thick seams (5) – (6)	(8) Maximum number in situ developments (7) – 180x10⁶ tons resources	(9) Satisfy process criteria? #4 (10 ft)	#7 (suitable terrain)	#8 (remote location)
Alaska	110,666	109,227	5,447	103,780	14,736	4,421	10,326	57	?	?	?
Colo.	19,733	19,477	4,121	15,356	2,180	654	1,537	8	?	?	
Mont.	176,819	174,520	103,417	71,103	10,096	3,028	7,079	39	?	?	
N. Mex.	50,639	49,981	2,736	47,245	6,708	2,012	4,707	26	?		
Oreg.	284	280	18	262	37	11	26	0			
Utah	173	171	1	170	24	8	16	0			
Wash.	4,180	4,126	1,317	2,833	402	120	293	1	No		No
Wyo.	123,240	121,638	51,369	70,280	9,979	2,993	6,997	38	?		
Others	32	32	5	5	2	2	3	0			
Total	485,766	479,847	168,425	314,054	44,178	13,260	30,995	180			

See also footnotes to Table 30.

Table 32 Maximum subbituminous coal resources for underground coal gasification (million tons)

	(1) Total estimated identified resources 0–3000 ft (1/1/74)	(2) Resources 2000 ft (1) x 98.7%	(3) Total reserve base 0–1000 ft (1/1/76)	(4) Resources < 2000 ft not suitable for mining (2) – (3)	(5) Resources not suitable for mining in thick beds (4) x 14.2%	(6) Potential additions to reserve base (5) x 30%	(7) Remaining unmineable thick seams (5) – (6)	(8) Maximum number in situ developments (7) – 180x10⁶ tons resources	(9) Satisfy process criteria?		
									#4 10 ft	#7 (suitable terrain)	#8 (remote location)
Alaska	110,666	109,227	5,447	103,780	14,736	4,421	19,157	106	?	?	?
Colo.	19,733	19,477	4,121	15,356	2,180	654	2,834	15	?	?	
Mont.	176,819	174,520	103,417	71,103	10,096	3,028	13,124	72	?		
N. Mex.	50,639	49,981	2,736	47,245	6,708	2,012	8,720	48	?		
Oreg.	284	280	18	262	37	11	48	0			
Utah	174	171	1	170	24	8	32	0			
Wash.	4,180	4,126	1,317	2,833	402	120	522	2	No		No
Wyo.	123,240	121,638	51,369	70,369	9,979	2,993	12,972	72	?	?	
Others	32	32		32	5						
Total	485,766	479,847	168,425	314,054	44,178	13,260	57,260	315			

See also footnotes to Table 30.
Note: Column 6: Potential deletions from reserve gas calculated by assuming that 30% of reserve base may become targets for UCG.

Table 33 Minimum lignite resources for underground coal gasification (million tons)

	(1) Total estimated identified resources 0–3000 ft (1/1/74)	(2) Resources 2000 ft (1) x 98.7%	(3) Total reserve base 0–1000 ft (1/1/76)	(4) Resources 2000 ft not suitable for mining (2) – (3)	(5) Resources not suitable for mining in thick beds (4) x 14.2%	(6) Potential additions to reserve base (5) x 30%	(7) Remaining unminable thick seams (5) – (6)	(8) number in situ developments (7) – 180x10⁶ tons resources	Minimum Satisfy process criteria?		
									#4 10 ft	#7 (suitable terrain)	#8 (remote location)

Ala.	2,000	1,974	1,083	891	126	37	89	0	
Ark.	350	346	26	320	45	13	32	0	
Mont.	112,521	111,058	15,767	95,291	13,531	4,059	9,472	52	?
N. Dak.	350,602	346,045	10,145	335,900	47,697	14,309	33,308	185	?
S. Dak.	2,185	2,156	426	1,730	245	74	171	0	
Tex.	10,293	10,159	3,182	6,977	990	297	693	3	?
Wash.	117	116	8	108	15	5	10	0	
Others	46	45		45	6	2	4	0	
Total	478,134	471,899	33,617	441,378		18,796	43,859	240	

See also footnotes to Table 30.

Table 34 Maximum lignite resources for underground coal gasification (million tons)

	(1) Total estimated identified resources 0 – 3000 ft (1/1/74)	(2) Resources 2000 ft (1) x 98.7%	(3) Total reserve base 0 – 1000 ft (1/1/76)	(4) Resources 2000 ft not suitable for mining (2) – (3)	(5) Resources not suitable for mining in thick beds (4) x 14.2%	(6) Maximum number in situ developments (7) – 180x10⁶ tons resources	(7) Satisfy process criteria? #1 (thickness 10 ft)	#7 (suitable terrain)	#8 (remote location)
Ala.	2,000	1,974	1,083	891	126	0			
Ark.	350	346	26	320	45	0			
Mont.	112,521	111,058	15,767	95,291	13,531	75			
N. Dak.	350,602	346,045	10,145	335,900	47,697	264			
S. Dak.	2,185	2,156	426	1,730	245	0			
Tex.	10,293	10,159	3,182	6,977	990	5			
Wash.	117	116	8	108	15	0			
Others	46	45	8	45	6	0			
Total	478,134	471,899	33,617	441,378	62,781	345			

See also footnotes to Table 30.
Note: Column 5. All resources not suitable for mining assumed to be targets for in situ development.

Fifteen states apparently have insufficient unminable coal resources in thick seams to support underground coal gasification (Table 35).

A total of 14 states apparently have sufficient unminable coal resources to support underground coal gasification, but they are estimated as failing to satisfy one or more criteria for a successful project (Table 36).

Some eight states apparently have sufficient unminable coal resources to support underground coal gasification, but the likelihood of coals meeting project criteria is considered uncertain (Table 37).

In all, a total of more than 60 billion tons occurring in 27 of the principal coal-bearing states are judged to have a low potential for underground coal gasification for one or another of the above reasons; see Table 38 for a summary of these data. The table suggests that the bituminous coals of the eastern and midwestern coalfields are particularly unfavorable prospects for underground coal gasification, either being present in insufficient quantities or failing to satisfy essential criteria (or both).

Only five states, Montana, New Mexico, North Dakota, Texas, and Wyoming appear to have sufficient coal resources which may satisfy most of the essential criteria for underground coal gasification (Table 39). The principal targets for this technique are the lower-rank coals, subbituminous and lignite, for which minimum and maximum values are shown. (Although Alaska possesses large deposits, their remoteness and difficult conditions make development speculative.)

In the minimum case (where the entire reserve base is assumed to be dedicated to mining and additional coals are added to the reserve base through improvements in mining technology), it is estimated that underground coal gasification can process some 19.6 billion tons of lignite. In the maximum case (where as much

Table 35 States apparently having insufficient unminable coal resources in thick seams to support underground coal gasification

	Bituminous	Subbituminous Minimum	Subbituminous Maximum	Lignite
Alabama				x
Arkansas	x			x
Arizona		x		
Colorado		x		
Georgia	x			
Maryland	x			
Michigan	x			
Montana	x			
N. Carolina	x			
Oregon	x	x		
S. Dakota				x
Tennessee	x			
Utah		x		
Virginia	x			
Washington	x	x	x	x

Table 36 States apparently having sufficient unminable coal resources to support underground coal gasification, but estimated as failing to satisfy one or more criteria

	Criterion failed		
Rank, state	Thickness	Terrain	Remoteness
Bituminous:			
Alabama	x		x
Arizona	x		
Illinois	x		x
Indiana	x		x
Iowa	x		x
Kansas	x		x
Kentucky	x		x
Missouri	x		x
Ohio	x		x
Oklahoma	x		
Pennsylvania	x		x
Virginia	x		x
West Virginia	x	x	x
Subbituminous:			
Washington	x		x

Table 37 States apparently having sufficient unminable coal resources to support underground coal gasification projects, but meeting one or more criterion considered uncertain

	Uncertain criterion		
Rank, state	Thickness	Terrain	Acquifer
Bituminous:			
Alaska	x	x	
Colorado	x		
New Mexico	x		
Texas	x		
Utah	x	x	
Subbituminous:			
Alaska	x	x	x
Colorado	x		x
Montana			x
New Mexico	x		x
Wyoming			x
Lignite:			
N. Dakota	x		
Texas	x		

Table 38 Summary of states having low potential for underground gasification

0009 State	Bituminous Insufficient unminable resources	Bituminous Failed one or more criterion	Bituminous Uncertain	Subbituminous Insufficient unminable Resources	Subbituminous Failed one or more criterion	Subbituminous Uncertain	Lignite Insufficient unminable resources	Lignite Failed one or more criterion	Lignite Uncertain	Total amount coal with low potential, million tons B	SB	L
Ala.							x			1,101		89
Alaska	x		?			?				1,836	10,326	32
Ark.		F					x			134		
Ariz.				x						2,052		
Colo.			?			?				9,797	1,537	
Ga.	x									2		
Ill.		F								7,568		
Ind.		F								2,160		
Iowa		F								419		
Kan.		F								1,732		
Ky.		F								3,728		
Md.	x									9		
Mich.	x									8		
Mo.		F								2,561		
Mont.	x									87		
N.C.	x									8		
Ohio		F								2,287		
Okla.		F								612		
Oreg.	x									5	26	
Pa.		F								3,990		
S. Dak.							x					171
Tenn.	x									152		
Utah		F	?							1,624	16	
Va.		F		x						564		
Wash.										157	293	10
W. Va.		F								5,988		
Wyo.	x	F								848		
										49,429	12,198	302

61,929 x 10⁶ tons

Table 39 States apparently capable of supporting UCG projects in identified resources

Rank, state	Remaining unminable coal in thick seams, million tons		Number of in situ developments		Total gas production, trillion std. ft³, at 100 x 10⁹ std. ft³/yr for 20 yrs	
	Minimum	Maximum	Minimum	Maximum	Minimum	Maximum
Subbituminous:						
Montana	7,079	13,124	39	72	78	144
New Mexico	4,707	8,720	26	48	52	96
Wyoming	6,997	12,972	38	76	76	144
Subtotal	18,783	34,816	103	142	206	384
Lignite:						
Montana	9,472	13,531	52	75	104	150
N. Dakota	33,388	47,697	185	264	370	528
Texas	693	990	3	5	6	10
Subtotal	43,553	62,218	240	344	480	688
Total	62,336	97,034	343	536	686	1,072

Wyoming could fail to satisfy criterion 4 regarding aquifers and water content.

as 30 percent of the reserve base may be developed through underground coal gasification instead of mining), it is estimated that underground coal gasification can process some 72.6 billion tons of subbituminous coal and about 62.6 billion tons of lignite. In either case, UCG development of subbituminous coal would be centered in Montana and Wyoming, while lignite activity would be largely in North Dakota and Montana.

Clearly, the magnitude of the range between minimum and maximum estimates (a factor of almost 4 in subbituminous coal and nearly 1.5 in lignite) needs to be reduced before serious attempts to carry out large-scale operations can be organized.

Recapitulating the above analysis, a comparison of coal resource magnitudes by potential recovery method is given in Table 40. The table shows that, under the assumptions employed in this analysis, from 35 to 42 percent of the nation's total identified coal resources could be developed by a combination of mining and underground coal gasification. The largest development potential appears to be for mining, doubtless reflecting the assumption that the coal deposits composing the reserve base would be mined. However, the main benefit of this assumption is to permit estimating the magnitude of coal that could be added to the development total through underground gasification. It is somewhat discouraging to find that, even allowing for an optimistic development prospect for underground coal gasification, so few resources are added to the total amount of coal which may experience development. Even when it is assumed that underground coal gasification would be practical on part of the reserve base, the amount of additional coal involved is still not great.

While it is possible that some of the coal in the reserve base (either as originally estimated by the Geological Survey or extended as suggested in this analysis) could experience development by underground gasification, it is also possible that some of the coals identified for underground gasification could be mined. Therefore, it is suggested that the development portion of the total coal resource will not change significantly from that given in Table 40. Furthermore, it does not appear very likely that the proportions will change very much between mining and underground coal gasification during the foreseeable future.

The estimates of coal resources favorable for underground gasification developed in this chapter are significantly less than those reported by other workers. For example, Glass[1] estimated more than 3 trillion tons of potential reserves for this method of development. ERDA estimated that the United States sits atop 1.2 trillion tons of unminable coal that the process could tap.[2] Those estimates, however, were made on a gross national basis, not on a detailed state and rank breakdown as used here. Localized information required for an operation may reduce reserves further. Although the maximum estimate derived in the

---

[1]G. B. Glass, "Coal Resources for In Situ Gasification," presented to the American Nuclear Society, April 1977.

[2]Quoted in R. Arnold, On-the-Spot Energy: Coal Burning in Earth Looks Promising as Gas Source for Utilities and Factories, *Wall St. J.*, p. 40, Apr. 26, 1977.

Table 40 Comparison of coal resource magnitudes by potential recovery methods (million tons)

Rank	(1) Total identified resources	(2) Estimated reserve base for mining	(3) Possible additions to reserve base	(4) Total coal for mining (2) + (3)	(5) Not presently recoverable by mining (1) − (2)	(6) Minimum target for UCG	(7) Maximum target for UCG	(8) Development potential as % total resources UCG		
								Mining	Minimum	Maximum
Bituminous	747,357	228,925	21,825	250,750	518,432			34	0	0
Subbituminous	485,766	168,425	13,260	181,685	304,081	34,816	37	4	7	7
Lignite	478,134	33,617	18,796	52,413	444,517	43,553	62,218	11	9	13
Total	1,711,257	430,967	53,881	484,848	1,267,030	62,336	97,034	(Av)27	(Av)7	(Av)10

Summary data for cols. 1 and 2 from *US Geol. Surv. Bull.* 1412, 1975.
Summary data for cols. 3, 6, and 7 from Tables 21 through 24.
Column 8 calculated as follows:
Mining: (4)÷(1)x100
Mining: (6)÷(1)x100
Maximum: (7)÷(1)x100

present study is *only about one-tenth* the amount of coal which ERDA regards as amenable to underground gasification, it is nevertheless a sizable amount of coal. Clearly, extensive geological work is required to arrive at a definitive and agreed-upon estimate of the size of the target for UCG technology.

Potential Resource Recovery

The analysis reported above considers the total amount of coal in place that may experience development by mining or UCG technologies. For each technology, development requires commitment of the entire amount of a given coal seam in a particular site for the lifetime of the operation, even though only a portion of the material or energy values may be extracted for use. In completing an assessment of resource utilization, it is essential to examine the vital question of recoverability.

Mining. Actually, the amount of coal that can be recovered through mining a given deposit varies from about 25 to 90 percent of the coal in place. Therefore, as discussed earlier in this chapter, to arrive at a reasonable estimate of the amount of recoverable coal, the reserve base data must be reduced by an appropriate amount to allow for incomplete recovery. It was pointed out above that coal reserves recoverable by mining are estimated to be only a relatively small part of the reserve base. The total estimated recoverable coal resources as indicated by the above data is 136 billion tons, or about 8 percent of the total U.S. coal resources. Clearly, the quantity of recoverable reserves is still substantial. Employing the estimated recoverable reserves (refer to Table 1, this section) and typical heating values for each principal rank of coal, it is possible to calculate the total recoverable heating value of mined coal; data are given in Table 42. The table shows that a total of nearly 3000×10^{15} Btu is contained in recoverable coal reserves. The largest amount, roughly half the total, is in bituminous coal, with another third in subbituminous coal and the remainder in anthracite and lignite.

Clearly, the amount of energy in coal recoverable through mining is a substantial quantity. To be sure, this coal must be further processed to complete extraction of its contained energy. Assuming that the efficiency of conversion of the energy content of recovered coal is only about 33 percent, then only about one-third of the total recoverable energy is transformed into useful work (Table 41, column 4).

Underground coal gasification. Estimating the potential for recovery of energy values from underground coal gasification is even more uncertain than for mining. There is little experience upon which to base a meaningful recoverability percentage.

If geological conditions are comparable to those encountered in ordinary mining operations, it may be that only about one-third of the total coal resource may be recovered by underground coal gasification. This estimate could be increased or decreased, depending on the geometry or geological conditions present in any given coalfield. Overall resource recovery may range from less than 20 to more

Table 41 Estimated recoverable energy values through coal mining

Rank	(1) Recoverable Reserves, billion tons	(2) Typical heating value, million Btu/ton	(3) Heating value recoverable coal, $\times 10^{15}$ Btu	(4) heating value, (3) $\times$ 33% $\times 10^{15}$ Btu
Anthracite	2.2	25.8	56.8	18.7
Bituminous	68.3	23.8	1625.5	536.4
Subbituminous	56.2	18.8	1056.6	348.7
Lignite	8.9	14.6	129.9	42.9
Total	135.6		2868.8	946.7

Table 42 Estimated recoverable energy values through underground coal gasification

Rank	(1) Optimistic reserves with potential for UCG (Table 40), billion tons Minimum	Maximum	(2) Estimated gasifiable reserves (1) x 30% Minimum	Maximum	(3) Typical heating value, million Btu/ton	(4) Heating value of gasifiable coal, x 10^{15} Btu Minimum	Maximum	(5) Heating value of actually gasified coal, x 10^{15} Btu (4) x 80% Minimum	Maximum
Subbituminous	18.7	34.8	5.8	10.8	18.8	109.0	203.0	87.2	162.4
Lignite	43.5	62.2	13.5	19.3	14.6	197.1	281.8	157.7	225.4
Total	62.2	97.0	19.3	30.1	32.4	313.3	706.2	244.9	387.8

than 40 percent, according to conditions.[1] For purposes of the present analysis, however, the estimated recovery percentage derived above will be used. Table 42 shows the estimated recoverable energy values through underground coal gasification. The above-derived recovery percentage was used to calculate the heating value of gasifiable coal. The largest values are for lignite and subbituminous coal (each near 200×10^{15} Btu), with bituminous coal at about half that value. The coal actually gasified will probably be less than the maximum possible, owing to variable geological features or other impediments, and only about four-fifths of the heating value may be ultimately recovered, as shown in the last column of the table.

Summary comparison. A summary comparison of the recoverable energy values through mining and underground gasification is shown in Table 43. The table shows that the greatest recovery of energy values appears to be through mining, which accounts for about three-quarters of the total. The largest single recovery of energy values is for mining bituminous coal, with the next largest for mining subbituminous coal; lignite and anthracite account for small portions of the energy recovery from mining.

The potential energy recovery from underground coal gasification appears to increase with decreasing rank. Accounting for little over one-tenth the total in bituminous coal, underground coal gasification increases to nearly one-third the recovery of subbituminous coal, and is estimated to make up more than four-fifths the recovery potential of lignite (Table 43). Of course, these data are estimates only, and it may well be that they will require revision as more definitive data are obtained. This attempt at quantifying the potential for underground coal gasification only serves to underscore the importance of advanced surveys and research into parameters that control the successful operation of the process.

Synthesis

The results described in the previous sections provide an estimate of the recoverable reserves of two different classes of bituminous coal. However, to address the question posed by how much steam coal may be recovered in the United States, it is necessary to combine bituminous coal data with those for other ranks that could also be employed in steam-raising applications. Table 44 presents such a synthesis of data. As in the previous analysis, remaining identified resources were taken from Averitt's[2] work, and the demonstrated reserve base values were those of the U.S. Bureau of Mines.[3] Estimated recoverable reserves of anthracite, subbituminous coal, and lignite were derived earlier[4] from the published data through a

[1] A. J. Moll, "The Economics of Underground Coal Gasification," presented at the Second Underground Coal Gasification Symposium, Morgantown, W. Va., Aug. 10, 1976.

[2] P. Averitt, Coal Resources of the United States, January 1, 1974, *US Geol. Surv. Bull.* 1412, 1975.

[3] U.S. Bureau of Mines, Demonstrated Coal Reserve Base of the United on January 1, 1976, *Miner. Ind. Surv.*, August 1977.

[4] See also R. A. Schmidt, Electric Utility Industry Strategy for Research in Coal Geology, presented at "Coal Geology and the Future," a symposium organized by the U.S. Geological Survey, Reston, Va., Sept. 27-28, 1976.

Table 43 Summary comparison of recoverable energy values through mining and underground coal gasification (10^{15} Btu)

Rank	Mining	UCG		Total		UCG as % total for each rank	
		Min.	Max.	Min.	Max.	Min.	Max.
Bituminous	551.4	0		551.4	551.4	0	33
Subbituminous	332.5	87.2	162.4	419.7	494.9	21	87
Lignite	34.2	157.7	226.4	191.9	259.6	82	
Total	918.1	244.7	387.8	1163.0	1305.9		

Table 44 Synthesis of coal resources and recoverable reserves, all ranks (million tons)

Rank	(1) Remaining identified resources Jan. 1, 1974	(2) Demonstrated reserve base Jan. 1, 1976	(3) Estimated recoverable reserves, all methods	(4) Estimated recoverable reserves deep mining	(5) Estimated recoverable reserves surface	(6) Estimated maximum reserves processed by underground gasification*	(7) Total estimated recoverable coal reserves, all methods (3) + (6)
Anthracite	19,662	7,371	2,234	2,166	68	0	2,234
Bituminous:†							
Coking	183,552	42,677	13,840	10,825	3,117		
Steam	563,085	186,249	54,398	43,771	10,627		
Subtotal	746,637	228,926	68,238	54,596	13,744	0	67,138
Subbituminous	485,766	168,425	56,227	32,320	24,318	10,800	67,027
Lignite	478,134	33,617	8,895	0	8,895	19,300	28,195
U.S. total	1,730,199	438,339	135,594	89,082	47,025	30,100	165,694

*R. A. Schmidt, "Underground Coal Gasification to Produce Fuels for Power Generation: A Review and Assessment of Processes and Reserves," EPRI manuscript, table 18, p. 60, September 1977.

†Bituminous coal data in this table assume that total coking coals will be dedicated to metallurgical uses.

Totals may not agree exactly with table 1 because of independent rounding.

procedure identical to that used in the present analysis.

Table 44 shows that the estimated recoverable reserves of coal of all ranks by all mining methods is nearly 136 billion tons. The total recoverable reserves are less than one-tenth the total identified resources and less than one-third of the demonstrated reserve base. Deep mining is required for recovery of almost two-thirds of the reserves, with the remainder being recovered by surface mining methods. Deep mining is the predominant method for recovery of anthracite and bituminous coals (of both classes), whereas surface mining is nearly equal to deep mining of subbituminous coals and is the only present method for recovery of lignite.

So far, the focus of this analysis has been on coals recoverable through mining. It is possible that additional reserves may be processed through underground gasification. A recent analysis estimated the maximum reserves processable by UCG methods.[1] Assuming that only very thick coals could be processed effectively and economically by underground gasification techniques, as well as other conditions essential for such processing, it was concluded that only some subbituminous coals and lignites in certain western states would be recoverable by underground gasification methods. About 30 billion tons of equivalent reserves are recoverable through underground coal gasification, or less than one-quarter of the total recoverable reserves through mining.

The total estimated recoverable coal reserves by all methods is estimated at about 165 billion tons. This is less than one-tenth of the remaining identified coal resources.

Considering only minable coal, the recoverable reserves would be about 120 billion tons as determined in this analysis. (The sum of anthracite, steam bituminous, subbituminous, and lignite, Table 44). If coals for underground gasification are counted in the steam-coal total, then there would appear to be about 150 billion tons of recoverable reserves (not counting coking coals).

Conclusions About Reserves

Clearly, 120 billion tons of recoverable steam coal is a substantial amount. However, the lifetime of even these reserves could be limited at annual production levels greatly in excess of those prevailing at present. For example, with steam-coal demand at the current level of about 600 million tons per year, the recoverable reserves would last 200 years. However, it is projected that domestic steam-coal demand will double or triple before the end of the twentieth century; this would place the lifetime of presently estimated American recoverable reserves somewhere between 100 and 67 years, respectively. Should the higher growth rate be realized, and no additional reserves be located, children living today would witness the utilization of the last recoverable coal present in the United States.

There are several ways additional coal reserves could be located. One way is through improved recoverability from known deposits. This, however, would require innovation, typically a time-consuming process (especially in empirical

---

[1]R. A. Schmidt, "Underground Coal Gasification to Produce Fuels for Power Generation: A Review and Assessment of Processes and Reserves," EPRI manuscript, September 1977.

activities such as coal production). It does not seem likely that much reserves could be added to the estimated total from improved technology, at least over a reasonable time frame. While it may be possible to locate new additional coal reserves, this is by no means certain. Much work remains to be done to delineate coal resources whose presence is only inferred. It may be that such efforts could expand the reserve base and increase the recoverable reserves, although it would be somewhat risky to proceed on the assumption that inferred deposits could be proven. There appears to be no substitute for thorough geological fieldwork to measure the presence of coal deposits, even in identified areas. A further need is exploration to identify domestic coal deposits whose existence is only hypothesized or speculated. Such efforts are needed in both known coalfields as well as in areas of potential coal deposits. Because exploration is time-consuming as well as uncertain, it must be undertaken (successfully) several years in advance of prospective developments. Recent efforts of the U.S. Geological Survey in mapping coal deposits are a valuable step in the right direction, but they should probably be expanded and intensified. Furthermore, a cooperative means to share public data with the private sector needs to be worked out to avoid duplication of work (or gaps in data coverage).

Optimists would find it reasonable to anticipate that technological improvements and exploration will add to the estimated U.S. recoverable reserves of steam coal, although the amount of added reserves remains unknown. In this event, the recoverable reserves estimated in this study would constitute a lower bound. With the location of additional coal reserves, the United States could remain essentially self-sufficient in coal supplies for an indefinite period. This would provide breathing space to develop new energy technologies that, ultimately, may replace coal as its supplies are diminished.

Pessimists, on the other hand, would maintain that technological developments would fall short of their objectives and exploration would probably be imperfectly successful in adding to recoverable reserves. As a result, the estimated recoverable reserves derived here would represent an upper bound. The United States could begin to lose its self-sufficiency in coal supplies as reserve exhaustion approaches in the next century. Industries dependent on coal would probably seek to maintain supplies, even if it meant importing coal in considerable quantities. This, of course, could lead to a reprise of the history of oil development—foreign exploration, development, world market standards, import quotas, entitlements, etc. Clearly, such an eventuality is not reassuring.

At present, it is probably prudent to be conservative in regard to coal; this, it is suggested, implies awareness of the consequences of a pessimistic outcome while attempting to identify as much recoverable reserves as possible. Fundamentally, this is a geological problem. Therefore, it is the responsibility of geologists to carry out the necessary work if the nation is to be assured of adequate supplies of coal for an acceptable period of time.

Reserve Ownership

Access to coal resources and reserves is the first requisite in their development. Reserves may be (1) owned outright, (2) rights to their exploitation purchased or leased from their owners, or (3) rights to access and production granted as a part of a cooperative or joint undertaking with the owners. Many alternative approaches to acquiring rights to coal reserves are employed for each of the above major classes.

Coal reserves are owned by both public and private organizations and institutions; these will be described separately below, followed by an analysis of the ownership of remaining recoverable reserves.

Public Organizations

The federal government is the largest single owner of coal resources and reserves. These government holdings occur almost entirely in states west of the Mississippi River, and have yet to experience even a fraction of the development which is potentially possible. The amount of coal resources and reserves on federal lands was estimated in the Department of the Interior's environmental impact statement.[1] Table 45 shows that about 187 billion tons of remaining U.S. coal reserves in place (roughly one-third of the total resources) is owned by the federal government. Of these, the largest reserves are in Alaska, North Dakota, Wyoming, Colorado, and New Mexico.

In recent years, significant amounts of federal coal lands in Western states have been leased for development, mainly in Montana, Wyoming, and Utah. A leasing program for federal coal lands was conducted in six Western states until recently.

This effective "moratorium" on coal leasing has been in force since the early 1970s. The moratorium continues, although a limited number of lease applications for special cases are under review and nominations for (and against) federal coal leasing were received by the Bureau of Land Management. Such nominations are one of the initial steps in the Department of the Interior's competitive coal leasing process, which remains to be developed fully in the event that leasing is later resumed in the 1980s.[2] Actually, it is not at all certain that leasing will be resumed at an early date. The Department of Energy's Leasing Programs Office concluded that a resumption of leasing of federal coal lands will not be needed to increase the U.S. coal supply before 1990.[3]

This effort to obtain basic information about the coal-bearing public lands of the West is essential to provide information necessary to comply with the requirements of the National Environmental Policy Act of 1970. Even then, it cannot be assumed that all such land will be targets for development as cognizant agencies may preclude certain areas: roughly 6 billion tons of coal in southern Montana is not recommended for development so that the land can be used for other pur-

---

[1] U.S. Department of the Interior, "Final Environmental Impact Statement for the Proposed Federal Coal Leasing Program," 1975.

[2] See "Interior Department Review of Coal Leasing Is Behind Schedule," *Energy Daily*, p. 2, March 24, 1978.

[3] U.S. Department of Energy "Federal Coal Leasing and 1985 and 1990 Regional Coal Production Forecasts," p. 103, June 1978.

Table 45 Estimate of federal coal resources* and values in principal leasing states for surface and underground deposits (million short tons)

State, deposit	Total resources†,‡	Federal resources†
Alabama:		
Surface	134	
Underground	7,537	
Alaska:		
Surface	4,411	4,279
Underground	60,629	58,810
California:		
Surface	25	
Underground	294	
Colorado:		
Surface	500	265
Underground	38,829	21,111
Montana:		
Surface	6,897	1,700
Underground	103,940	
New Mexico:		
Surface	2,457	1,450
Underground	28,239	16,661
No. Dakota:		
Surface	2,075	519
Underground	173,240	43,310
Oklahoma:		
Surface	111	4
Underground	1,529	61
Oregon:		
Surface		
Underground	167	
Utah:		
Surface	150	123
Underground	11,714	9,605
Washington:		
Surface	135	
Underground	2,984	
Wyoming:		
Surface	13,971	6,706
Underground	46,357	22,251
Total	507,325	186,855

*Refers to coal that can be recovered with existing technology and equipment or that may be available in the foreseeable future. Only those coals less than 3000 feet in depth are included. Strippable coal reserves are adjusted to conform to the stripping ratio, which varies with area. Coal that cannot be mined because of proximity to natural or artificial features is excluded.

†U.S. Department of the Interior, Final Environmental Impact Statement for the Proposed Federal Coal Leasing Program (using data from Strippable Reserves of Bituminous Coal and Lignite in the United States, *US Bur. Mines, Inf. Circ.* 8531, p. 23, 1971).

‡P. Averitt, Summary of U.S. Mineral Resources, *US Geol. Surv., Prof. Paper*, p. 820, 1972.

poses.[1] This practice, if extended, would remove substantial portions of federal reserves from development. Unless present practices are changed, it would seem that western coal deposits would be preferentially developed on private lands. These are largely held by railroad companies, but are in a "checkerboard" pattern that would lead to costly operations and potential losses in reserve recovery.

Private Ownership

The *Keystone News Bulletin* compiled data on organizations owning, leasing, or controlling coal reserves.[2] These data, together with more recent information about the holdings of some oil companies compiled by the American Petroleum Institute (API), are shown in Table 46. The table shows that nearly 125 billion tons of coal reserves is held by the firms listed. The listing, while comprehensive, is not necessarily complete. An estimate of the magnitude of reserves yet to be accounted for is given in a following section.

Although the compilation points out that "the figures reported for each organization are estimated totals and do not differentiate between recoverable or in-place reserves," representatives of the *Keystone News Bulletin* point out that these data are for coal that is "basically recoverable." This appears reasonable in view of the fact that companies would have to pay taxes on their coal holdings; there would be no incentive to report other than the actual expected recoverable reserves to minimize tax liability. Accordingly, it is assumed that the reported data on coal reserves are equivalent to remaining recoverable reserves as used in an earlier section.

Table 47 presents a summary of coal reserve control by class of parent company activity. The table shows that more than one-third of the remaining recoverable coal reserves are held by oil companies (especially by their coal subsidiaries). The average oil company holdings are also the largest of any class. The next largest holdings (both in percentage and in average size of reserves) are those of railroads. While coal companies hold the third largest portion of reserves, the average company's holdings are the smallest of any. Electric utility holdings reported[3] to the *Keystone News Bulletin* represent less than one-tenth of the total, and the average company's reserves are modest.

In general, most of the coal lands east of the Mississippi are owned privately. "Information on coal ownership may be so complex as to be unattainable without the cooperation of the individual owner."[4] In the Appalachian region, many large tracts of land are held by railroads, mining, manufacturing, and landowning companies. As we have seen, many western lands are held by the federal government,

---

[1] U.S. Department of the Interior, Bureau of Land Management, "Summary Resource Study: Decker-Birney Area, Montana," 1972.

[2] The Coal Reserves Picture: Estimated Tonnages Held by Individual Firms, *Keystone News Bull.*, p. 35, June 1976. For this analysis, data for Canadian firms were deleted.

[3] Note that this listing does not include reserves known to be held by Texas utilities, Southern California Edison, Pacific Gas & Electric, Arizona Public Service, and San Diego Gas and Electric, to name just a few organizations.

[4] Averitt, *loc. cit.*

Table 46 Control of coal reserves (ownership, lease, other) in United States (billion tons)

Parent company	Coal operating company	Keystone News Bulletin*	API†	Adopted value this section	Parent Company Industry							
					Oil	Rail	Steel	Gas	Util.	Mining	Coal	Other
Continental Oil	Consolidation Coal	10.800	13.350	13.350	13.350							
Burlington Northern		11.400	11.400	11.400		11.4						
Union Pacific	Rocky Mtn. Energy	10.000	10.000	10.000		10.0						
Newmont et al.	Peabody Coal	8.900	9.000	9.000						8.9		
Exxon Corporation	Monterey Coal	7.000	7.500	7.500	7.0							
AMAX	Amax Coal	3.134	5.045	5.045						5.045		
N. American Coal	N. American Coal	5.000	5.000	5.000							5.0	
Occidental Petroleum	Island Creek	4.430	3.400	4.430	4.43							
U.S. Steel	U.S. Steel	2.700	3.000	3.000			3.0					
Kerr-McGee	Kerr-McGee Coal	1.500	2.800	2.800	2.80							
Gulf Oil	Pittsburg & Midway	2.600	2.600	2.600	2.60							
Eastern Gas & Fuel	Eastern Associates	1.192	2.600	2.600				2.6				
Pacific Power & Light	Pacific Power & Light	2.500	2.500	2.500					2.5			
Mobil Oil		2.500	2.500	2.500	2.50							
Sun Oil		2.200	2.271	2.271	2.271							
ARCO		2.200	2.200	2.200	2.20							
Texaco		1.650	2.000	2.000	2.0							
Phillips Petroleum			2.000	2.000	2.0							
Bethlehem Steel	Bethlehem Mines	1.800	1.800	1.800			1.8					
AEP	Central Appalachian	1.500		1.500					1.5			
Tenneco			1.700	1.700	1.70							
Pittston Company	Clinchfield Coal	1.500		1.500							1.5	
Norfolk & Western Rwy.	Pocahontas Land Corp.	1.400		1.400		1.4						
Utah International	Utah International	1.100		1.100							1.1	
Westmoreland Resources	Westmoreland Resources	1.100		1.100							1.1	
Hillman Coal & Coke		1.000		1.000							1.0	
Houston Natural Gas	Ziegler Coal	1.000		1.000				1.0				
Montana Power	Western Energy	1.000		1.000					1.0			

Table 46 Control of coal reserves (ownership, lease, other) in United States (billion tons) (continued)

Parent company	Coal operating company	Keystone News Bulletin*	API†	Adopted value (this section)	Parent Company Industry							
					Oil	Rail	Steel	Gas	Util.	Mining	Coal	Other
Westmoreland Coal	Westmoreland Coal	0.849		0.849							0.849	
Standard Oil of Ohio	Old Ben Coal	0.825		0.825	0.825							
Greenwood Stripping Corp.	Greenwood Stripping	0.735		0.735							0.735	
General Dynamics	Freeman United	0.600		0.600								0.600
Montana-Dakota Util.	Knife River Coal	0.600		0.600					0.600			
D. D. Stewart	Kentucky Home Coal	0.600		0.600								0.600
Panhandle Eastern	Youghiogheny & Ohio	0.500		0.500				0.500				
Columbia Gas		0.484		0.484				0.484				
Valley Camp Coal	Valley Camp Coal	0.475		0.475							0.475	
MAPCO	Webster Country Coal	0.473		0.473	0.473							
Consolidated Nat. Gas		0.450		0.450				0.450				
TVA		0.412		0.412					0.412			
Duke Power		0.401		0.401					0.401			
Armco Steel	Eastover Mining	0.400		0.400			0.400					
Coastal States Energy	Southern Utah Fuel	0.400		0.400								0.400
Penn Pocahontas Coal	Penn Pocahontas	0.400		0.400							0.400	
Southern Electric Gen.	Southern Electric Gen.	0.400		0.400					0.400			
Kentucky King Coal	Kentucky King Coal	0.395		0.395							0.395	
International Harvester	Wisconsin Steel	0.370		0.370								0.370
Santa Fe Industries		0.370		0.370		0.370						
Reynolds Metals		0.350		0.350						0.350		
Jim Walter Corp.	Jim Walter Corp.	0.350		0.350								0.350
Mintech Corporation		0.337		0.337						0.337		
St. Joe Mineral	A. T. Massey Coal	0.323		0.323						0.323		
Southern Railway		0.280		0.280		0.280						
Bates Manufacturing	Virginia Iron. Coal & Coke	0.276		0.276								0.276
Ill. Central Gulf RR	Madison Coal	0.276		0.276		0.276						
Union Carbide	Union Carbide Metals	0.265		0.265						0.265		
ALCO Standard	Barnes, Tucker & Upshur Coal	0.255		0.255								0.255

Company	Property				
Blue Diamond Coal	Stearns Mining	0.250			0.250
A.T. Walker Estate	Allegheny River Mining	0.230				0.230
Merchants Petroleum		0.221	0.221		
Gulf Resources & Chemical	Charter Coal	0.203		0.203	
Bane Coal	Bane Coal	0.200			0.200	0.200
Donan Joint Venture		0.200				0.200
Great Northern Nekoosa	Brillian Coal	0.200			
Jones & Loughlin	Jones & Loughlin	0.200		0.200	
Kentucky River Coal	Kentucky River Coal	0.200			0.200	0.200
McAllester Fuel	McAllester Fuel	0.200				0.200
New Mexico & Arizona Land		0.200			
Palmer Coking Coal	Palmer Coking Coal	0.200			0.200
Pinson Coal Company	Pinson Coal	0.200			0.200
Solar Fuel	Solar Fuel	0.200			0.200
Zapata Corporation	Zapata Corporation	0.200				0.200
Black Hills Pwr & Light	Wyodels Resources	0.188		0.188	0.188
Lykes-Youngstown	Emerald Mines	0.160		0.160	0.160
Public Service (NM)	Western Coal	0.160			0.160
Red Ash Pocahontas	Red Ash Pocahontas	0.153			0.153
Ashland Oil	Arch Minerals	0.150	0.150		0.153
California Portland Cement		0.150			
New Era Resources	New Era Resources	0.150			0.150
Rochester & Pittsburgh	Rochester & Pittsburgh	0.150			0.150
Neely & Gibson Coal	Neely & Gibson Coal	0.140			0.140
B&H Elkhorn Coal	B&H Elkhorn Coal	0.125			0.125
Allied Chemical	Semet-Solvay Div	0.125				0.125
Kaiser Steel	Kaiser Steel	0.120		0.120	
Drummond Company	H. E. Drummond	0.110			0.110	0.110
Interstate Lumber		0.110			
Slab Fork Coal	Slab Fork Coal	0.108			0.108
Carbon Fuel	Carbon Fuel	0.100			0.100
Mead Corporation	Mead Coal	0.100			0.100
Penna P&L		0.95		0.095	
Allegheny Power Service	Allegheny-Pittsburgh Coal	0.90		0.90	

Table 46 Control of coal reserves (ownership, lease, other) in United States (billion tons) (continued)

Parent company	Coal operating company	Keystone News Bulletin*	API†	Adopted value (this section)	Parent Company Industry							
					Oil	Rail	Steel	Gas	Util.	Mining	Coal	Other
Wise Development		0.90		0.90								0.90
Southeast Coal	Southeast Coal	0.082		0.082								0.82
Cambria Manufacturing		0.080		0.080					0.80			
Washington Water Power	Washington Irrig & Dev.	0.080		0.080					0.080			
Rapoca Energy		0.080		0.080								0.080
Joseph Orlandi		0.076		0.076								0.076
Bergoo Coal	Bergoo Coal.	0.075		0.075							0.075	
Corley Company	Corley Company	0.075		0.075							0.075	
Cedar Coal	Cedar Coal	0.070		0.070							0.070	
Falcon Seaboard	Falcon Coal	0.070		0.070							0.070	
Guaranty Gas		0.070		0.070			0.070					
Scholl & Wilcher	Coal Power Corp.	0.070		0.070								0.070
Solar Fuel	Solar Fuel	0.070		0.070							0.070	
Apollo Corp/Gysegem	Golden Rod Coal	0.065		0.065								0.065
ASARCO	Midland Coal	0.060		0.060						0.060		
Shamrock Coal	Shamrock Coal	0.060		0.060							0.060	
Shannon Land & Mining		0.060		0.060								0.060
Red Jacket Coal	Red Jacket Coal	0.052		0.052							0.052	
CRN Mining	CRN Mining	0.050		0.050							0.050	
Dexter-Carpenter Coal	D&C Mining	0.050		0.050							0.050	
Iowa Public Service	Energy Development Co.	0.050		0.050					0.050			
General Energy	Buckhorn Hazard Coal	0.050		0.050								0.050
McCulloh Oil	Braztah Coal	0.050		0.050	0.050							
Public Service Indiana		0.050		0.050					0.050			
Lehigh Valley Anthracite	Lehigh Valley Anthracite	0.048		0.048							0.048	
United Nuclear	Platcon Mining	0.042		0.042								0.042
Airco Coals	Kodak Mining	0.040		0.040							0.040	

Company	Company	Value
CDR Enterprises	CDR Enterprises	0.040
Chapperal Coal	Chapperal Coal	0.040
Kentucky United Mining	Kentucky United Mining	0.040
Manor Mining & Contracting		0.040
Burford, Inc.	Burford, Inc.	0.038
Lucas Coal	Mineral Hill Corp.	0.037
New River Company	New River Company	
W. R. Grace	Race Fork Coal	0.034
Missouri, Kansas, Texas RR		0.036
Mt. Victory Coal	Mt. Victory Coal	0.032
Adventure Coal	Adventure Coal	0.031
Bills Coal	Bills Coal	0.030
Cairnes Coal	Cairnes Coal	0.030
Chicago & NW Rwy		0.030
Douglas Pocahontas Coal	Douglas Pocahontas Coal	0.030
Hepburnia Coal	Hepburnia Coal	0.030
Jeddo-Highland Coal	Jeddo-Highland Coal	0.030
PBS Company		0.030
Canon Coal	Canon Coal	0.028
Henry Clay Mining	Henry Clay Mining	0.025
Caney Branch Coal	Caney Branch Coal	0.022
Glen Burn Colliery	Glen Burn Colliery	0.020
Kentucky Elkhorn Coals	Kentucky Elkhorn Coals	0.020
Penn Allegheny Coal	Penn Allegheny Coal	0.020
Tarheel Coals	Tarheel Coals	0.020
Lawson Heirs		0.018
Aloe Coal	Aloe Coal	0.015
Brook Coal	Midway Coal	0.015
Kentucky Prince Coal	Reliable Coal	0.015
Middle States Coal	Kentucky Prince Coal	0.015
	Middle States Coal	0.015
Cardinal Mining	Cardinal Mining	0.014

Table 46 Control of coal reserves (ownership, lease, other) in United States (billion tons) (continued)

Parent company	Coal operating company	Keystone News Bulletin*	API†	Adopted value (this section)	Parent Company Industry							
					Oil	Rail	Steel	Gas	Util.	Mining	Coal	Other
Osborne Mining	Osborne Mining	0.014		0.014							0.014	
Tenn-Tex Coal	Tenn-Tex Coal	0.014		0.014							0.014	
Golden Glow Coals	Golden Glow Coals	0.013		0.013							0.013	
Moshannon Falls Mining	Moshannon Falls Mining	0.013		0.013							0.013	
Chafin Coal	Chafin Coal	0.012		0.012							0.012	
R. G. Mining	R. G. Mining	0.012		0.012							0.012	
Arcadia Company	Arcadia Company	0.010		0.010							0.010	
Buckhannon River Co.		0.010		0.010								0.010
Cedarbrook Coal	Cedarbrook Coal	0.010		0.010							0.010	
Great Basins Petroleum		0.010		0.010	0.010							
Green Brook Coal	Green Brook Coal	0.010		0.010							0.010	
Gysegem Enterprises	Gysegem Enterprises	0.010		0.010							0.010	
Lucas Coal	Lucas Coal	0.010		0.010							0.010	
Marguette Company	Southern Energy Resources	0.010		0.010								0.010
Mineral Development Co.	Penn-Mar Coal	0.010		0.010								0.010
Missouri Poupe RR		0.010		0.010		0.010						
Peggo Run Coal	Peggo Run Coal	0.010		0.010							0.010	
Potter Coal	Potter Coal	0.010		0.010							0.010	
James Spur Coal	James Spur Coal	0.010		0.010							0.010	
Penna P&L	Tunnelton Mining	0.010		0.010					0.010			
Robertson & Associates	Robertson & Associates	0.010		0.010								0.010
Valley Coal	Valley Coal	0.010		0.010							0.010	
Bane Mining	Bane Mining	0.009		0.009						0.009		
Canamex Commodity	Canamex Coal	0.009		0.009								0.009
Flanary Coal & Land		0.008		0.008								0.008
Husky Industries	Husky Industries	0.009		0.009	0.009							
Bebe Coal	Bebe Coal	0.008		0.008							0.008	

Company	Value	Company	Value	
Dixie Mining	0.008	Dixie Mining	0.008	0.008
Grove City Construction	0.008	Grove City Construction	0.008	0.008
Longwall Mining, Inc.	0.008	Longwall Mining	0.008	0.008
Boich Mining	0.008	Boich Mining	0.008	0.008
Reclamation & Air Survey	0.008	Reclamation & Air Survey	0.008	0.008
C. H. Snyder	0.008	C. H. Snyder	0.008	0.008
Swistock	0.008	Swistock	0.008	0.008
Leon's Coal	0.007	Leon's Coal	0.007	0.007
General Energy	0.006	General Energy	0.006	0.006
Ohio River Collieries	0.006	Ohio River Collieries	0.006	0.006
R. E. M. Coal	0.006	R. E. M. Coal	0.006	0.006
S&D Construction	0.006	S&D Construction	0.006	
Donovan Companies	0.005	Alumbaugh Coal	0.005	0.005
Energy Producers of Amer.	0.005	Energy Producers of Amer.	0.005	0.005
Jones & Brague Mining	0.005	Jones & Brague Mining	0.005	0.005
McDowell Enterprises	0.005	Medlin Energy Corporation	0.005	0.005
North Cambria Fuel	0.005	North Cambria Fuel	0.005	0.005
Carter McCall Enterprises	0.005		0.005	0.005
Southern Pacific Trans.	0.005		0.005	
Wyoming Mining	0.005	Wyoming Mining	0.005	0.005
Ambrosia Coal & Constr.	0.004	Ambrosia Coal & Constr.	0.004	0.004
Henry B. Coal	0.004	Henry B. Coal	0.004	0.004
Karst-Robbins Coal	0.004	Karst-Robbins Coal	0.004	0.004
Belva Coal	0.003	Belva Coal	0.003	0.003
Bridgeview Coal	0.003	Bridgeview	0.003	0.003
Bull Creek Coal & Dock	0.003	Bull Creek Coal & Dock	0.003	0.003
Farrell-Cooper Mining	0.003	Farrell-Cooper Mining	0.003	0.003
Keller Steel	0.003	Industrial Mining	0.003	
King Knob Coal	0.003	King Knob Coal	0.003	0.003
Markle-Bullers Coal	0.003	Markle-Bullers Coal	0.003	0.003

Table 46 Control of coal reserves (ownership, lease, other) in United States (billion tons) (continued)

Parent company	Coal operating company	Keystone News Bulletin*	API†	Adopted value (this section)	Parent Company Industry							
					Oil	Rail	Steel	Gas	Util.	Mining	Coal	Other
Louilia Coal	Louilia Coal	0.003		0.003							0.003	
Natisco Company	Natisco Company	0.003		0.003							0.003	
Moshannon Falls Mining	Moshannon Falls Mining	0.003		0.003							0.003	
Penna-Ky Mining	Penna-Ky Mining	0.003		0.003							0.003	
Perry Ross Coal	Perry Ross Coal	0.003		0.003							0.003	
Smith & Stover Coal	Smith & Stover Coal	0.003		0.003							0.003	
Willowbrook Mining	Willowbrook Mining	0.003		0.003							0.003	
Anthony Mining	Anthony Mining	0.002		0.002							0.002	
Assoc. Drilling	Assoc. Drilling	0.002		0.002							0.002	
Boyle Coal	Boyle Coal	0.002		0.002							0.002	
Earl M. Brown	Earl M. Brown	0.002		0.002							0.002	
Champion Coal	Champion Coal	0.002		0.002							0.002	
Chose Eaton Company	Jefferson Co. Coal	0.002		0.002							0.002	
Dudek Coal Mining	Dudek Coal Mining	0.002		0.002							0.002	
Jader Fuel	Jader Fuel	0.002		0.002							0.002	
Monroe Coal Sales	Monroe Coal	0.002		0.002							0.002	
PIC Company	PIC Company	0.002		0.002							0.002	
Apache Coal	Apache Coal	0.002		0.002							0.002	
S&D Trucking	S&D Trucking	0.002		0.002							0.002	
Ralph Veon	Ralph Veon	0.002		0.002							0.002	
Wasson Coal Mining	Wasson Coal Mining	0.002		0.002							0.002	
Big Ben Coal	Big Ben Coal	0.001		0.001							0.001	
Buckeye Coal Mining	Buckeye Coal Mining	0.001		0.001							0.001	
Concoal Corporation	Congleton Brothers	0.001		0.001							0.001	
Preston Energy		0.001		0.001							0.001	
Princess Coal Sales		0.001		0.001								0.001
Alabama Electric Coop	Abston Construction	0.001		0.001						0.001		
B. H. & H	B. H. & H	0.001		0.001							0.001	

Empire Coke	0.001	0.001							0.001	
Joseph Grodin Coal	0.001	0.001							0.001	
Keffler & Rose Enterprises	0.001	0.001								0.001
H. L. Kennedy	0.001	0.001							0.001	
McKim Coal	0.001	0.001							0.001	
C. A. Ogden Coal	0.001	0.001							0.001	
Sequatchie Valley Coal	0.001	0.001							0.001	
Trans-Air	0.001	0.001								0.001
Margarita Fuels	0.001	0.001								
H. R. Wood Coal	0.001	0.001							0.001	
United Coals	0.001	0.001							0.001	
Zimnox Coal	0.001	0.001							0.001	
Total	112.310	124.804	44.59	23.8	5.68	5.10	7.54	15.19	16.97	5.36

*June 1976. A. Hersh, "Concentration Levels in the Production and Reserve Holdings of Crude Oil.

†Natural Gas, Coal and Uranium in the U.S. American Petroleum Institute Working Paper, Nov. 26, 1976.

Table 47 Control of private recoverable coal reserves by parent company classification

Classification by industry	Reserves, billion tons	% of total	No. of companies	Average company reserves, billion tons
Oil	44.59	36	18	2.48
Railroad	23.80	19	10	2.38
Steel	5.68	5	7	0.81
Gas	5.10	4	6	0.85
Utility	7.54	6	16	0.47
Mining	15.19	12	9	1.69
Coal	16.96	14	138	0.12
Other	5.36	4	42	0.13
TOTAL	124.22	100	246	0.50

Source: Keystone News Bull., June 1976.

but there are substantial private holdings in the West as well. These private lands in the West are largely held by railroads.

In the early days of construction of transcontinental railroads, the railroad companies received as a form of subsidy considerable areas of land, including coal rights, adjoining the rights-of-way. The Burlington Northern received alternate sections in a similar pattern for a distance of 40 miles on both sides of the right-of-way. Although much of this land was sold to settlers, the Western railroads as a group probably hold the second largest acreage of coal land in the West.[1]

It may be expected that the reserves held by these private companies are among the thickest and most accessible coal deposits. The list of companies in Table 47 includes those actively engaged in coal mining, as well as those who merely own the coal reserves and lease rights to their development; the major railroads historically were especially important in this regard. For example, the four largest landowners in West Virginia [Pocahontas Land Corporation (Norfolk & Western Railway), Western Pocahontas Company (Chesapeake & Ohio Railway), Georgia Pacific Corporation, and Charleston National Bank] together controlled more coal lands than all the mining companies combined. These landowners frequently lease their lands for mining. The extent of land ownership by nonmining companies suggests that the establishment of leases for developing coal reserves on these lands is an important factor in the mining industry.

A schematic of relationships among landholding companies and operators is shown in Figure 5, representative of the situation existing in southern West Virginia. In this case, railroad companies (or their wholly owned subsidiaries) own extensive coal reserves, as we have seen. Prohibited by the Interstate Commerce Act of 1887 from engaging in coal mining, they can lease coal lands to operating companies for coal production (from which a royalty is received). Railroads participate indirectly in the marketing process, providing information to operators and sales

[1] *Ibid.*

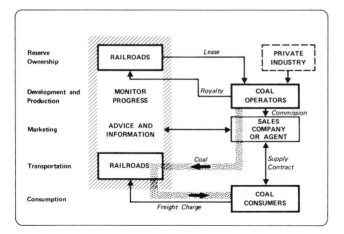

Figure 5. Schematic of institutional relationships.

agents. This is largely because their coal reserves are concentrated in the area they serve with transportation facilities. The railroads are also naturally engaged in transporting coal to consumers for which the consumers pay a freight charge. Thus, although not directly engaged in mining, railroads with coal holdings can and to enjoy financial benefits from coal production as well as from its transportation.

As noted above, the data on coal reserves held by electric utilities is acknowledged to be incomplete. A recent survey of utility captive coal performed by the Federal Power Commission is given in Table 48. The table shows that some 24 utility companies produced coal from their own reserves in 1975, with total production amounting to nearly 47 million tons. This is slightly higher than the total included in the *Keystone News Bulletin* report. It will be important to monitor developments in utility coal ownership closely in the near future.

Ownership of Recoverable Reserves

The preceding data on ownership or control of coal reserves permit an analysis of recoverable reserves in terms of the coal reserve base. The term *reserve base* refers to the total quantity of coal in place under specified depth and thickness criteria.[1] Coals in the reserve base are those whose occurrence is reserved and indicated through detailed geological and engineering studies[2] (see Figure 2). It is reasonable to conclude that the statistics on public and private coal reserves cited above pertain to the well-defined deposits of the reserve base. It is, under these assump-

---

[1] Bituminous coal and anthracite 28 inches thick or more; subbituminous coal and lignite 60 inches thick or more, occurring at depths less than 1000 feet. Z. E. Murphy, et al., Demonstrated Coal Reserve Base of the United States on January 1, 1974, *Minerals Ind. Surv.*, p. 6, June 1974.

[2] Averitt, *op. cit.*, p. 3.

Table 48 Average prices of captive coal delivered to electric utilities

Utility company	Name of coal property[a]	1975 coal receipts		Total cost $ FOB plant
		Tons	Av. unit price $/Ton	
Southern Electric Generating Co.[b]	Segco #1 Mine	552,787	24.06	13,301,900
Alabama Power Co.		470,892	24.06	11,331,249
	Total	1,023,679	24.06	24,633,149
Iowa Public Service Co.	Energy Development Inc.	900,264	15.71	14,146,027
Montana-Dakota Util. Co.	Knife River Coal Mining Co. Welch Coal Co.	1,160,684	5.61	6,507,808
The Montana Power Co.	Western Energy Co.	834,543	4.32	3,609,214
T. V. A.	T. V. A. owned land	4,498,329	9.51	42,794,835
Utah Power & Light Co.	Desert Coal Mine	985,689	7.94[c]	7,823,282
Public Service Co. of N. Mex. with Tucson Gas & Elec. Co. for San Juan Plant	Western Coal Coal	1,262,200	4.51	5,692,522
Pacific Power & Light Co.	Dave Johnston Mine	3,195,855	2.46	7,856,058[d]
Pacific Pwr. & Light Co. with Washington Water Pwr. Co.	Centralia Operation (jointly owned by P. P. L. and W. W. P. Co.)	1,760,655	7.60	13,384,592[d]
Pacific Pwr. & Light Co. with Idaho Power Co.	Bridger Coal Co.	682,989	4.71	3,215,969[d]
Dallas Power & Light Co. with Texas Elec. Service Co. and Texas Pwr. & Light Co.	Big Brown Operation (lignite)	9,150,233	2.97	27,172,993
Black Hills Power & Light Co.	Wyodak Resources Development	728,098	4.50	3,276,991
Virginia Electric & Power Co.	Laurel Run Mining Co.	271,480	15.27	4,145,640
Cleveland Electric Illuminating Co.	North American Coal Co.	1,232,861	25.32	31,216,132
Tampa Electric Co.	Cal-Glo Mining Co.	402,763	32.50	13,090,552
Pennsylvania Power & Light Co.	Greenwich Collieries Co.	2,672,301[e]	21.82	58,296,851
	Tunnelton Mining Co.	436,754[e]	23.08	10,080,104
	Rushton Mining Co.	716,825[e]	21.67	15,534,465

Company	Mine			
	Lady Jane Collieries Inc.	269,946 e	20.80	5,613,782
	Oneida Mining	562,937 e	44.63 f	25,122,784
	Total	4,658,763 e	24.61	114,647,986
Appalachian Power Co.	Central Appl. Coal Co.	400,147	26.75	10,705,377
	Central Coal Co. g	49,784	35.39	1,761,638
	(Produced by contractors on company-owned lands)			
	Southern Appl. Coal Co.	302,225	17.41	5,262,528
	Cedar Coal Co.	436,565	25.23	11,013,838
		672,173	21.48	14,435,681
	Total	1,860,894	23.20	43,179,062
Capco h	Quarto Coal Co. i	840,000	19.24	16,161,600
Ohio Power Co.	Windsor Power-House Coal Co.			
	Central Ohio Coal Co.			
	Central Coal Co. j			
	Southern Ohio Coal Co.	4,733,158	18.95	89,693,043
Ohio Electric Co.	Southern Ohio Coal Co.	2,049,772	21.67	44,426,694
Ohio Edison Co.	Ohio Edison Mine	157,528	10.32	1,626,293
Duquesne Light Co.	Warwick Mining Co.	1,249,143	17.64	22,034,690
Duke Power Co.	Eastover Mining Co.	1,903,827	26.41	50,271,999
Columbus and Southern Ohio Elec.	Simco Inc. (joint venture with Peabody Coal)	934,418	18.73	17,503,808
	National total	46,477,823	$13.08	608,110,939

a Includes owned coal mines and mines owned by affiliated companies (including subsidiaries).
b Segco is owned equally by the Alabama Power Co. and the Georgia Power Co.
c Return on investment not included.
d Includes only direct costs of mining operation.
e Includes owned coal mines and mines owned by affiliated companies (including subsidiaries).
f Actual 1975 production from Oneida mine was only half of anticipated production, therefore the fixed costs of the mine were allocated to a small total tonnage resulting in an inflated per unit cost.
g Joint control with Ohio Power Co.
h Capco consists of the Ohio Edison Co., the Cleveland Electric Illuminating Co., the Toledo Edison Co., the Duquesne Light Co., and the Pennsylvania Pwr. Co.
i The Quarto Coal Co. has a loan and loan guarantee arrangement with the Capco group.
j Joint control with Appalachian Power Co.
Source: Federal Power Commission.

tions, possible to assess the prospects for future coal development.

Table 49 summarizes coal reserve data. The total federal reserve base cited above is some 187 billion tons. Not all this amount, however, can be recovered. Employing an average recoverability factor from the reserve base for both surface and underground mining, the estimated recoverable reserves from federal deposits is estimated to be about 71 billion tons. Already leased recoverable reserves were listed in the Department of Interior's Environmental Impact Statement at about 27 billion tons; when these are deducted from the total estimated recoverable reserves, a balance of 44 billion tons of recoverable federal coal reserves remains available for lease.

The table also shows the total estimated recoverable reserves held by private organizations at about 125 billion tons. This total includes the above-mentioned 27 billion tons of federal reserves and some 98 billion tons of private recoverable reserves. At the same recovery rate assumed for federal deposits, an estimated private reserve base of about 251 billion tons is indicated.

A summary of data on recoverable coal reserves from measured and indicated deposits is given in Table 50. The table shows that estimated remaining recoverable reserves derived in Chapter 3 range from 136 to 166 billion tons, depending on the technology employed. Also shown are the 125 billion tons of recoverable coal owned, leased, or controlled by identified companies. Therefore, there appear to be between 11 and 41 billion tons of remaining recoverable coal reserves which are either held by companies not included in the *Keystone News Bulletin* survey or are in federal reserves that remain to be acquired by prospective developers, probably for application at advanced technology such as underground gasification. The extent to which potentially recoverable reserves may be obtained could spark a new "coal rush" as organizations seek to secure future fuel supplies.

For the most part, however, it seems likely that prospective new entrants into coal reserve acquisition or development face formidable obstacles. The measured and indicated deposits are largely in the hands of other organizations, who may be expected to be, at best, tough bargainers. Even the promise of new federal leases

Table 49 Summary of coal reserve base data (billion tons)

1. Federal	
a. Total federal reserve base	187
b. Estimated recoverable reserves (at 38% of reserve base)	71
c. Less leased recoverable reserves	27
d. Recoverable reserves remaining available for lease	44
2. Private	
a. Total estimated recoverable reserves (including federal leases)	125
b. Less recoverable leased federal reserves	27
c. Total private recoverable reserves	98
d. Estimated private reserve base	251
3. Totals	
a. Total reserve base	438
b. Total remaining recoverable reserves (all methods of development)	166

Table 50 Summary of recoverable coal reserves (billion tons)

1. Estimated recoverable coal reserves (all ranks)	136 to 166
2. Calculated total remaining recoverable coal reserves (Table 49)	169
3. Recoverable coal reserves that are owned, leased, or controlled by identified companies (*Keystone News Bull.*, June 1976)	125
4. Estimated recoverable coal reserves held by companies not responding to *Keystone News Bulletin* Survey (includes, but is not limited to, Texas Utilities, Pacific Gas & Electric, Southern California Edison, San Diego Gas & Electric, Arizona Public Service)	11 to 41

appears to account for only about one-third of the total remaining recoverable reserves, and there is no assurance that their development would be without costly conditions or spirited legal challenges. Nevertheless, the need of consumers for future coal supplies will probably necessitate dealing with both private and public organizations to obtain the coal they require.

Only one alternative appears open, and that is for such organizations to direct their attention to coal deposits presently considered outside the reserve base. As indicated in Figure 5, these would be economic deposits that are inferred, hypothetical, or speculative and subeconomic deposits of all stages of definition. This alternative poses severe problems to prospective new entrants, because the examination and evaluation of these less-well-known or subeconomic deposits places a premium on knowledge about coal operations which most firms not actively engaged in coal operations will not have. There will probably be few such organizations having the means to acquire or establish such essential expertise. It seems reasonable to conclude, therefore, that unless intensive efforts are undertaken by public (or private) organizations to add to the potential reserves, present patterns of producer-consumer relations will be continued for the foreseeable future (at least until the end of the century).

TWO

PRODUCTION

Coal production is an enterprise in which the efforts of many diverse participants are combined to deal with an array of natural, technical, and operational problems. Clearly defined areas of interest and basic criteria guide each participant's actions. Often the concerns of one key participant may be in conflict with those of another, impairing production operations until the conflict has been resolved. It is no easy matter to ensure the cooperation of essential participants and carry out coal production operations.

Methods in current use for coal production evolved through a long sequence of trial and error. As such, they represent those few approaches that were proven successful in extracting coal economically; many more methods were tried, were deficient in some respect, and were discarded. The trial-and-error process is based largely on empirical expertise acquired through familiarity with coal production operations (and adds to such empirical knowledge, as well). The principal reason for such a pattern of development is that coal remains a poorly understood commodity despite hundreds of years of use and study (Chapter 2). Production is thus concerned with a complex array of natural phenomena and operating uncertainties. It seems reasonable to expect that developments of new and improved production technology will be evolutionary, as in the past. Accordingly, an important first step toward improved methods of coal production is a review and analysis of existing methods and their practice.

Production methods are strongly influenced by the physical features of coal deposits. Position of coal relative to the surface of the earth, thickness of seams, attitude of seams, degree of fracturing, continuity, and other factors all affect the choice of methods for coal extraction. Further, coal characteristics influence working conditions in mines and contribute to social and environmental impacts that are of increasing public concern. In many respects, these nontechnical aspects of coal production represent the most difficult area of operations today and in the future.

Statistics on coal production operations are compiled for a variety of subjects. Output of coal is, of course, the principal statistic measured, but data are collected on equipment types and sizes, labor forces, and productivity, to mention just a few. The volume of statistical data about coal production alone presents formidable problems in analysis. National data provide a useful introduction to details of coal production, but it must be kept in mind that there are important regional and local differences that could cause departures from overall trends in production or utilization.

Trends in production statistics serve two purposes. First, they record the evolution of operations and the improvements in technology that occurred in the past. This is valuable in learning how—and why—the industry evolved as it did. Second, trends are useful in guiding forecasts of the dimensions and character of future production. With a history of evolutionary changes in production methods, it is logical to expect relatively slow changes to present-day technology. Thus, with a knowledge of production trends and their historical rates of change, it should be possible to estimate future requirements with a degree of confidence, and it should be possible to assess the likelihood that forecasts can be realized.

FOUR

OVERVIEW OF INDUSTRY COMPONENTS

PARTICIPANTS IN MINING AND AFFECTED PARTIES

Six groups—the chief participants and the most significantly affected parties—are critical if production of coal is to expand to meet projected demands. From an analysis of the potential impact of expansion on these six groups, and their "stakes" in the outcome, it is clear that for each group there is a pacing parameter—critical conditions or demands which must be satisfied if future development is to occur on a large scale and without excessive political, institutional, and social costs to the nation as a whole. The six groups are (1) electric utility coal consumers, (2) the mine owners (and their parent companies and investors), (3) labor, (4) the local mining community, (5) the environmentalists, and (6) the government. It must be understood, however, that each of these "groups" is in fact a social abstraction—that is, each of the groups is made up of individuals, organizations, and subgroups with somewhat different priorities, objectives, strategies, and modes of operation, in practice often disparate and conflicting.

For the electric utilities, already the principal consumer of coal, shortages in supplies of other fossil fuels and delays in realization of prospective nuclear capabilities mean that renewed attention will be devoted to coal for combustion and conversion. Utilities are concerned with availability of coal, reliability of supply, ease of use, and a reasonable coal cost. Unless assurance can be provided that these conditions can be achieved and maintained, it will be very difficult for utilities to continue to employ coal as a principal fuel in existing plants, to reconvert plants for coal use, or to construct new facilities dependent on coal. Uncertainty on the part of electric utility consumers will be reflected to other participants in the coal production process.

For the mine operators, expansion means that new mines must be opened or existing operations extended. Of principal concern is the credibility of demand (and price) projections over the next 20 to 30 years. Unless operators are persuaded (and investors and lending institutions are also persuaded) that this demand will exist and be firm, new mines will not be opened in a swift and orderly fashion, the necessary support facilities such as new rail spurs will not be built, and conditions necessary for an experienced labor force will not develop. For projected demand and prices to have credibility, a clearly articulated federal energy policy must be formulated and implemented with appropriate incentives, and acceptable assurance must be given as to long-range environmental and safety criteria. It is not clear that existing legal obstacles must be relaxed or changed, but at a minimum the guidelines for implementation must be firm and the prospects for more stringent criteria in the future must not prejudice the expectations for price and profits.

A second and almost equally important condition for full participation of mine operators and the supporting industry is improved productivity. Although the coal industry tends to place most of the blame for decreasing productivity on safety and health regulations, it appears that they are in fact prepared to live with the present regulations. A more troublesome difficulty in the future will be to reduce the high rates of absenteeism and wildcat strikes. Mine owners tend to place the burden of responsibility for this factor on organized labor, but it is likely that the prerequisite for controlling it is improved management-labor relations in general, perhaps some innovative management practices such as flexible work scheduling, autonomous work teams, etc. Whether these practices can be adapted to mine operations or whether there are technological solutions to the productivity problem needs much study.

Labor demands are wage increases which stay ahead of inflation, increased benefits, and improved safety and health. A more generalized demand is increased autonomy in work assignments and scheduling and improved working conditions. Given full employment and competitively rising wages, these do not appear to be severe constraints on expansion of coal mining. A more serious potential constraint, although not yet articulated as a labor demand, will be the acceptability of living conditions in the mining community, including availability of moderately priced housing, public services, schools, employment for spouses and older children of the miners, etc. Cooperative planning by community leaders and mine owners will be necessary to avoid this constraint if expansion of mining activity occurs rapidly in a small community, especially with development of new coalfields or greatly expanded operations in already-producing areas.

The rate of growth and the resources and planning to manage such growth are the critical parameters for the local community. In general, such communities will welcome expansion of mining operations and the secondary economic development which accompanies it. However, it appears that communities where new mining operations would be developed are not expecting it, and thus not preparing for it. Informal communication by mine owners of plans for development, with local planning officials, and cooperation in helping the community work out the problems associated with rapid expansion, will be useful to avoid social dislocations and deteriorated quality of life in the community, which in turn can lead to worker dissatisfaction, increased absenteeism, excessive labor turnover, and declining productivity. Some protection against deleterious effects of mine close-downs may also eventually be sought by mining communities.

At the national level, the critical factor in avoiding strong and effective environmentalist opposition is enforcement of the Clean Air laws. Any serious degradation of the criteria or failure to enforce the Acts will provoke opposition to the essential users of the coal, the electric utilities. Aside from this factor, environmental opposition is likely to be minimal because underground mining is considered by most environmentalists as preferable to the risks of nuclear plant accidents or oil spills, and also preferable to strip mining. In some cases, however, there will be local opposition to mines, based on the threat of subsidence, acid mine drainage, gob piles, ponds and dams, aesthetic degradation, or construction of roads or bridges related to the mines. Environmentalists will also make common cause with labor unions to oppose relaxation of health and safety laws.

Full participation by government (primarily the federal government, but also state governments) would mean (1) a strong energy policy emphasizing coal and backed by incentives for coal mining, (2) realistic environmental and safety regulations, (3) strong funding for R&D related to coal mining and utilization, (4) university and lower-level training programs for mining engineers and miners, (5) technical and/or financial assistance for communities adversely impacted by rapid growth, and (6) action to prevent abandonment of railroad lines, or to encourage needed branch lines or spurs.

INDUSTRY STRUCTURE

The "coal industry" comprises several elements. These include landowners, mining companies, equipment suppliers, transportation companies, consumers, and labor.[1]

"So far as the bituminous coal industry is concerned, it's structure is compellingly determined by geology. ... Geological differentials will determine the ownership, financial patterns, and employment patterns in the coal industry [as well as indicate the thrust of criticism of its activities]."[2]

Landowners play a critical role. Those that lease coal rights typically require their lessees to mine "to exhaustion" according to a negotiated or set percentage of recovery of estimated original minable reserves. The royalty structure called for in the lease usually provides an incentive to achieve maximum coal recovery, as leases commonly include provisions for payments to the landowner in terms of the negotiated recovery rate regardless of whether such recovery is actually attained.

Mining companies may be described in four categories:

1. Integrated companies mining coal largely for their own use. These are the so-called *captive* mines.
2. Interstate commercial companies operating mines in several states (e.g., Con-

[1]See, for example, "Energy Research and Development—Problems and Prospects", U.S. Senate Committee on Interior and Insular Affairs, Serial No. 93-21, 1973.

[2]C. L. Christensen, "Economic Redevelopment in Bituminous Coal," Harvard, Cambridge, Mass., 1962.

solidation, Peabody).
3. Intrastate commercial companies mining coal for sale but operating more than one mine within a single state (e.g., Whitesville A&S in West Virginia).
4. Single-unit commercial companies operating only one mine.

In recent years the smaller operators have been going out of business at an increasing rate. The integrated companies mine coal concentrated in large blocks and have large annual production.[1] Commercial companies that operate in several states dominate this aspect of the industry. Intrastate and single-unit producers have the smallest capacity of all. The company size and degree of coal development is related to the available reserves. The existence of large reserves of high-quality coals will tend to attract the investment which will make possible large mines and may result in large multiunit companies. The selection process will be such that those who have coal lands at the margin (with poor quality and less readily minable reserves) will be those who must be content to operate small mines and remain small companies.

This appears to have been the problem faced by the oil companies who were seeking to acquire coal lands in the late 1950s and early 1960s. Existing coal companies controlled the best reserves through ownership or unbreakable long-term leases with landowning companies, and the prospective new entrants were thus limited to the fringes of the minable reserves (and thereby to the fringes of the industry). Faced with this situation, the noncoal companies who wished to gain a position in the industry followed the classic advice of "if you can't beat 'em, join 'em" and undertook a wide-ranging program of acquiring coal companies (and the reserves which they controlled) (Table 1).

For example, the Continental-Consolidation acquisition was financed by "production payment" arrangements, under which a loan to finance the acquisitions was secured by the proceeds of the acquired coal companies' future production. The security was deemed adequate if the lending institution was satisfied that there were sufficient long-term contracts in force to ensure that the coal would be marketed as produced. As a result of the acquisitions:

Fifteen of the largest companies control more than half the nation's coal output.
Independent coal companies' share of the market decreased from 31.5 percent in 1962 to 9.7 percent in 1969.
Oil and gas companies' share rose from 2.1 to 23 percent.
Other large firms' shares rose from 2 to 15 percent.

These percentages are based on national figures, and the degree of concentration in certain parts of the nation is even greater. "The big coal corporations thus dominate the market places, leaving the smaller operators to either take what is left or sell through agencies controlled by these larger companies."[2]

[1] *Ibid.*

[2] C. D. McDowell, president of Harlan County (Kentucky) Coal Operators Association, statement before the Subcommittee on Special Small Business Problems of the Select Committee on Small Business, U.S. House of Representatives, Oct. 2, 1970.

Table 1 Acquisition of coal companies by other firms

Company	Coal company acquired	Date of acquisition
General Dynamics	Freeman Coal	Dec. 31, 1959
	United Electric Coal	Dec. 31, 1959*
Gulf Oil	Pittsburg and Midway Coal	Late 1963
Continental Oil	Consolidation Coal	Sept. 15, 1966
Occidental Petroleum	Island Creek	Jan. 29, 1968
	Maust Properties	Aug. 8, 1969
Newmont, Williams, Bechtel, Boeing, Equitable Life	Peabody Coal	July 1, 1977
Standard Oil (Ohio)	Old Ben Coal	Aug. 1968
	Enos Coal	Aug. 1968
	Winding Gulf	Nov. 1968
Westmoreland Coal	Imperial Smokeless	Jan. 31, 1969
Wheeling-Pittsburgh Steel	Omar Mining	Dec. 1968
Eastern Gas & Fuel	Joanne Coal	June 18, 1969
	Ranger Fuel (30%)	Jan. 1970
	Sterling Smokeless	Apr. 15, 1970
Pittston Company	Eastern Coal	Oct. 1969
Amax	Ayrshire Collieries	Oct. 31, 1969
Gulf Resources & Chemical	C & K Coal Company	Jan. 6, 1970
Alco Standard	Barnes & Tucker	July 1970

*25% interest in 1959, increased to 37% July 1, 1962, to 52.9% Dec. 31, 1963, to 100% in November 1966.
Source: American Public Power Administration

Few small companies have their own sales department, and previous studies in West Virginia (Thompson) have shown that they use the sales arm of large companies in marketing their production.

Small operators frequently are not affiliated with the United Mine Workers of America (UMWA). This combined with the fact that they typically sell their coal through the sales units of larger, unionized companies, has important economic implications for the small company. There is not too much difference in wages paid to union or nonunion miners. The principal difference is that union mines make payments into the UMWA benefit and pension funds while nonunion mines do not. However, the National Bituminous Coal Wage Agreement of 1978 provides that any union-affiliated company that procures or acquires coal from a nonunion company must pay the equivalent UMWA fund payment per ton *plus* an additional $0.50 per ton. In other words, the sales unit of a large company that handles nonunion coal must allow for a charge of normal payments plus a penalty per ton for this clause alone, clearly a disincentive from dealing with nonunion mines.

There are also a number of independent sales agents who handle transactions of smaller coal producers. These sales agents commonly deal with smaller coal producers (see, for example, the "Keystone Coal Industry Manual." It is possible that at least some of the smaller, nonunion producers use the independent sales agents to avoid the welfare fund and penalty charges.

Assuming that union-produced coal sets the prevailing market prices as a ceiling, the effect of this charge to nonunion coal (on top of any sales commission and handling charges due to the sales agent in the transaction) is to depress the price paid to the nonunion company and to seriously squeeze its margin of profit. Many small mining companies have gone out of business or were absorbed by larger firms as a result. Note, however, that the profitability of larger companies is not affected, and may even be enhanced by this practice.

Equipment suppliers are essential to the industry as they supply the tools for coal recovery and processing. Generally, the equipment suppliers do not mass-produce mining machines, whether used for surface or for deep mining. Instead these machines are custom-built and thereby costly, resulting in low unit profits for the manufacturer. The equipment suppliers make their profit (according to *Fortune* of May 1972) through sales of spare parts to service their equipment. This would appear to constrain new developments to some degree.

Transportation of coal is largely by railroads. With many railroads' joint interest in development of their coal reserves and in shipment of this coal on their system, it would be consistent with their objectives to encourage developments that continue the need for transportation of coal to consumer installations located elsewhere. The transportation and distribution of coal is very much affected by the structure of freight rates, which are typically paid directly by the consumers (coal costs are quoted as FOB mine).

In recent years, there has been an apparent shortage in transportation equipment (mainly railroad hopper cars) for moving coal from mines to markets. "There is little or no storage of bituminous coal at the mines, and coal mines cannot operate without regular supply and a sufficient number of railroad cars."[1] This problem appears to be particularly acute for the small operator, who:

> ... has been denied his fair share of available railroad cars by the railroads that are oriented towards the needs of the big operators. Not only does the small operator pay higher rates but he is forced out of business because the cars he should receive are dedicated to those mines that ship unit trains (fixed numbers of coal cars that make regular shuttle runs between mine and market) to the big consumer.
>
> Most of the shortage [of cars] in 1970 was a 35,000 decrease in the number of railroad hopper cars ... attributed to (retirement) of the old 50−60 ton capacity class...[2]

and insufficient replacement with newer cars of 100-ton capacity. The net effect of the rail car shortage was to contribute to the increase in coal prices and dramatize the economic plight of some of the eastern railroads. Although there is an obvious need for more complete information, preliminary data[3] suggest that railroads which both own coal reserves and transport coal to consumers are in an advantageous and profitable position, whereas those that merely transport coal are not. Norfolk & Western and the Burlington Northern would be examples of the former, while the Penn Central would exemplify the latter.

[1] U.S. Bureau of Mines, "Restrictions on the Uses of Coal," June 1971. (Manuscript, 57 pages.)
[2] McDowell, *loc. cit.*
[3] *Forbes,* Nov. 15, 1972.

However, the coal car "shortage" in the early 1970s was probably more apparent rather than real. *The San Jose Mercury* reported on January 12, 1972, that some 20,000 of the 35,000 "retired" coal cars would be pressed into service to carry the grain sold to the Soviet Union to ports for shipment. It might be concluded from this development that there is no technical constraint upon coal transportation given certain economic considerations. In other words, it could be argued that the railroad companies sought to take advantage of increased coal demand to obtain newer cars that would provide greater capacity and lower operating costs, rather than attempting to achieve a relatively lower rate of profit through higher-volume shipments.

As noted above, the coal mining industry comprises mining companies and satellite organizations that provide services and support to mining operations. There are a number of mining companies of differing sizes. In an attempt to provide further details about the industry, the work of Thompson[1] is cited. Thompson's work covered both surface and underground mining, and it is assumed that the data on characteristics of different-sized companies remain relevant to the situation of the present day.

Thompson established four categories of company by total annual production:

Large companies, 1 million tons and greater
Medium-sized companies, 500,000 to 999,999 tons
Small companies, 100,000 to 499,999 tons
Very small companies, less than 100,000 tons

Based on a questionnaire survey, Thompson analyzed data on production sales from noncaptive mines in West Virginia and found that these mines accounted for more than 85 percent of total state production. Table 2, compiled from Thompson's report, shows that large and medium firms enjoy a wide range of users for their coal, and that their production is widely distributed to a number of destinations. In contrast, small and very small firms have most of their production consumed by a few users located in a more limited geographical area. As will be noted in a later section, in 1963 and earlier, sales were typically made by relatively short-term or "spot" contracts, whereas most mines at present have their production dedicated to a particular consumer. It is noteworthy that a high proportion of coal mined by small and very small companies (nearly 50 percent) is consumed in West Virginia and other nearby Eastern states.

Thompson's data on marketing methods used by coal mining firms of different sizes also have significance, although they are about 15 years old (Table 3). The table shows that large firms sold more than 85 percent of their production directly to the consumer or to a distributor, and that only about 7 percent was sold through independent sales agents. Direct selling was equally important for medium-sized firms, although roughly two times as much coal was handled by independent sales agents as for large firms. The situation is greatly different for small companies,

[1] J. H. Thompson, The Changing Markets for West Virginia Coal, 1951-1963, *W.Va. Univ. Bus. Econ. Stud.,* vol. 9, no. 2, December 1964.

Table 2 Percentage distribution of sales of noncaptive West Virginia mines by size of mining company, 1963

	Large firms	Medium firms	Small firms	Very small firms
User				
Electric utilities	34.6	12.7	47.4	46.4
Manufacturing	17.5	28.2	17.7	21.5
Steel and coke	21.1	18.0	5.2	2.7
Retail	4.0	8.2	3.5	1.9
Exports	19.5	28.2	17.7	24.0
Others	3.5	4.7	8.5	3.5
	100.0	100.0	100.0	100.0
Shipment and destination				
Great Lakes:				
U.S.	10.8	14.9	8.1	7.1
Canada	4.5	2.4	1.0	2.6
Tidewater:				
Export	19.5	28.2	17.7	23.6
Coastal trade	8.6	3.2	8.6	1.2
Rail, river, truck:				
W. Virginia	6.9	0.5	11.1	19.0
W. Pennsylvania	6.1	1.3	2.3	3.5
Other Eastern States	19.7	20.9	30.7	27.3
Midwest	11.0	20.4	14.9	10.1
South	12.5	8.2	5.5	5.5
Canada	0.4		0.1	
	100.0	100.0	100.0	100.0

Source: J. H. Thompson, The Changing Markets for West Virginia Coal, 1951-1963, *W. Va. Univ. Bus. Econ. Stud.,* vol. 9, no. 2, December 1964.

which relied upon independent sales agents to market more than 60 percent of their production. The small companies handled their own sales for only about 35 percent of production. Very small companies also relied heavily upon independent sales agents and sold only about 25 percent of their production directly. Additionally, very small companies market about 32 percent of their production through the sales department of large or medium-sized companies.

Although the specific percentages determined by Thompson may have changed somewhat since his analysis was completed, the relative proportions are less likely to be altered. Therefore, company size seems to exert a considerable influence on the business patterns followed in the coal mining industry.

According to Thompson's categories, the West Virginia surface mining companies as of 1970 were as shown in Table 4.

Table 3 Percentage distribution of output of noncaptive West Virginia mines by size of mining company, 1961

	Large firms	Medium firms	Small firms	Very small firms
Marketing method:				
Producer or con- trolled sales company to user	76.5	81.5	29.7	14.2
Independent sales agent	6.9	16.6	60.8	40.0
Producer or con- trolled sales company to distributor	10.1		8.0	11.3
Producer or con- trolled sales company to retailer	6.1	1.9	1.0	0.5
To truckers at mine	0.2		0.5	2.0
All other methods	0.2			31.9
Totals	100.0	100.0	100.0	100.0

Source: J.H. Thompson, The Changing Markets for West Virginia Coal, 1951-1963, *W. Va. Univ. Bus. Econ. Stud.,* vol. 9, no. 2, December 1964.

The data for surface mining companies are shown in expanded form in Table 5 and compared to production. The table shows that most production is accounted for by companies that produce from 100,000 to 500,000 tons per year (34 percent), with the next largest production from companies that produce from 50,000 to 100,000 tons and from 500,000 to 750,000 tons (about 18 percent each). Companies that produce over 1 million tons account for roughly 15 percent of total surface-mined production. It is apparent from these data that the small and middle-range companies are the principal producers of surface-mined coal in West Virginia. In contrast to other states, in West Virginia larger surface mining companies amount to a rather low part of total production, although their individual production is great.

Table 4 Summary of company data for 1970 surface coal mining operations in West Virginia

Production category	Number	Percent
Large companies	3	1
Medium-sized companies	11	5
Small companies	48	23
Very small companies	150	71
Total	212	100

Source: West Virginia Department of Mines.

Table 5 Summary of company data for 1970 surface coal mining operations in West Virginia

Total production, tons	No. of companies	Total companies, percent	Percent of total surface production 1970
Less than 10,000	49	23	0.1
10,000−50,000	64	30	6.7
50,000−100,000	37	18	17.5
100,000−500,000	48	23	34.0
500,000−750,000	8	4	17.8
750,000−1 million	3	1	8.9
More than 1 million	3	1	15.0
Totals	212	100	100.0

PATTERNS OF COAL INDUSTRY ASSOCIATION

The coal industry is one of the nation's basic industries, one which is of importance to the conduct of many other industries and individual businesses that they comprise. As a result, it is not surprising that members of the coal industry would have established long-standing relationships with consumer industries as well as various other industries that provide goods and services essential to coal production operations. These relationships, based upon basic everyday operations, extend into concepts for modification to improve these operations through research, development, and engineering as well as into planning for expanded and new facilities in the future.

Most of the participants in the coal industry have established informal channels of communication, by which ideas and innovations may be shared for the general benefit. This is consistent with the evolutionary nature of coal production and use, and is in keeping with the historical practice of trial and error in perfecting new approaches to common problems. Given the nature of coal as described in Chapter 2 and our present understanding of its formation and occurrence, it seems likely that these patterns will continue for an indefinite time.

Even the advent of new organizations such as oil companies into the coal industry seems unlikely to alter such established patterns of industry association—rooted in characteristics of the resource itself—very greatly in the near future. Moreover, massive governmental expenditures for research are not likely to lead to wide-ranging changes in these patterns, because even a success in research will require a considerable time for adoption in a significant share of the industry owning to the sizable investment represented by present facilities and the dependence on present-day technology for projected expansion. In short, it appears likely that present patterns of industry association will persist for some time. Clearly, much more intensive work is required to display and comprehend the structural relationships that compose the leadership of the coal industry.

PATTERNS OF COMPANY ASSOCIATION

In an attempt to understand better the framework in which transactions take place in the coal mining industry, the association of companies listed in the industry's standard reference work may be cited.

The "Keystone Coal Industry Manual"[1] lists coal producers and sales agents in a comprehensive and cross-indexed fashion. Inspection of entries in this valuable reference reveals that several organizations are related through common dealings. For example, many coal producers share the same sales agents (p. 35-138 of the manual). Other companies may be affiliated through common ownership, investment, production, or management (or any combination of these (p. 558 of the manual). If plotted on one chart, these associations would show an extensive and interconnected array of companies that compose the coal industry of the United States. The array includes major companies such as the Consolidation Coal Company and Eastern Associated Coal Corporation and small companies such as the Ten-A Coal Company and Queen Victoria, Inc., each apparently interrelated through patterns of common dealings. Although there are exceptions, the data suggest that the sales agents/producers appear to act as media for facilitating communication among their client companies that confine their operations to producing coal. Obviously, however, there are important exceptions to such generalizations.

Thompson was one of the first to point out that small mining companies (of all types of mining) in West Virginia were interrelated to larger companies through sales agreements to market their production. Drease and Bryant[2] determined that a small surface mining company in southeastern Ohio (in general quite similar to West Virginia from an economic sense) had its demand controlled by "the residual demand of electric utilities which is not provided by their long term supplies." The small company's production was to meet demands created either through contractual agreements or through short-term inability of the long-term supplier to meet production requirements.

A further relationship, that of land holding to mining companies is revealed through data on surface mining permits.[3] For each permit, the acreage, surface mining company, and tract holder (landowner or lessee) are listed. Using these data, it is possible to analyze the relationships of surface mining companies to landowners and deep mine companies. Several different types of organizations were involved; land companies, mining companies operating both deep and surface mines, and mining companies operating only deep mines are shown in addition to surface mining companies.

In West Virginia, for example, major land companies such as the Pocahontas Land Corporation (a subsidiary of Norfolk & Western Railway), Western Po-

[1]"Keystone Coal Industry Manual," McGraw-Hill, New York, 1976.

[2]G. R. Drease and H. L. Bryant, "Costs and Effects of a Water Quality Program for a Small Strip Mining Company," a report submitted to the U.S. Army Engineer Institute for Water Resources, report number IWR 71-7, 150 pages, August 1971.

[3]West Virginia Department of Natural Resources, Division of Reclamation, permit data for 1971, 1970, 1969.

cahontas Corporation (a subsidiary of the Chesapeake & Ohio Railway), the Rowland Corporation, C. C. Dickinson, and the Charleston National Bank played an important role in coal mining through their ownership of minable coal lands. Additionally, major coal companies also were significant in holding reserves; among these were Consolidation Coal Company (a subsidiary of Continental Oil Company), U.S. Steel Corporation, Ranger Fuel Corporation (a subsidiary of the Pittston Company), Bethlehem Mines Corporation (a subsidiary of Bethlehem Steel Corporation), and Cannelton Coal Company (a subsidiary of Algoma Steel Corporation).

In the early 1970s, for example, some major coal companies that operated only deep mines participated in surface mining through their control of lands permitted for mining by other companies. This can be an effective mechanism for recovery of coal from properties that may be too small or otherwise unfavorable for development by a major corporation, yet which still contain valuable coal deposits. Without such arrangements with smaller companies, it is not at all certain that such coal reserves would experience development at all, and valuable reserves could be by-passed and lost. Thus, although these companies did not directly carry out surface mining operations, they were nonetheless valuable, active, (although indirect), participants in surface mining through leases granted to other companies. It seems reasonable that similar patterns of association would be continued in the future, to serve the interests of the several participants.

Finally, and by no means least, the coal industry is dependent on labor. The United Mine Workers of America, which has experienced an active and eventful history, represents about half the mine workers. Entire volumes could be devoted to study of the UMWA alone. At present, it will be important to observe the new leadership of the union to ascertain its potential new directions and their implications for the coal industry as a whole.

The UMWA has had a turbulent existence, including a number of bitter battles with government, industry, other unions, and itself. Since 1950, however, there has been a period of exceptional calm in the UMWA's relations with the industry (for one analysis of the possible reasons behind this unprecedented development, see Bethell's paper[1]). Part of the reason for the calm was the private agreements reached between the UMWA and the Bituminous Coal Operator's Association (BCOA). Little has appeared in public about the BCOA—UMWA relationships that so control the coal industry. However, an article by a former official of the BCOA[2] sheds considerable light on these practices, although it is addressed to the National Bituminous Coal Wage Agreement of 1971. Several important facts about this agreement, 20 years after the initial UMWA—BCOA agreement, are worthy of note:[3]

It was "not subject to termination by any signatory party" prior to November 12, 1974.

[1]T. N. Bethell, Conspiracy in Coal, *The Washington Monthly*, vol. I, no. 2, March 1969.
[2]S. W. Zanolli, Labor Relations—How It Works in the Bituminous Coal Mining Industry, *Min. Eng.*, pp. 34—39, December 1972.
[3]All quotes from *ibid.*

It was the first "one document *national*" [original emphasis] agreement that sorts out provisions of earlier agreements. However, the complete "contract" includes the terms and conditions of all various district agreements, except provisions changed. Also, "prior custom and practice not in conflict" with the agreement may be continued. Finally:

> As the parties from time to time since November 12, 1972 have jointly executed addenda, supplements, or joint interpretations with respect to the 1971 National Agreement, these have also become part of the complete contract. Occasionally the parties mutually recognize an ambiguity or deficiency in some bit of contract language and agree on an addendum or joint interpretation. To the extent that such joint action is taken by authorized agents of the parties they become binding on all covered by the contract and also on umpires.

Seniority provisions were expanded and refined to include layoff and recall, employment rights of laid-off miners to other mines in the same area, and job bidding.

Internal political strife within the UMWA in recent years has not improved matters. The national wage agreement negotiated following the strike of 1974 attempted to provide new mechanisms for dealing with labor grievances as one step toward greater stability and higher productivity. Unfortunately, the chaotic state of UMWA affairs and the unwieldy nature of the procedures rendered this approach ineffective. This was a major factor contributing to all-time high levels of absenteeism and wildcat strikes that plagued the industry. As an example, miner-days lost to wildcat strikes increased nearly fivefold from 1973 to 1977, exceeding 2.4 million miner-days in 1977. It hardly seems realistic to expect to reach projected levels of coal production unless the roots of these critical problems can be identified and corrective actions taken. Stability in mine labor relations is vital to every component of the coal industry and its customers.

The several components of the coal industry interact with one another in production operations. Output is determined by how efficient this interaction is with respect to the mining methods employed. An introduction to coal mining methods is given in the next chapter.

CHAPTER FIVE

MINING METHODS

GEOGRAPHICAL/GEOLOGICAL INFLUENCES ON MINING METHODS

Coal mining technology has to be evaluated in terms of geographical and geological perspectives. Simply stated, there are major differences in the physical and chemical characteristics of coal deposits that separate the eastern and midwestern fields from those of the northern Great Plains and Rocky Mountains.[1] To avoid repeating these cumbersome expressions in the following discussion, the terms *East* and *West* will be used instead.

Geologically speaking,[2] the coalfields of the East are older than those of the West (roughly 300 million years versus 100 million years). Furthermore, in one degree or another, the eastern coalfields have been subjected to important tectonic stresses for much of the interval since their formation. As a result, the process of coal formation (as described in Chapter 2) is considered to be more complete in the East. The product of these processes is relatively thin seams (typically in the range of 4–6 feet) that contain indurated and compact coal of relatively high heating value (commonly of the order of 10,000–12,000 Btu per pound or higher) but high sulfur content (typically of the order of 2–3 percent). A further consideration is that subsequent to the deposition of the vegetable matter ultimately transformed to coal, additional sedimentary deposits were laid down in the same area, with the result that the eastern coals were deeply buried beneath the surface. In places, tectonic forces have uplifted portions of the eastern coalfields to where they occur relatively near the surface; also erosion has exposed certain coal seams. Erosion

---

[1]See E. Faltermayer, Clearing the Way for The New Age of Coal, *Fortune*, p. 215, May 1974; E. Faltermayer, It's Back to the Pits for Coal's New Future, *Fortune*, p. 137, June 1974; J. G. Phillips. Energy Report/Environmentalists, Utilities Argue over East, West Mining *National Journal Reports*, p. 1014, June 6, 1974.

[2]See P. Averitt, Coal Resources of the United States, *US Geol. Surv. Bull.* 1412, 1975.

has also removed a portion of the overlying strata, again bringing some seams near the surface. Still, most eastern coal resources occur at depths of several hundred feet beneath the surface.

In summary, the eastern coalfields are characterized by:

1. Relatively thin seams
2. High heating value
3. High sulfur content
4. Deep burial of the bulk of the coal seams

As a result of these fundamental geological factors, development of coal deposits in the eastern coalfields has been primarily be deep mining methods, with lesser amounts of surface mining until recent years.

Development of the eastern coalfields (especially those in Appalachia) dates from pre-Revolutionary days, and today these fields remain as the principal source of American coal production. Coal production methods used today were developed for working the eastern deposits, with the result that:

Deep mining methods are oriented toward the relatively thinner seams of the East (this applies to both domestic and European deep mining technology, where similar conditions occur).

Surface mining methods are designed either for the large-volume, deep digging required to expose coal seams for recovery, or for the relatively small-volume, shallow digging or augering needed to gain access to coal seams along the contour of mountains. Relatively smaller-volume coal loading and haulage equipment is required owing to the thin coal seams of the East.

The western coalfields, as noted above, are geologically younger than the eastern ones. The process of coal formation had less time to operate on the western deposits of vegetable matter, most coalfield areas had less time to be affected by tectonic stresses, and relatively smaller volumes of subsequent sediments were deposited. The product of these processes in the West is relatively thick seams (typically in the range of 10–30 feet or more) that contain friable and porous coal of relatively low heating value (ranging from about 7000–9000 Btu per pound) but with relatively low sulfur content (typically less than 1 percent). Many of the western deposits occur close to the surface, although there are important reserves at greater depths.

In summary, the western coalfields are characterized by:

1. Relatively thick seams
2. Low heating value
3. Low sulfur content
4. Shallow burial of large reserves

These geological factors exerted strong influences upon the development of western coals. Remote from major industrial markets, the coals were developed initially to serve railroad and home-heating requirements. Although some deep mining was practiced in the past, most production has been from surface mines (especially in recent years). The technology employed for western coal development was primarily a straightforward extension of equipment and practices established through experience in the East; to be sure, there were minor local modifications made to adapt better to some western conditions, but by and large the same practices meant that:

Deep mining is practiced in the West only where seam and roof conditions permit the direct application of existing technologies which have been developed primarily to work the thin seam deposits of the East. At present, deep mining technology for working in thick western seams under relatively incompetent roof conditions does not exist.

Surface mining in the West requires relatively low-volume, shallow digging to expose thick coal seams for recovery. The giant excavators used in the East do not appear to be necessary, at least for the foreseeable future. There are two options for acquiring the requisite excavating equipment for working western deposits: (1) obtain new equipment tailored to western deposit characteristics or (2) use older, smaller-capacity equipment retired from service in eastern operations. Both options have been employed in developing western deposits, although the availability of used equipment is now probably small.

Although low-volume overburden excavation is required in the West, the thick seams could be most efficiently recovered through high-volume, continuous coal loading and haulage. The deposits are presently worked through the extension of eastern-developed, cyclical-type technology developed to work thin seams.

Assessment

The foregoing suggests that the different geological conditions occurring in eastern and western coalfields exert major influences upon the manner of their development. In the ideal case, mining methods should be tailored to the characteristics of the deposits to obtain optimum efficiency of operation and resource recovery. The evolution of mining technology has been such, however, as to emphasize the development of eastern coal deposits and then to attempt to extend such technology to the western coalfields. It is not unreasonable to suggest that there may be a limit to which eastern-oriented technology (surface or deep mining) can be modified for application to the different conditions of the West. Whether such a limit exists, and if so what consequences for resource recovery or costs (or both) may result, should be determined at an early date. One result of such an analytical process may be to identify needs for R&D to work the western coal deposits better.

By the same argument, there may be similar limits to the degree of improvements in existing eastern-type mining technology from automation or further mechanization. The potential for innovation in technology needs to be evaluated for this case also.

With the foregoing as background, a brief description of the principal deep and surface coal mining methods and major external effects of each method is presented below.

UNDERGROUND ("DEEP") MINING METHODS

Geologic factors relative to the occurrence of coal seams control mining methods and influence technology and recovery of reserves. Generally speaking, most coal reserves occur at sufficient depth as to require underground or deep mining methods, with relatively smaller amounts occurring sufficiently near the surface where strip mining may be employed. Also, operations are constrained by the thickness of the coal seam. Roughly four-fifths of all coal mined in the United States is obtained from seams ranging in thickness from 3 to 8 feet.

Mine Design and Auxiliary Systems

Practices for mine design and auxiliary systems may limit the use of new systems in present mines or in mines designed to employ present-day operating technology. Underground mines are commonly operated for 20 to 50 years. The initial mine design may preclude modifications to accommodate new systems that might be developed for increasing the rate of coal extraction. An understanding of principles for mine design and auxiliary systems specification to determine their effect on the long-term extraction of coal is therefore important.

Present status. Computer programs have been experimented with in connection with the design of mines (including such aspects as access openings, production openings, and auxiliary air power equipment), but mines continue to be designed primarily by the empirical expertise of design engineering groups. Mine design takes about 1 to 2 years. Innovations in mine design are hampered to a considerable extent by the lack of major developments in auxiliary equipment. For instance, the fans being used in ventilation systems to get air to the mine face in the quantities specified by law are of the same design and of essentially the same air-moving capabilities as those designed and built 30 years ago. The air-volume capacity necessary to minimize dust and to carry safely the released methane from the face of the longwall would be the limitation on a mechanized longwall capable of mining coal at the rate of 3000 tons per day per shift.[1]

It should also be noted that as mining extends to greater depths, the ability of the fans to bring needed air down to the faces and large accessways will seriously limit the capabilites of the current system designs. Several major explosions in the past have been blamed on fan failure and the subsequent buildup of dust and gas. Although stringent maintenance and inspection procedures have been instituted in coal mines to prevent major explosions, no major improvements in fan design have resulted.

Current practice in mine design has partly resulted from requirements of present laws and regulations, which in turn reflects available technology. For instance, to increase safety more access openings have been required. At the same time, this has resulted in more roof-support problems, since there is more roof area exposed

---

[1]"Mining Engineering Handbook," Society of Mining Engineers, Salt Lake City, 1973.

per operating face. Mine design might best be improved by reducing the number of access openings, thus decreasing roof falls and simplifying the ventilation problem.

The ideal situation where all facets of mining can be satisfied optimally with one specific system does not exist. As a result, a variety of mining systems and equipment have been developed to take advantage of the differences in natural conditions as much as possible. All facets of mining (and the interaction of each with other facets) must be evaluated to provide proper comparisons and trade offs.

Mining Variables

Basically, seven major independent mining engineering variables can be identified, excluding the human element. These are:

1. Seam height
2. Bottom quality
3. Roof quality, rock structure, partings
4. Methane liberation
5. Hardness of seam
6. Depth of seam
7. Water

To some extent these are interrelated—for example, roof quality is partially a function of the depth of the seam, and floor quality may result from the presence of water—however, each can also be a factor independent of any other—for example, the roof may simply be extremely weak, and water may cause problems even though the bottom is firm.

Each of these items can be subdivided into logical groups such that significant changes in the production system can be identified with the change from one subdivision to the next. However, it must be considered that these independent variables also affect a secondary set of dependent variables which themselves affect the techniques and methods to be employed. Some of these "semi-independent" variables are:

1. Pillar sizes
2. Opening widths
3. Cut depths
4. Percent recovery
5. Roof-support techniques

As an example, loading and hauling efficiency in a cut is affected to a great extent by the dimensions of the cuts (the more tons per cut the greater the efficiency). The dimensions are determined by the height, width, and depth of the cut. While the former is a direct result of the seam height (an independent variable), the latter are often determined by the roof quality and depth of seam (and thus are semi-independent).

Planning and Developing a Mine

The mining plan is often dictated by one of the key independent variables. However, the plan may also be strictly a function of management preferences.

All the information gathered about a coal property must be carefully analyzed. It is assumed that exploration of adjacent mines (if any), core drilling, and other surface geologic surveys have established most of the variable factors listed above. Based on the market conditions that determine needed extraction rates and the life of the mine, certain questions must be resolved in proceeding with mine development.

Portal and surface-facility location. The selection of a portal site involves factors such as method of access, method of ventilation, type of haulage system, and the lifetime of the mine. Certain rules are used as guidelines. The portal area should be free of the danger of flooding (low spots) and be close to the geographical center of the haulage. However, it should be accessible to workers (near highways) as well as close facilities such as parking spaces, bathhouses, supply yards, preparation plants, refuse disposal, and mine-water treatment ponds. These main structures, being of the longest mine life, should be located in the most favorable strata to be easily supported and maintained.

Portal types. Access to the coal seam may be obtained by three general types of entries depending upon coal occurrence (Figure 1):

Drift entry, where the coal is exposed on a hillside or outcrop or can be rendered horizontally
Slope entry, where the coal seam lies between about a 300- and 600-foot depth and conveyor haulage from the mine is employed
Shaft entry, where the coal seam lies at depths greater than 600 feet, and hoists are used for loading out the produced coal

A drift entry is a preferred choice but is limited to those seams that outcrop; thus it is a special case becoming increasingly rare as the shallower seams are depleted. Since it is merely an extension of the underground entry system, it will generally be the most economic overall. However, in certain situations, and usually with an irregular property, a drift portal may be so remote that it will not be feasible and thus a complete evaluation becomes necessary.

The decision as to whether a slope or shaft will be employed can be a very difficult one and reflects its use as well as the overall economics. The vertical shaft provides the least length of passageway from the surface to the seam. Footage to be sunk and the materials for lining and equipping the shaft are both minimized. In addition, for air, it will provide the least pressure drop for openings of the same size. For these reasons, air shafts are universally employed.

Haulage, man-trip, and supply needs require a careful analysis of the two possible portals. A slope configuration is used to take advantage of belt haulage. The maximum angle for belt transportation of coal is 18%, and this means a slope will

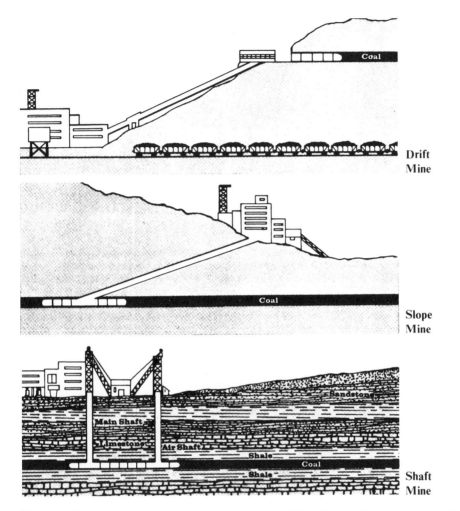

Figure 1. Three types of underground coal mine entries. (After National Coal Association, *Bituminous Coal Facts*, various years.)

be three times the length of the shaft. Fortunately, a slope usually can be driven faster and approximately at one-third the cost of the vertical shaft per foot, therefore providing an economic stand off. The deciding factor becomes the condition of the ground. If the ground is poor, requiring continuous support, the greater length of the slope will place it at a disadvantage relative to the shaft.

Mine development. Mine development requires a systematic procedure of laying out a mine for services and to provide an organized system of attack. A series of parallel openings called *entries* separated by blocks of coal to provide roof support is generally driven from the portal in a central location of the property. These are comparable to the main avenues of a city wherein lie power, piping, haulage, ventilation, etc. The large number of parallel headings is necessary to keep the air velocities down to a reasonable limit, usually 600 to 800 feet per minute, with 4 to 6 tons of air required for every ton of coal mined in a modern coal mine.

From an engineering standpoint, it would be desirable to drive these entries directly to the property line and then extract the coal from both sides on the way back, the so-called *full-retreat system*. In this manner, no active openings need be maintained between caved ground, greatly simplifying roof control and minimizing roof falls which would lead to production delays. However, this would require tying up considerable capital in rail, wire, pipe, etc., without compensating production and, therefore, would generally be financially prohibitive for most companies. Therefore, a compromise between technology and economics is usually affected by utilizing the half-advance, half-retreat system. Here, when the main entries have been driven inward sufficiently, panels will be turned off to one side. These panels are usually 2000 to 3000 feet long, being limited by the haulage system, and minimizing the time in the panel required to hold up the top. At the end of the panel, rooms will be driven from one or both sides on retreat or the pillars only may be pulled back, referred to as a *slicing system*. The first panel will be followed by others until one side is done. Then, the panels will be pulled consecutively from the back of the property outward on the other side, extracting the main entries also on the way. Since percentage extraction on development is only about 30 percent, the combined low extraction ratio and high percentage costs of services makes this uneconomic, and thus the development/production ratio is very closely watched for a coal mine. Sufficient development is maintained for production purposes, but driving ahead too far and tying up capital investment as well as the cost of maintaining the entries are to be avoided. Laying out the mine on a coordinate system has obvious simplifying advantages for both mining and support systems.

Mining systems. From the points of entry, coal is removed in a systematic pattern of "rooms," where the coal has been removed and "pillars" are left to support the overlying rocks or roof. The room-and-pillar approach is the basic technique for coal recovery by deep mining; particular mining methods differ only in the way coal is removed to form the rooms and pillars, whose dimensions are determined by local geology; typically, rooms and pillars will be laid out in an orthogonal pattern with dimensions of the order 20 to 30 feet, determined largely by roof support, haulage, and ventilation requirements. (The latter are for the disposal of methane released as the coal is mined, which represents a health and explosive hazard.)

The room-and-pillar system, utilizing both conventional and continuous mining equipment, remains the dominant technique in the United States. Presently, longwall and shortwall constitute only 5 percent of the total underground production, with only 4 shortwall units and about 90 longwall units in operation.

Conventional mining Figure 2 shows the *conventional* deep mining method, which is the oldest of those currently used in deep mining to produce substantial tonnages of coal, accounting in the early 1970s for about 100 million tons of production. The distinguishing characteristic of conventional deep mining is its sequential

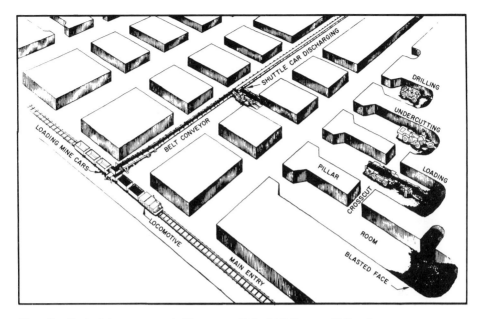

Figure 2. Coal mining—room-and-pillar system. (After U.S. Bureau of Mines.)

utilization of specialized machines to perform individual operations. As the figure shows, separate machines are used at the coal face for drilling, undercutting, blasting, loading, and haulage. Not shown in the figure are roof bolters (who drill and insert steel rods into the exposed roof to tie the strata together—much as a toothpick holds together the several layers of a club sandwich) and rock dusters (who spread crushed limestone to suppress potentially dangerous coal dust).

A complete set of the individual mining machines constitutes a *face unit*, operated by a crew of from 12 to 14 workers. The face crew is the basic production unit in all deep mining.

The basic mining operation is to undercut the mining face with a coal cutter to facilitate blasting by providing space for expansion and allowing gravity assistance in breakage. A coal cutter is similar in principle to a chain saw and is in fact simply a large one. It is equipped with a long flat arm, or "cutter bar," from 8 to 14 feet in length, around whose edge a chain armed with hard-metal cutting teeth is driven by an electric motor. The cutter bar is first inserted endwise into the end of the face at the bottom for its full length and is then moved across the bottom of the face, leaving a kerf about 5 inches thick and the length of the cutter bar in depth along the bottom of the coal seam. The ground coal, or "bug dust," brought out by the cutting teeth is removed from the face, which is then ready for the blast-hole drill. Coal cutter bars may be mounted on boxlike frames that contain the electric drives, reduction gears, and winches. They are moved toward and across the face by winching and moved from face to face on low cars. They may be mounted on rubber-tired vehicles with arms enabling them to cut in any direction desired and at any desired height on the face. Sometimes, kerfs are also cut along the top or vertically along the sides of the face to make blasting easier, to induce breakage in large lumps, to leave some coal with the roof for better roof conditions, or to avoid breaking down a portion of unwanted material.

Blast-hole drilling in coal is done with electrically driven auger drills often mounted on rubber-tired vehicles to facilitate movement from face to face. The holes are loaded with various types of "permissible" explosives; the word *permissible* means that the explosive has been tested and approved by the U.S. Bureau of Mines for coal blasting. Permissible explosives may be ordinary dynamites diluted with salt to reduce flame or cartridges of compressed air, liquid oxygen, or carbon dioxide. Coal blasting is usually done rather lightly and with slow explosives to encourage breakage in large lumps, which still command a premium price in some space-heating uses.

A ramp-type loader is moved in to load the shuttle cars. Such a loader consists of a crawler-mounted inclined ramp that thrusts itself into the bottom of the coal pile. On each side of the ramp is a clawlike arm, mounted and driven to make a sweep across the lower corner of the ramp, pushing the coal toward the middle onto a chain conveyor. The conveyor carries the coal up the ramp incline and out to the end of the cantilever arm overhanging the shuttle car. The shuttle car is a long, low rubber-tired vehicle, with a body open at the far end. The bottom consists of a chain conveyor that moves the load toward the open end as the near end is loaded. The near end of the body is flared out to increase capacity, and the farther portion is straight-sided to facilitate movement of the load with the conveyor. The driver's seat is mounted on the side of the body.

The loaded car carries the coal to a transfer hopper at a point on the main haulage system, where it discharges out the open end by activating the conveyor bottom. Two shuttle cars are commonly worked together so that one can be loading while the other is moving. The usual drive is electric, with the current received through a trailing cable that is automatically reeled out and in as the car moves away from or toward a fixed connection placed midway along its route. Storage-battery-powered cars are also used.

After loading is completed, a roof-bolting machine is commonly moved into the area from which the coal has been removed to provide support for the roof and prevent caving. Holes are drilled 4 to 8 feet into the roof, and long bolts are placed in the holes. The bolts have expansible devices on their ends to anchor them. Wide, flat washers are placed over the projecting ends of the bolts, which are threaded. Nuts screwed on the threaded ends hold the washers against the roof, and the bolts are placed in tension by tightening the nuts. The effect of the bolting is to provide support for loose chunks of rock that might otherwise fall, to strengthen the roof by tying the strata into a thick beam, and to tie the flat, comparatively weak arch to a higher, more competent one above. Roof bolting has done a great deal to supplant props in ground support and is much more convenient, since it does not obstruct the opening. Roof-bolting machines are commonly wheel-mounted for easy movement.

The six units described—cutter, drill, loader, two shuttle cars, and roof-bolting machine—constitute a conventional mining unit. Such a unit will serve up to 26 mining faces in a single shift and may account for as much as 1500 tons of production with 9 to 14 workers, but usually about half this amount (and has been decreasing since 1970).

The sequential nature of conventional mining results in a lower productivity than other common deep mining methods, but it compensates in part for this because it can mine *selectively,* lessening the amount of wastes introduced into coal that must be later removed.

As mining progresses into a seam, pillar supports are left which represent about 50 percent of the total coal. However, when the mining limits are reached, further mining is done in "retreat" back toward the entry, in which pillars are mined and the roof is allowed to collapse. This practice may lead to extraction of up to about 75 to 85 percent of the coal, depending on local conditions.

Production from conventional sections   Production from a conventional section results from the interaction of the production units with the independent variables listed earlier. The variables affect each unit operation. The result is that one of the operations becomes the "bottleneck" behind which the other units normally queue. This bottleneck can be eased or shifted by inserting an additional unit to eliminate the bottleneck or through overtime work by the bottleneck unit. The goal is to have the production controlled by the loading and hauling cycle, that is, to have this operation as the bottleneck.

The precise production rate cannot be predicted as a function of the variables without a great deal of fieldwork to categorize each independent variable and list the output of the units. Even if this were done, the human element would serve to introduce variability which would cause the relationships to be obscured. Some of the determinants of production which are largely human-controlled are maintenance, operator efficiency, and coordination between units.

THE USE OF TIME In the analysis of conventional mining, or any system of mining, concern is with loading- (and hauling-) time utilization.

Conventional mining is inherently a place-change system. Unless a new technique is devised to replace blasting, unit operations will be required to place change frequently. Efficient moving is thus one of the prime requisites to high production. To be efficient, moves must be kept as short as possible. Cable handling (by all operations) and minimum ventilation rerouting are also needed to keep move time to a minimum.

Breakdowns consume fairly large amounts of time, and a trade off between service time and breakdown time (i.e., preventive and breakdown maintenance) is evident, although studies must be made at each operation to determine this trade off.

Within a cut, nonloading time is predominantly change-out time and wait-on-car time. The only methods available to eliminate the former are continuous haulage or the driving of entries sufficiently wide to permit shuttle cars to pass in the same roadway. Practically, the time may be minimized by installing the largest practicable capacity shuttle cars, thus cutting down on the number of cars to be loaded and hence the number of change outs.

To cut down the wait-on-car time, additional cars, larger cars, improved dumping facilities, more frequent dump move up, or a redesigned system to permit multiple dump points could alleviate the problem. It should be noted that comments on hauling delays are applicable to continuous as well as conventional mining.

Continuous mining Continuous mining differs from conventional mining in that the drilling and cutting machines and blasting are not used, and the basic coal loader is combined with high-speed power-driven wheels or chains that tear coal from the face mechanically. Although several types of continuous miners are in use, the most popular is a "ripper" machine that mounts three or four cutting wheels all on the same level and turning in vertical planes on arms that can be raised and lowered and moved sidewards. This movement allows the wheels to reach all parts of the face. The wheels are studded with cutting teeth to rip out the coal. All continuous miners are crawler-mounted and have ramp-type loaders built into them. Other types have double, triple, or quadruple auger heads combined with chain cutters. These are called *borers* and are used principally in driving entries. Another ripper type consists of a wide arm, movable up and down, on which is mounted a number of chain cutters close together. Unlike the conventional units, a continuous miner usually stays in one working place throughout a shift, thus avoiding loss of production from moving from face to face.

Because a continuous miner digs and loads steadily, it should feed a continuous transporting medium, like a conveyor belt. However, conveyor belts are not easily extended and withdrawn to accommodate the movements of the miner and to proceed with it as a face is advanced. Extendible-retractable conveyors and mobile bridge conveyors have been developed and used for this purpose but have not proved dependable enough for general acceptance. Thus, in many places the continuous miners simply dump their loads on the floors, and the coal is picked up by ramp-type loaders serving shuttle cars. This is an awkward compromise, wasteful of machinery and workers, and continuous mining cannot be conceived to be fully developed until a more compatible, flexible transport scheme is devised and proven. Another unsatisfactory compromise is to use shuttle cars and to stop the continuous miner while a loaded car is moved out and an empty one is being positioned for loading.

Continuous mining has grown substantially in the last 22 years, reaching about 175 million tons of production in 1969 and increasing slightly to 187 million tons in 1976. Although able to mine at a rapid rate, continuous miners do not have the ability to mine selectively, and typically include greater amounts of waste matter (that must be removed through mechanical cleaning) than does conventional mining. Additionally, slight irregularities in seam character or operator actions can lead to inclusion of significant amounts of roof or floor rocks as further wastes to be removed.

Whether the conventional steps of cutting, drilling, blasting, and loading are employed with multiple machine units or whether a continuous miner rips the coal from the seam directly and loads it in one step, room-and-pillar systems are more or less the same, modifications being more a function of seam and roof conditions then anything else. Typically, vertical shafts are used in the middle of the property for down and upcast ventilation, main entries are driven, and production panel entries are developed on a half-advance, half-retreat system. After developing the panels, the pillars are extracted on retreat. This is a distinguishing feature of room-and-pillar systems. At great depth, narrow entries are necessary to minimize spans, leaving large blocks of coal (pillars) for support. In shallow thin seams and under good top it was common to drive very wide entries or rooms with small intervening pillars which remained behind with no attempt at pillar extraction. Between complete and no-pillar extraction, there are a variety of partial extraction techniques. Because of recently enacted subsidence legislation, the trend will be to less full-extraction techniques to minimize surface damage.

Production from continuous sections In recent years, continuous mining has been growing at the expense of conventional mining. By replacing the unit operations of cutting, drilling, blasting, and loading into one operation by a single machine, cycling equipment becomes less of a problem as do the delays associated with it. Therefore, the need of operating many mining places simultaneously is reduced. Thus, continuous mining is a concentrated activity which minimizes many of the service problems, but these also become more critical, affecting some machines more so than others. One other obvious advantage of concentration is that a reduction in the work force is possible for a continuous mining production unit as compared to conventional.

Therefore, the very name continuous mining is a misnomer since the operation of the machines is intermittent. The available operation time of the continuous miner has been found to have a weighted average of 34.2 percent, which includes tram time, nearer 20 percent without its inclusion. Most delays are attributed to roof control, ventilation, haulage, and maintenance. Motors on continuous mining machines are vastly oversized, and thus load factors are in the range of 20 to 50 percent. Since nearly all these machines are ac-powered and use squirrel-cage motors, operating these machines under light loads creates adverse power factors that have a very deleterious effect on the overall electrical system. As a result, many companies are converting their old machines to motors of smaller size and machine manufacturers are reducing motor sizes on new equipment.

The horsepower craze in mining machinery has been an unfortunate one. Too many operators have equated productivity to horsepower. However, the power in the motors cannot be fully utilized because of limitations in traction capability when the machines are being driven into coal. For example, power measurements reveal that more power is consumed in the downward shearing cycle of milling machines than in sumping, proving conclusively that traction effort is the limiting factor in sumping, not horsepower of the machine. In the downward shearing cycles, the weight of the machine is more effectively utilized to provide the hydraulic downward thrust of the head.

As with conventional mining, roof bolting is the prime bottleneck, probably even more so because of the limited places worked. Unlike conventional, only a few places are worked at any given time, usually only two, to cut tramming time. Thus, there is less margin for errors in design, and with all the eggs in one basket, downtime on a continuous miner produces a complete cessation of activity, not true with conventional mining where it is easier to make up the lost availability of a single piece of equipment by operating many faces and thus mining somewhat ahead.

There is virtually no correlation between the manufacturer-stated loading rate and the actual shift production of a continuous miner which is affected widely by the variables already discussed. Also, haulage cycles are not much different than specified in conventional mining. The continuous miner availability in the average mine is extremely low. While intuitively, shuttle-car haulage has been given the lion's share of the blame, this is probably exaggerated. As with conventional mining (but even more so), a good deal of work is accomplished during change out that does affect the production rate. The operator will use this time to trim the top and scoop the coal into piles for faster loading. Since these activities are required with continuous haulage systems, the production rate would be decreased also.

The major delay elements are due to the required moving of machines from place to place because of ventilation and roof-control requirements. A system of concurrent bolting and extension of ventilation in a place to permit advances of say 100 feet would improve production greatly. Only then will the miner operate probably more than the 20 to 30 percent shift time observed now.

Variation of conventional and continuous production with the independent variables As stated earlier, it is hypothesized that production is a function of the seven independent variables of seam height, bottom quality, roof quality, methane liberation, hardness of seam, depth of seam, and water. Each of these and its relation to production potential are discussed individually below.

Production is related to seam height. As the seam height increases, shuttle-car payloads will increase (even with the same car). This will decrease the number of change outs required per ton and also serve to decrease the wait time per ton since fewer "waits" will be encountered. Since more tons are mined in each cut, tram time per ton will also decrease since the tram time per cut should not change. Finally, since all support operations tend to be a constant time per cut, any wait-on-bottlenecks time will decrease, as the loading and hauling operation will take longer to load a cut of coal. It should be noted however, that as seam heights exceed 180 inches, conventional equipment and methods are no longer considered feasible.

Fair or poor bottom quality will generally impair conventional section production. The face equipment used is generally cat-mounted or four-wheel drive, relatively light, and not susceptible to easily becoming mired or seriously slowed by poor bottom. Shuttle cars will slow somewhat in fair bottom and may slow 30 to 50 percent (or more on occasion) in poor bottom.

In excellent or good top one bolter will generally suffice without becoming a production bottleneck. In average conditions, two bolters or one twin-boom bolter will be required to avoid a bolting bottleneck. In fair top, two bolters will restrict production, and in poor top, production will be restricted severely by the roof-support function. Except for maneuverability restrictions, poor top will not affect the cutting and drilling operations. Shooting will also not be affected by poor top.

Loading and hauling may have delays while scaling top, and shuttle-car speeds may be reduced if clearances are decreased by increased roof support, but the overall cycle time will still normally be controlled by the roof-support cycle.

Methane liberation is normally less of a problem with conventional mining than with continuous mining. Because the coal is shot into a few relatively large pieces, less gas is released. In addition, the intermittent nature of the process tends to allow the gas level to reduce before the face is once again shot and loaded. While a gas inrush may be experienced immediately after blasting, with good ventilation it will return to normal levels by the time the loader is ready to load the first shuttle car. The primary effect of gas is the need to maintain tight line and check brattices in the face area. This may delay the loading and hauling cycle, possibly for several minutes after each shot.

Hardness of coal, like methane liberation, presents less problems to conventional sections than to continuous miner units. Drilling, shooting, and cutting are the affected operations, with the effect on the first two noticeable only if additional holes are required over those normally expected. In addition, these operations often experience a large wait for other bottlenecks, and the presence of hard coal only serves to decrease this wait time. The opposite is also true in that soft coal will not serve to increase production from a conventional unit.

The effects of seam depth are experienced indirectly in most cases. As seam depth increases, pillar sizes also increase, thus increasing the average change-out distance and haul distance in a given cut cycle and the average tram distance from cut to cut. The loading and hauling cycle will be affected most because of this. A second indirect effect of seam depth may be heaving bottom or shearing of the roof; however, these are treated under roof and floor quality. At great depths (several hundred to well over 1000 feet) a point is reached in a given area at which room-and-pillar mining cannot economically be accomplished.

Water will normally affect operations only if standing and then will affect maintenance and breakdowns more than cycle times, assuming that the bottom is hard.

SELECTION OF CONVENTIONAL UNITS Conventional units may have advantages over continuous units where hard seams, gaseous seams, or variable seam heights are encountered. Since conventional units are lighter than continuous miners, marginal floor quality may also warrant the selection of conventional equipment. As seam heights decrease and tram time per ton becomes higher, continuous mining should exhibit an increasing advantage as moves are made twice as often with conventional (Figure 3).

Conventional units are generally more reliable and have a greater availability than continuous mines but also require better planning and coordination for efficient use.

INTERMITTENT HAULAGE Intermittent or modular haulage has been recognized as a bottleneck in materials handling in underground coal mining ever since the first shuttle cars were introduced. Conveyor schemes of many types have been introduced, lauded, and have faded away, while this seemingly inefficient method has remained. The reasons for this are primarily flexibility and reach. Flexibility is exhibited by the ability of the haulage unit to follow the miner or loader through

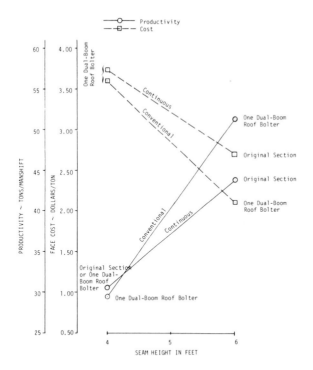

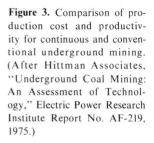

Figure 3. Comparison of production cost and productivity for continuous and conventional underground mining. (After Hittman Associates, "Underground Coal Mining: An Assessment of Technology," Electric Power Research Institute Report No. AF-219, 1975.)

any mining configuration and the ability to continue hauling even though one of the units is disabled. Reach is simply the ability to extend out from the dumping point as far as the miner must go. Continuous haulage schemes have always fallen short on one or both of these points.

Time studies and simulations of room-and-pillar mining systems indicate that change-out time will represent from 15 to 25 percent of the *available time for production*. (This is defined as the shift time less travel, face preparation, scheduled meetings, breakdowns, lunch, servicing, etc., that is, the time in which the units and personnel are actually capable of coal production.) In general, available time for production will range from 175 to 300 minutes per shift with an "average" value at 225 minutes. Thus, 30 to 60 minutes could be saved if suitable continuous haulage units were available. It must be recognized, however, that not all this time will be additional loading time. In general, this time will be distributed proportionally among the remaining loading and hauling activities.

Longwall mining Longwall mining developed in a similar fashion to the other deep mining methods but is based, as its name implies, on long coal panels (from 250 to 600 feet wide) that may be the order of 1500 feet long. The coal in these huge panels is mined by a cutting drum or coal plow which is winched along the face from the ends. The cutting tool cuts the entire height of the seam, and the broken coal falls on a chain conveyor that is parallel to the face and held against it by hydraulic jacks. Perpendicular to the face across the chain conveyor is a series of hydraulic roof supports that have cantilever beams extending over the conveyor.

The supports can be advanced forward as the face is mined. As the coal is mined and the support moved from beneath the roof, it is allowed to collapse directly behind the mining area.

Longwall mining still retains the room-and-pillar system in the entry development, a source of concern at increased depths of mining. A tract of coal is first blocked off by entries and then a longwall between the entries is mined back on a retreat system.

A shortwall system is somewhat similar to longwall. The difference is that in longwall the face length averages from 350 to 600 feet while in shortwall it is only 150 to 200 feet. However, there are notable differences in equipment employed between the two systems, primarily affecting the thickness of the coal mined on a single pass and also producing bidirectional mining on longwall faces but usually only unidirectional mining with shortwall.

While there are many reasons for deploying one system over another and each has to be picked on its own merits, the following is a capsule view of some of the trends. The oldest system in regular use has been the room-and-pillar system employing conventional equipment. This is because at the shallower bituminous and lignite seams mined in this country, a great deal of flexibility can be achieved with various modifications of the room-and-pillar system while still being able to support the top adequately. While a continuous miner was in use for driving miles of entries in Illinois in the 1920s, a detriment to continuous mining was the finer product which was not marketable in the then-prevailing domestic market, and it took the rise of the utility market in the post-World War II period plus better machine manufacturing technology producing greater reliability.

Continuous mining in room-and-pillar systems has made great strides because although the amount of production per shift may not be signficantly different than with conventional, the unit-shift tonnage is accomplished with fewer personnel, affecting greater economies. However, where a coarser product is still desired and the seam conditions are especially difficult to cut, the choice tips to conventional. Conventional mining is far from obsolete.

One of the most important factors influencing the choice of longwall is depth of seam. Since the vertical overburden pressure increases at a rate of 1.1 psi per foot of depth, entries must be driven narrower and pillars wider for roof control until a practical limit is reached for typical workings. Therefore, the immediate roof conditions influence longwall selection, mining taking place today in seams that formerly could not be worked with room-and-pillar system. However, uniformly thick and contiguous coal seams are a requirement for longwall and preclude its use in the mining of variable seams. Not only will faults and barrier areas preclude the use of longwall, but the presence of gas wells will also negate its use because of the need to leave 300-foot barrier pillars around each well.

Shortwalling can overcome some of the disadvantages of longwall. The shorter wall can be laid out more easily in a seam with greater variability and it also minimizes the financial risks as some of the equipment from the room-and-pillar system can be employed without having to start from scratch by purchasing all components of the system (in particular, the continuous mining machine and ancillary haulage equipment).

Longwall mining has had a long history in Europe where adverse conditions have frequently mandated its use. In the United States, this method has had to compete economically with the highly productive room-and-pillar systems. While longwall accounts for only 4 percent of present underground production, the deeper deposits and areas with poor conditions which must be mined in the future suggest that longwall will increase its share of production.

Longwall mining consists of driving one or more entries or gates approximately 300 to 600 feet apart, mining an interconnection, then mining the rib of the interconnection of a longwall; hence, the name *longwall* mining. The retreat system is used almost exclusively in the United States since the entries do not have to be maintained for travel in by the longwall face, thus simplifying support and ventilation. Modified advance systems, which do not require haulage through the caved-in areas or "gob," have been tried to minimize moving costs; however, the chain of pillars in the gob tended to squeeze and disrupt the airflow and the mirror-image effect of subsequent panels tended to confuse mechanics and wipe out most or all of the benefits anticipated.

Because of the time-dependent deterioration of rock and coal, the longer a given area must be supported the greater the likelihood of roof deterioration. Although the exact effect of time and speed of face advance on the caving characteristics of a longwall panel is somewhat controversial, it is agreed that a uniform rate of extraction without long periods of idleness is best. In addition, the gain in production from increased face length relative to the additional capital investment required decreases as the face length increases.

One of the major problems with longwall is being able to develop sufficient entries as well as to maintain them. With high-capacity jacks on short centers, roof control at the face is rarely a problem. The greatest difficulty exists in supporting the tail entries. The tail entry at the end of the active face is subjected to great ground pressures because of the superpositioning of two major abutment stresses at this point. First is the side abutment pressure resulting from the previously mined panel upon which is superimposed the face abutment from the active panel. This frequently results in such deterioration in the tail entries that considerable supports including cribs and hydraulic jacks must be installed. This then interferes with turnaround time and moving of the conveyor. In addition to the tail entry problem with such small pillars, only one entry remains in the gob area for bleeding if a three-entry system is used, and this generally deteriorates so badly as to be unusable. Thus, the tendency is to drive four entries with a large pillar located adjacent to one end of the face, providing a potential shear plane in the roof and caving to relieve the pressure on the edges of the panel. However, while this might improve roof conditions, with weak bottoms it could create severe heave conditions, and therefore the pillars are generally rearranged so that the two smaller pillars are placed between the large pillar and the active panel in the tail entries and act as yield pillars relieving pressure on the bottom.

In comparing production rates and operating costs with room-and-pillar costs, it must be remembered that longwall replaces only the rooming and pillaring portions of the former. Thus, longwall costs and production rates should only be compared with performances in the rooms and pillars where supply and operating costs are normally the lowest and production the highest for most miners. Viewed in this respect, longwall performance often is less spectacular, particularly when the high capital investment is considered.

Face width must be selected so that panel development can match the longwall extraction rate. Panel depths can also be used to balance development with panel extraction although one belt length is often a standard depth, again to save on capital. Capital costs are generally in excess of $1½ million for a longwall face 450 to 600 feet long.

NEW DEVELOPMENTS Longwall development has been rapid during the past decade. Shearer horsepower and support capacities have increased greatly, and pan and chain designs have been much improved. These trends will probably continue though at a slower rate in the future.

Future developments may include the semiautomation of prop advancement, allowing moves to be made from the head gate. Some means of moving the equipment for development, make it uncertain that longwall will account for a sizable longwall, but this development is probably well in the future.

With its potential for true continuous mining, high production rates, and apparent potential for automation, longwall should continue to grow. However, its inflexibility, high capital cost, and the fact that longwall requires auxiliary equipment for development, make it uncertain that longwall will account for a sizable amount of U.S. production for the remainder of this century.

Shortwall mining Shortwall mining can be considered to be a compromise between room and pillar and longwall, with both technical and economic reasons for the choice. First, if a company desires to change from room and pillar to some type of wall operation, a large capital investment is usually required without any assurances of its success. Therefore, rather than proceed directly to longwall with its huge capital outlay, a corporation may turn first to shortwall, since only the supports need to be added, the shuttle cars and continuous miners being utilized from existing room-and-pillar operations.

Second, however, there may be technical reasons for choosing shortwall over longwall. Many seams are relatively shallow and overlain by massive sandstones and limestones that cannot be broken. If a longwall face is established under such conditions, props of prohibitive size would be required.

The shortwall system probably cannot be adopted as widely as either longwall or continuous mining room-and-pillar systems. It is suspected that poorer roof conditions would permit the mining of such a wide web (10 feet). Recently, a number of manufacturers have produced narrower miners, and an 8-foot mined web is now practicable and should improve conditions. However, probably a 5-foot width would be better, but this would undoubtedly preclude the use of shuttle cars.

Shortwall mining being largely experimental, considerable development work remains for optimizing shortwall systems, but the successes with three such units to date would indicate that considerable effort is warranted.

Comparison Comparing the several types of underground mining, longwall operation calls for the highest capital cost but yields the greatest productivity per worker and permits the highest percentage extraction. Thus, properly used, it has the best potential for low total cost per ton. However, it is only properly used where the roof will break safely, where the seam thickness is between 4 and 7 feet and quite uniform, and where the seam does not contain resistant or abrasive partings.

Continuous mining requires the lowest investment for a given capacity and under proper conditions can provide somewhat higher productivity per worker than conventional mining. However, as noted above, it loses this advantage when a compatible conveyor system cannot be used and is at a disadvantage where the seam contains tough or abrasive partings. Also, it is somewhat more vulnerable to poor roof conditions, because it must commonly work farther ahead of bolted areas than conventional mining or else stop digging while the roof is bolted. Probably it has a somewhat better future than conventional mining in large mines where seam conditions are good, particularly after more effective bridge or extendible conveyors are developed. In the hands of many operators or with poor seam conditions, conventional mining excels, and this is likely to be a good competitor for the foreseeable future.

The seam conditions exert a strong influence on mining methods, as found in a relatively recent study of West Virginia deep mines.[1] Seam thickness exerts an important influence on mining methods, with conventional mining concentrated in thinner seams, mixed conventional and continuous in intermediate seams, and the largest percentage of continuous mining in thick seams (Figure 4). Continuous mining has fewer workers in a face crew and higher output, thereby giving higher productivity (Table 1). Figure 5 shows the estimated ranges of the available percentage of equipment availability for conventional and continuous mining. The figure leads to the conclusion that conventional mining is generally more efficient in seams less than 65 inches high, while continuous mining is more effective in seams of 75- to 80-inch thickness and greater. The different mining systems are essentially comparable at thicknesses from 65 to 75 inches.

Although longwall mining accounts for a rather small percentage of American coal production at present, it appears to have promise for the future.

There are two vitally-important advantages to longwall mining today. The first is that ventilation problems are greatly reduced, as the air must be coursed-over 5 to 7 or more working places in conventional or continuous systems.

Based on actual experience, another main advantage is that men with little or no mining experience can be trained much more quickly than is possible with the other types of coal mining. If the current shortage of skilled miners continues, this can be vitally important.[2]

Along the same lines, it may be noted that:

New concepts being considered may make longwalling still more productive, while aiding roof control at the same time. Two examples would be: (1) simultaneous mining of development pillars, and (2) shortwall mining of the development pillars, using continuous miners and special jacks.

[1] K. E. McElhattan, "Mining Efficiency and Equipment Analysis as Affected by Mining Conditions", presented at 1969 Annual Meeting of AIME, Washington, D.C., Feb. 16-20, 1969, Preprint No. 69AU50.

[2] Mining and Preparation in 1971, *Coal Age*, pp. 66–71, February 1972.

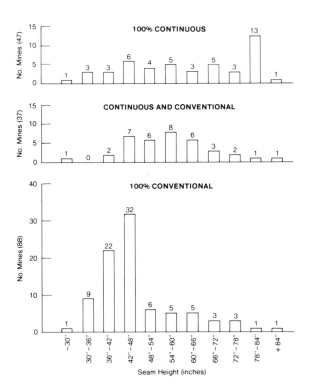

Figure 4. Mining methods of 172 West Virginia mines by seam heights. (After K.E. McElhattan, "Mining Efficiency and Equipment Analysis as Affected by Mining Conditions," AIME Preprint No. 69AU50, 1969.)

Well-plugging tests carried out last year by the Bureau [of Mines], and a coal company may mean quite a bit to those operating longwalls. Present law states that abandoned oil or gas well must be surrounded by a pillar of coal to protect miners. This might complicate the operation of a longwall not to mention the loss of production. A survey indicated that there are 80,000 of these abandoned wells in the West Virginia coal fields alone. The tests revealed that a plugged well could be mined through without any gas release.[1]

Should these tests prove more generally applicable, then the pace of longwall development would be further accelerated.[2]

The *products* from the three main deep mining methods were studied recently.[3] It was noted that conventional mining has fewer fine particles and dust than either continuous method studied. Further, it was pointed out that:

Any change in mining method that results in a coarser product at the coal face, has at least three potential advantages:
1. The decreased surface areas retard methane diffusion;
2. The quantities of dust in the respirable range [are] reduced and
3. The reduction in energy consumed leads to more efficient extraction.

[1] *Ibid.*
[2] *Ibid.*
[3] R. L. Schmidt, W. H. Engelmann, and R. R. Fumanti, A Comparison of Borer, Ripper, and Conventional Mining Products in Illinois No. 6 Coal, *US Bur. Mines, Rep. Invest. No.* 7687, 1972.

Table 1 Estimated productivity of conventional vs continuous mining 48″,60″, and 70″ seam height

Production data	Conven-tional	Con-tinuous	Conven-tional	Con-tinuous	Conven-tional	Con-tinuous
Seam height, inches (3)	48″	48″	60″	60″	72″	72″
Width of place, feet	20	20	20	20	20	20
Depth of cut, feet	8	18	8	18	8	18
Tons per cut	25.6	58	32	72	38	86
Cuts per Shift	20	8.7	20	8.3	18	8.2
Tons per shift	512	500	640	600	680	700
Work Minutes per Shift	400	400	400	400	400	400
Face Crew						
Continuous miner	—	1	—	1	—	1
Loading machine	2	1	1	1	2	1
Shuttle cars	2	2	2	2	2	2
Cutting machine	2	—	2	—	2	—
Drill	1	—	1	—	1	—
Shooting	1	—	1	—	1	—
Roof bolt machine	2	2	2	2	2	2
Total face crew	10	6	10	6	10	6
Man Minutes Per Cut (1)						
Continuous miner	—	31.0	—	33.0	—	33.5
Loading machine	30.0	31.0	30.0	33.0	34.0	33.5
Shuttle cars	30.0	62.0	30.0	66.0	34.0	67.0
Cutting	30.0	—	30.0	—	35.0	—
Drilling	13.0	—	13.0	—	15.0	—
Shooting	17.0	—	17.0	—	20.0	—
Roofing bolting	30.0	72.0	30.0	72.0	30.0	75.6
Total man minutes per cut (1)	150.0	196.0	150.0	204.0	168.0	209.6
Man minutes per shift at the face (1)	3000	17000	3000	1700	3024	1720
Man minutes per ton (1)	5.86	3.38	4.69	2.86	4.42	2.44
Tons per man shift (2)	51.2	83.3	64.0	100.0	68.0	116.6

(1) Working at the Face—Does not include moving or delays
(2) Tons per 8 hour Man Shift
(3) Good mining conditions suitable for either conventional or continuous

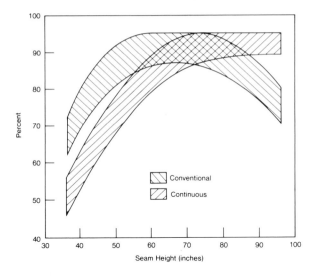

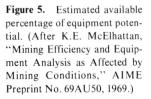

Figure 5. Estimated available percentage of equipment potential. (After K.E. McElhattan, "Mining Efficiency and Equipment Analysis as Affected by Mining Conditions," AIME Preprint No. 69AU50, 1969.)

It seems clear that the more mechanized mining methods contribute both to larger methane release from certain coal beds and to increased quantities of dust; both can present hazards to workers.

Ventilation. In ordinary industrial ventilation applications, ducts are chosen to provide the most effective air distribution system and a fan is selected to operate at its maximum efficiency with this static system. In mining, the excavated openings in coal constitute the ventilation circuit. These are constantly being extended or reduced as mining progresses. Therefore, the ventilation system in underground coal mining is dynamic, resulting in a range of operating conditions which make planning and maintenance extremely difficult.

The starting point for ventilation design is the desired quantities of air at the face and the methane liberation rate for the seam being mined.

The primary function of mine ventilation is to dilute, render harmless, and carry away dangerous accumulations of gas and dust from the working environment. As a result of mining at greater depths, poorer natural conditions, a higher degree of mechanization, and greater concern for miner health and safety, more rigid ventilation requirements have been enacted in recent legislation. Newer continuous mining equipment operating at greater depth, advancing more rapidly, and producing a finer product results in a higher liberation of gas and dust. At the same time, the greater bulk of the machine and the need to maintain necessary auxiliary functions make ventilation implementation even more difficult.

Under federal law, a minimum velocity of 60 feet per minute in working places is required, and respirable dust levels (-10 micrometers) cannot exceed 2 milligrams per cubic meter average per shift as measured on a standard collecting instrument. Methane accumulations are not allowed to exceed 1 percent in the working area. The minimum volume of air at the last open crosscut has been increased to 900 cubic feet per minute, with 300 cubic feet per minute required at the face.

These more stringent face requirements are coupled with regulations which make distribution more difficult. Belt conveyors cannot be placed in main airways, and the maximum velocity of air on trolley entries is limited to 250 feet per minute.

Splitting the air is necessary for safety as well as minimal power cost. Placing each working section on a separate split ensures that each crew will have a fresh air supply, uncontaminated by dust and gas accumulated on a previously ventilated section. Splitting also has the desirable effect of sectionalizing portions of the mine and minimizing the likelihood of an explosion propagating from one section to another. Finally, by regulating splits, better control of local ambient conditions is possible. Without regulation the constantly moving sections have resistances which are too variable to otherwise provide reliable ventilation. Within a split, if both development and a pillar line must be ventilated, mining should be planned in such a manner that the development is ventilated first and the pillar line last so the return air passes directly into the gob, and not vice versa.

In operating mines, it is common to lose 50 to 70 percent of the air between the fan(s) and last open crosscuts on the working selection where the major job of diluting and carrying away gases and dusts is conducted. The more poorly maintained airways result in even greater fugitive air losses, causing greater quantities of air to be handled by the fan at higher pressures with resultant high power costs.

Control devices used to course the air through the mine are stoppings, overcasts, and regulators. Stoppings are walls constructed to separate intake and return airways and are usually composed of concrete or cinder blocks. Construction methods used are either cemented joints or dry stacking with a subsequent plaster coating. Overcasts permit the crossing of intake and return air by an over-and-under arrangement. Walls of the overcasts are concrete block, and the roof is generally steel beams supporting concrete block or precast slabs. A secondary use for overcasts is to balance pressures in separate parallel return entries. Regulators are used to control and redistribute the airflow through the mine. These usually consist of a frame with a sliding door and are arranged so that each split is controlled by one regulator.

Ground control. Together with mine ventilation, ground control affects the productivity of coal more than any other factor. Not only are delays incurred during production to permit normal support installation, but hazards and production losses due to accidents are great.

Basically, parallel mine excavations are made with intervening blocks or pillars to withstand the major overburden pressures which may be considered to be 1.1 psi per foot of depth. Spans must be limited to prevent destructive stresses in the intermediate top so that the overburden over the excavation may be transferred through an arching effect to the pillars. Thus, limited spans (maximum 20 feet by law) and pillars of adequate size are the keys to roof control. However, since the immediate top over the excavation may be so weak as to preclude complete stability at any span, artificial supports will be required.

There are too many imponderables to be able to design a foolproof mining system, and therefore artificial supports will be required to support excavations. In fact, because roof conditions can change so quickly, it is absolutely necessary to invoke the law which states that no one is to go under unsupported roof. It is well-documented that most injuries and fatalities occur under so-called good roof because personnel do not apply proper caution.

Timber supports were the oldest method of support used in coal mines. A simple prop with a flat cap piece and wedge to install it tightly frequently was all that was required, and a support pattern of 4 by 4 feet was common. However, if the top is weak and brittle, the roof will fail between props and therefore larger headers might be employed. Over roadways, where minimum spans of 8 feet are required for maneuvering, three-piece sets would be employed. While wooden sets are common, steel beams and channel irons and rails are also used to some degree.

Since shortly after World War II, the use of roof bolts in coal mines has become widespread. Roof bolts have been more successful than timber props. If roof bolts are inserted immediately in the roof with sufficient installed tension before the beds can separate, a monolithic beam of thickness equal to the length of the bolt will be established, creating a much stronger structure. Although the thickness of the beam has been established by nature and is determined by the spacing of bedding planes, its effective thickness may be made greater if the individual beds are not allowed to separate, and therefore the overlying bed acts as a monolithic beam. For this reason, roof bolts can be considered an active type of support whereas wooden timbers are passive, i.e., they do not prevent failure but instead support the broken material.

Hydraulic props have gained favor in recent years as a support. In addition to being able to provide a setting load, they have good rigidity and strength and can be provided with bypass or yield valves to prevent self-destruction. Finally, in the longwall system, they can be provided with double-acting rams for self-advancing. In room-and-pillar full-extraction systems, they are easily triggered and withdrawn remotely.

Mine expansion. Faced with a national goal of energy self-sufficiency and large resources of coal amenable to underground mining, it must be decided whether to expand existing facilities or open new mines. There are obvious advantages to obtaining additional production by expanding a mine but this has some serious limitations. Assuming a mine is producing 5000 tons per day from 10 machine units on each of two operating shifts per day, it is not realistic to expand this to 10,000 tons by adding an additional 10 machine units. Because of the interaction among all unit and auxiliary operations, a change such as this creates a domino effect. That is, more units require more air, power, haulage capability, etc., that may not be achieved as cheaply as opening a new mine. For example, it is very difficult to drive parallel entries since the space may not be there and closer spacing of air shafts is expensive. The haulage may have to be completely junked and replaced. For example, 6- or 8-ton cars hauling on 60-pound rail with smaller locomotives may have been adequate to serve the 10 units. However, doubling the production would probably necessitate going to larger cars, say 20 tons, which would require larger rail, better ballast, and alignment, and possibly greater top clearance, not to mention larger locomotives, more passing tracks, better signaling systems, etc. Another possibility would be to go to full three-shift operation. Again, however, there are some offsetting disadvantages. Invariably, a preventive maintenance program, usually on the third shift, would have to be abandoned, eventually leading to a greater number of mechanical delays. Supplying the mine and doing dead work such as belt extension, track laying, etc., would have to be done on a production shift, again creating problems. A viable compromise is a partial third shift with the crews rotated nightly so that maintenance and supplying could be done. In any event, it may be more economical to open a new mine but the 5- to 12- year lead time for development must be considered. In the near future a 15 to 20 percent increase in product is possible with mine expansion, but over the long run, new mines must go in production.

New Deep Mining Technology to the Year 2000

No large degree of innovative substitution in mining technology is expected in the next quarter century; this topic is discussed in detail in Chapter 6. One very strong reason against wholesale technology substitution is the tendency for mining operators to retain their machines in place as long as possible. Evidence for this is found in the unwillingness of some operators to replace their nonpermissible machines.[1] New machines are a substantial financial burden and have high set-up costs. Since mining systems are often tailored to the capabilities of the hardware, a change in hardware type frequently means a redesign of the mine system. The continued use of loading machines behind continuous miners and of all-track haulage systems are examples of operations which maintain original mining systems despite improvements in equipment that would permit new systems to be installed.

A shortage of manufacturing capacity has delayed delivery of new equipment in recent years. This situation was largely corrected by an expansion of production capacity by manufacturing companies. Still, with design and construction capacity fully utilized, new machines can be made only by discontinuing to make existing units. There is no incentive for this switch as long as operators continue to use existing units and replace or repair them. Instead, there is every incentive to continue present patterns of manufacturing unchanged because of a steady and secure market.

Yet another reason for slow substitution is the conservative approach of operators and miners to innovation. Examined fully, these fears are quite rational. Because of the inherently high risks (capital, as well as health and safety) in coal mining, operators and miners like to have good proof of performance for a new machine. There is no competitive edge which results from being first. This wait-and-see attitude, of necessity, results in long lead times.

The future. Although mining methods in the year 2000 will have a similar appearance to those of today, new machinery will incorporate many changes. Indeed, mining methods in those mines which are designed and opened at that date by in-

[1]Permissible mine equipment is that formally approved by the U.S. Bureau of Mines after having passed the inspections, the explosion tests, and other requirements for use in gassy mines. U.S. Bureau of Mines, "Dictionary of Mining, Mineral, and Related Terms," p. 809, 1968.

novative operators may be significantly different from the normal methods of mining in vogue at that time. Factors influencing the rate of introduction of innovations will continue to be the demand for deep-mined coal, the availability of capital, and thus the rate of opening of new mines and replacement of old mines.

The mix, or percentage makeup, of mining methods that will exist in the year 2000 based on knowledge of present systems is estimated. It is projected that room-and-pillar mining will represent 70 to 80 percent of all underground U.S. coal production. This percentage will be divided, with continuous taking 50 to 60 percent of all deep mining, or approximately 65 to 85 percent of room and pillar, and conventional taking from 20 to 30 percent of all deep mining. Longwall mining will have 10 to 25 percent of the total with the upper figure being reached only if there is a thick-seam adaptation available. Shortwall and other novel methods may have up to 10 percent of the total.

R&D opportunities. The foregoing assessment of present underground mining technology suggests several opportunities for R&D to improve operations. A brief summary of selected technical factors is presented below, followed by a discussion of potentials for R&D in the application of technology.

New technology In looking for improvements in underground mining, intermittent haulage is usually examined first and place-changing delays next. Yet conventional mining appears destined to remain with both problems since blasting requires that no machinery be present near the coal face.

One alternative might be the development of long-hole blasting. This would require the use of drills which could sense the floor and roof positions; such a drill has been tested and apparently works well. Since cutter bars and chains could not follow rolling bottoms and would become unwieldy in any case, the blasting pattern would more likely follow a burn cut where one or more large holes are drilled to serve as free faces. The feasibility of shooting holes 20 to 100 feet deep would have to be demonstrated, of course.

Should this prove feasible, a second problem—roof support—would immediately be faced. Unless continuous-support methods could be developed, place changing would still be necessary; with continuous roof support it is possible to envision a loading machine advancing 100 feet through broken material, although a third problem would be to ensure that all explosives are indeed discharged. Continuous transportation could then be feasible since place changing would be rare.

On a shorter term, research is currently underway to develop units which will combine the functions of several conventional units. Among these are self-loading shuttle cars and combination cutter-drilling machines. While these will probably not serve to increase production, productivity per worker would increase and section management would be simplified with these units.

More research needs to be conducted in the area of applied geology and rock mechanics for the better design of underground methods. A better understanding of stress in the rock overlying excavations as well as in the pillars and their effects would lead to more rational design. The lack of suitable instrumentation underground has not permitted confirmation or rejection of the various ground-support theories.

There are two basic philosophies with regard to roof control underground. The first is the development of an early-warning monitoring system so that proper remedial action can take place prior to an accident, while the other philosophy is to treat all roof as dangerous, and thus provide support. While there has been considerable research conducted to obtain monitoring devices, the results have been very discouraging. Because of the large number of variables, it is questionable whether a fully reliable system of monitoring can be reasonably secured.

The use of supports is a positive way to prevent roof accidents. However, existing supports must have improved effectiveness and new techniques must be developed in conjunction with the mining scheme. Presently, too much production is lost in place changes required with today's support schemes. Methods must be developed to permit the continuous miner to remain in one place to mine a lift greater than the 10 to 20 feet presently employed. Some combination of a surge car with temporary canopy support and integral roof bolters combined with remote operation of the continuous miner ahead of it should allow for concurrent support with mining and an increase in machine availability, thus improving production greatly.

To eliminate delays within a cut it appears that the fan should be mounted on the continuous miner, the atmosphere rendered inert, or the gas and dust suppressed prior to mining. Mounting the fan on the miner not only will eliminate the job of moving the fan between cuts and extending the tubing at the face within a cut, it will also permit the use of collapsible tubing out by the miner since this tubing will be pressurized. It is likely that this tubing could rest on the ground during the cycle and simply be rolled up and stacked on the miner when it is trammed from cut to cut.

Experiments with mining in an inert atmosphere have been attempted with personnel dressed in "space units" with self-contained life-support units. While this eliminates exposure to dust and renders methane inexplosive, the workers are subject to additional dangers from roof falls since their senses are impaired and they are exposed to the sudden failure of their artificial atmosphere. It appears that a more hostile environment has been substituted for one which, except for the danger of an explosion, was less hostile. Thus, it seems that automated mining must be a forerunner to the inert-atmosphere concept.

It would appear that degasification and/or water or chemical infusion to suppress gas and dust formation during mining are worthwhile avenues of pursuit. Several degasification projects are in the experimental stages. These would primarily prevent the stopping of mining due to the failure of the ventilation current to dilute the gas below 1 percent. The effective area of degasification wells remains to be proven.

Water cutting of the coal would appear to offer the advantages of a low dust formation rate and safety from explosions. Several research groups are currently looking at water cutting.

To eliminate the inefficiency and danger of running equipment through brattice lines, transparent material may be effective. Air curtains are also being tested to determine if they are capable of diverting air within a mine.

Technology applications There are several areas for investigation in the application of technology.

1. Given the variability in mining conditions and resulting uncertainty in operations, it would be worthwhile to carry out an analysis of the relative costs and benefits of alternative regulatory approaches to the several participants in underground mining. A principal purpose of such an analysis would be to determine the impact of uncertainty in natural conditions upon the likelihood of attainment of performance standards.

2. Hypothesizing that systematic geological information would be valuable in guiding ongoing operations, it would be worthwhile to carry out an analysis of the manner in which such data might be routinely collected and employed. With mining already a complex place-change process, can sufficient time be found to enable geologic mapping to proceed without disruption of the production cycle and exposure of workers to hazards? Assuming the data can be collected, how will it be factored back to guide the operations? To what extent will training (or retraining) of workers be required to perform the needed tasks? What can (or should) be the relative roles of government, industry, labor, and the mining profession in such activities?

3. Recognizing that many mining machines and facilities are continued in use well beyond their efficient operational lifetime, it would be worthwhile to evaluate the relative costs and benefits of encouraging more effective modernization of operations. A principal purpose of this evaluation would be to examine the manner of transfer of existing and new technology. For example, should government establish the equivalent of an "urban renewal" program for underground mines by purchasing old equipment that is in use only because of "grandfather" clauses and assisting operators in acquiring modern replacement equipment? Alternatively, what programs or incentives could be devised by government to encourage equipment manufacturers and operators to upgrade obsolete equipment and accelerate the transfer of technology resulting from advanced R&D? What can be done to deal with the concerns of organized labor over health and safety issues as well as job security in the introduction of new technology?

4. Much practical information about underground mining is gained only by experience of workers, and while valid for given conditions, is difficult to relate to new or different circumstances. It would be worthwhile to intensify efforts to place this knowledge on an analytical basis so that training of new workers could be improved and the benefits from such information could be more widespread.

5. For the immediate future, the focus of underground coal mining is likely to be in the East. Much of this development appears likely to be undertaken with technology much like that of the present day. However, there are substantial underground reserves in the West that appear to require new technology in their development, and it would be worthwhile to analyze the significance of

this fact. For example, do western underground reserves offer the prospect of development of new or improved mining methods that can be, in turn, adapted to upgrade eastern operations? What is the relationship between western coal reserves projected for surface development and those requiring underground mining? What innovative mining systems and approaches to regulation can be devised to maximize resource recovery and minimize adverse environmental impact?

External Effects of Deep Mining

Deep mining causes impacts on the physical environment that are matters of public concern; these include (among others) acid mine drainage, subsidence, mine fires, and disposal of wastes from coal preparation or treatment. Important as these impacts may be, they pale in comparison to the public concern over the social effects of deep mining, in particular the health, safety, and well-being of miners as they pursue their occupation. Salient aspects of the health and safety issue are presented next to complete the discussion of deep mining.

Accidents. Deep mining for coal is among the most hazardous occupations in the nation, if not *the* most hazardous. In the early 1970s, large deep mines in the United States had about 0.5 fatalities per million tons of production. Small deep mines were four times more hazardous, having nearly two fatalities per million tons. Deep mining was similarly hazardous in terms of nonfatal injuries, with about 75 nonfatal injuries per million tons of production.

There have been many attempts at the state and federal levels to legislate conditions leading to increased safety in deep mines. For example, the West Virginia Coal Mine Safety Law requires certification of miners in an attempt to ensure reasonable safety to the miner and fellow employees. To be certified, miners must have at least "6 months practical experience as a miner or as a miner's apprentice." In a personal communication, the Director of the Department of Mines pointed out that some large deep mining companies conduct on-the-job training programs for their new employees. Mainly, however, these large companies seek experienced miners so as to maintain production and safety standards. Prospective new workers unable to demonstrate education or experience to qualify them for certification or apprenticeships at large mines can get this experience only by working at smaller mines. As noted, smaller deep mines have fatality rates four times than that for large deep mines and nonfatal injury rates that are about the same as the large mines.

Many prospective new miners thus receive training only by surviving a testing period in small mines, after which they can be certified by the state and, if fortunate, advance to a job with a larger, more highly productive, and, presumably, safer mine. However, it is important to bear in mind that in the process of becoming certified, the worker who enters a small mine becomes part of a working crew, a close-knit group in which individuals depend on their buddies for their well-being in the mines; patterns of friendship are often developed that extend beyond working associations.[1] Many miners will be reluctant to break up such associations in a larger, less independent (but perhaps safer) mine. Consequently, many miners who enter small mines may well remain there, exposed to demonstrably greater hazards over the lifetime of the operation, or their own, whichever ends first. It remains to be seen whether improvements in deep mine health and safety programs in response to new laws and regulations will lead to changes in these proportions. However, it seems likely that the present relations of injury pattern will persist, at least for the short term.

Immediate deep mine hazards include roof falls, explosive hazards from methane and/or coal dust, and equipment-related accidents. Chronic hazards include black lung and other debilitating effects of deep mining. Although both hazards must be included in a comprehensive program of R&D to improve coal mine health and safety, the following discussion emphasizes operational hazards as being perhaps more immediately influenced through improved technology or practice.

In a study completed for the U.S. Bureau of Mines in 1971, Theodore Barry and Associates reported on operational deep mine hazards. The major findings of this important study are:

Many operators view safety training as an expensive luxury that detracts from vital production time: [consequently, at large numbers of mines] probably as much as half the total mine population, [safety training is] virtually non-existent.

Experienced miners often exercise their seniority to bid onto the day shift and away from swing and midnight shift positions. This results in a disproportionate number of new and relatively inexperienced miners working these shifts. The absentee and turnover problems . . . are compounded for these shifts, especially midnight, with a corresponding increase in the fatality rate.

[For a 50 mine sample] normalized figures showed that 19.8 percent of non-roof fall fatalities occurred between 8 A.M. and 4 P.M.; 22.2 percent occurred between 4 P.M. and 12 A.M.; and 58 percent occurred between 12 A.M. and 8 A.M. *If these estimates are true for the industry, the term "graveyard shift" has real meaning in the mining industry."* [Emphasis added.]

Experienced miners exercise seniority by bidding away from [jobs such as roof bolting] because they are dangerous, difficult, uncomfortable [dust and noise] and pay less than other crew positions [more directly related to production].

The foreman's instructions seem to be followed in most cases. The overwhelming majority of incidents in which the supervisor's instructions were contrary to federal regulations were roof fall fatalities involving non-compliance with the roof support plan . . . . This suggests that many first line supervisors apparently are not convinced that unsupported roof is extremely dangerous.[2]

The first 1 to 3 weeks of a job are extremely hazardous when compared to a worker's career at a particular task. This danger becomes even greater when the trainee is working in a highly responsible crew-dependent position such as roof bolting or shuttle car operation. [Figure 6.]

Fatalities were about evenly divided among conventional and continuous mining.

Small mines had more than 15 percent of total injuries occurring during the first week of job experience.

[1]E. E. Knipe, and H. M. Lewis, "The Impact of Coal Mining of the Traditional Mountain Sub-Culture: A Case of Peasantry Gained and Peasantry Lost," paper presented at 1969 Meeting of Southern Anthropological Society, New Orleans, La., Mar. 14, 1969.

[2]This finding appears consistent with industry practice to improve the quality of produced coal through selective mining. "Frequently it has been found necessary to leave part of the bed at the top to form a coal roof . . . until the cut has been loaded out." J. C. Anderson, J. V. Leonard, and C. T. Holland, New Coal Preparation, Chap. 6, Leonard and Mitchell (eds.), in "Coal Preparation," AIME, New York, 1968.

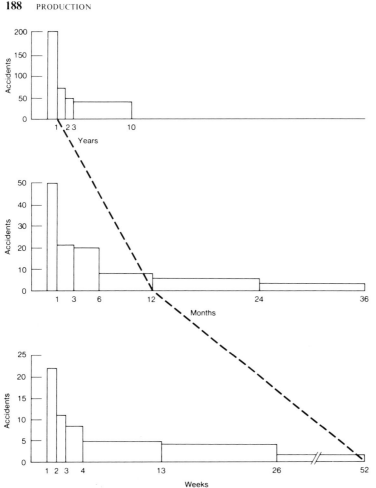

Figure 6. Task experience for all accidents compared on a yearly, monthly, and weekly basis. (After Theodore Barry & Association, "Industrial Engineering Study of Hazards Associated with Underground Coal Mine Production," prepared for U.S. Bureau of Mines, 1971.)

One of the most fundamental adjustments a new miner must make, and one which may contribute in some part to higher injury rates for such personnel, is to a working environment in which available light is relatively limited. Therefore, in addressing the reduction of accidents, better illumination deserves serious investigation.

Illumination. While the technology of mining coal has evolved during the past 30 years, most of this work is literally performed in the dark, because mine illumination has not progressed beyond the miner's cap lamp. Bockosh[1] pointed out that:

[1]G. R. Bockosh, "Mine Illumination," presented at 1st Symposium on Underground Mining, NCA/BCR Coal Conference and EXPO II, Louisville, Ky., Oct. 21-23, 1975.

Mine illumination today consists solely of the miner's cap lamp and in some cases, machine head lamps. Although the incandescent cap lamp has performed admirably in the past as a reliable source of light, its narrow beam of light provides essentially no peripheral vision. In an environment where hazards may present themselves from roof, floor, or rib, peripheral vision becomes essential. The introduction of additional lighting in the working place will provide this needed improvement in the miner's ability to visually detect potentially dangerous situations before an accident occurs. Also, the additional lighting effectively improves the working environment, causing better employee morale.

The miner's cap lamp provides very limited illumination. With the face area illuminated to approximately the same level as that provided by the cap lamp for close tasks, the miner would suffer a loss in peripheral vision only when leaving the face area. This would reduce problems in adapting to lighting conditions. Unfortunately, U.S. mining experience with area illumination has been unsatisfactory in the past because of problems with glare and adaptation. At present, however, progress with fluorescent lighting, mercury-vapor lamps, and high-pressure sodium-vapor lamps in recent years offers promise that "soft" light of low glare may be employed to illuminate the major working areas of underground coal mines in the near future. The ability to see one's surroundings more clearly should benefit both miner safety and production.

Longer-term risks. Hazards of death or physical injury associated with some discrete event or accident during operations are not the only risks to the well-being of workers who pursue occupations in coal production. Less obvious but equally as serious hazards stem from the long-term exposure of workers to conditions associated with production operations, with the result often being an impaired ability to perform basic bodily functions such as breathing or hearing. A brief discussion of the apparent causes of these disabilities is given below in terms of their immediate agents, dust and noise.

Dust Production of coal, especially in underground mines, results in the generation of many fine coal particles, or dust.

> Inhalation of dust has long been recognized as a health hazard leading to pulmonary diseases such as coal workers' pneumoconiosis [CWP] . . . CWP is the most severe health and safety problem facing the coal mining industry today, for the number of permanent disabilities and deaths of coal miners due to CWP is 3.5 times the disabilities and deaths due to *all* other mine accidents (1964-1970 Pennsylvania data). [Original emphasis.][1]

The mining method employed has a direct influence upon dust production. Courtney pointed out that "continuous mining machines were designed to mine coal at a fast rate. They are very efficient mining machines. However, by using blunt high-speed bits, they probably are the best machines for forming dust that could be invented, except for a grinding stone."[2]

---

[1] W. G. Courtney, "New Developments in Respirable Dust Control," presented at 1st Symposium on Underground Mining, NCA/BCR Coal Conference and EXPO II, Louisville, Ky., Oct. 21-23, 1975.

[2] *Ibid.*

Research by the U.S. Bureau of Mines shows that continuous mining yields approximately 5000 grams of respirable dust at the face per ton of mined coal. About 2 grams of this dust becomes airborne at the face, and the remainder adheres to the broken coal. The amount of dust produced varies among different coal seams, but the basic explanation for such differences remains to be determined.

Considerable investigation of technology to limit dust production or to control dust that is produced has been underway in the United States and other countries for many years. Laboratory studies by the Bureau of Mines show that the formation of airborne respirable dust is reduced greatly as the bit's depth of cut increases. It was found that dust formed by a 1-inch deep cut was about 5 percent of that formed with a ¼-inch deep cut and about 20 percent of that formed with a ½-inch cut. The angle of cut did not make any difference in the amount of dust generated. Furthermore, reduction in cutting speed can also result in a significant reduction in dust production. The combination of increased depth of cut and lower cutting speeds may lead to significantly lower rates of dust production.

Reduction in the amount of coal dust produced in mining is an essential step in dust control; if less dust is produced, the problems of dust suppression should be lessened. However, it will probably be impossible to prevent dust production entirely. Therefore, means of dust control will continue to be required. Methods employed at present include water sprays, secondary ventilation, various collection devices and/or materials, and personnel protective equipment. The variety of control methods is dictated by the diversity of mining operations; it is unlikely that a single technique will be suitable for all circumstances.

Aggressive pursuit is required of means to limit dust production and to control what dust is produced. The urgency of this need is evidenced by statistics maintained by the Bureau of Mines showing that between 10 and 15 percent of working underground coal miners suffer from pneumoconiosis.[1] At present, this amounts to from 15,000 to nearly 23,000 workers.[2] Unless the percentage of work force affected by pneumoconiosis can be reduced significantly by the preventive and control measures noted above, an increased work force necessary to accomplish expanded production could lead to substantial increases in the numbers of workers afflicted with this disease. It is difficult to estimate the potential magnitude of the problem, owing to uncertainty whether the amount of underground mining practiced with today's technology will retain its present share. If so, it is possible that the numbers of workers suffering from pneumoconiosis could fall in the range from 30,000 to 46,000 (if no improvement in dust control is realized and projected expansion in production takes place).

Noise Coal production, as noted in earlier parts of this chapter, employs machinery to a considerable degree; this machinery typically emits a great deal of noise in routine use. "Undoubtedly the noisiest location in an underground coal mine is at the working face. The primary activity at the face, which is the brute force extraction of coal, requires a tremendous amount of mechanical energy. Un-

---

[1]Cited in *Coal Age,* July 1976.

[2]The U.S. Bureau of Mines reports the average number of personnel working daily during 1976 in underground coal mines was about 152,900.

fortunately, a byproduct of this force expenditure is the generation of noise."[1]

Typical variations in noise level and operating times for underground face equipment are shown in Figure 7. It was found by the Mining Enforcement and Safety Administration (MESA) that the average noise levels between different makes of the same machine type are relatively small. Thus the noise of a given machine type is essentially independent of the manufacturer or of varying operating conditions.

The effect of noise on mine workers is to impair hearing, and can result in permanent hearing loss. It was found by the National Institute for Occupational Safety and Health (NIOSH) that coal miners have measurably worse hearing on the average than workers not subjected to excessive occupational noise (Figure 8). The figure shows that coal miners in every age group have worse hearing than other people of the same age.

Reduction of the noise intensity of the underground mining environment is essential to safeguard workers against the risk of permanent hearing impairment or loss. MESA noted that "obviously, the equipment manufacturers are the key to keeping the equipment operators in compliance [with noise level standards]. Redesigned mining equipment, which will produce lower levels of noise, is needed." However, such redesigns will be difficult to implement. Manufacturers need firm guidelines as to tolerable levels of noise, and the assurance that they will not be altered greatly. Roughly 5 years is typically required for major redesign of mining equipment; at least for the near term, noise control in underground mining will be forced to rely on attenuation of noise produced by existing equipment. The

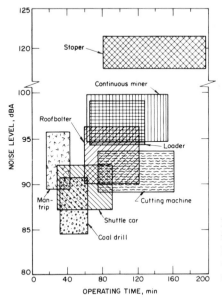

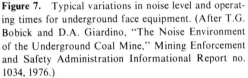

Figure 7. Typical variations in noise level and operating times for underground face equipment. (After T.G. Bobick and D.A. Giardino, "The Noise Environment of the Underground Coal Mine," Mining Enforcement and Safety Administration Informational Report no. 1034, 1976.)

[1]T. G. Bobick and D. A. Giardino, "The Noise Environment of the Underground Coal Mine," Mining Enforcement and Safety Administration Informational Report no. 1034, 26 pages, 1976.

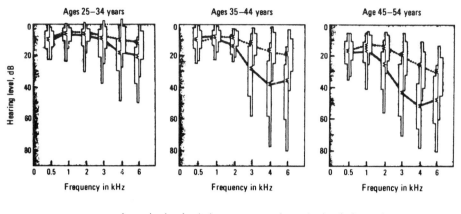

Average hearing of coal miners ·········· Average hearing of other people

Figure 8. Average hearing of coal miners and other people. (After NIOSH, cited in *Coal Age*, p. 154, July 1976.)

goal of a quieter underground mining environment can be approached eventually only by shifting to widespread use of inherently quieter machines.

Assessment of the Future of Deep Coal Mining

This review of the state of the art of deep mining technology would be incomplete without an assessment of its possible future. Present production is nearly evenly divided between conventional and continuous mining, with a relatively small amount contributed by longwall or shortwall methods. Roughly 20 years was required from the introduction of continuous mining until it achieved about half the total deep coal production. If this pattern is repeated by longwall technology, then it will be early in the 1990s before longwall deep mining accounts for comparable amounts of coal production. While the pace of introduction of longwall technology could be accelerated through government action[1] or incentives, it does not appear likely that the general trends in deep-mining equipment development and application could be altered in substantial degree.

The consequence of such a situation appears to be that, for all practical purposes, the nation has no recourse but to rely upon existing methods of deep coal mining for the remainder of the present century. To be sure, these existing methods—conventional, continuous, longwall, and shortwall—can be improved upon, refined, and even automated to some degree to provide increased production efficiency as well as improved health and safety. Still, even these improvements would be just that, and the basic mining methods would remain essentially as known at present.

[1]It was noted by Mr. John Corcoran of Consolidation Coal Company that revision of existing regulations against subsidence and for leaving barrier pillars around oil and gas wells would be required prior to the advent of a real increase in longwall mining. *Min. Congr. J.*, pp. 69-70, July 1973.

Without a breakthrough in deep mining methods (which cannot be completely discounted although the application of such innovations on a large scale in the next 25 years would be, at best, a formidable undertaking), some version of present mining methods will probably be employed in the future. This implies that, since such methods were developed primarily to work the deposits of the East and Midwest, their principal application will be in these regions. The potential for recovery of deeply buried thick western coal seams occurring under different geological conditions will probably remain unrealized unless new mining technology or in situ recovery methods perfected in a short time are demonstrated.

In terms of R&D on coal mining, this assessment suggests that it will be concerned with incremental improvements in present systems to realize benefits in productivity and health-safety factors. This will be especially true for relatively modest R&D efforts sponsored by the coal producers and equipment suppliers and, similarly, the more extensive programs undertaken by agencies of the federal government. Such an emphasis is logical in terms of the economic, political, and social interests of the research-sponsoring organizations. Yet, substantial areas for innovation in deep mining R&D will remain to be pursued by other organizations, in particular, work on novel methods to work thin eastern deposits as well as work on perfecting a technology for recovery of thick western seams. As noted elsewhere in this chapter, successes from the present R&D programs would appear to accelerate the depletion of eastern and midwestern coal deposits. There appears to be a real need for a better balance in R&D to improve recovery of known reserves as well as to add to the reserves by perfecting means to exploit deposits which are not developable with current technology. Overall, this is a somewhat pessimistic conclusion, but it is consistent with patterns of recent experience.

There is some encouraging evidence that the process of developing mining equipment for coal production is becoming more systematic. For example, Krupp[1] employs a questionnaire to compile detailed technical and engineering data on the nature of coal deposits and associated strata to guide the design of large bucket-wheel excavating equipment for surface mining. In addition, data on hydrology and climates are collected, as well as planned mining methods and schedule. These are all used in determining the most satisfactory equipment parameters for a given site. In the future, it seems reasonable to expect more extensive use of such approaches in selecting optimum equipment designs for effective coal recovery.

Conclusions and Implications—Underground Mining

Variability in geological conditions and uncertainty in operations are consistent themes which are encountered in every phase of underground coal mining. Technological developments have succeeded in mechanizing several mining functions, but the integration of these functions into a production system requires flexibility in application that can only be provided by skilled and experienced people.

As a research hypothesis, it is suggested that the precise natural conditions

---

[1]Krupp International, Inc., "Planning Data and Information For Development of Mining Equipment."

associated with mining are essentially unpredictable. These may be wide differences in fundamental parameters such as coal characteristics, roof or floor conditions, and seam height (even in different parts of the same seam in the same mine). This variability in natural conditions has led, through a tradition of trial and error, to a great variety of mining systems, equipment, and practices.

A considerable amount of quantitative technical measurements and analyses have been carried out in attempts to aid underground mining operations. Most of this work was (and is) oriented toward equipment or practices that may be applicable more or less universally in nominal operations. The thrust of this approach is toward the transformation of underground mining to an industrial activity and away from its traditional trade or guildlike approach. While promising strides have been made in applying new technology to improve operational efficiency and safety, there appear to be limits imposed on technology by the inherent uncertainty in natural mine conditions. It is obvious that technology has improved operations by relieving burdens from the workers, but it has not realized its full potential because the variability in natural conditions preclude its ability to predict the effects of its application with certainty.

In practice, there, present coal development is little different from that of the past; we have, in short, mechanized many of the tasks but remain unable to accurately forecast their working environment or the consequences of their activities on that environment. This is an unbalanced situation—sophisticated machines operating in an imperfectly specified working environment that is described principally by generally accurate but nonanalytical information gleaned by the practical experience of relatively untrained personnel and which is difficult to relate to new or different circumstances.

One explanation of the present inability to forecast mining conditions is the absence of geologic mapping in underground coal mines to identify joints, rock types, etc., and map them systematically. Coal mines thus expose rocks but do not extract information from them; this is at odds with a basic principle of geology and contrasts vividly with metal mining in which extensive mapping is done regularly. Engineering principles have dominated operations because of their immediate and direct relationship to production, and the potential value of geology as an operational aid has been unrealized. Nevertheless, this is understandable in terms of the coal.industry's concern with production and with the shortage of geologists available or willing to work in the mines. Still an enormous amount of potentially useful information about coal, its occurrence, and effects of mining have been lost.

The evolution of coal mining technology is consistent with the above interpretation. First to be mechanized were haulage tasks unrelated to geologic conditions. As equipment was perfected, face production tasks more critically dependent on seam, roof, and floor conditions were mechanized. For the immediate future, the imperfect state of knowledge about coal deposits and their characteristics limits the degree to which essential operations may be mechanized or automated. In short, the unpredictable variability in deposits appears to require the presence of workers in the vicinity of operations to make essential judgments about conditions so as to realize full benefits from the application of machine systems. Thus, although R&D in improving mining techniques can make operations more productive, it is unlikely that operations can be automated to the degree where workers are no longer essential in view of the uncertainty about mining conditions.

Recent work by the U.S. Bureau of Mines indicates that increasing emphasis is being placed on geologic studies in underground coal mines.[1] The objective of this work is to develop a means to apply geological data in the prediction of roof conditions as an aid in mine design as well as in operations. Still, these additional data will only supplement the know-how of experienced mining personnel. Far more extensive work in the geology of underground coal mining is required. As shown in Chapter 3, the bulk of recoverable reserves will require deep mining methods in their development. Therefore, it appears likely that deep mining will once again increase its share of total output as these larger reserves are exploited to meet expanding demands.

Expansion of coal production and utilization will be based largely on the increased use of existing technology. Advanced technology is not expected to come into commercial operation until the latter part of the 1980s. Even then, existing technologies will continue to be the mainstay of coal utilization at least for the remainder of this century.

Large numbers of new workers and new equipment will be required to compensate for retirements as well as to increase production capacity. If the projected increases are to be realized, increased reliance must be placed on existing equipment and procedures. The significance of this finding is that it would appear to eliminate uncertainty about future coal development approaches, and enable concrete plans and programs for worker training and equipment manufacture to be formulated and implemented by private industry. Furthermore, since such equipment would be in use for a considerable time (roughly to the end of the century), this would promote stability in the industry and assure relative constancy in jobs and practices. As a result, the level of effort required to accomplish the production increases could absorb excess productive capacity in heavy industries and be a further force acting toward economic stabilization, relatively independent of the actions of the federal government.

A critical pacing parameter in expansion of underground coal mining is directly related to the potential secondary consequences of rapid growth, namely, the ability of affected local communities to absorb and manage such growth. Detrimental impacts on the quality of life in local communities resulting from unforeseen, uneven, and possibly temporary growth in a short time can produce employee discontent, labor turnover, and falling productivity, which in turn become constraints on future expansion of the stimulating industry. These impacts can perhaps be avoided or moderated by the creation of mechanisms or processes of communication and cooperative planning between mining companies and community leaders, and by some technical and financial assistance to affected communities during the period of most rapid growth. The long-range potential impacts on communities of a subsequent decline in coal mining, if innovative new sources of energy are developed, must also be foreseen and planned for, if societal benefits

[1] J. W. Corwine, Roof Control is More Than Just Protection At The Mine Face, *Coal Min. Process.*, pp. 48-52, November 1976.

are to outweigh societal costs. For large measure, these concerns also apply to areas where surface mining is practiced. A review of surface mining methods is presented next.

SURFACE MINING METHODS

Surface mining refers to the set of activities carried out upon the earth's surface for recovery of an underlying mineral deposit. The principal operation entails removal of earth, rock and other strats (*overburden*) to uncover the deposit sought. Removal of overburden is also known as *stripping,* giving rise to the term *strip mining.*[1] Three main methods of surface coal mining are practiced at present: area strip mining, contour strip mining, and auger mining.

Area Strip Mining

Area strip mining is usually carried out on relatively flat terrain. A trench or "box cut" is dug through the overburden to expose a portion of the coal seam, and this coal is removed. Next, a series of parallel cuts are made, and the overburden from each is deposited in the previous excavation. The resulting effect is a series of parallel ridges of displaced overburden or *spoil*, with an average elevation usually somewhat higher than the original surface because of expansion in unit volume from disturbance. The resulting terrain, unless graded or leveled, "resembles the ridges of a gigantic washboard" (Figure 9).

The overburden is stripped by power shovel, dragline, or bucket wheel. Bulldozers are commonly used in ordinary stripping to clean the coal surface preparatory to taking the coal and for leveling the spoil piles. Draglines are the most common stripping machines because of their long reach and versatility. For a given digging capacity, they are also less expensive in the larger sizes. Draglines with booms up to 300 feet long and with bucket capacities up to 250 cubic yards are in use or under construction. Because draglines dig best below grade, they usually move or "walk" on top of the undisturbed overburden or on a bench cut into it.

Shovels are somewhat better diggers than draglines, both as to cost and in terms of ability to dig tough material. However, a shovel can dig only above grade. Thus, its usual position in stripping is on the top of the coal seam. Shovels up to 180 cubic yard bucket capacity and 200-foot reach are in use.

The bucket wheels used in strip mining of coal are long bridge structures that may stand on top of the coal seam or on a bench in the undisturbed overburden. The digging wheels are on fairly short booms, which are extensible and retractable. The rest of the structures are rigid and simply provide support for conveyor belts that carry the spoil from wheels to the spoil areas. Some bucket wheels are mounted on old shovel substructures and, lacking swiveling devices, long booms,

---

[1] U.S. Bureau of Mines, "A Dictionary of Mining, Mineral, and Related Terms, p. 1090, 1968. Note that the term *strip mining* may also refer to the removal of overburden in narrow bands from the area being mined. Thus, the term *strip* has dual meaning—removal of overburden in general and the manner of removal specifically.

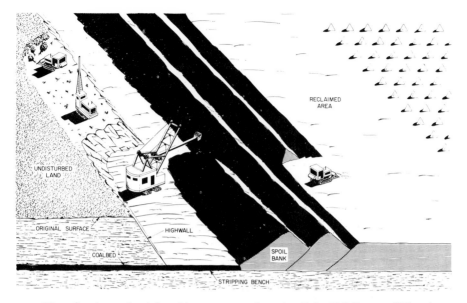

Figure 9. Area strip mining with concurrent reclamation. (After U.S. Bureau of Mines.)

and counterbalances, are comparatively inexpensive, whereas modern bucket wheels manufactured in Germany are more expensive than shovels and draglines of equivalent weight. Bucket-wheel tests by U.S. coal operators have produced the general conviction that they are not properly used in difficult digging, although they do very well in readily dug material. Thus, in Illinois strip mining, they are used in stripping the upper, more diggable portions of overburden, being followed by shovels that dig the deeper, tougher overburden, usually after blasting.

Blasting with light charges is usually done in preparation for stripping to improve the diggability of ground. Blasting is necessary in solid formations and is often done where not absolutely necessary, as it reduces costs by easing the difficulty of digging. Blasting is done in drill holes, usually 6 or 8 inches in diameter, using fertilizer-grade ammonium nitrate fuel oil (ANFO), mixed in bulk at the mine site. (Explosives are discussed later in this chapter.)

As the coal beds are exposed by stripping the overburden, smaller digging machines follow, loading the coal into trucks for transport.

Trends in stripping equipment development[1] have moved rapidly upward toward larger-capacity bucket sizes in recent years (Figure 10). However, it may be questioned whether indefinite growth in equipment size can be continued, for the following reasons:

---

[1]For a comprehensive description of surface mining equipment, see R. Stefanko, R. V. Ramini, and M. R. Ferko, "An Analysis of Strip-Mining Methods and Equipment Selection," Pennsylvania State University, Research and Development Report no. 61, prepared for the Office of Coal Research, May 21, 1973.

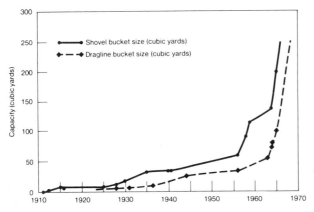

Figure 10. Trends in stripping equipment development. (From U.S. Bureau of Mines, *Miner. Yearb.*, various years.)

- There appears to be a natural balance between effective size, weight, and the structural strength of equipment.
- Larger machines are more complicated and have more potential failure points.
- The geology of coal occurrence is such that favorable sites for giant equipment to operate effectively and economically appear to be limited.

Area strip mining is currently practiced extensively in Illinois, Ohio, western Kentucky, North Dakota, Arizona, and New Mexico. Prospective areas for area strip mining at substantial production levels include Wyoming, Montana, and Utah.

Contour Strip Mining

Contour strip mining is practiced where horizontal or gently dipping coal seams occur in hilly or mountainous country, such as in West Virginia, eastern Kentucky, western Pennsylvania, and eastern Ohio. Prospective areas for contour strip mining include parts of Wyoming, Colorado, Utah, and Montana. Overburden is removed from the coal seam starting at the outcrop and moving at the same level along the hillside. This is continued until the ratio of overburden to coal becomes uneconomic. The result of this type of mining is a bench on the hillside at the level of the coal seam occurrence. The downslope side of the bench is commonly covered by displaced overburden. The upslope side of the bench is bordered by a high wall that varies in height according to topography and seam thickness.

Owing to the nature of the deposits and topography in places such as West Virginia, most of the mining equipment used in contour strip mining is small by standards of area strip mining activities in other states with more gentle topography. In other words, the surface mining industry of West Virginia has not been characterized by giant earthmoving machinery such as that presently operating in Ohio and Illinois. It does not appear likely that the physical conditions in areas having high topographical relief would be amenable to such equipment, because the relatively short duration of a contour mining operation does not provide economic justification for purchase of the giant area strip mining machinery plus the high costs of dismantling, moving, and reassembly of these machines in inaccessible mountainous terrain.

Overburden removal during contour strip mining creates a *bench* on the hillside, composed of two parts. The *solid bench* is the portion from which overburden was removed and is underlain by solid rock and at this stage in operations, coal. The *fill bench* is the top portion of the spoil bank from the initial excavation. The inner limit of the solid bench is bounded by a *highwall* of unexcavated rock (Figure 11).

An initial evaluation suggests that the topographic conditions would impose severe, if not insurmountable, limitations on giant equipment. Also, several major problems in certain giant machines have been noted even in the relatively flat areas of other states. It does not appear that either of these problems regarding giant machines for West Virginia surface mining operations would be resolved quickly. It is far more likely that surface mine operators would continue to make use of existing technology in their activities.

Auger Mining

Auger mining is practiced when the overburden ratio in contour strip mining becomes uneconomic and where slope and/or bench-width restrictions limit the use of contour mining. In this method, coal is produced by boring mechanically into the seam and is usually the last phase of surface mining in a particular location. As auger mining is limited to the coal itself, little additional land disturbance is caused directly.

A coal auger is a mechanical borer that drives horizontally into coal seams that may be exposed through contour strip mining. Under favorable conditions of coal seam uniformity and thickness, auger mining can yield additional production for 150 to 200 feet farther into the hillside from the base of the highwall. Often, however, augers achieve lesser efficiency owing to irregularities in the coal seam, and can produce a high proportion of rejects if they should also remove waste rock from the roof or floor. In this circumstance, cleaning of coal would definitely be required to remove the waste matter prior to use. Auger mining requires sufficient bench width to allow for maneuvering trucks around the auger machine to receive coal production.

Emerging Surface Mining Technology

There are emerging alternatives to the conventional contour strip mining method.

Box-cut method. The box-cut method differs from the conventional contour strip mining method in that overburden material which the conventional method would remove as a second cut is mined first. In other words, the box-cut method begins excavations upslope from the cropline where the final highwall will be, digs down to the seam, and casts spoil downslope (Figure 12a). This normally requires earth-moving shovels or draglines rather than the bulldozers or scrapers used in conventional contour strip mining. Later cuts in the box-cut method involve rehandling of spoil cast from the first (or "box") cut, placing it back against the highwall in the area where coal has been removed, and then removing overburden from the re-

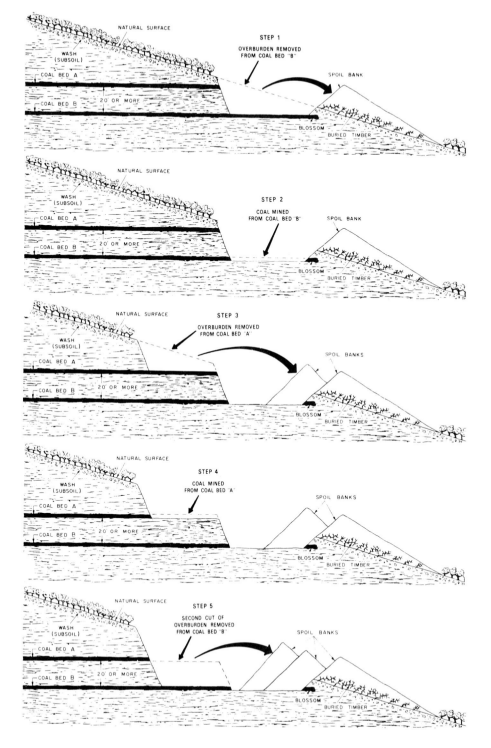

STEP 1
OVERBURDEN REMOVED
FROM COAL BED "B"

NATURAL SURFACE

WASH
(SUBSOIL)

COAL BED A

COAL BED B

20' OR MORE

SPOIL BANK

BLOSSOM

BURIED TIMBER

STEP 2
COAL MINED
FROM COAL BED "B"

NATURAL SURFACE

WASH
(SUBSOIL)

COAL BED A

COAL BED B

20' OR MORE

SPOIL BANK

BLOSSOM

BURIED TIMBER

STEP 3
OVERBURDEN REMOVED
FROM COAL BED "A"

NATURAL SURFACE

WASH
(SUBSOIL)

COAL BED A

COAL BED B

20' OR MORE

SPOIL BANKS

BLOSSOM

BURIED TIMBER

STEP 4
COAL MINED
FROM COAL BED "A"

NATURAL SURFACE

WASH
(SUBSOIL)

COAL BED A

COAL BED B

20' OR MORE

SPOIL BANKS

BLOSSOM

BURIED TIMBER

STEP 5
SECOND CUT OF
OVERBURDEN REMOVED
FROM COAL BED "B"

NATURAL SURFACE

WASH
(SUBSOIL)

COAL BED A

COAL BED B

20' OR MORE

SPOIL BANKS

BLOSSOM

BURIED TIMBER

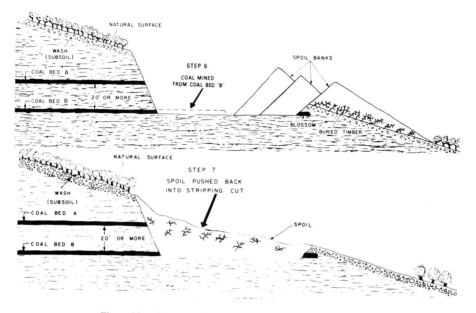

Figure 11. Contour stripping. (After U.S. Bureau of Mines.)

mainder of the seam to complete the recovery of the lift of coal (Figure 12b). If augering is to be done, the box cut must be wide enough to allow trucks to pass by the auger machine. Also, augering would have to follow removal of the part of the lift of coal exposed by the box cut, and another cut would have to precede recovery of the remaining lift. This is necessary because replacement of spoil against the highwall would cover the coal seam and preclude the opportunity to carry out augering operations, unless the operation is carefully planned in a sequential manner along a coal seam.

The advantage of the box-cut method is that the amount of spoil cast downslope is minimized and retained at the level of the bench for use in backfilling to reduce or cover the highwall. The disadvantages are that it appears to require earthmoving shovels not necessarily available to small operators and that it requires careful planning, especially if augering is to be carried out.

Block-cut method. The block-cut method employs the same type of machinery used in conventional contour strip mining. In this method, mining begins at or near the cropline (except for the bloom) and works into the hillside as in conventional contour strip mining. However, only a minimum amount of overburden is placed downslope from the coal seam. Instead, overburden removed from the advancing face of the mine along the contour is hauled to the mined-out area where coal was removed (Figure 13). In other words, the technique is to backfill the mined bench with spoil produced as the bench advances along the contour (Figure 13). The method is thus similar to that employed in area strip mining, where spoil is placed behind mining operations. A larger amount of haulage is involved in this method than in conventional contour strip mining because of the need to transfer

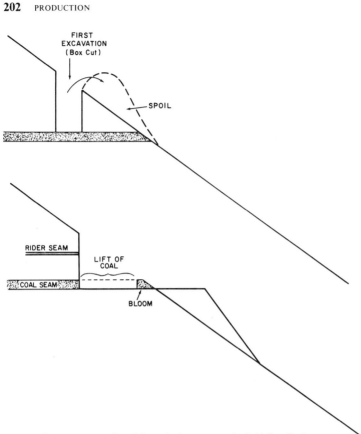

Figure 12. Contour strip mining: the box-cut method. (After R. A. Schmidt and W.C. Stoneman, "A Study of Surface Coal Mining in West Virginia," prepared by Stanford Research Institute for the West Virginia Legislature, 1972.)

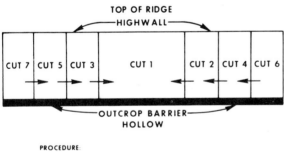

PROCEDURE:

1. SCALP FROM TOP OF HIGHWALL TO OUTCROP BARRIER, REMOVE AND STORE TOPSOIL.
2. REMOVE AND DISPOSE OF OVERBURDEN FROM CUT 1.
3. PICK UP COAL, LEAVING AT LEAST A 15 FOOT UNDISTURBED OUTCROP BARRIER.
4. MAKE SUCCESIVE CUTS AS NUMBERED.
5. OVERBURDEN IS MOVED IN THE DIRECTION, AS SHOWN BY ARROWS, AND PLACED IN THE ADJACENT PIT.
6. COMPLETE BACKFILL AND GRADING TO THE APPROXIMATE ORIGINAL CONTOUR.

Figure 13. The block-cut method of contour strip mining. (After E. Grim and R.D. Hill, "Environmental Protection in Surface Mining of Coal," *US Environ. Prot. Agency Rep. EPA* 670/2-74-093, October 1974.)

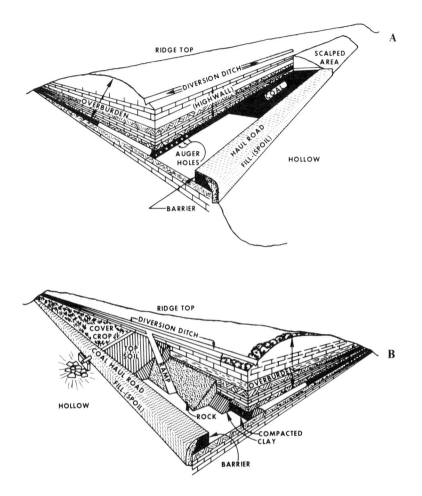

Figure 14 Block-cut method. (a) Stripping phase; (b) backfilling phase. (After E. Grim, and R.D. Hill, "Environmental Protection in Surface Mining of Coal," *US Environ. Prot. Agency Rep. EPA* 670/2-74-093, October 1974.)

overburden along the bench. These added haulage costs have to be evaluated to determine their magnitude. It would seem possible, however, for operational scheduling to efficiently accomplish such haulage, and if overburden could be handled in backhauling, the level of costs might be reduced.

The advantages of the block-cut method are that it largely eliminates the problems of spoil banks and that it accomplishes backfilling, highwall reduction, and return to approximate original land contour as a regular part of ongoing mining operations. Operational disadvantages will include location of haulage roads as well as maintaining spoil stability. It would appear possible that backfilling could compact the spoil so that revegetation may be impaired. However, these and other possible operational problems have to be evaluated through field trials.

Advantages and disadvantages of the block-cut method were discussed by Ramani[1] as follows:

Benefits and advantages of the block-cut method over conventional contour strip-mining have been demonstrated at producing mines under varying conditions and are:

1. Spoil on the downslope is totally eliminated. Since no fill bench is produced, landslides have been eliminated.
2. Mined area is completely backfilled, and since no highwall is left, the area is aesthetically more pleasing.
3. Acreage disturbed is approximately 60% less than that disturbed by conventional contour mining.
4. Reclamation costs are lower, as the overburden is handled only once instead of two or three times.
5. Slope is not a limiting factor.
6. The block-cut method is applicable to multi-seam mining.
7. At present, this method does not require the development of new equipment. As new mining technology develops, however, modified or new types of equipment may be needed.
8. Regular explosives are used, but blasting techniques had to be developed to keep shot material on the permit area.
9. Bonding amounts and acreage fees have been reduced.
10. Size of the disturbed area drainage system is smaller.
11. Size and number of sediment control structures have been reduced. Total life of structure usefulness is increased.
12. No new safety hazards have been introduced. However, the increased number of pieces of moving equipment in a more confined area may negate this point.
13. Revegetation costs have been considerably reduced and it is easier to keep the seeding current with the mining. Bond releases are quicker.
14. [Acid mine drainage], siltation, and erosion is significantly reduced and more easily controlled because of concurrent reclamation with mining.
15. Total amount of coal recovered is equal to that recovered by conventional methods.
16. Overburden is easily segregated, topsoil can be saved, and toxic materials can be deeply buried.
17. Equipment, materials, and manpower are concentrated, making for a more efficient operation.
18. The method allows for early removal of equipment from the operation and placing it back in production at another site.

Disadvantages of the block-cut method are:

1. Complicated and time-consuming methods of drilling and blasting to maintain control of the overburden and get proper fragmentation for the particular types of equipment being used in spoil removal.
2. Economics may limit use of this method; i.e., thin seams of steam coal cannot be recovered profitably if the overburden must be shot.
3. Special precautions must be taken in scheduling the various phases of mining and reclamation so as to realize the maximum recovery of coal and at the same time eliminate any dead time for equipment.
4. It is very important that the location of the initial box cut be properly selected. In some areas there will be no place to back haul the material taken at the beginning of the block cut or to dispose of the excess spoil at the end of the operation. Head-of-hollow fill is not always possible, as it can only be done in a restricted set of circumstances.
5. Long-term environmental consequences are not known and will require a monitor program of a pilot block-cut operation to determine if stream siltation and mineralization can be eliminated.

[1]R. V. Ramani, Surface Mining Methods, Techniques, and Equipment, in E. C. Grim and R. D. Hill (eds.), "Environmental Protection in Surface Mining of Coal," *US Environ. Prot. Agency Rep. EPA* 6780/2-74-093, October 1974.

6. Investment costs for spoil haulage equipment are increased. Some small mines cannot afford this additional expense.
7. The block-cut method develops no broad bench that has a high land use potential in mountainous terrain. No access is left for forest firefighting crews, timbering operations, or recreational purposes.
8. Augering must be conducted concurrently with mining.

Explosives Used in Coal Production

In all but a few uncommon cases where natural coal occurrences are particularly favorable, or where mechanical excavation is feasible, coal and/or its overlying strata must be blasted as the first step in extraction. Therefore, explosives are essential in coal production operations, especially in surface mining. This section provides a brief overview of the principal types of explosives used in coal production, presents a review of trends in explosive use, especially with respect to coal mining, and analyzes relationships between explosive use and elements of production operations.

Types. Explosives are chemical compounds capable of releasing large amounts of energy rapidly under controlled or semicontrolled conditions.[1] The ingredients of the explosive (which may exist as a solid, liquid, or a mixture of the two) are transformed into other products, mainly gaseous, which occupy a much larger volume than the original configuration. Also, the explosive reaction generates considerable heat, expanding the gaseous products to the extent that they exert enormous pressure on their surroundings. The result is fragmentation of the medium in which explosives are employed.

Explosives exist in three main classes: mechanical, chemical, and nuclear (Figure 15).

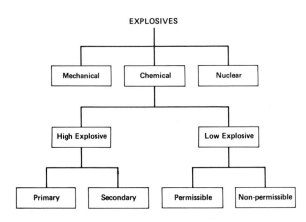

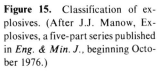

Figure 15. Classification of explosives. (After J.J. Manow, Explosives, a five-part series published in *Eng. & Min. J.*, beginning October 1976.)

[1]For an introductory treatment of explosives, refer to a series of articles by J. J. Manow published in *Eng. Min. J.* in October 1976 (pp. 85–85), December 1976 (pp. 60–68), January 1977 (pp. 74-75), February 1977 (pp. 76–78), and May 1977 (pp. 82–93).

1. *Mechanical* explosives consist of inert materials which are caused to vaporize very rapidly by the introduction of very hot matter.
2. *Chemical* explosives may be of high or low types:
   a. *High explosives* are characterized by very high rates of reaction and high pressures. Included are *primary* explosives (detonated by low-energy ignition services such as spark, flame, or impact) and *secondary* explosives requiring a considerably greater energy input for ignition.
   b. *Low explosives* have much lower rates of reaction and much lower pressures. Included are certain types of *permissible* explosives approved for use in mining, and *nonpermissible* explosives.
3. *Nuclear* explosives consist of fissionable materials such as uranium, plutonium, or the like which are capable of extremely destructive explosions.

The chemical composition of explosives is related to organic compounds of carbon, hydrogen, and nitrogen, although there are numerous materials and mixtures having explosive properties but which contain no nitrogen. From the point of view of coal mining explosives, however, nitrogen-based compounds are used almost exclusively. In particular, ammonium nitrate mixtures are widely used in various configurations. The remainder of this section will concentrate on ammonium nitrate-based explosives.

Trends. Trends in explosive use by consuming industry over the last quarter century are shown in Figure 16. During this time, total explosive use increased more than threefold. Except for brief decreases in 1954, 1958, and 1967–1968, the total quantity of explosives used in the United States increased progressively. It is reasonable to expect that the total amount of explosives used will continue to

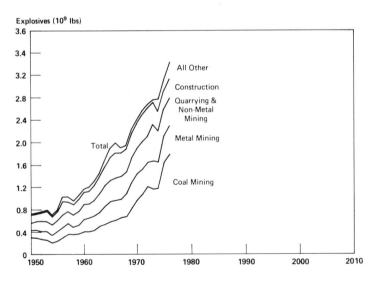

Figure 16. Trends in explosive use in the U.S. (From U.S. Bureau of Mines, *Miner. Yearb.*)

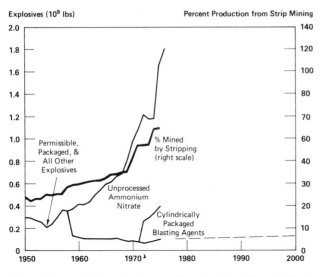

Figure 17. Trends in explosive use of coal mining. (From U.S. Bureau of Mines, *Miner. Yearb.*, 1940-1974.)

increase throughout the remaining years of the twentieth century, although no specific projections are shown.

The coal industry is, and throughout the entire interval has been, the largest consumer of explosives. Explosive use in coal mining nearly doubled during the decade of the 1950s, roughly doubled again by the end of the 1960s, and already is close to a third doubling in the latter 1970s. This rapid growth in explosive use for coal production is the principal reason for the overall increase in consumption, because other consuming sectors grew at much more modest rates. It seems apparent that coal mining will remain as the largest single explosive consumer throughout the rest of the century, and beyond.

Trends in the types of explosives used in coal mining are shown in Figure 17. Important changes have occurred. While *permissible* and other packaged explosives were used almost exclusively in the 1950s, strong inroads were made by what the U.S. Bureau of Mines classifies as "unprocessed" ammonium nitrate beginning as early as 1959.[1] The use of ammonium nitrate, especially as a mixture with a small amount of fuel oil (ANFO), expanded rapidly throughout the 1960s, amounting to all but one-tenth of total explosive consumption by the end of the decade and reducing the once-dominant explosives to a relatively insignificant position. The early years of the 1970s saw continued expansion in the use of unprocessed ammonium nitrate, as well as the onset of rapidly increasing use of cylindrically packaged blasting agents made largely from the same material. At present, explosives employing ammonium nitrate constitute all but about one-twentieth of the total explosives used in coal mining. This rapid and massive substitution of ammo-

[1] *Permissible* explosives are explosives that are broadly defined as having "slow rates of reaction and low explosive pressure and which have been tested for safety and handling and approved for use in mines by the U.S. Bureau of Mines." U.S. Bureau of Mines, *op. cit*, p. 809.

nium nitrate for other explosives used in coal mining represented a change in approach to fragmentation, which, together with the advent of improved mining machinery, enabled the industry to develop as it has in recent years. Particularly noteworthy is the growth in the portion of total coal production from surface mines, which parallels the explosive consumption curve.

Figure 18 shows the relationship between total coal production and explosive use. For most of the quarter century, coal production and explosive use were in direct proportion to one another; the greater the coal production, the greater the explosive use. However, each decade had its own individual characteristics. In the 1950s, explosive use ranged from 0.5 to 1.0 pound per ton of coal produced. During the 1960s, this amount increased to more than 1.5 pounds per ton. By the mid-1970s, roughly 2.5 pounds of explosive was used for each ton of coal. The consequence of this situation is more extensive fragmentation of overburden, creating more fine particles. Unless properly handled and monitored, this could promote severe erosion and sedimentation problems in some parts of the nation. On the plus side, however, is the fact that more finely divided overburden may facilitate rehabilitation under careful management procedures.

Heavy blasting can also break up coal into fine particles, leading to a certain amount of losses (depending on the nature of the coal). While possibly an advantage in certain preparation or consuming facilities, finely divided coal is difficult to handle and transport without suffering additional losses. A further problem is that heavy blasting may introduce finely divided rocks into the coal and lead to the need for cleaning (which might not have been required otherwise). Alternatively, uncleaned coal with introduced rocks from blasting may cause operational problems in power plants, countering any prospective advantage from being

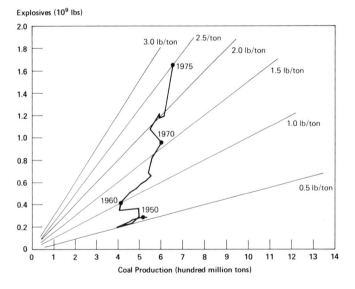

Figure 18. Relationship between coal production and explosive usage. (From U.S. Bureau of Mines, *Miner. Yearb.*)

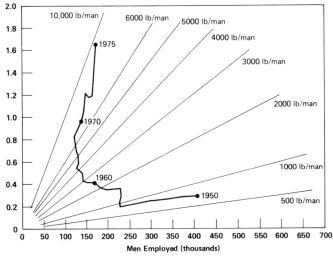

Figure 19. Relationship of coal mining work force and explosive usage. (From U.S. Bureau of Mines, *Miner. Yearb.*, various years.)

finely divided at the mine. Clearly, this problem requires careful analysis on a case-by-case basis.

The relation of explosive use in coal mining to the magnitude of the work force is shown in Figure 19. In the early 1950s, less than 1000 pounds of explosive was used for every person working in the mines, but this grew in the latter part of that decade to more than 2000 pounds per person. At least part of the reason behind this increase was the rapidly shrinking work force during this period; although the use of explosives per person roughly doubled, the work force was reduced by more than half. During the 1960s, explosive use per person continued its increase, reaching more than 6000 pounds per person. This increase is probably more "real" than that of the 1950s, because the work force remained relatively constant during this decade. The increase in amount of explosive per person continued in the early 1970s, reaching nearly 10,000 pounds per person in 1975.

The increase in quantities of explosive employed per person is an indication of the changes in mining methods that occurred over this quarter century. With a smaller work force, coal production was maintained and even increased to all-time maximum levels, at least in part, by greatly increased use of explosives (compare Figure 19). In a real sense, operators found it possible to substitute for a large work force by using mechanical energy from machines and chemical energy from explosives. So far, none of the recent trends show any indication of reversal; thus, for the future it may be postulated that increased coal production will be carried out by a slightly larger work force using increasingly larger amounts of explosives. While it seems reasonable to expect that there exist practical limits to the effective use of explosives, there is no present indication that these have been approached (much less exceeded). Probably, such limits as do exist are economic ones, pertain-

Pounds of Explosive per Ton of Coal

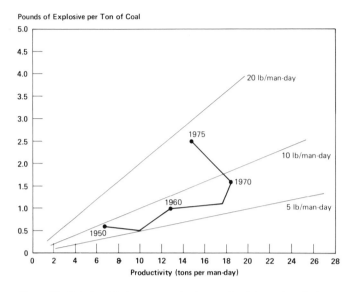

Figure 20. Relationship between coal mine productivity and explosive usage. (From U.S. Bureau of Mines, *Miner. Yearb.*, various years.)

ing to the cost of explosive supplies on the one hand and/or to the economic efficiency of their use on the other. Again, this is a topic requiring careful case-by-case analysis beyond the scope of the present section.

The relation of explosive use per ton of coal to productivity is shown in Figure 20. Productivity is useful because it integrates several physical and operational variables but does not require discrimination among them for purposes of analysis. It also serves as an indicator of the overall efficiency of the operations. For the 1950s and most of the 1960s, productivity increased directly with increased use of explosives: for every 0.1 pound of explosive per ton of coal, productivity increased 1.2 tons per miner-day. Yet, for nearly one decade explosive usage remained in the relatively narrow range from 5 to 10 pounds per man-day. Following 1969, however, productivity decreased significantly at the same time that explosive use was roughly doubling, an *inverse* relationship; for every 0.1 pound of explosive per ton of coal, productivity decreased 0.4 ton per miner-day. These relations, however, must be analyzed very carefully to avoid misleading conclusions.

Obviously, many other factors connected with mining had some influence upon changes in productivity in the early 1970s. In fact, it is not at all unlikely that the accelerated use of explosives in the 1970s was undertaken in an attempt to lessen the impact of declining productivity; note that while explosive use doubled in the 1970s, productivity declined by only about one-quarter. One can only speculate about the possible magnitude of the productivity decline that might have been experienced in these years had it not been possible to expand explosive use so rapidly and so greatly. However, it is not at all clear whether expanded explosive use can even partially compensate for lower productivity levels indefinitely, especially in underground mines.

Looking to the future, it hardly seems reasonable to expect a continued decline in productivity and continued increases in explosive use as industry attempts to compensate. If there are to be sufficient supplies of coal to meet projected requirements, there appears to be no substitute for a return to improved productivity (and by the same token, lower rates of explosive usage).

Forecast. As indicated earlier, the principal explosive used in coal mining is composed mainly of ammonium nitrate. Therefore, in reviewing past and projected supply-demand relations for coal mining explosives, it is appropriate to concentrate on production and consumption of ammonium nitrate. Ammonium nitrate is employed to meet several demands. Its largest use, accounting for roughly four-fifths of the total, is a fertilizer in agricultural applications.[1] Agriculture is projected to remain as the largest user of ammonium nitrate throughout the rest of the century, and probably beyond (Figure 21).

Explosives applications are only a minor use for ammonium nitrate, representing roughly one-twentieth of the present total. While it may be possible to expand the share of ammonium nitrate consumed as explosives, this would depend largely on price competition, and to a lesser extent on the available capacity in production of ammonium nitrate. There appears to be sufficient, if not excess, capacity for the production of ammonium nitrate.

Thus coal mining explosives represent a small part of the total consumption, and

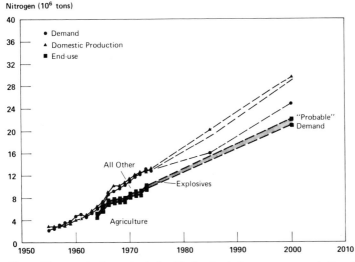

Figure 21. Supply-demand relationship for fixed nitrogen compounds (in million tons of contained nitrogen) (From "*Mineral Facts and Problems*," *US Bur. Mines Bull.* 670, 1976.)

[1]"Mineral Facts and Problems," *US Bur. Mines Bull.* 670, p. 749, 1976.

there appears to be a strong likelihood that there would be sufficient supplies of ammonium nitrate available to meet coal production requirements. The ultimate magnitude of these requirements, however, remains to be determined.

Implications. The importance of explosives for power generation can be illustrated with a simple example. Assume a power plant of 1000 megawatts electric (MWe) annual capacity, consuming roughly 3 million tons of coal per year. As shown in Figure 19, present explosive usage in coal production amounts to about 2.5 pounds per ton. Therefore, the following relation is valid for annual consumption:

$$\frac{3 \text{ million tons coal}}{1000 \text{ MWe}} \times \frac{2.5 \text{ lb explosives}}{1 \text{ ton coal}} = \frac{7500 \text{ lb explosives}}{\text{MWe}}$$

These relations are illustrated (for a range of explosive use in coal production) in Figure 22.

All projections indicate expanded coal production to serve present and emerging consumer requirements. If past trends are any guide, this production will be accomplished with an increasing use of explosives per unit of coal. This, in turn, will increase the ratio of explosive use per unit of power generation.

Nitrogen fixation, by ammonia synthesis, the basic element of the process from which nitrate explosives are derived, is an energy-intensive process. The energy must be supplied in a clean and efficient fuel; natural gas is the principal fuel used for this purpose. Total gas consumption in ammonia manufacture ranges from 32,000 cubic feet per ton of ammonia up to about 40,000 cubic feet per ton. Additional energy consumption is in the form of electrical energy (15 kilowatt hours per ton) and water supply (2000 gallons per ton).

In terms of power generation, the gas required for ammonia production is re-

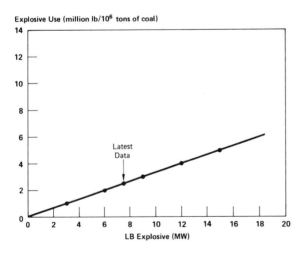

Explosive Use (million lb/10⁶ tons of coal)

Figure 22. Relationship of explosive use in coal production to power generation. (From U.S. Bureau of Mines, *Miner. Yearb.*, various years.)

lated to power generation as follows:

$$\frac{7500 \text{ lb explosives}}{M We} \times \frac{ton}{2000 \text{ lb}} \times \frac{40{,}000 \text{ ft}^3 \text{ gas}}{ton \text{ ammonia}} \times \frac{0.4 \text{ lb ammonia}}{lb \text{ explosives}} = \frac{60{,}000 \text{ ft}^3 \text{ gas}}{M We}$$

Thus even power generation from coal is dependent (albeit indirectly) on supplies of natural gas. If supplies of natural gas are sufficient, it may be possible to obtain the necessary gas for explosive manufacture through coal gasification, but at a higher price. In fact, ammonia synthesis is the main application of current commercial coal gasification plants operated abroad. Use of higher-cost fuels to produce ammonia would lead to greater explosive costs, and this would be reflected in the patterns of usage in surface mining operations.

External Effects of Surface Mining

Surface mining is inherently less hazardous than deep mining to the workers employed in operations. The hazards are not comparable in intensity to those encountered in deep mining, such as roof falls, methane release, coal dust explosions. Although surface mining does require ordinary prudence to avoid injuries and even fatalities, the record of the recent past indicates that the numbers and rates of injuries or fatalities are but a fraction of those related to deep mining. Manageable as the industrial safety aspects of surface mining may be, the impacts of surface mining operations upon the physical environment have been often severe. As a result, the environmental effects of surface coal mining have become matters of intense public concern, both in areas of the East where such operations have been in progress for many years and in areas of the West where new operations are planned for the future. Salient aspects of the environmental impacts of surface coal mining in both regions of the nation are presented next to complete the discussion of surface mining.

In introducing this controversial subject, it is useful to distinguish between *environmental change* through surface mining activities and *environmental damage* caused by such operations.[1] Environmental changes from mining operations may be the target of legitimate control activities, depending on the character and extent of the impacts. Such control activities may be accomplished by revised mining practices and procedures or by improved technology. In the control case, the application of alternate methods or equipment would allow potentially adverse environmental effects to be managed within accepted limits to minimize the amount of change to nature and mitigate the potential of such changes to present risk to society.

Environmental damages from surface mining operations, on the other hand, imply that mining-induced impacts on the physical environment are beyond the reach of controls. Furthermore, the term *damages* implies that these impacts are

---

[1]The term *environmental changes* implies that, while the character of the environment may be altered by mining operations, such alteration is of relatively short duration. The changes may be reversed under proper attention, and the changes are subject to being controlled through adoption of suitable technical practices.

irreversible and cause irreparable changes to the natural environment which represent substantial risks to society, whether immediately or over a longer period of time.

The root of the controversy over environmental effects of surface mining, then, could be in the identification of such environmental changes as opposed to damages. In the discussion which follows, an attempt is made to distinguish, (in gross terms) among changes and damages associated with surface mining in eastern and western coalfields. The humid environment of the eastern coalfields where surface mining is practiced may be characterized simply as one having abundant surface moisture. Frequent but relatively gentle rains lead to physical runoff of water which can physically remove as sediment the rocks and soil disturbed from their original position during surface mining operations. Runoff can lead to failure of spoil banks, resulting in slides. Sediment can also clog streams and watercourses, resulting in flooding. Serious as these physical effects of weathering in the humid East may be locally, they appear to be amenable to control by applying revised procedures, practices, or technologies; according to the definitions introduced earlier, these would be termed environmental changes.

The abundant moisture of the East also induces chemical changes in the rocks and soils disturbed by surface mining. Water can penetrate into the interstices of surface mine spoils. The process of fragmentation of rocks in preparation for their excavation leads to the creation of many particles of various size, each having many surfaces upon which water can adhere and possibly react with the mineral constituents to leach out soluble components. These chemical effects of weathering are manifest as phenomena such as acid mine drainage and spoils barren of nutrients which will not support vegetation. Despite attempts to arrest chemical weathering, surface and ground water serves as a means to transport weathering products, and there remain substantial areas of the East where such impacts have persisted for some time. As far as can be determined, the products of chemical weathering do not appear to be controllable either in degree or in areal extent with available technologies; according to the above definitions, these would represent environmental damages.

The fact that the smaller total rainfall of the West occurs in relatively short but intense periods means that the ability of runoff water to pick up and transport rocks and sediments is great. Physical weathering is facilitated if rocks and soil are broken up, as in excavation of overburden to expose coal for extraction, because smaller particles are more readily transported by running water (actually, in flash floods, huge boulders can be moved as well as enormous volumes of smaller sediments). Despite attempts to contain sediments, there appears to be no available means to check the erosive power of running water in the West; according to the definitions used here, these would be environmental damages.

The smaller amount of moisture in the West means that chemical weathering is retarded in degree and scope compared to the East. Moreover, the lesser amounts of running water lead to limited dispersal of weathering products. Thus the chemical effects on disturbed lands in the West are likely to be relatively localized to the immediate vicinity of the area mined. Because of their local character there appears to be promise in realizing control over adverse chemical effects; according to the definitions used here, these would be environmental changes.

The different environmental conditions of the eastern and western coalfields result in different environmental impacts as a consequence of surface mining. These may be summarized in gross terms, as follows:

Type of impact	East	West
Physical	Environmental change	Environmental damage
Chemical	Environmental damage	Environmental change

To be sure, individual localities in each region may be identified as exceptions to the above generalizations. Nevertheless, these classifications as to type of impact and environmental consequences are regarded as useful in guiding attention to topics where R&D activities can be most effective in minimizing adverse environmental effects of surface coal mining.

The National Academy of Sciences[1] provided data on the relationship of land disturbance to coal production. Historical data on coal production and acres disturbed in surface mining were employed, together with average seam thickness, to calculate acreage disturbed per million tons of production by state in the West. As shown in Figure 23, greater land disturbance is required to produce a million tons in states where thin seams predominate, with lesser disturbance where thick seams are present. The Academy employed these data in projecting possible future land disturbance in these states to the end of the century. The total amount of disturbance was estimated to be less than 200,000 acres for mining operations (other activities related to mining were not included, but it was estimated that their total might be twice the acreage disturbed in mining itself). Still, these totals are rather modest in comparison to the total area involved, although the effects of mining would likely be concentrated in certain areas. Clearly, evaluation of potential effects would have to be performed for specific sites.

Rehabilitation of Spoil Banks

The development of technology for the rehabilitation of spoil banks and control of erosion and sedimentation has been pursued for many years. Most of our knowledge results from agricultural research. With the rapid expansion in surface coal mining in recent years, there has been increasing public concern over control of erosion and sedimentation from mining operations and spoil banks in various stages of rehabilitation. The present state of technology is presented in a com-

[1]National Academy of Sciences, "Rehabilitation Potential of Western Coal Lands," a report to the Energy Policy Project of the Ford Foundation, Ballinger Publishing Company, Cambridge, Mass., 1974.

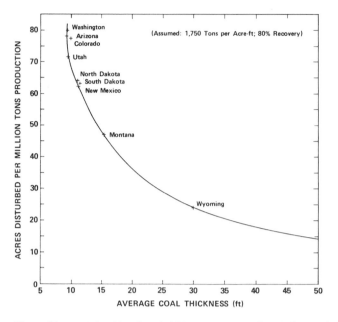

Figure 23. Relationship of coal thickness to acres disturbed per million tons production. (After National Academy of Sciences, "Rehabilitation Potential of Western Coal Lands," Ballinger Publications, Cambridge, Mass., 1974.)

prehensive recent report intended as a guide to operators.[1] The discussion in this section presents an overview of the subject.

Surface mining for coal requires the removal of overburden, the soil and rock covering the coal seam. As noted earlier, overburden is commonly drilled and blasted with explosive mixtures of ammonium nitrate and fuel oil or other high explosives in preparation for removal. The efficiency of rock breakage in blasting is determined by the properties of the rock and by the total amount of explosive charge used; larger amounts of explosive will usually produce more fragmentation and result in a greater proportion of finer materials that are easier to excavate than large blocks of rock. Breakage of rock increases its volume by increasing the surface area of individual units, commonly from 25 to 40 percent.

Overburden removed from coal seams in common strip mining is usually placed in spoil piles. The spoil is a heterogeneous mixture of sandstone, shale, siltstone, clay, coal, and soil. Mineral matter occurring in the spoil includes the common rock-forming minerals such as quartz, feldspar, and ferromagnesian silicates as well as such water-soluble sulfur compounds as may be present.

Spoil texture varies. A common range of sizes of spoil materials would extend from boulders to sand and silt-sized particles; the finer materials usually predominate, especially with heavy blasting. Additional fine material may be

[1]Erosion and Sediment Control: Surface Mining in the Eastern U.S., Vol. 1, Planning; Vol. 2, Design, *US Environ. Prot. Agency Rep.* EPA-625/3-76-006, October 1976.

produced during the mining operation as equipment moving over the spoil causes further disintegration of rock materials.

The manner of operations determines the character of the spoil-bank surface, and this represents the primary control on drainage and runoff. Most spoil banks have an irregular and chaotic surface. Surface runoff forms a pattern of small channels down the slope, which can lead to sheet erosion or gullying.

Spoil-bank materials are relatively impervious and offer little capacity for groundwater storage. Material is without the protection of a vegetative cover immediately following excavation and is subject to rapid erosion. Sheet erosion, the removal of sediment particles by overland runoff from precipitation, is the dominant process by which sediment is produced from surface-mined lands in the East.[1]

Sheet erosion removes the finer particles from the surface of the spoil bank and exposes new material to agents of chemical weathering. Where sulfides are present, this can lead to acid drainage. Also, it is noted by the U.S. Geological Survey that the rates of sheet erosion in eastern Kentucky are about the same order of magnitude as the amounts of suspended sediment leaving their study areas.

Sheet erosion can lead to the formation of channels as erosion progresses. Over time, such channels can become enlarged into gullies. More commonly, however, gullies form from depressions gouged in spoil surfaces as large rocks and boulders are pushed downslope during operations. These depressions serve as initial drainage courses for runoff, concentrating erosive forces at a few places and resulting in very large sediment yield from those areas. In general, gullies form in proportion to the size of the area they drain, as well as the runoff this area produces.

A difficulty in assessing the impact of surface mining on the environment lies in the fact that most available data are derived from case studies, and it is often difficult to apply values obtained for one area in a general manner. The relative magnitude of pre- and post-mining levels of erosion provides a useful comparison, but even this is somewhat limited as the comparison deals only with effects and does not include consideration of their causes. Knowledge of the causative factors is required if technology is to be modified or operational sequences revised to minimize adverse or undesirable effects. Still, the case history data provide the only quantitative information about the effects of mining.

The U.S. Geological Survey[2] has noted that the amount of material removed from untreated spoil banks by sheet erosion decreases over a 4-year period, although the loss of material by gullying increased greatly during the same interval. This is explained by the concentration of large quantities of surface runoff into a single channel, where turbulence and high water velocity can erode and transport large volumes of material from the gully walls in the spoil bank.

A summary of numerical data for erosion and sedimentation data as reported by

---

[1]U.S. Geological Survey, "Catalog of Information on Water Data," edition 1970, appendix B.

[2]Council on Environmental Quality, "Environmental Quality: The First Annual Report of the Council on Environmental Quality," pp. 37-38, August 1970.

the U.S. Geological Survey for contour strip mining in similar geological, topographic, and climatological areas of eastern Kentucky is presented in Table 2. These data show that each factor is increased substantially over the conditions present in unmined areas. The largest difference is in sediment yield, which is about 1 to 2000 times as great for mined areas as for unmined areas. The derivations of major effects and trends are suggested in the table to give a better insight into the time a mined area would require to recover from the effects of disturbances.

The table indicates that coal-mine access roads represent the largest sediment yield from surface mining sites in the Appalachian region. The Council on Environmental Quality[1] determined that the estimated sediment yield during a rainstorm at highway construction sites was about 10 times that of cultivated lands, 200 times that for grass areas, and 2000 times that of forested areas, depending on rainfall, land slope, and exposure of banks. Highway construction sites are thus comparable to surface-mine spoil banks and access roads as a source of sediment, but with o ie important difference. Following the completion of construction, a systematic program of regular highway maintenance is commonly carried out, so that there appears to be a strong likelihood of significant reductions in sediment yields from highway sites over relatively short times. Such maintenance programs are not carried out for areas disturbed by surface mining.

Suspended sediment in streams. In humid climates like the northern Appalachian region, the amount of material exposed at the surface by natural processes for weathering or erosion has achieved relative equilibrium with patterns of rainfall and runoff. It was estimated[2] that 40 to 50 percent of precipitation remains as runoff that can carry with it dissolved and suspended matter derived from the soil and rock at the land surface. Surface mining of coal, especially by the contour strip mining method, generally disrupts the landscape and the natural cycle of drainage, leading to an increase in the amount of sediment present in streams.

The sediment load of a stream is influenced by the amount and intensity of precipitation, the rate of runoff, vegetative cover, and society's pattern of land use. Most of the annual sediment load of West Virginia is transported during the few days of high runoff in the spring and fall of the year, although the quantity of sediment in any given drainage basin varies and is different from year to year.

Suspended and bed-load sediments in streams have been increased as a result of surface mining. Several studies[3] have shown that the suspended-sediment content in surface-mined watersheds is more than 1000 times that in similar drainage basins where significant mining has not occurred. Bed-load sediment has also increased, filling in the stream channel, reducing its volume for carrying water, and

[1]Council on Environmental Quality, "Environmental Quality: The First Annual Report of the Council on Environmental Quality," pp. 37-38, August 1970.

[2]W. L. Doll; G. Meyer; and R. J. Archer, Water Resources of West Virginia. U.S. Geological Survey and West Virginia Department of Natural Resources, Division of Water Resources, 1963.

[3]W. R. Curtis "Strip Mining, Erosion, and Sedimentation," paper presented at 1970 Meeting of American Society of Agricultural Engineers, Minneapolis, 1970. Also *US Geol. Surv. Prof. Pap.* 427-A,B,C, 1963, 1964, 1970.

Table 2 Summary of erosion and sedimentation data from contour strip mining

Factor	Typical value	Comparison with unmined areas	Duration of major effects
Sheet erosion, spoil bank*	4.86−7.82 tons/acre	5−13 times as much	3−5 years,† decreases
Sediment yield, spoil bank†	400-600 tons/acre	1000 times as much	5−1(years, decreases
Sediment yield, access road†	90-400 tons/acre	2000−9000 times as much	n.e.‡
Erosion rate, spoil bank†	14.8 yd³/acre	5−10 times as much	3−5 years, decreases
Erosion rate, gully†	159 yd³/acre	5−10 times as much	3− years, decreases
Net dissolved solids, drainage area†	2.1 tons/acre	10 times (+) as much	n.e.
Net dissolved solids, spoil bank†	22 tons/acre	126 times as much	n.e.
Suspended sediment concentration†	5,000−19,000 ppm		2−5 years, decreases

*C. R. Collier et al., Influences of Strip Mining on the Hydrologic Environment of Parts of Beaver Creek Basin, Kentucky, 1955-1959, *US Geol. Surv. Prof. Pap.* 427-B, 1964.

†C. R. Collier, et al., Influences of Strip Mining on the Hydrologic Environment of Parts of Beaver Creek Basin, Kentucky, 1955-66, *US Geol. Surv. Prof. Pap.* 427-C, 1970.

‡n.e. = no estimate given.

enhancing the likelihood of flooding.

The character of suspended sediment washed from surface-mined areas changes with time. At first, sediment is composed mainly of fine-grained material that is produced in the breaking of rocks and movement of soil as a result of mining activities. Later, the breakdown of soil is less rapid, and larger-sized particles are predominant in the sediment. This can be attributed to the stabilization of slopes through reclamation or through the approach to a new equilibrium of weathering of the disturbed material, or both.

Sediments occurring in the bed load of streams will represent relatively larger and heavier particles that will travel generally short distances from their sources. On the other hand, the smaller particles that are commonly present in far greater numbers travel significantly greater distances owing to their lesser weight.

Revegetation

Revegetation of surface-mined lands has become virtually synonymous with reclamation for many people. This is not surprising, as much of the work in reclamation emphasized the search for plants that could be relied upon to establish themselves and survive in surface mine spoils.

Initial revegetation efforts attempted to directly reestablish climax or intermediate species on lands disturbed by surface mining. These efforts included attempts to plant numerous seedlings and trees, but the results were generally unsuccessful as most woody species either did not survive or failed to achieve soil stabilization. The U.S. Department of Agriculture's Soil Conservation Service[1] noted that even where such plantings have become established, insufficient litter for erosion control was produced, and there was continued active erosion in certain plantings 9 to 12 years old.

Present revegetation practices emphasize the early establishment of a series of vegetative species on spoil areas following mining operations as quickly as possible to provide a foundation for a more or less natural progression toward an intermediate or climax condition.

There are two fundamental topics that are essential to successful revegetation of surface-mined areas. First, it is essential to know the basic characteristics of the "seed bed," in this case the surface mine spoil, so that it can be prepared properly with the nutrients necessary to support plant growth. Second, it is critical to know the environmental tolerances of a variety of plant or seed species to select those varieties that will have the highest prospect for successful growth under the conditions present in the spoil. Each of these topics is considered in turn.

Spoil character. Information about spoil character is necessary for planning revegetation operations. In particular, it is important to have data on pH, slope, stoniness, position in mined area, and typical coal seams. Each factor can exert an important influence on the potential for vegetation to become established, and their interactions with one another often prove to be critical in determining the longer-range survivability of the vegetation.

Another important constraint upon vegetation reestablishment is related to slope aspect, e.g., the direction which the slope faces. In most U.S. localities, north- and northeast-facing slopes are commonly cool and wet, offering relatively favorable sites for vegetation, while south- and southwest-facing slopes are usually hot and dry, presenting a far more severe environment for vegetation. Vogel[2] notes that weeping lovegrass (a common species used in revegetating spoil areas in Appalachia) died out after 1 year on south-facing slopes but lived as long as 4 years on level benches and north-facing slopes. Other species fare similarly, although each would have somewhat different survival times. The problem with small seedlings is that they normally grow in deep shade; when exposed on a spoil bank, they literally are sunburned and die.

Elevation of disturbed areas is an important consideration in selecting species

[1]U.S. Department of Agriculture, Soil Conservation Service "Strip Mine Spoil Plantings," Aug. 31, 1967. (Manuscript.)

[2]W. G. Vogel, Weeping Lovegrass for Vegetating Strip-Mine Spoils in Appalachia, *Proc. First Weeping Lovegrass Symp.*, Apr. 28-29, 1970. (The Samuel Roberts Noble Foundation, Ardmore, Okla.)

for replanting, and the Soil Conservation Service[1] recommends different species for sites, depending on their elevations.

Spoil age exerts an important influence over its receptiveness to revegetation. The permeability of spoils decreases with age as weathering produces increasing amounts of fine-textured spoil, leading to poor aeration and internal drainage that may be harmful to plant development. Too much aeration would also be adverse to plant success. Grading of spoils results in compaction of spoil from 8 to 12 inches, impairing the ability of plants to establish root systems and effectively advancing the aging process. Spoils require at least 2 years to settle to fairly well-fixed angles of repose when no special precautions are taken. Chemical weathering of spoils often leads to relatively high acidity in spoils for 5 to 6 years after mining when no spoil treatment to neutralize such acidity is applied. Bare spoil areas are hotter, drier, and more windswept than other planting areas; in other words, these areas have a "southern aspect" by virtue of their physical and chemical character, and present a harsh environment for reestablishment of vegetation.

Features and phenomena present at individual sites will determine the degree of difficulty in reestablishing vegetative cover at these sites. However, it is possible for operators to control adverse effects of spoil material by proper placement in accordance with recognizable properties during mining operations and regrading.[2]

Spoil chemistry. Research in revegetation indicates that "success in establishing various types of vegetation on strip mine spoils is often limited by spoil acidity, especially in the East. Thus, for planning revegetation programs on strip mined areas, a knowledge of the relative spoil acidity is essential."[3] There are several simple techniques to rapidly carry out measurements of soil acidity in the field, and many are routinely carried out on operations in Appalachia.

The characteristics of Appalachian surface mine spoils were recently investigated to assess the opportunities for successful reestablishment of vegetation and the probability of surface mining affecting the chemistry of associated streams.[4] The soil-sized fraction (less than a 2-millimeter particle size) averaged 37 percent for all spoils studied. Although certain Appalachian spoils thus have sufficient soil-sized materials to retain adequate amounts of water during normal weather conditions, they are vulnerable to erosion, chemical weathering, and leaching of soluble compounds.

Experiments to study the nutrient regime of spoils indicate fertilizer treatments incorporating nitrogen and phosphorous would effectively increase the yield of plantings on a majority of spoils. However, leaching of fertilizer from spoils can result in a return to initial nutrient-deficient conditions and an adverse effect on

[1] U.S. Department of Agriculture, Soil Conservation Service, "Report of Interagency Evaluation of Surface Mine Reclamation in West Virginia," July 26-30, 1971. (Manuscript.)

[2] Richard M. Smith, "Interagency Evaluation on Surface Mine Spoil Reclamation," memorandum, July 26-30, 1971.

[3] W. A. Berg, Determining pH of Strip-Mine Spoils, *US Dep. Agric., Forest Serv. Res. Note* NE-98, 1969.

[4] W. T. Plass, and W. G. Vogel, "The Chemical Properties and Particle Size Distribution of Thirty-nine Southern West Virginia Surface Mine Spoils," U.S. Department of Agriculture, Forest Service, Northeastern Forest Experiment Station, Berea, Ky., manuscript, 20 pages, 1971.

vegetation survival unless maintenance or other forms of continued treatment are provided.

Assessment of the Future of Surface Coal Mining

Surface mining's share of total national production increased steadily over recent years, until it now accounts for roughly half the total. During this time, the capacities of surface mining equipment increased steadily, culminating in giant overburden excavators and coal-haulage units. This equipment was developed through the time-honored coal mining approach of trial, error, and refinement. As a result, a strong technological base has been established.

The capacities of existing surface coal mining equipment thus cover a wide range and appear capable of dealing with most prospective future mining situations. The giant equipment developed in the 1960s, it is suggested here, represents an upper practical limit to capacity that will probably be duplicated rarely if at all in the future. The reason for this was stated concisely as follows:

> While [giant] equipment is physically capable of moving deeper and deeper overburden, the performance increase is not always proportional to the investment cost. For example, a 100 cubic yard shovel operating at a depth of 92 feet can handle somewhat more than twice the volume of a 45 cubic yard shovel operating in 52 feet of overburden. But operating under these conditions for the same thickness of coal, the net increase in coal availability would be less than 20 percent.[2]

An additional, nontrivial concern is that if a giant machine represents the most productive capacity at a given property, failure of the machine could curtail or at best seriously impair production.

In view of these facts, it seems likely that future surface mining for the remainder of the century will employ the array of equipment types in existence at present. Surely, equipment improvements are to be expected to increase efficiency and operation, but it seems clear that the basic equipment types and classes have been perfected through the developments of recent years, and that the resulting technology will be employed in prospective future operations.

In terms of R&D on surface mining methods, there appears to be little real need for much effort in giant excavating equipment. Rather, effort appears to be revived in perfecting the manner in which such equipment is employed, especially in new geological and geographical locales, to minimize adverse environmental impact and optimize coal recovery.

Although the capability of surface mining equipment is great, the coal reserves amenable to its deployment are not great in comparison to those accessible primarily by underground methods. As pointed out in Chapter 3, roughly one-third of the total recoverable coal reserves can be developed through surface mining. It is somewhat paradoxical that highly efficient equipment has been perfected to work these limited reserves (and that the rapid expansion of such equipment will merely accelerate the depletion of these finite deposits). As a result, it hardly appears likely that surface mining can maintain its present share of total coal output, let alone increase it to meet greater demands.

This chapter has served to introduce coal mining methods used in production operations. With this foundation, it is appropriate to review trends in the application of coal production technology, presented in the following chapter.

CHAPTER SIX

TRENDS IN COAL PRODUCTION TECHNOLOGY

Trends in coal production technology illustrate patterns of coal development in the United States. This chapter contains such data, compiled from annual issues of *Minerals Yearbook*, published by the U.S. Bureau of Mines. The compilation extends from 1940 to the early 1970s; this period of time was chosen to present essential recent information describing the changes experienced by the industry in recent years. This historical record provides a basis for recognizing the potentials for future evolution of the industry.

The proportion of coal produced by the principal mining methods has changed in the past 30 years. The total marketed production ranged between 400 and 600 million tons.

1. The production from surface mining increased from about 50 million tons in 1940 to over 300 million tons in 1977, a sixfold increase (Figure 1).
2. The production from deep mining declined from over 500 million tons in the early 1940s to about 275 million tons in 1977, almost half its maximum value. In deep mining, continuous mining increased its share of the total deep mining production, finally exceeding that from conventional mining in the late 1960s.

The U.S. Bureau of Mines recently noted that "much of the potential of mechanization appears to have been reached" in deep mining. However, these data were based on averages and the conclusion may be overly pessimistic. Accordingly, it is appropriate at this point to examine trends in surface and deep mining methods.

TRENDS IN DEEP MINING METHODS

Methods currently used for deep mining of coal have evolved through a number of developments, physical and economic conditions, and circumstances that are difficult to isolate and analyze. Therefore, attention in this chapter is focused on

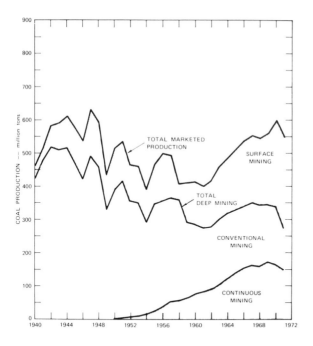

Figure 1. Trends in coal production by mining method. (From U.S. Bureau of Mines, *Miner. Yearb.*, various years.)

production statistics for various methods or technologies as reported by the Bureau of Mines. Regardless of the nature or characteristics of the method, its degree of success and acceptance by the industry may be regarded as directly proportional to the amount of coal production it achieves.

Figure 2 show trends in deep mining methods. In the 1940s all deep-mined coal was produced by conventional mining. Shortly after that decade began, power drilling of shotholes exceeded hand drilling. In the following years, hand drilling declined rapidly and at present represents a very small tonnage. Power drilling of shotholes became the dominant method of conventional mining in the late 1940s and most of the 1950s, but its production level started a decline in the late 1950s, which continues to the present day. Starting in the late 1940s and continuing to the present, the production achieved by continuous mining was increased to the point in the late 1960s where it surpassed conventional mining by all methods of shothole drilling. Starting in the late 1960s, longwall mining began in the United States, but at present its production is small.

These trends are instructive regarding the state of deep mining. A few key factors are listed below:

1. Each new method is more mechanized than the older methods, providing the capability of achieving production with fewer workers.
2. There is a time lag of at least 10 years from the introduction of a new technology to its widespread application resulting in substantial production. This is best illustrated by continuous mining. It may be that longwall mining represents the start of another cycle.

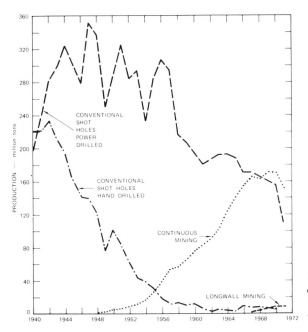

Figure 2. Trends in methods for deep mining of coal. (From U.S. Bureau of Mines, *Miner. Yearb.*, various years.)

3. Introduction of new technologies such as continuous mining as a replacement for older technologies such as conventional mining. This results in total production being relatively constant, and the total capacity of the industry is not significantly increased through the new technology.

4. The data suggest that, in a period of economic stress or changed regulations (such as that following enforcement of the Federal Coal Mine Health and Safety Act of 1969), older technologies that require larger work forces will be most severely affected, as seen in the much sharper drop in production from conventional mining. This marked reduction may be viewed as an attempt to control labor cost, while the relatively smaller decline in continuous mining probably reflects the smaller work force required. Another factor in the smaller decline in continuous mining (but quite difficult to assess) is the degree to which operations were continued in spite of increased costs to satisfy investment or production commitments.

Similar trends are shown in mechanical loading (Figure 3). Hand loading declined in the 1950s, being replaced by mobile loaders. These rates, however, were not entirely the same as the advent of mining methods (compare Figure 4). This suggests that some components of deep mining operations systems yield less readily to improved technology. Stated another way, there are time lags of varying duration for the introduction of new methods at several stages of operation. This topic clearly requires comprehensive study; probably, both technical and institutional constraints control the application of new technologies, and these will need to be understood if real progress is to be made.

Figure 4 shows trends in deep-mine haulage equipment. This is primarily main

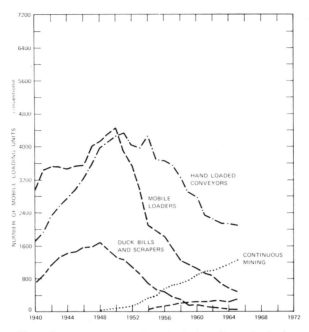

Figure 3. Trends in use of mechanical loading units in deep mining of coal. (From U.S. Bureau of Mines, *Miner. Yearb.*, various years.)

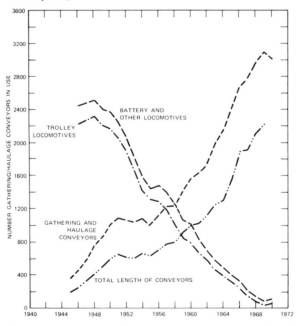

Figure 4. Trends in use of haulage equipment in deep mining of coal. (From U.S. Bureau of Mines, *Miner. Yearb.*, various years.)

haulage rather than face haulage. Although not directly expressed in terms of production, these data also suggest a rather substantial shift toward less labor-intensive operations in the post-World War II period. This shift toward more rapid haulage methods is consistent with the needs of the higher-capacity mining methods that were increasingly used during this time. As in the case of mining methods, however, the newer technologies appear to have replaced those used previously, and thus the total overall capacity remains relatively constant.

A principal reason for the replacement of deep mining technologies appears to be the economic advantages in lower labor costs and higher productivity. Operators that persist in using certain technologies may be at an economic disadvantage unless they are able to achieve production at costs comparable with their potential competitors. Yet, replacement of technologies does not necessarily improve resource recovery or add to overall capacity, especially during the interval when the replacement is in progress. Another crucial factor is that in important respects at least some new technologies pose greater health and safety hazards than those they replace. The balancing of these intricate economic, technological, and social factors is an institutional problem of the first magnitude. A careful analysis is required at an early date if the requisite coal production from deep mining is available to meet national energy needs.

Figure 5 shows trends in numbers of deep mine equipment in use. Mobile loading machines have decreased in numbers during the 1950s, but are showing a gradual increase in recent years. At the same time, there has been substantial

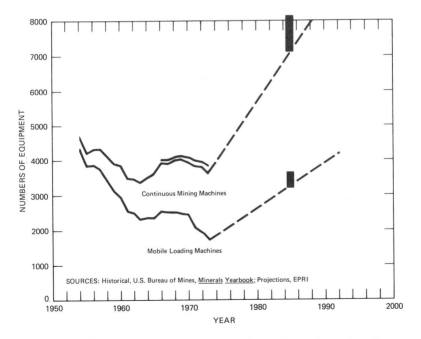

Figure 5. Trends in numbers of deep mining equipment in use. (From U.S. Bureau of mines, *Miner. yearb.*, various years.)

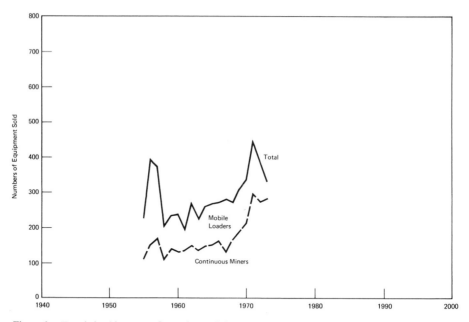

Figure 6. Trends in shipments of new deep mining equipment. (From U.S. Bureau of Mines, *Miner. Yearb.*, various years.)

growth in continuous miners. In recent years, a growing number of longwall machines have been used in deep mines.

These data on equipment in use need to be compared with trends of shipments of new deep mining equipment (Figure 6). The figure shows that the numbers of continuous miners shipped in recent years is more than five times that of mobile loaders (and, presumably, other conventional mining equipment). The fact that coal loaders still comprise such a large amount of equipment in use, coupled with a relatively small number of new shipments, suggests that most of those machines are old and likely to be of lower capacity. In contrast, continuous miners are more likely to be of more recent vintage and of higher capacity (although it is rare to find actual operations using more than a fraction at this capacity).

TRENDS IN SURFACE MINING METHODS

Figure 7 shows trends in surface mining methods. Most surface production is from area strip mining, with relatively small amounts from augering. The growth in strip mining was especially significant in the 1960s, leading to the situation where, in the early 1970s, surface mining production actually surpassed that from deep mining.

The growth in surface mining is directly related to the types and capacities of excavating equipment used to strip away soil and rock to expose coal seams for removal. Figure 8 shows trends in surface-mine excavating equipment. Power shovels are predominant, although in recent years draglines have become more

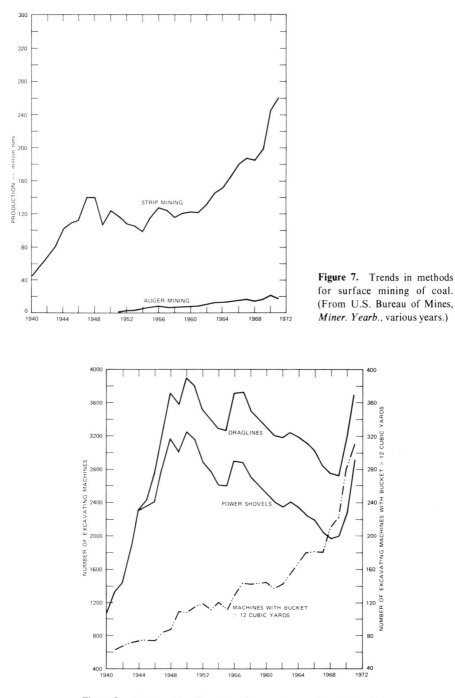

Figure 7. Trends in methods for surface mining of coal. (From U.S. Bureau of Mines, *Miner. Yearb.*, various years.)

Figure 8. Relationship of number of excavating machines to bucket capacity in surface mining of coal. (From U.S. Bureau of Mines, *Miner. Yearb.*, various years.)

numerous. These machines are inherently different in concept. Power shovels travel on the coal seam, and their excavations are above and away from the machine. Draglines, on the other hand, travel on the soil and rock above the coal and dig down and toward the machine. Each has certain advantages for particular conditions, although in many respects operator experience and preference are the determining factors in choice of excavating equipment.

The number of excavators declined in the 1950s and 1960s, with this trend reversing only in the early 1970s as surface mining spurted upward (Figure 1). Probably more significant, however, is the steady increase in large-capacity excavating equipment during the same interval. The number of machines with buckets greater than 12 cubic yards capacity roughly doubled during the 1960s. Although the Bureau of Mines changed the reporting practices slightly in 1970, this increase in the number of high-capacity equipment appears to have continued in the present decade.

Ancillary earthmoving equipment in use at surface mines was historically relatively constant until the 1970s, when a substantial increase occurred (Figure 9). Most of these smaller earthmovers are bulldozers, with fewer scrapers. The size of these machines also increased during this interval, although the Bureau of Mines has reported no quantitative statistical information on their capacities.

Haulage data for surface mines show similar trends (Figure 10). The number of trucks decreased in the last 20 years, while the average capacity and average distance hauled increased. Thus the haulage capacity was at least retained and most likely expanded.

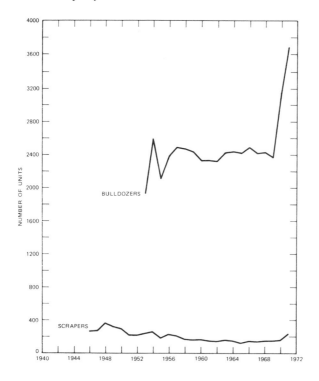

Figure 9. Trends in use of bulldozers and scrapers in surface mining of coal. (From U.S. Bureau of Mines, *Miner. Yearb.*, various years.)

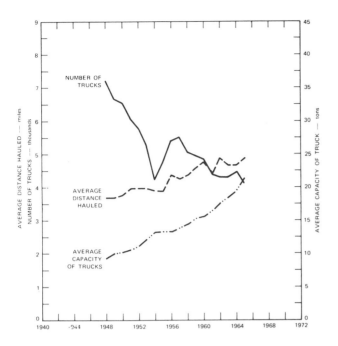

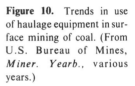

Figure 10. Trends in use of haulage equipment in surface mining of coal. (From U.S. Bureau of Mines, *Miner. Yearb.*, various years.)

In contrast to the trends in deep mining technology, developments in surface mining were such as to greatly expand the production capacity through development of new and giant equipment. The increased technical capability was greatly in excess of increases in work force related to larger numbers of mines. While deep-mine technical improvements enabled maintenance of production levels with a smaller work force, surface mining technology greatly augmented the production attainable by the present work force. This difference in the developments of the two coal mining methods is central to the character of new operations for achieving increased production levels to supply coal to meet future needs. Clearly, automation of deep mining will be most costly and time-consuming because of the need to develop new and improved technologies. On the other hand, surface mining technology already exists to augment supplies from favorable deposits; the principal limitation on applying such technology lies in the yet-to-be-realized approaches for mitigation and control of adverse environmental impacts from surface operations.

Figure 11 compares capacity to monthly production for draglines and power shovels. The data show that, for machines of comparable size, shovels have slightly higher monthly production. This may be attributed to the lower precision of dragline bucket maneuverability. At comparable excavating capacity, draglines also have greater power requirements than shovels and have had an increasing growth in recent years, largely as a result of other excavating considerations (Figure 12).

There are strong economic reasons for relying upon smaller-sized excavating

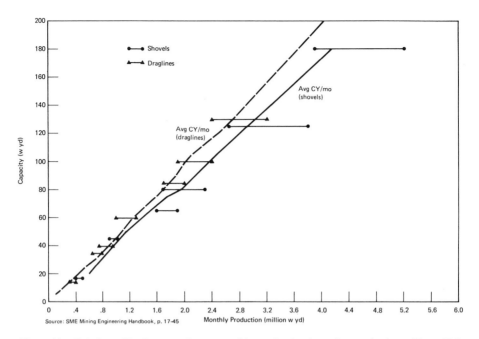

Figure 11. Relation of bucket capacity to monthly production in surface coal mines. (From U.S. Bureau of Mines, *Miner. Yearb.*, various years.)

equipment. Cone et al.[1] showed the importance of combining engineering cost analyses with econometric analysis. While the unit cost of moving overburden decreases as machine size increases, this does not tell the whole story. It was found that marginal productivity decreased as machine size is increased; in other words, for each unit of weight added to larger machines, less than a unit of overburden is moved. Accordingly, as the size of the machine is increased, its unit cost increases. The authors state that "economies of scale do not exist in larger machines. The economic machine at present is smaller than the maximum size now in use." In engineering terms, the "optimal" size machine is between 105 and 130 cubic yards, but in economic terms, the optimal size is between 25 and 50 cubic yards capacity.

Two important conclusions are drawn from this analysis. It is pointed out by the authors that (1) diseconomies of scale do exist with respect to stripping equipment, and (2) the portion of the coal-supply curve contributed by stripping cost is inelastic. This latter point is critical, because decreasing returns can occur; small increases in output can be obtained at greather than proportional increases in cost. In conclusion, they noted that "if it is necessary to mine coal from beneath deeper layers of overburden and no improvements are made, this mining operation will result in a greater than proportional cost. As the demand for coal increases, given an inelastic supply, coal prices will tend to rise for this operation only."[2]

[1]B. W. Cone, L. J. Defferding, and W. I. Enderlin, "An Economic Analysis of Shovels and Draglines Used in U.S. Surface Coal Mines," Battelle Pacific Northwest Laboratories, June 1976.
[2]*Ibid.*

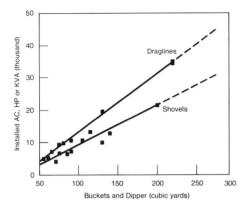

Figure 12. Growth rate of load on a power system as deeper coal is stripped with shovel and dragline. (From U.S. Bureau of Mines, *Miner. Yearb.,* various years.)

The surface coal mining industry thus runs the risk of being overcapitalized, with too much money invested in fewer, larger, but relatively inefficient machines. These factors, more than any outside pressures about environmental quality, will be the real determinant controlling the magnitude and type of surface coal mining.

Actually, we already may have reached the point where coal reserves most readily accessible to the smaller, "optimal" machines may be approaching full development (or the limits of public tolerance toward their development, which is effectively the same thing). To avoid overcapitalization, producers may again turn to underground operations. Of course, should underground operations be undertaken, the problem is to avoid overcapitalization there as well (caused by investment in machines with high theoretical capacity is rarely approached in practice, such as continuous mining machines).

In view of these facts, it seems likely that surface mining for the remainder of the century will employ the existing array of equipment types. Surely, equipment improvements are to be expected to increase efficiency and operation, but it seems reasonable to conclude that the basic equipment types and classes have been perfected through the developments of recent years, and that the resulting technology will be employed in prospective future operations.

In terms of R&D on surface mining methods, there appears to be little real need for much effort in giant excavating equipment. Rather, effort appears to be revived in perfecting the manner in which such equipment is employed, so as to minimize adverse environmental impact and optimize coal recovery.

TRENDS IN COAL CLEANING

Trends in coal cleaning are directly related to trends in mining methods. As noted earlier, raw coal produced by certain mining methods (notably continuous mining) contains wastes and refuse that must be removed from the coal prior to use. To clean the coals, a variety of mechanical processes are used that rely upon the difference in density of coal and other rocks or minerals to separate them from the coal. However, the cleaning methods are imperfectly discriminatory among coal and wastes (in similar fashion to mining), and roughly 20 to 30 percent of raw coal may be lost as a result of cleaning. This lost coal and waste material is termed *refuse* and is discarded near coal-cleaning plants.

Thus, total coal production is represented by the raw coal figure, while total marketed production is raw coal less refuse. In 1970, the total raw coal production was about 700 million tons, but the total marketed production was only about 600 million tons—this latter figure is the commonly reported number, because it refers to coal actually entering the markets.

The 30-year period since 1940 shows a steady increase in refuse of nearly 10-fold (Figure 13). The amount of uncleaned coal was substantially reduced in the mid to late 1950s and early 1960s (or in other words, most coal was cleaned). This was a time of relatively low production, and it is likely that cleaning was employed to present the highest quality product to remaining consumers. The amount of uncleaned coal increased again in the late 1960s, and continues to increase in the 1970s. This may be because cleaning causes coal losses and diminishes the total available to be sold. In a period of heavy demand for coal, certain consumers such as electric utilities might have been willing to accept uncleaned coal to ensure their supply. Also, in time of increasing coal prices, they may have found that the added cost for cleaning coal was more than they could afford to pay.

Figure 14 shows trends in the methods of coal cleaning. In the last 30 years, jigs maintained their principal role as the most common cleaning method, accounting for nearly half the total. The same period has seen the growth of dense-medium separation and concentrating tables to the point where they represent, respectively, the second and third most used methods. Relatively little coal is cleaned by pneumatic methods or by wet classifiers and launders.

Figure 15 shows trends in coal crushing. Although the numbers of plants crush-

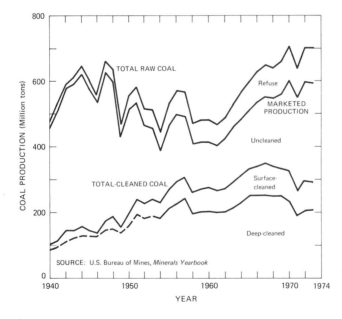

Figure 13. Trends in coal cleaning. (From U.S. Bureau of Mines, *Miner. Yearb.*, various years.)

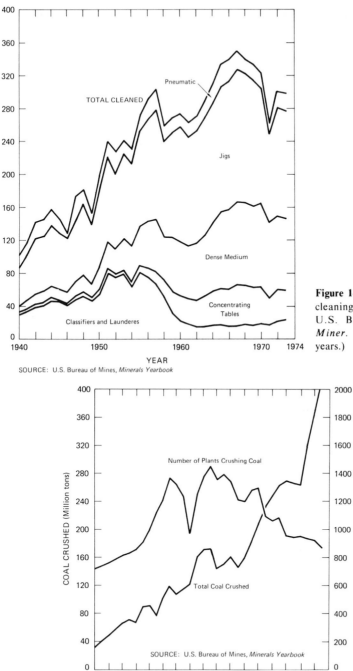

Figure 14. Trends in coal-cleaning methods. (From U.S. Bureau of Mines, *Miner. Yearb.*, various years.)

SOURCE: U.S. Bureau of Mines, *Minerals Yearbook*

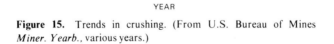

Figure 15. Trends in crushing. (From U.S. Bureau of Mines *Miner. Yearb.*, various years.)

ing coal has declined in recent years, the total coal crushed has increased steadily (leveling off only recently).

These data suggest that the rated growth in coal cleaning and crushing capacity in recent years will probably not represent a constraint upon conversion to other fuels. Indeed many conversion processes are able to process coal without resort to cleaning, so that this would not even be required in those circumstances.

It is important to bear in mind that heating values remain in the material discarded as refuse. With roughly 100 million tons of this material being produced annually, it would be worthwhile to examine ways to employ this in connection with energy conversion processes.

TRENDS IN PRODUCTION BY MINE CAPACITY

Most coal in recent years has been produced from large-capacity mines (Figure 16). This is a recent development. The share of total production by mines producing more than 500,000 tons annually has grown from about one-quarter in 1950 to nearly two-thirds in 1970. During the same time, the production from the next largest mines (200,000–500,000 tons) has declined. As a result, much of current

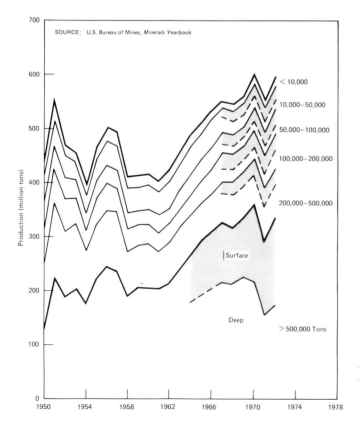

Figure 16. Coal production by mine capacity. (From U.S. Bureau of Mines, *Miner. Yearb.*, various years.)

coal production is represented by sizable operations, a change from prior patterns where producing units were relatively small. One consequence of this trend is to emphasize the "baseload" production capacity of the larger mines and to deemphasize the "intermediate" or "peaking" production from smaller mines (by analogy with electric utilities). This trend is consistent with a basic trend of the electric utility industry, the coal industry's largest customer. However, with so much production capacity in large mines, the historical coal industry problem of overcapacity could reappear in the future should conditions change.

It may also be noted that the sizes of mines are adjusted to "satisfy recognized consumption patterns."[1] The increase in the size of utility plants as pointed out above was paralleled by an increase in the amount of production from large coal mines (Figure 16). Intermediate-sized mines diminished, while smaller mines appeared to remain at relatively constant number, serving to supplement coal produced by the large operations that bear the principal responsibility for coal supply.

This point was summarized[2] as follows:

An important factor in coal supply, particularly in emergencies, is the size of mines . . . in 1972, over 56% of production came from less than 6% of the mines, and 73% from 12% of the mines. On the other hand, only 16.8% of total output came from 79% [3870] of the mines. *Of significance in this respect is that smaller mines, many of which are surface operations, provide the greatest flexibility for increased coal production to meet emergency requirements, as demonstrated effectively in 1970.* They are not as difficult to open and close as are larger mines, and their production is not so highly bound to contracts, such as at large mines. [Emphasis added.]

The decrease in the numbers of intermediate and small mines in recent years thus reduced a degree of flexibility essential in responding to changed situations.

If recent trends continue, future increases in production capacity will probably be in large, baseload mines to the extend that reserves and available capital and firm supply contracts will permit. Smaller mines will probably continue to be developed as well, where reserves are more limited or where secure markets may not be identified.

Figure 16 also illustrates the increase in production share by surface mining (although data by mining method are limited only to recent years). The largest increase in surface mine production took place in large mines during recent years. It is interesting to note that surface mining accounts for the bulk of production in the four smallest production categories. This is consistent with the "peaking" analogy in that small surface mines can be opened in a relatively short time, and thereby their production can be available to augment major supplies from other sources. Only the intermediate-sized mines (200,000−500,000 tons) have more deep production than surface, probably because of the more steady demand for coal that they serve.

In terms of mining technology, it is reasonable to expect that, generally speak-

[1]C. L. Christensen, "Economic Redevelopment in Bituminous Coal," Harvard, Cambridge, Mass., 1962.

[2]U.S. Bureau of Mines, Assessment of the Impact of Air Quality Requirements on Coal in 1975 and 1980, *Bit. Coal Lignite Rep. Suppl.,* January 1974.

ing, smaller operations employ older, less mechanized equipment while larger mines may be expected to have larger numbers of more modern equipment. There are numerous exceptions to this situation, of course. However, because of the capital requirements, it seems most likely that the larger mines would have the wherewithal to acquire newer, improved technology as it becomes available. Unless steps are taken to aid in upgrading the technology at smaller mines (especially deep mines), it would be increasingly difficult for them to fulfill their role in supplying "peaking" coal. As noted above, this would mean that larger mines would have to add to their capacity to compensate for the production, and this could lead toward the re-creation of a situation of overcapacity in the industry as existed in earlier years.

TRENDS IN EMPLOYMENT AND PRODUCTION

The age distribution of current miners as of January 1971 was analyzed by Leo Kramer, Inc.[1] It was found that the following existed:

Starting age	% of current miners
Under 20	42.1
20–24	32.5
25–29	14.3
30–34	7.5
35+	5.7

These data suggest that many young people have found the mining industry their initial employer in the coalfields. Fewer older men start work in the coal mines. This could be attributed to the nature of the work and to the level of skills of the older workers.

A significant decrease in the numbers of miners under 20 years of age who started in the industry took place around the late 1940s or early 1950s (refer to Table 1); note that the numbers of workers age 35–39 in 1971 who started when they were under 20 years old are about half the numbers of workers aged 40–44 who started when they were under 20. The exact reason for this sharp drop (which has continued and intensified up to the present) is not known, although it is probably related to changed conditions in the coalfields that lead to alternate opportunities in a diversifying economy. It may be, however, that this is related to the BCOA–UMWA wage agreement of 1950 and to the protection of workers already in the industry, through their seniority rights, from layoffs due to mechanization. This could have reduced the numbers of new entrants into the industry at that time, and this reduction in opportunities for new entrants into the coal industry appears to have continued for roughly 20 years. As a result, young people native to the coalfields who would normally have entered the industry as a new "class" each year were forced to seek other employment starting in the early

[1]Kramer Assoc., "Determination of Labor Management Requirements to Meet the Goals of Project Independence." Report to Federal Energy Administration, 1975.

Table 1 Starting age of miners, January 1971

Current age group	Total current miners	Under 20	Starting age				Average age at start
			20−24	25−29	30−34	35+	
Total number	104,600	44,022	31,873	14,955	7,819	5,931	22.7
Percentage	100.00	42.09	30.47	14.30	7.47	5.67	
Under 20	1,151	1,151					18.8
20−24	8,713	2,748	5,965				21.1
25−29	11,035	1,966	4,844	4,225			23.6
30−34	10,261	2,180	2,095	3,378	2,608		25.7
35−39	9,644	3,696	2,195	788	1,714	1,251	25.0
40−44	12,887	6,236	3,893	830	340	1,588	22.9
45−49	15,429	7,994	4,618	1,504	455	858	22.1
50−54	15,847	7,924	4,184	2,212	887	634	22.2
55−59	12,813	6,399	3,160	1,327	1,280	647	22.3
60 and over	6,820	3,728	919	685	535	953	23.6

Source: UMWA Welfare and Retirement Fund survey.

1950s, leading to a substantial out-migration from several mining areas. There is evidence, however, that there has been a shift to larger numbers of young miners in recent years (Table 2). It remains to be seen whether this shift can reverse the trend of the previous 20 years.

The Kramer study also examined the number of workers who would leave the coal industry by 1980. It was concluded that work force "attrition" would be as follows to 1980:

1. Retirement: 5500 workers per year (4500 miners, 1000 supervisory, etc.)
2. Disability: 4000 in 1973, 2000 in 1974, 1000 annually thereafter.
3. Turnover: 1 percent of work force per year (separations, deaths, etc.)
4. Total workers leaving industry annually as of 1975 = 7500, or about 6−7 percent of the work force.

Table 2 Age distribution of bituminous coal miners, 1961−1970

Year ending Dec. 31	Percent of total in age group				Weighted average age
	Under 30	30−44	45−59	60 and over	
1961	2.9	40.8	49.5	6.8	46.0
1962	2.8	39.1	52.0	6.1	46.2
1963	3.8	36.7	53.1	6.4	45.1
1964	5.5	35.2	52.7	6.6	46.2
1965	6.6	33.8	52.9	6.7	46.1
1966	9.0	31.0	53.1	6.9	45.9
1967	11.4	32.5	49.6	6.5	44.9
1970*	20.0	31.4	42.1	6.5	43.0

*The Dec. 31, 1970, data are the same as those presented by the UMWA Fund for Jan. 1, 1971.

Source: Bituminous Coal Operators Association. Data derived from the UMWA Welfare and Retirement Fund.

These figures are lower than a previous estimate by Given,[1] who stated that "on a strictly mathematical basis, without allowance for any change in the averages created by enlargement of the working forces, the industry could lose some 6 to 7 percent of its people a year because of *retirement alone.* In certain specialized classifications, such as maintenance supervisors and technicians, the rate may be even higher." [Emphasis added.] It seems apparent that, as long as people mine coal, the work force situation will continue to be a "factor potentially limiting supply."

This review of trends in coal production technology presented data on how much coal was produced or processed by different methods. While useful, knowledge of the amount of coal produced by each method does not indicate how effectively operations were carried out. As an attempt to address this facet of coal production, trends in productivity are discussed in the following chapter.

[1] Ivan A. Given, Manpower for Coal, *Coal Age,* pp. 60-66, May 1967.

CHAPTER SEVEN

TRENDS IN COAL MINE PRODUCTIVITY

INTRODUCTION

Even a casual consideration of coal characteristics, occurrence, and recovery methods reveals the variability of deposits, coal quality, and mined material. This variability greatly complicates analysis of important aspects of the coal industry, as it tends to frustrate attempts to employ simplifying concepts—there are just too many exceptions, and there has been a tendency to deal either in special cases (which are not generally applicable) or in averages (which are not representative of real conditions).

Productivity can be employed as a unifying basis for expressing many key aspects of mining operations, including costs, facilitating analysis of these factors. In this chapter, productivity is defined as coal produced per miner-day (alternatively, it may be defined as coal produced per unit shift[1] or per miner-hour). Productivity is useful because it incorporates the several variables in coal occurrence and mining methods but does not require discrimination among them for purposes of analysis. Productivity can be considered in the aggregate or for individual mines (in which case the sensitivity of local factors would be of obvious importance). Finally, productivity may be readily determined from statistics commonly published by state agencies for each mine, giving annual coal production, number of employees, and number of days worked.

The Significance of Averages

Most production and productivity data reported by the U.S. Bureau of Mines are averages for all mines in a certain county, state, or nation. These average data are heavily influenced by the larger number of relatively smaller or older operations and accordingly present a very conservative indication of the present capability of mining technology. Although most pronounced for deep mines, the same is true for surface mines. The effect of using average productivity data is to understate the

---

[1] A unit shift is defined as the operation of all equipment in a face-crew unit for an 8-hour shift.

present mine capacity; the amount of misstatement is determined by the difference between the average productivity and the actual productivity achieved at an individual mine.[1]

The average statistics reported for coal mining are rather similar to those employed by the Department of Agriculture. In a recent assessment of programs it was noted that "including these small farms [substitute 'mines'] in the statistics tends to exaggerate the low-income position of commercial farmers [substitute 'large mining companies'] . . . relative to the rest of the economy and hence adds pressure to raise prices of farm commodities [substitute 'coal']."[2] Obviously, raised prices would lead to increased profits, if costs were held constant.

In spite of these limitations of average productivity data, the status of much publicly available statistical information on the coal mining industry is such that there is little practical alternative to their use in analysis. This is an institutional problem. The following consequences of using average productivity data are noted.

1. It is not possible to assess the range of productivity, leading to uncertainty about industry capacity.
2. Averages understate production capacity but overstate costs.
3. Averages understate productive capacity but overstate the need for labor. The amount of overstatement is determined by the difference between average and actual productivity.

In the subsequent discussion, we shall seek to explore the significance of productivity, both in averages and actual cases. Therefore, although this chapter necessarily employs average productivity data, and while the analysis suggests the significance of these data, it was not possible to assess the range of productivity values and the uncertainty this may bring to interpretation of the data. It will be important to keep this fact in mind in reviewing the subsequent discussion.

TRENDS IN PRODUCTIVITY

Coal mine productivity has increased steadily throughout most of the last 30 years (Figure 1). This increase has been experienced in both surface and deep mine operations, and an indication of the magnitude of the increase may be suggested by inspection of average data (with full allowance that these are not representative of any particular mine).

The largest increase in productivity was experienced in surface mining, resulting from the introduction of giant equipment in the 1960s. A smaller increase in productivity occurred in deep mining, a result of the growth in continuous mining.

[1]See also H. E. Risser, Coal Mine Productivity—Some Things the Averages Don't Tell, *Proc. Counc. Econ., AIME,* 1966.

[2]U.S. Department of Agriculture, quoted by Burt Schorr, Cash-Crop Decline? Butz Seeks to Reduce Subsidies to Farmers and May Well Succeed, *Wall St. J.,* p. 1, Jan. 16, 1973.

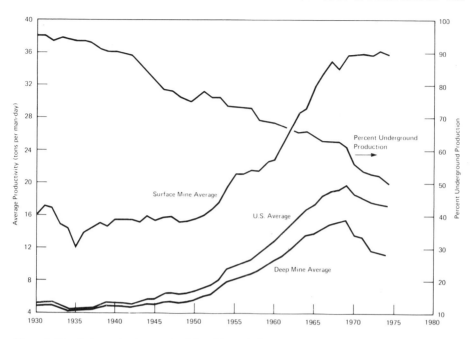

Figure 1 Trends in coal mine productivity. (From U.S. Bureau of Mines, *Miner. Yearb.*, various years.)

The importance of deep mining production to the total national output may be appreciated by the fact that although average surface mining productivity is roughly twice that of deep mining, the national figure is much closer to that for deep mining. Furthermore, the greater departure of the national average from the deep mining average in recent years coincides with the period in which surface mining's share of the total production increased markedly over past levels, with a corresponding decline in the proportion of deep mine production.

Productivity has declined in the last few years, however, related to changes in regulatory requirements, especially the Federal Coal Mine Health and Safety Act of 1969.

> Indications are that compliance [with the Act] has slowed the mine crews only slightly and that workers at the face are still quite productive [within limits of machine availability]. The decline in employee productivity is *almost entirely due to the fact that nonproducing workers have had to be hired*. Included in this category are additional numbers of ventilation men, maintenance and cleaning men, roof-bolting men, and supervisors. These workers reduce the computed average tonnage per employee; they also add an estimated 50 cents or more to the cost of mining a ton of coal. [Emphasis added.][1]

[1]S. A. Schweitzer, "The Limits to Kentucky Coal Output: A Short Term Analysis," University of Kentucky Institute for Mining and Minerals Research TR 81-74-IMMRZ, March 1974.

Trends in Productivity and Employment

Trends in productivity and employment (see Figure 2) are indicative of coal's production capacity. The figure shows average productivity plotted versus the number of workers employed in the industry. In the 30 years from 1940 to 1970, productivity increased from about 5 tons per miner-day to nearly 20 tons per miner-day; at the same time, the work force decreased from nearly 500,000 workers to slightly more than 100,000 workers. The magnitude of productivity increase and work force decrease is approximately the same, a factor of 4. Therefore, the daily capacity of the coal industry has remained in the relatively narrow range from 2 to 3 million tons per day for three decades. If past trends can be relied upon to forecast future conditions, it appears likely that further increases in productivity will help to meet expanded coal production requirements. However, industry potential for raising production capacity will probably require additions to the work force as well. Clearly, future production capacity will be determined by striking a balance of productivity and work force, and neither aspect should be placed in precedence over the other.

The U.S. Bureau of Mines reported recently[1] that:

Because of the implementation of recently enacted health and safety regulations, *and because much of the potential of mechanization (in deep mines) appears to have been reached,* future gains in productivity will probably not exceed 2 percent annually and may even be closer to 1 percent. In fact there is some speculation that productivity may remain at about the 1969 rate, or actually decline slightly, until about 1985. [Emphasis added.]

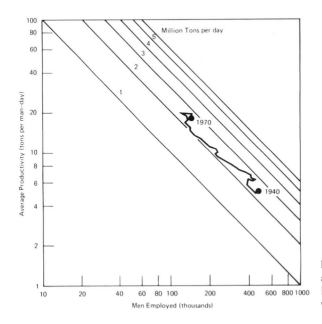

Figure 2 Trends in productivity and employment. (From U.S. Bureau of Mines, *Miner. Yearb.,* various years.)

[1]U.S. Bureau of Mines, "Restrictions on the Uses of Coal," manuscript, 57 pages, June 1971.

More recent events have shown this speculation to be quite optimistic; deep mine productivity for the late 1970s is roughly half that achieved in 1969.

The National Petroleum Council stated that "the future ability of the coal industry to supply its overall share of U.S. energy demand will depend on its ability to produce coal from deep mines. In this connection, the manpower problem will be controlling."[1] In view of the foregoing, it is apparent that the degree of work force problems facing the coal industry is critically dependent on the productivity frame of reference. Actually, work force could be a problem for the coal industry at both extremes:

Low productivity requires too many workers to achieve desired production levels, and a work force shortage may be faced if production demand continues to grow while present "average" productivity levels are maintained.

Increased productivity requires fewer workers to achieve state production goals, and a work force surplus could be created by rapid shifts to more mechanization. This could cause severe social effects similar to those experienced in the Appalachian region in the 1950s.

Figure 3, a graph of mining work force versus production, is useful in projecting the magnitude of labor force required to achieve future production levels at different productivities. If historical productivity improvements of the 1960s were to be continued, then substantially increased production could be realized with essentially the same-sized work force as at present. If on the other hand, as seems more likely, future productivity levels are not significantly different from those which prevail today, then a major increase in work force will be required to achieve increased production.

Evaluation of coal mine productivity has been hampered by the special features of individual coal mines, which have made it very difficult to arrive at a common data base from which analytical comparisons can be made. Seam characteristics, equipment, and section conditions vary greatly, and these influence other significant factors that contribute to the resulting productivity. By investigating the time required to perform discrete events in a series of conventional mining operations, Douglas and Herhal[2] both (1) demonstrated a simple yet effective analytical method for such studies and (2) discovered meaningful and important results. The method is based on a set of event-activity networks related to each machine in the conventional mining section. Observers then use digital watches and record the time of each activity or event on a tape recorder. The resulting data are then computer-processed for analysis. This simple approach yielded the following conclusions in a test sample of mines:

1. Production at underground coal mines using the conventional method may vary widely, depending on the organization of operations. Some mines seem to

[1] National Pet. Council, "US Energy Outlook: Coal Availability," 1973 p. 48.

[2] W. J. Douglas and A. J. Herhal, "Productivity Measurement in Conventional Mining Systems," presented at Third Conference on Mine Productivity, Pennsylvania State University, June 1976.

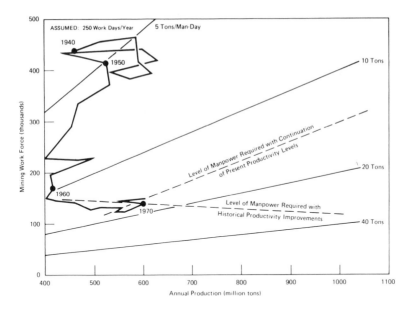

Figure 3 Projections of production and employment. (From U.S. Bureau of Mines, *Miner. Yearb.*, various years.)

work to an implicit, "internally acceptable quota" which is achieved, somehow.

2. Operator performance varies widely, and different machines may represent "bottlenecks" in different mines.

3. Equipment reliability (or its lack) represents an important constraint upon coal mine productivity. Failures of from once to twice a shift are not uncommon, and reduce productivity seriously in many mines.

4. System performance, i.e., the integrated operation of several different machines, reveals that as much as half the shift time is spent in delays resulting from system imbalance and waiting times. Delays may be caused by traffic, place waiting, safety, systems and/or logistics, or maintenance. Recognition of delay points enables formulation of new approaches to solve these problems and improve machine availability (the percentages of time that a machine is available to perform a job function).

5. Overall, it was found that less than 50 percent of shift time was spent on job functions, with over 30 percent on unnecessary delays. Safety delays did not cause the system to back up. Better system management would reduce delays and increase production and productivity.

Unfortunately, such operational, reliability, and maintenance information as compiled in the above-cited study is not collected routinely in most mines (or, if done, is not suitable for detailed analysis). Better information on the manner of conducting actual operations should permit improvement of the output (and productivity) of existing mines, regardless of the mining method used. Clearly, a relatively small effort in this regard could be of substantial benefit to the industry.

Productivity and Technology

The technology available at the time a coal mine is opened appears to influence the productivity throughout its lifetime. Figure 4 shows current coal mine productivity for a representative sampling of surface and underground mines plotted versus the year the mine was opened. The data show that productivity increases steadily over time; lowest productivities are found for select mines, while highest productivities are recorded for newer mines. Data for deep mines show relatively less scatter than those for surface mines. Surface mine productivity is greater than deep mine productivity because of the use of large-capacity equipment.

Figure 5 shows trends in productivity at large deep mines in Illinois, derived from data provided through the cooperation of the Illinois Geological Survey. The data indicate that some large deep mines in Illinois have reached (and sustained) productivities between 20 and 25 tons per miner-day for roughly 20 years. (Recall that Figure 1 showed deep mine average productivity rising from about 6 tons per miner-day to about 15 tons per miner-day during the same interval of time.)

Not every mine shows the same trend, and the rapid rise and decline of Old Ben No. 21 is attributed to the effect of increased haulage distances from the entry. Even these fluctuating levels are significantly greater than the averages.

The principal conclusions from a recent study of coal mine productivity in Illinois[1] are summarized below:

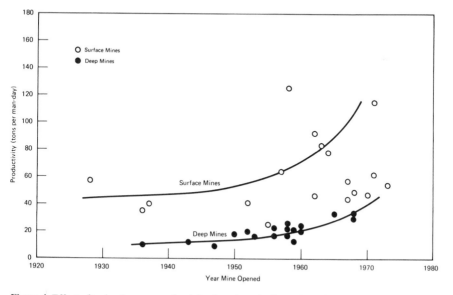

Figure 4 Effect of technology on productivity for selected mines. (Data from *"Keystone Coal Industry Manual," Coal Age,* and U.S. Bureau of Mines, *Miner. Yearb.,* various years.)

[1]*Ibid.*

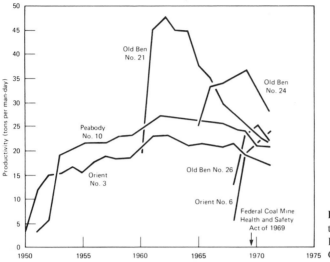

Figure 5 Trends in productivity at large deep mines in Illinois. (Data from Illinois Geological Survey.)

Underground mines

1. Productivity increases with seam thickness at a rate of about 5 tons per miner-day per foot for thicknesses from 4 to 7 feet but levels off at higher thicknesses.
2. Bad roof or floor conditions could result in a loss of 10 to 35 percent in productivity in a given year.
3. Productivity increases with size of operation at a rate of about 10 tons per miner-day per million tons of production up to about 3 million tons per year. "Very little gain in productivity can be realized from designing [an underground] operation with a capacity of more than 3 million tons per year."[1]
4. Productivity increases with mine development up to an age of about 7 years but subsequently declines for the remainder of mine lifetime.
5. Productivity decreases with increasing percentage of reject materials at a rate of about 1 ton per miner-day per 2.5 percent of reject.

Surface mines

1. Productivity increases as stripping ratio decreases at a rate of about 1 ton per miner-day for each increment of overburden. The nature of overburden varies widely, in turn affecting productivity.
2. Productivity increases with increased annual output at a rate of about 10 tons per miner-day per million tons of additional production. Unlike underground mines, there does not appear to be an optimum size surface mine from the productivity standpoint.
3. Productivity declines with increasing age of operation following the initial 5 to 7 years of production.
4. Productivity decreases with increasing percentage of reject materials at a rate of about 1 ton per miner-day for every 2 percent of reject.

[1]R. Malhotra, Factors Responsible for Variation in Productivity of Illinois Coal Mines, *Ill. State Geol. Surv., Ill. Miner. Note* 60, 18 pages, August 1975.

Productivity and Health and Safety

The preceding data show that productivity in coal mining increased by roughly four times during the period from the 1930s to the late 1960s. During this time, the number of injuries (both fatal and nonfatal) declined. Figure 6 shows data for non-fatal injuries. A steady decline in the number of injuries per million tons of production was realized, and it would appear that there has been real progress in improving coal mine safety. However, a more accurate measure of the risk of injury is to consider the number of injuries per amount of exposure time. While the number of injuries per million miner-hours of exposure have declined since the 1930s, the rate of this decline appears to be slowing.

During the 1930s and 1940s, the nonfatal injury rate per million miner-hours parallel that measured per million tons. Those curves cross during the early 1950s, probably related to the changes in mining methods which began around that time as mechanization became more complete. For all practical purposes, the numbers of nonfatal injuries per million miner-hours has been relatively constant over the last 20 years regardless of the level of productivity.

At present, there are about half as many nonfatal injuries per million miner-hours of exposure as there were during the 1930s. However, there are at present only about one-fourth as many workers as there were during the 1930s. Because the decline in the rate of nonfatal injuries is slower than the rate of decrease in number of workers, the real risk of nonfatal injury actually has increased with increased productivity for those workers remaining in the industry. Moreover, data for recent years suggest that the rate of nonfatal injuries is increasing again.

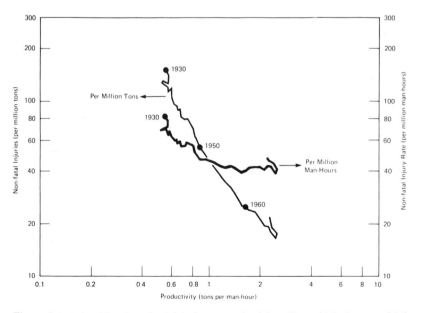

Figure 6 Relationship of nonfatal injuries to productivity. (From U.S. Bureau of Mines, *Miner. Yearb.*, various years.)

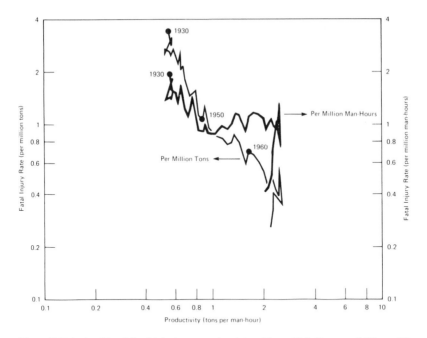

Figure 7 Relationship of fatal injuries to productivity. (From U.S. Bureau of Mines, *Miner. Yearb.*, various years.)

Figure 7 shows data for fatal injuries. Again, a steady decline in the number of fatal injuries per million tons of production is evident for most of the period examined. As was found with nonfatal injuries, there was a change in the number of fatal injuries per million miner-hours of exposure with increasing productivity beginning in the early 1950s. Prior to that time, the data on fatal injuries per million tons was roughly parallel to that per million miner-hours. Subsequent to 1950 and until the 1970s, the numbers of fatal injuries per million miner-hours has remained relatively constant regardless of improving productivity. Significant reductions in the numbers of fatal injuries per million miner-hours of exposure were realized in the early 1970s as the Federal Coal Mine Health and Safety Act of 1969 was implemented. The fatal injury rate per million miner-hours in 1974 is about half that of the 1960s. It is interesting and perhaps significant that these low rates of fatal injury per million miner-hours appear to return to the historical pattern established in the 1930s.

The reason for the existence of this situation, which makes deep coal mining the most hazardous industry in the nation (a fatality rate nearly 10 times that for manufacturing industries), appears to be related to the fact that safety costs money and detracts from production time. *The Wall Street Journal*[1] quoted the head of one large captive coal operation having a good safety record as follows: "Safety is

[1] J. V. Conti, Safety Underground: Coal-Mine Study Shows Record Can Be Improved When Firms Really Try, *Wall St. J.*, p. 1, Jan. 18, 1973.

a cost we're willing to bear. It can be said that if more money has been spent on safety, profit has been less." Asked by the reporter to comment whether cost and profit considerations have led to unsafe conditions elsewhere in the industry, the same man replied: "I don't know what else to say. If your stockholders expect to get a certain rate of return, you've got to get it. And therefore you've got to be content with less safety if you're going to get more profit."

APPARENT RELATIONSHIP BETWEEN PRODUCTIVITY AND PRICE

The relationship of coal price to productivity is shown in Figure 8. Actual dollars are used for each year for comparison with the average productivity that year. No attempt has been made to compensate for effects of inflation in either parameter. The figure shows that, in terms of prices per unit of productivity,[1] there have been important changes over the last several decades. Prices were between 25 and 50 cents per unit productivity during the 1930s but escalated during the 1940s to more than 75 cents per unit productivity. The 1950s and 1960s were periods of steady improvement in productivity and relatively uniform prices, leading to a steady decline in the costs per unit productivity, reaching 25 cents per unit in the late 1960s.

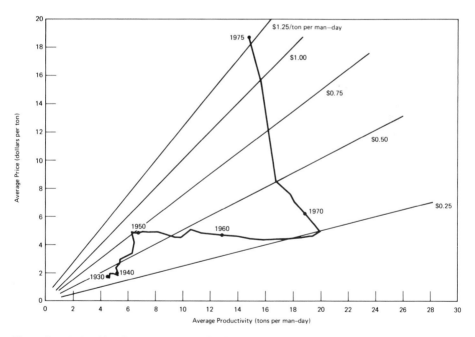

Figure 8 Relationship of coal price to productivity. (From U.S. Bureau of Mines, *Miner. Yearb.*, various years.)

---

[1] In this discussion, *unit productivity* refers to output measured in tons per miner-day.

Dramatic changes occurred during the early 1970s; productivity declined and prices soared. The average price per productivity unit exceeded $1.25 in 1975.

Every indication is that these recent trends are likely to continue, at least for the immediate future. Because of the relationship between productivity and price, the continued decline in coal mine productivity seems to correlate with higher prices.

The relationship of coal production to mining equipment price index is given in Figure 9. The figure shows data for overall equipment used in the coal industry, as well as that employed only in surface mining, and mechanical cleaning. Since 1969, the equipment price index for coal mining equipment nearly doubled in magnitude. This increase occurred at a period when overall coal production increased only by about 10 percent.

Increases in equipment price indices were also shown for major aspects of production operations. Underground mining equipment prices experienced the greatest increases during the early 1970s, roughly doubling the previous value. Noteworthy is the trend of price increases, because they took place at times of decreasing underground production. Trends in the price index of mechanical cleaning equipment parallels the pattern for underground mining equipment, reflecting the fact that most underground production requires cleaning prior to use.

Surface mining equipment price indices also increased, though not as much as those for underground equipment. Because of steady increases in surface mining production, the price index pattern is distinctly different from underground mining.

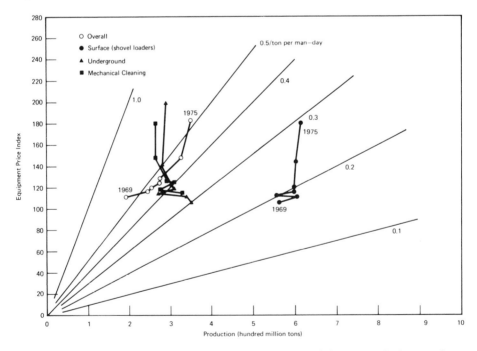

Figure 9 Relationship of coal production to mining equipment price index. (From *Coal Age,* various years.)

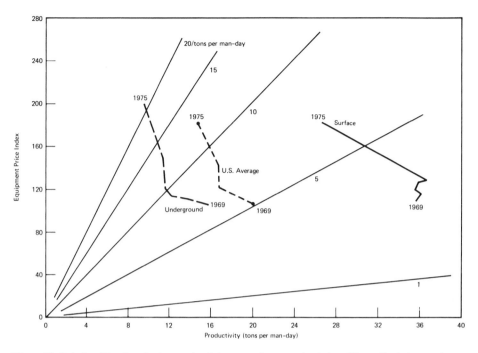

Figure 10 Relationship of coal mine productivity to equipment price index. (From *Coal Age,* various years, and U.S. Bureau of Mines, *Miner. Yearb.,* various years.)

Figure 10 shows that during the early 1970s lower coal mine productivity occurred at the same times as higher equipment prices were being experienced (as measured by price indices). For example, average productivity declined by roughly one-fourth while the overall equipment price index was nearly doubling. Similar trends are shown for surface and underground mining.

Mining equipment represents a substantial capital investment, which, if it is to be recovered in an orderly fashion, must be employed effectively. In an attempt to investigate the relationship of coal mine productivity to capital investment, we have computed the units of price index per unit of productivity (shown by diagonal lines on Figure 10). (This parameter may be somewhat artificial in that it compares the price of a new piece of equipment with average productivity derived from equipment representing a range of ages. However, because mining operations are integrated systems, and because the pace of technological change is slow, it does not appear likely that the performance of a new piece of equipment will differ significantly from other, similar units already in service.)

In the late 1960s, U.S. average data indicate 5 units of price index per unit of productivity. During the early 1970s, increases in equipment price and declines in productivity brought this value to nearly 13 units of price index per unit of productivity. Changes in surface mining were relatively modest, going from 3 to 7 in these derived units. In contrast, enormous changes took place in underground mining, with the above units increasing from 7 to more than 21 over the same interval of time. These data are interpreted as representing a relatively inefficient use of capital; present requirements lead to substantial (and increasing) amounts of capital invested in mining equipment which is employed to produce fewer tons per miner-day. Stated another way, the coal industry at present is overcapitalized in relation to its productivity. This statement may come as a surprise to those who have been accustomed to the conventional wisdom that the coal industry has always been (or always will be) chronically undercapitalized. However true that may have been in the past, it does not apply today.

To illustrate the above point further, it is appropriate to cite data presented by Wearly.[1] Comparing performance characteristics of two continuous mining machines, one made in 1967, the other in 1975, he pointed out that "while price has not quite doubled, power has doubled, and *output [capacity] has almost tripled.*" [Emphasis added]

Unfortunately, at the same time the output capacity of such equipment was increasing, productivity per operating unit was declining, as shown above. Thus the additional capital investment provided expanded production capacity having decreasing likelihood that it will be employed; certainly, the same productivity could have been achieved by less costly machines of more modest capability. In this sense, therefore, there appears to be significant overcapitalization in the coal industry over what is required to maintain production levels. The situation is not unlike the "horsepower craze" once prevalent in the automobile industry. In coal mining, the equivalent is "output capacity," which may be attractive but which is not, by itself, indicative of the capability to produce coal.

SUMMARY AND OUTLOOK REGARDING PRODUCTIVITY

In terms of production per miner-day, there have been major improvements in coal mine productivity until 1970. As a result, it has been possible to maintain overall productive capacity within relatively narrow limits with only about one-fourth as many workers. It would be possible to continue present levels of production with current productivity if the size of the work force remained relatively constant. However, Given[2] found that "on a strictly mathematical basis, without allowance for any change in the averages created by enlargement of the working forces, the industry could lose some 6 to 7 percent of its people a year because of retirement alone. In certain specialized classifications, such as maintenance supervisors and technicians, the rate may be even higher." Therefore, it appears that major efforts would be required to maintain the work force at its present levels; in short, the industry would have to run very hard to return to recent high levels of productivity and to increase production.

If efforts to attract the numbers of people with appropriate skills to sustain the work force at its present levels are unsuccessful, then the industry would be unable

[1] W. L. Wearly, Implications of Escalating Capital and Development Costs, *Min. Congr. J.,* pp. 33–40, June 1976.

[2] Ivan A. Given, Manpower for Coal, *Coal Age,* pp. 60–66, May 1967.

to achieve its production goals. It could revert to lower productivity operations that require less sophisticated skills, but this would imply the need for an even larger work force and this appears even less likely of realization. A more probable situation would be that the industry would seek to achieve further gains in productivity so as to alleviate the work force problem. Increased productivity would also provide for higher overall capacity should additional work force be available at some future time. However, there are nontechnical restrictions upon the degree to which productivity can be increased, apart from the technical aspects of equipment design. This problem was discussed by Saalbach,[1] who noted that the principal reason why innovation is resisted is because workers "fear what will follow change." Alteration in present mining practices to increase productivity will require technical innovation and changes in working patterns. These could represent threats in the minds of workers who lack knowledge, have a narrow range of skills, and have limited employment objectives.[2] In response to such attitudes, it is apparent that technological changes to increase productivity could not realize their potential because of a lack of commitment to accomplish their purpose through concerns over job security. Alternatively, this situation could so constrain the pace of technological change as to impair (if not preclude) its ability to keep pace with either the work force shortage or production demands. The public does not often associate such insights into the characteristics and motivations of its workers with the coal industry, and in the past too few industry officials were inclined to pay much attention to such matters. However, Saalbach's thoughtful discussion is indicative of new progressive thinking in the industry that should be supported.

In view of all these problems, what can be done to increase productivity in coal mining? If limited to "averages" the answer is fairly simple: increase the degree of strip mining where giant equipment can recover substantial tonnages with a minimal work force. Actually, however, reserves that can be mined by surface methods are limited, and those that can be surface-mined with minimal adverse environmental effects are further restricted. Accordingly, it seems unrealistic to rely upon increased surface mining for substantial coal production in the future, although it may prove locally important (and certainly makes averages look better).

Thus the requirements for future coal production suggest that there will be a persistent need for expanded deep mining, although this is no reason to suspect that this would actually occur. The traditional deep miners, in every sense of the word, are skilled workers who know the "personality" of the coal seam and roof conditions for their workings, not necessarily in accurate technical terminology but in practical terms that are designed to protect them and their fellow workers. Miners must be willing and able to learn these essential factors of deep mining, primarily by drawing on the experience of older workers, since there are no textbooks from which to learn them. Miners who have no other work alternative than deep mining may be less receptive to the subtle techniques of their trade (or may consciously ignore them), presenting a hazard to themselves and to all those in the

---

[1] W. F. Saalbach, Can Workers Accept Innovation? *Coal Age,* pp. 114–115, July 1972.

[2] There is good reason for this. Mechanization during the 1950s resulted in loss of jobs for three-quarters of the work force of the previous decade.

vicinity of their work areas.

If coal production seeks to maximize efficient recovery of available reserves to meet demands, it seems apparent that deep mining will be required. Increased deep mine productivity within tolerable health and safety risks will be necessary in this regard. Accomplishment of increased coal mine productivity will be possible only with a systematic comprehensive and cooperative effort among operating companies, equipment manufacturers, labor organizations, and cognizant public and private institutions knowledgeable about the coal industry. Without such an integrated attack on these problems it hardly seems reasonable to expect that the industry will be able to fulfill its role in providing raw materials to meet the nation's energy needs at economic, environmental, or social prices that the people would be willing to pay.

Achievement of improved productivity will not be a simple matter because of the state of technological development. The role of existing technology in coal production is discussed in the following chapter.

CHAPTER EIGHT

ROLE OF EXISTING TECHNOLOGY IN COAL PRODUCTION FOR ELECTRIC POWER GENERATION

Coal production is a rather simple activity conceptually, yet it is intensively complex and intricate of detail in actual practice. A common public attitude is that the coal industry is backward, persisting in the use of outmoded technology in disregard of the prospective benefits from advanced research and development. The extent to which such views might be held is an indication of a serious lack of knowledge about the manner and people of the coal industry.

Far from being a set of cut-and-dried operations, coal production as an enterprise is replete with uncertainties in fundamental aspects such as deposit characteristics, mining conditions, labor relations, market economics, equipment performance, transportation availability, financial security, and governmental regulations. This array of natural and institutional uncertainties is such that coal production is described in the profession as *winning*. The term reflects the struggle of the coal producers with the imperfectly understood processes of nature that created the deposits they labor to exploit.

Estimating the role of existing technology in such operations is a difficult task. Many estimates are either so general as to preclude application to individual areas or so specific that useful generalizations cannot be derived.

This chapter discusses estimated future coal production and consumption requirements for electric power generation and analyzes the projected deployment schedule for accomplishing coal production targets. The magnitude of future coal development activities is estimated by the use of factors for production components per million tons. This methodology is employed as a contribution to greater understanding about the complexities of the coal industry, and to enable readers to construct their own estimates should they choose.

ELECTRIC UTILITY COAL CONSUMPTION

The electric utility industry is the largest coal consumer, accounting for nearly 400 million tons in 1974 (roughly two-thirds of total production). It was estimated[1] that 780 million tons of coal would be required by the electric utility industry in 1984, and that by 1985 the amount would be nearly double that of the present. It was also estimated that about 253 million tons of coal would be produced from western surface mines in the mid-1980s. As noted above, situations could develop to make such estimates optimistic and unrealizable. In that event, either projected demands would need to be reduced or increased production from eastern underground mining would be required.

Two basic coal uses are anticipated: conventional coal combustion and advanced coal conversion (see Part Three). For the near term (to 1985) and at least a large part of the intermediate term (1985 to 2000) coal will continue to be used in the following conventional ways:

1. In existing boilers adapted to use either established coal supplies that are treated or prepared in some fashion to satisfy environmental requirements or new coal supplies to achieve compliance with pollution control standards
2. In oil-fired boilers reconverted to use coal
3. In new coal combustion systems

For the rest of the intermediate term (1985 to 2000), probably the latter part of this interval, the following advanced coal uses may be proven to be economically feasible:

1. Gasification
2. Liquefaction
3. Fluidized-bed combustion
4. Other advanced coal uses

It remains to be determined whether the advanced coal uses will substitute for conventional uses or whether they will be in addition to them. For purposes of this analysis, it is assumed that the historical pattern of substitution[2] will be repeated, and that the projected coal production levels will be sufficient to supply both conventional and advanced uses.

[1]National Electric Reliability Council, "Estimated Fossil Fuel Requirements for the Electric Utility Industry of the United States, 1974–1984," manuscript, July 1975.

[2]Historically, coal production has been in the range of 400 to 600 million tons for more than 50 years. During this time, important markets such as rail and household use have been lost, but expanded coal use in other sectors has maintained the overall production level.

TECHNOLOGY FOR COAL PRODUCTION

The foregoing projections of doubled coal production for electric utility use in only 10 years place important constraints upon the manner of attaining production targets. Clearly, if proposed 1985 production levels are to be realized, efforts should already be underway or should start without delay. Mines must be planned and designed and orders placed for equipment. The work force to operate this equipment must be recruited and trained. All these activities, it is emphasized, will be carried out of necessity with *existing coal development technology* to meet projected requirements. "We all agree that totally new mining methods are needed, but we cannot meet our 1985 goals with systems that will require 25 years to develop. Thus, we must devote a part of our efforts to more modest types of improvement that can be achieved quickly. Even research successes that we may achieve in the next five years will have little impact on 1985 production."[1]

Reliance on existing technology will not be a temporary condition. Equipment and facilities are costly, and it is reasonable to expect their continued use for sufficient time to recover the investment they represent. Many coal mines are commonly developed with lifetimes of 20 to 30 years or longer; thus it seems likely that technologies of the present day will persist beyond the turn of the century (probably accounting for a substantial volume of coal). The mere fact that mines and production facilities were designed to employ certain machines or methods will constrain the amount and character of perspective changes resulting from later improvements.

In this regard, note that coal production already is heavily mechanized.

We have to a large degree reached the technological limits of productivity increases under existing conditions and with presently available equipment. *Future increases, in the short run at least, will depend more upon managerial and manpower inputs than upon technology.* [Emphasis added.] [2]

Greater utilization of our current machinery is the most immediate solution to coal's declining productivity. Forty percent of the nation's underground coal is still being mined by conventional methods. *The 60 percent that has gone [to] continuous [mining methods] is getting less than 11 percent of its theoretical production.* [Emphasis added.][3]

There are, in short, many opportunities for improvement in applying existing technologies, and these potentials need to be pursued.

Still, it is recognized that R&D on new coal production and utilization methods is required to break through the present technological ceiling, and large amounts of money are being spent for such work. However, R&D programs require time; the federal program plans for equipment and process demonstrations to the mid-1980s. R&D is also risky, in the sense that the effort may fail to achieve development specifications.

[1]W. N. Poundstone, What's Needed on Research, *Coal Min. Process.,* pp. 54—56, January 1975.
[2]J. P. Brennan, "Human Factors in Coal—A Historical View," presented at 1st Conference on Productivity in Mining, University of Missouri at Rolla, May 13-15, 1974.
[3]W. L. Wearly, "Technological Solutions to Declining Productivity in Underground Mining," presented at 1st Conference on Productivity in Mining, University of Missouri at Rolla, May 14, 1974.

Even if new coal technology can be demonstrated successfully by the mid-1980s, there will be additional time required to construct facilities necessary for commercial production. Present experience is that roughly 10 years is required for new plant construction, and there is nothing on the horizon to suggest that this time can be shortened significantly.[1]

ESTIMATE OF FUTURE COAL EXTRACTION TECHNOLOGIES

Three estimates of future coal demand to meet electric utility industry requirements are shown in Figure 1. The lowest estimate is one prepared on behalf of the federal government, taking into account the potential impact of severe curtailment of new coal production, mainly in the West. The middle estimate is for a 15-year doubling time for electricity generation, assuming that there is rapid development of nuclear power so that coal and nuclear generation are about equal in the year 2000. The upper curve is for a 15-year doubling time in electricity generation but with curtailed nuclear development, requiring very rapid growth in coal to meet the overall generating target.

The figure also shows as horizontal bands the portions of coal production output represented by different sets of technology. Clearly, present production is from present facilities. Also, it seems apparent that much future production will be from present facilities. Furthermore, it seems apparent that expanded production in the

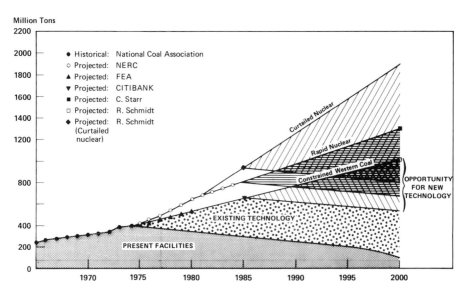

Figure 1 Projected coal production requirements for electric utility use.

[1]Actually, all signs point to even longer lead times for plant construction. See, for example, U.S. Coal-Liquefaction Use Seen 4–10 Years Away, *Oil Gas J.*, p. 48, Sept. 16, 1974.

next decade will require expanded use of existing technology. Assuming that present efforts in R&D are successful and that new technology is demonstrated during the early 1980s, the earliest opportunity for new technology appears to be around 1985. However, if the new technology is not ready to be employed in commercial operations at this time, then there will probably be further expansion in the use of existing technology. This will push back the "window" of opportunity for new technology, as well as shrink the size of the potential market for that technology. The figure shows that magnitude of this window for each of the alternative cases illustrated, assuming that coal production facilities are retired at a rate of 25 percent every 10 years as reserves are exhausted. The figure illustrates remarks by Claybourne Mitchell of Detroit Edison to the effect that federal R&D agencies should emphasize current technology for utilization of coal rather than future technology "which may take many years to develop."[1]

The areas in Figure 1 labeled "opportunity for new technology" are just that — opportunities. They represent the largest contribution that new technology could make to future coal production, assuming that there is a complete replacement of existing technology. Actually, however, this assumption is unrealistic as operating conditions and operator preferences will lead to continued expanded use of existing technology in future years. Additionally, there are likely to be several constraints imposed on the adoption of new technology; capital, operating costs, labor, environmental impact, and safety all will adversely influence the adoption of new technology and lead to continued reliance upon existing technology. In view of these apparent limitations to the widespread introduction of new technology, it seems prudent to give renewed attention to the prospects of achieving improvements in the efficient employment of currently available technologies.

Projected Deployment Schedule

The projected deployment schedule of technologies for coal production to serve the electric utility industry suggested by the above information is presented qualitatively in Figure 2 (quantitative data are given in the following section). The figure suggests that conventional coal combustion can be expanded through use of existing plant technology and existing mining and/or transport technology; expansion of capacity is achieved merely by construction and/or manufacture of larger numbers of present units. These units, as indicated in the figure, would continue in operation at least throughout the remainder of the century.

Advanced coal uses such as conversion are shown in a development and demonstration mode until the mid-1980s, after which time their operational capacity would increase from a low level. Improved coal production technology would be undergoing similar development and demonstration. Ideally, such new technology would become available at about the same time. It seems apparent that either more units of existing types of equipment will be required or that improved mining and/or transportation equipment with capacities greatly in excess of

[1] Cited in *Skillings' Mine Rev.*, p. 27, Nov. 15, 1975.

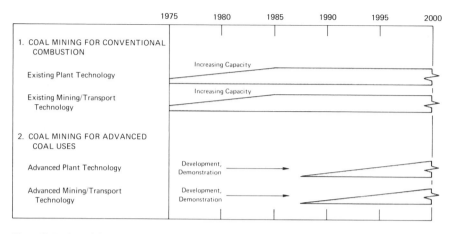

Figure 2 Projected deployment schedule — coal mining and transportation.

present machines will be needed to supply the enormous needs of advanced coal utilization processes.

The projected deployment schedule suggests that a two-tier coal production industry will result. First, the industry will be based on existing technology at least until 1985 and probably beyond. A continued, strong market for existing technology could well persist to the end of the century. Second, the industry will experience later contribution of new facilities as well as later replacements for compatible operations using existing technologies.

Magnitude of Future Coal Production Efforts

The magnitudes of future coal work force and production equipment were estimated through the same principle used in estimating future production:

Existing capacity − depletion/retirement + new additions × factor = 1985 capacity

Based on estimated production in each of the above cases, magnitudes were calculated using factors per million tons derived for each element from historical experience.

Sample results of calculations employing these factors are shown for the rapid nuclear development case by 1985 in Tables 1 and 2; data for the same case in the year 2000 are given in Tables 3 and 4. The tables show that important increases in each category are required. For example, Table 1 shows that the work force must be roughly doubled by 1985 in rapid western development, while Table 2 indicates that a tripling in work force is necessary with expanded underground mining.

An important part of each estimate is the magnitude of personnel or equipment required merely to maintain the present levels in the face of retirements or turnover. For example Table 1 shows that 84,000 new underground mine workers will be required in the next decade; about 35,000 of this total will be replacements

Table 1 Estimate of labor requirements for utility coal production by 1985

Rapid nuclear development case

Item	Underground*	Surface†	Total
1973 work force	119,900	37,900	157,800
Additional capacity (+): Deep: at 350 workers/million tons Surface: at 100 workers/million tons	84,000	16,000	100,000
1985 work force	203,900	53,900	257,800

*At 60 percent of new production because of impediments to expanded western operations, 240 million tons.
†At 40 percent of new production, 160 million tons.

for workers constituting the present work force.[1]

Similar large increases in coal production and transportation equipment are required to meet projected utility requirements. For example, Table 2 shows that nearly as many continuous mining machines will be required in the next 10 years as are in service at present.

The magnitude of future coal production labor and equipment requirements would be greater in the event of curtailed nuclear development and lesser in the event of curtailed western coal development (assuming that there would be no offsetting increase in coal production from other regions). For purposes of this discussion, only one example is sufficient to illustrate the methodology. The next section continues the above example to derive an estimate of capital requirements for future coal production.

Table 2 Example estimate of equipment requirements for utility coal production by 1985

Rapid nuclear development case

Item	Underground continuous miners*	Surface excavating equipment	Transportation† Rail cars	Locomotives
1974 amount	1900	130	354,608	27,418
New equipment (+): Factor per million tons	10	0.5	180	10
Amount	1440	80	54,000	3,000
1985 amount	3340	210	408,608	30,418

*Assumed that 60 percent of new production will be continuous miners (144 million tons).
†Assumed that 75% of new production will be rail-shipped (300 million tons).

[1]This estimate may be too high; it includes workers who move from one coal company to another without being lost to the industry as a whole.

Table 3 Estimate of labor requirements for utility coal production by 2000

Rapid nuclear development case

Item	Underground*	Surface†	Total
1973 work force	119,900	37,900	157,800
Additional capacity	273,000	52,000	325,000
2000 work force	392,900	89,900	482,800

*60 percent of new production is underground because of reserve shortages, 780 million tons.
†40 percent of new production is surface, 520 million tons.

CAPITAL REQUIREMENTS

Capital requirements for new coal development facilities were estimated recently.[1] Table 5 shows capital costs for mine production and infrastructure facilities (including the environmental and/or reclamation costs) to produce a ton of coal by each mining method. Because western coals have only about three-quarters the heating value of eastern coals, the western estimate must be increased by between one-quarter and one-third to become equivalent to eastern coal for comparative purposes. The table shows that, on an equivalent heating-value basis, the capital cost for production of western surface-mined coal is only about one-third that of eastern coal.

Capital costs for transportation are not included in the above data. It was estimated[2] that an additional $5 to $6 per annual ton would be needed for equipment

Table 4 Example estimate of equipment requirements for utility coal production by 2000

Rapid nuclear development case

Item	Underground continuous miners*	Surface excavating equipment	Transportation† Rail cars	Transportation† Locomotives
1974 amount	1900	130	354,608	27,418
New equipment (+):				
Factor per million tons	10	0.5	180	10
Amount	5850	260	121,500	6,750
2000 amount	7750	390	476,100	34,168

*Assumed that 75 percent of new underground production will be continuous miners (585 million tons).

†Assumed that 75 percent of new production will be rail-shipped (675 million tons).

[1]G. W. Land, "Capital Requirements for New Mine Development," presented at Third Conference on Mine Productivity, Pennsylvania State University, Apr. 5-8, 1976. It is noted that these figures are averages and that actual capital costs for a given mine may vary considerably.

[2]Source is testimony by Frank Milliken of Kennecott Copper Corporation at FEA hearings on Project Independence, New York City, Aug. 19, 1974.

Table 5 Estimated capital costs for new coal mines

Dollars per ton of annual capacity

Mining method	Eastern	Western
Underground	$57.20	57.20
Surface	$48.30	$18.00
Western surface, equivalent heating-value basis		$21.60

Source: Modified from G. W. Land, "Capital Requirements for New Mine Development," presented at Third Conference on Mine Productivity, Pennsylvania State University, Apr. 5-8, 1976.

to transport the coal to market (Table 6). Costs are higher for western coals because their lower heating value necessitates handling of greater volumes of material for an equivalent energy content.

Total estimated capital costs for mining and transportation (equivalent heating-value basis) are presented in Table 7. The table shows that even after adjustment for low heating value, the capital costs for western coal are only about half those of eastern coal development. It is emphasized, however, that these data are incomplete in that capital costs for coal utilization facilities are not included, being beyond the scope of this section. Because coal development is part of an integrated

Table 6 Estimated capital costs for coal transportation

Dollars per ton

Mining method	Tonnage basis only	Equivalent heating-value basis
Eastern underground	$6	$6
Eastern surface	$6	$6
Western surface	$6	$8

Source: Testimony by Frank Milliken of Kennecott Copper Corporation at FEA hearings on Project Independence, New York City, Aug. 19, 1974.

Table 7 Total estimated capital costs for coal mining and transportation equivalent heating value basis

Dollars per ton of annual capacity

Mining method	Eastern	Western
Underground	$57.20	57.20
Surface	$48.30	$18.00
Western surface, equivalent heating-value basis		$21.60

Source: Modified from G. W. Land, "Capital Requirements for New Mine Development," presented at Third Conference on Mine Productivity, Pennsylvania State University, Apr. 5-8, 1976.

Table 8 Relation of capital costs to mining method

Mining method	Capital costs,* $/annual ton	Heating value, million Btu/ton	Capital cost $/million Btu
Underground:			
Appalachia	65.85	23	2.86
Illinois Basin	48.45	21	2.31
Surface:			
Appalachia	46.50	23	2.02
Illinois Basin	50.29	21	2.39
Western	18.00	18	1.00

*From G. W. Land, "Capital Requirements for New Mine Development," presented at Third Conference on Mine Productivity, Pennsylvania State University, Apr. 5-8, 1976.

systems operation, an accurate accounting of total capital costs must take account of all parts of that system.

The relation of capital costs to mining method is summarized in Table 8. Estimated capital costs for underground and surface mining in different regions as determined by Land[1] are shown, together with average heating values of coals typical to each area. These data were used in calculating capital costs per unit of heating value (dollars per million Btu). The table shows that underground mining in Appalachia is the most capital-intensive of all methods, especially when compared to surface mining in the same region. In contrast, the Illinois Basin's underground mines are less capital-intensive than surface mines. Least capital costs of all are found for western surface mines.

On this basis alone, it would appear that coal mine operators would seek to open mines having least capital exposure (other things being equal). However, there are numerous other operational and regulatory factors that contribute to the overall cost of coal production and utilization, so it is incomplete to focus attention on the mining capital cost alone. Unfortunately, many of these additional capital cost factors are poorly known and difficult to determine. It will be important to achieve better understanding of the total capital cost picture as the basis for a thorough analysis of possible alternatives to coal development.

EQUIPMENT PRODUCTION CAPACITIES

The capability of the mining-equipment manufacturing industry to achieve the indicated production levels is assessed in this section.

Table 9 shows statistics on continuous mining machines derived from data published annually by *Coal Age*. The numbers of machines in use and new machines shipped were added to give the maximum number of machines in service in any given year. This number was compared with the number of machines in service

[1] Land, *loc. cit.*

Table 9 Trends in production of continuous mining machines

Year	(1) Machines in use	(2) New machines shipped	(3) Maximum machines in service (1) + (2)	(4) Machines in use following year	(5) Retired machines (3)−(4)	(6) Ratio of new to retired (2) ÷ (5)
1950						
1951						
1952	152					
1953	219					
1954	325					
1955	385	109	494	510	(16)	6.81
1956	510	154	664	614	50	3.08
1957	614	168	782	679	103	1.63
1958	679	107	786	776	10	10.70
1959	776	140	916	879	37	3.78
1960	879	128	1007	927	80	1.60
1961	927	115	1042	961	81	1.42
1962	961	149	1110	1030	80	1.86
1963	1030	137	1167	1111	56	2.45
1964	1111	150	1261	1218	43	3.49
1965	1218	151	1369	1380	(11)	13.73
1966	1380	161	1541	1412	129	1.25
1967	1412	129	1541	1487	54	2.39
1968	1487	164	1651	1571	80	2.05
1969	1571	190	1761	1566	195	0.97
1970	1566	211	1777	1781	(4)	57.75
1971	1781	297	2078	1849	229	1.30
1972	1849	274	2173	1866	257	1.07
1973	1866	281	2147	1900	247	1.14
1974	1900	352	2252	2000 (est.)	252	
1975	2000	591	2591	2250 (est.)	241	
1976	2250					

Source: Coal Age, February Annual Review Issues.

the following year, indicating that many machines had been retired. Comparing the numbers of new continuous mining machines shipped with retired machines leads to the conclusion that most new machines are merely replacements for older equipment.

This interpretation of *Coal Age* statistics is confirmed by a representative of one of the major continuous miner manufacturers.[1] In a paper presented to the 1975 Annual Meeting of the National Coal Association, it was pointed out by Kroehle that "about 250 replacement machines" are produced each year with "another 100" for export. These data agree almost exactly with those in Table 9.

Based on projections of future coal requirements, Kroehle estimated that the U.S. market for continuous mining machines would be from 550 to 600 per year

---

[1]T. P. Kroehle, Jeffrey Mining Machinery Company.

for 10 years. He estimated that 1976 capacity was greater than 600 machines, and wondered aloud whether the equipment manufacturers had expanded their capacity too fast. Citing a typical manufacturing sequence (Figure 3), Kroehle noted that 2 years was needed for optimum planning of equipment production capacity. This lead time is necessary in reducing manufacturers' costs because of the great number of equipment variations offered to meet different mining conditions. In recent years, a 4- to 6-month lag time has been experienced.

Table 10 shows comparable data for mobile loaders, the principal element of a conventional mining section. In this case, up to four times as many machines are retired as are produced each year. There would seem to be an opportunity to increase production of mobile loaders. However, it must be remembered that mobile loaders are manufactured by the same companies who make continuous mining machinery, and it is possible that greater emphasis on mobile loaders could detract from their ability to produce continuous miners (and conversely). The potential role of conventional mining equipment in contributing to coal production should not be overlooked. As shown in Chapter 5, conventional mining can (under given conditions) outperform continuous mining by providing higher productivity and lower cost.

In view of these findings, it would be prudent to reconsider the present momentum toward increased reliance on continuous mining for future underground coal production. Conventional mining, in addition to the above advantages, employs simpler equipment that is more readily manufactured in large quantities. To be sure, conventional mining requires more skilled workers, and an intensified training effort would be required. Training is feasible, however, because the mining technologies are well-known and logical programs to familiarize workers can be established.

The estimated manufacturing capacity for large excavating machinery to work surface coal mines is shown in Figure 4. The figure shows that in recent years production capacity was 200 to 600 cubic yards per year, out of a theoretical capacity of 1000 cubic yards per year.[1] The industry is presently expanding its production capacity, and it is estimated that by 1980 it will be capable of producing a theoretical 1500 cubic yards per year. This could, it is noted, be left high and dry by protracted litigation over western coal development. Future capacity is projected to be two to five times the present theoretical capacity.

The following estimate of U.S. surface coal mine excavating capacity was made by E. P. Berg of Bucyrus Erie Company:

Year, tons	Excavating capacity, yd^3	Surface coal production, million tons	Individual machine size, yd^3/million
1980	9,000	130	70
1985	11,000	230	50
2000	30,000	770	40

[1]To determine the number of machines, divide by the capacity of individual machines. For example, with a capacity of 600 cubic yards per year and an average size per unit of 60 cubic yards, 10 excavators would be constructed each year.

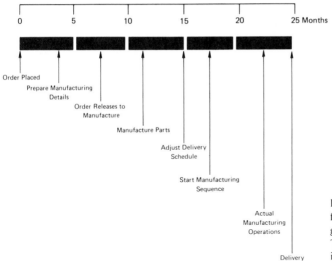

Figure 3 Typical manufacturing sequence − underground equipment. (After T. P. Kroehle, Jeffrey Mining Machinery.)

Table 10 Trends in production of mobile loading machines

Year	(1) Machines in use	(2) New machines shipped	(3) Maximum machines in service (1) + (2)	(4) Machines in use following year	(5) Retired machines (3)−(4)	(6) Ratio of new to retired (2) ÷ (5)
1950						
1951						
1952						
1953						
1954	4314					
1955	3819	120	3939	3854	85	1.41
1956	3854	239	4093	3755	338	0.71
1957	3755	209	3964	3424	540	0.39
1958	3424	97	3521	3121	400	0.24
1959	3121	95	3216	2952	264	0.36
1960	2952	110	3062	2583	479	0.23
1961	2583	84	2667	2502	165	0.51
1962	2502	113	2615	2345	270	0.42
1963	2345	89	2434	2396	38	2.34
1964	2396	111	2507	2394	113	0.98
1965	2394	115	2509	2579	(70)	1.64
1966	2579	111	2690	2518	172	0.65
1967	2518	151	2669	2542	127	1.19
1968	2542	110	2652	2466	186	0.59
1969	2466	120	2586	2420	166	0.72
1970	2420	126	2546	2065	481	0.26
1971	2065	147	2212	1959	253	0.58
1972	1959	114	2073	1786	287	0.40
1973	1786	54	1840	1600	240	0.23
1974	1600	65	1665	1600 (est.)	65	
1975	1600	102	1702	1650 (est.)	52	
1976	1625					

Source: Coal Age, February Annual Review Issues.

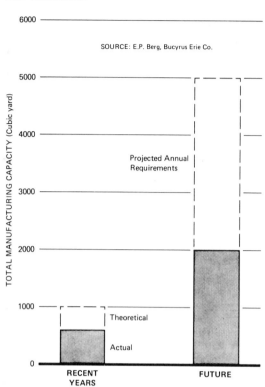

Figure 4 Estimated manufacturing capacity requirements for surface coal mine excavating equipment. (After E.P. Berg, Bucyrus Erie Co.)

This suggests that *giant* excavating equipment of 100 cubic yards capacity or greater is not likely to be a major factor in future surface coal production. Rather, the manufacturers are aiming toward more modest-sized equipment (and larger numbers of these) to provide a flexible capability to work the thick, near-surface seams of the Western states (assuming that potential delaying factors can be resolved expeditiously).

The business approach of the equipment manufacturers is noteworthy. As noted by Kroehle of Jeffrey Mining Machinery in the earlier-cited paper, "Customer service has historically meant spare parts availability in our industry." There is evidence to suggest that by serving the customer in this manner, the equipment suppliers are also serving themselves. In an article on one major supplier of mining machinery, it was reported[1] that:

> In the earth-moving industry the real profits are not in the equipment itself, but in the parts. A large crawler tractor chewing up rock in, say, an iron mine will use up parts worth as much as the original equipment within two years or so. Caterpillar has always refused to say publicly how much of its total sales volume consists of parts, but . . . it is hinted that the current figures are [from 30 to 45 percent]. An even more closely guarded secret is the proportion of *profit* attributable to this parts volume . . . . Sources in the industry indicate that the profit margin on parts is at least twice that on original equipment. If that is so, then over half, in some years perhaps even three-quarters, of Caterpillar's profit could come from parts.

[1]S. Rose, The Going Gets Tougher for Caterpillar, *Fortune,* p. 161, May 1972.

All forms of mining equipment are similar to the earthmovers of Caterpillar in that they are specialized, complex, and costly, and may be expected to require comparable maintenance and replacement of worn parts. By inference, suppliers of this equipment may also be expected to enjoy significant profit levels from parts sales. As a result, it would appear to be in the equipment suppliers' interest to continue to supply parts rather than to engage in development of new or improved mining equipment that would impair their ability to achieve present profit levels. This could represent an institutional factor that may constrain the pace of introduction of new technology, entirely apart from the ordinary technical problems of perfecting new equipment and demonstrating its commercial competitiveness.

The plight of mining equipment manufacturers was described by Wearly.[1] Noting that some 230 continuous mining machines are sold annually, amounting to some $46 million split among three major suppliers, he went on to estimate the potential for development of new equipment. Machinery manufacturers can afford to spend about 3 per cent of their income on new products, or, in this case, $1.5 million. Using data for a representative year, Wearly calculated net revenues from continuous miners at over $1 billion. Improvements in equipment could result in a 10 percent reduction of cost of production, or some $100 million in this example. Most of the benefits from reduced cost would be realized by the mining companies, and manufacturers would "be lucky" if their income increased as much as 10 percent. This, Wearly cautions, tends to dampen enthusiasm on the part of manufacturers for taking risks in developing new equipment.

Another problem was described by Wearly, relating to the patent and proprietary data of manufacturing companies. Such information was developed at company risk and expense and reflects the know-how derived from experience. Many old-line mining equipment manufacturers are reluctant to risk the potential loss of information they consider proprietary under terms of government contracts for advanced research and development of new or improved equipment. One consequence is that contract awards are made to firms having lesser experience in mining operations, and at least some of their effort must be devoted to a learning process.

While it may be worthwhile to have additional firms in the equipment field to contribute fresh approaches, it is a fact that there is a history of excess capacity in that industry. Although extraordinary conditions following the Arab oil embargo prompted a rush of orders for mining equipment that led to long waiting times and to consideration of equipment availability as a "constraint" to expanded coal production, the situation appears to be returning to normal. It was noted that today "new order rates and backlogs for mining equipment have fallen rapidly and [now] there's an overabundance of capacity."[2]

Bleak prospects are in the offing for equipment makers supplying both surface and underground operations, according to the referenced article. New federal strip mine legislation "would impose a morass of red tape on coal operators and

---

[1] W. L. Wearly, "Technological Solutions and Declining Productivity in Underground Mining," presented at 1st Conference on Productivity in Mining. University of Missouri at Rolla, May 14, 1974.

[2] G. Getschow, Outlook for Coal-Mining Machinery Concerns Is Clouded by UMW Election and Labor Talks, *Wall St. J.,* May 1977.

seriously delay new coal-mining projects in the West."[1] Underground operations would be affected as well. Noting that the equipment manufacturers doubled production of continuous mining equipment during the past 3 years at the same time that coal production per miner-day dropped an average of 10 percent per year, it was concluded that "it won't be a seller's market for mining machinery for some time."[2]

These events are indicative of the dynamic nature of the coal industry. Just a few years ago, it was common to encounter many articles[3] analyzing "constraints" to coal production; included in that category were numerous equipment and supply items, together with labor availability and other services essential to carry out coal production. The same approach is persistent with some[4] who conclude that there is no way to realize increased coal production or utilization because the constraints were too great. Circumstances suggest, however, that such writers failed to recognize the dynamic character of the coal industry and the normal response of aggressive businesses to perceived market opportunity. To be sure, one outcome of concerted actions to remove one set of apparent constraints can be to create a new set of problems (such as overcapacity) that, for a time, will represent a new "constraint." This illustrates the necessity of understanding the linkages among coal industry participants and the historical patterns of their relationships in the context of changing industry conditions. It also points out the importance of taking an integrated view of operations, rather than focusing on any one element of the industry. While the existence of "constraints" may be employed to justify governmental intervention to alleviate them, the absence of constraints would seem to call for entirely different governmental action, if any.

CONCLUSIONS

A discussion of future coal requirements for electric power generation was presented. The role of existing coal production technology in accomplishing production targets was examined, and estimated deployment schedules and magnitude of efforts was analyzed.

Variability in geological conditions and uncertainty in operations are consistent themes which are encountered in every phase of coal mining. Technological developments have succeeded in mechanizing several mining functions, but the integration of these functions into a production system requires flexibility in application that can only be provided by skilled and experienced people.

The precise natural conditions associated with mining are essentially unpredictable. There may be wide differences in fundamental parameters such as coal characteristics, roof or floor conditions, and seam height (even in different

---

[1] *Ibid.*

[2] *Ibid.*

[3] See, for example, National Academy of Engineering, "U.S. Energy Prospects: An Engineering Viewpoint," Washington, 1974.

[4] G. C. Gambs, cited in *Forbes,* pp. 73–74, June 1, 1977.

parts of the same seam in the same mine). This variability in natural conditions has led, through a tradition of trial and error, to a great variety of mining systems, equipment, and practices.

A considerable amount of quantitative technical measurements and analyses have been carried out in attempts to aid in mining operations. Most of this work was (and is) oriented toward equipment or practices that may be applicable more or less universally in nominal operations. The thrust of this approach is toward the transformation of coal mining to an industrial activity and away from its traditional trade or guildlike approach. While promising strides have been made in applying new technology to improve operational efficiency and safety, there appear to be limits imposed on technology by the inherent uncertainty in natural mine conditions. It is obvious that technology has improved operations by relieving burdens from workers, but is has not realized its full potential because the variability in natural conditions precludes its ability to predict the effects of its application with certainty.

Finally, it is emphasized that coal will remain as a mainstay energy source in the United States, at least for the remainder of the twentieth century, especially for the generation of electric power. Regardless of all the effort and money expended for R&D on solar energy, geothermal energy, advanced nuclear systems, and even coal conversion technologies, these would represent only a small share of the nations's energy sources, even if R&D was completely successful. It is suggested that a more efficient use of public funds, rather than being completely devoted to such R&D, would be to provide incentives for expanding existing coal production and transportation technology and facilities. Expenditures in such areas as miner training programs, cost sharing on high-risk new mine openings (especially in high-sulfur seams where market conditions may be clouded by pollution control regulations), and financial help to ensure adequate rail haulage would be far more productive.

Production of coal is merely the first stage in its utilization, as mentioned in Chapter 1. Prior to use, it is not uncommon to "prepare" the coal through various beneficiation approaches, described briefly in the next chapter.

Tables 11 to 18 present factors for estimating the magnitude of future coal production. A basic assumption is that existing technology will remain as the mainstay for coal production for at least the next decade and probably beyond. This permits calculation of production factors in considerable detail, based on present operations. Factors are presented per million tons of production to facilitate their use in assessing alternate production conditions. Note, however, that these data are subject to change through improvements in production technology.

Table 11 Factors used in estimating magnitude of coal labor elements

		Factor		
Element		Overall*	USBM†	Selected Value
1.	Work force workers (million tons):			
	Deep	430	250	350
	Production		140	
	Maintenance		50	
	Outside		20	
	Supervisory		39	
	Technical		1	
	Surface	140	60	100
	Production		35	
	Maintenance		14	
	Supervisory		9	
	Technical		2	
2.	Inspectors	2		2

*Total industry figures, "Keystone Coal Industry Manual," McGraw-Hill, New York, 1972.
†Large Modern Mines, *US Bur. Mines Inf. Circ.* 8535, 1972, and 8632, 1974.

Table 12 Factors used in estimating magnitude of underground coal equipment elements

Modern continuous mining operation

Item	Requirements per million tons
Continuous miner or loading machine	10 each
Shuttle car	10 each
Roof bolter	5 each
Ratio feeder	5 each
Auxiliary fan	5 each
Man-trip jeep	5 each
Mechanic jeep	2 each
Personnel jeep	2 each
Rock duster	6 each
Supply car	20 each
Main-line belt conveyor	9,000 feet
Secondary conveyors	25,000 feet
Main-line belt power center	5 each
Section belt power center	5 each
Section rectifier	5 each
Section switch house	5 each
High-voltage cable	15,000 feet
Coupler	15 each
Trolley wire	25,000 feet
Track	25,000 feet
Freshwater line	25,000 feet
Scoop tractor	6 each
Battery charger	7 each
All-service mask	10 each
Breathing apparatus	15 each
Self-rescuer	250 each
Stretcher set	10 each
Safety light	100 each
Methanometer	100 each
Fire-chemical car	5 each
Lamp (plus accessories)	250 each
Dust sampler	20 each

Source: Basic Estimated Capital Investment and Operating Costs for Underground Bituminous Coal Mines, *US Bur. Mines Inf. Circ.* 8632, 1974.

Table 13 Factors used in estimating magnitude of supplies for underground coal production

Typical continuous miner operation, Appalachia

Item	Requirements per million tons
Hydraulic oil	156,000 gallons
Gear oil	39,000 gallons
Grease	39,000 gallons
Fire-resistant oil	39,000 gallons
Timber	1,000 10-ft lengths
	1,000 14-ft lengths
	20,000 8-ft lengths
Wedges	102,000 each
Cap pieces	51,000 ea; 3 × 4 × 18 in
Plank	3,000 ea; 1½ × 6 in × 14 ft
	1,000 ea; 4 × 6 in × 14 ft
Header blocks	36,000 ea; 2 × 8 × 24 in
Crib blocks	15,000 ea; 5 × 6 × 30 in
Square posts	1,000 ea; 6 × 8 in × 8 ft
Resin cartridges	193,000 each
Rebar	97,000 each
Roof bolt plates	176,000 each
Roof bolt with shell	2,000 ea; 4-ft lengths
	13,000 ea; 5-ft lengths
	60,000 ea; 6-ft lengths
	4,000 ea; 8-ft lengths
	12,000 ea; 1.5-ft lengths
Roof channel	5,000 ea; 14-ft lengths
Pipe	13,000 ea; 2 in × 20 ft
Brattice cloth	3,000 yards
Ship lab boards	3,000 ea; 1 × 8 in × 12 ft
Plank	1,000 ea; 2 × 4 in × 14 ft
Rock dust	54,500 tons
Machine bits	76,000 each

Source: Pennsylvania State University

Table 14 Factors used in estimating magnitude of surface coal equipment elements

Typical area strip mining operation

Item	Requirements million tons*
Dragline	1 each
Overburden drill	1 each
Coal shovel	1 each
Coal haulers	2 each
Cable handler	1 each
Front-end loader	1 each
Coal drill	1 each
Bulldozers	2 each
Road grader	1 each
Explosives truck	1 each
Mechanics truck	1 each
Crane truck	1 each
Lubrication truck	1 each
Welding truck	1 each
Pickup trucks	4 each
Utility truck	1 each
Water truck	1 each
Substation	1 each

*Cost Analysis of Model Mines for Strip Mining of Coal in the United States, *US Bur. Mines Inf. Circ.* 8535, 1972.

Table 15 Factors used in estimating magnitude of coal transportation elements

Item	Requirements per million tons
Rail:	
Cars	180
Locomotives	10
Water:	
Barges	30
Tugs	2
Trucks	100

Table 16 Estimates of track capacities for various hypothetical rail-line configurations

1. These estimates are based upon several fundamental assumptions, such as average rolling terrain, a 50 mph track speed, total absence of priority trains and an average downtime of 25 percent.
2. The capacities are shown as number of trains per day, which is the sum of movements in each direction.
3. Coal unit trains would typically handle 10,000 to 11,000 tons per loaded train. Each loaded train movement must be matched with an empty return.

	Capacity, trains/day	Days for 1 million tons
Case I: Single track with 2.5-mile sidings with 11 miles between sidings and timetable train-order operations	10-15	10
Case II: Single track with 2.5-mile sidings with 7 miles between sidings and centralized traffic control (CTC)	30-35	3
Case III: Alternating segments of single and double track, each segment 10 miles long, with CTC	60-70	2
Case IV: Double track with CTC permitting movements in both directions on each track	75-125	

Source: Burlington Northern Railway Company.

Table 17 Basic material needs for rail-line construction

Approximate quantities required for heavy-duty single-track line

Item	Rate of installation	Quantity per mile
1. Rail	132 lb/yd (each track)	235 tons
2. Crossties	23−24 per 39-ft track panel	3,200 each
3. Tie plates	2 per tie	6,400 each
4. Spikes	8 per tie	25,600 each
5. Rail anchors	Variable	5,000 each
6. Ballast		3500−4000 tons

Source: Burlington Northern Railway Company.

Table 18 Factors used in estimating magnitude of coal preparation equipment

Item	Requirement per million tons	
	Level C	Level D
Bradfor breaker (10-ft dia. × 15-ft length)	1	1
Scalping screen (4 × 10 ft)	1	1
Primary screening coarse:		
Raw-coal screens (6 × 10-ft double deck)	2	2
Prewet screens (5 × 12-ft double deck)		
Coarse beneficiation:		
Heavy-medium vessel (4-ft width × 8-ft weir)	1	1
Refuse drain & rinse (4 × 14 ft)	1	1
Clean-coal drain & rinse		
(6 × 16-ft double deck)	1	1
Clean-coal crusher	n.a.	1
Coarse-coal centrifuge	n.a.	1
⅜ in × 28 mesh beneficiation:		
Desliming Screens (5 × 16 ft)	n.a.	5
Heavy-medium cyclones (24-in dia.)	n.a.	2
Refuse drain & rinse (5 × 16 ft)	n.a.	2
Fine-coal centrifuge (1100 million)	n.a.	1
Fine-refuse centrifuge (1100 million)	n.a.	1
Dilute-medium cyclone (24-in dia.)	n.a.	1
−28 mesh beneficiation:		
Froth flotation cells (5 cell × 300 ft³)	n.a.	1
Clean-coal filter (10 ft 6 in dia. × 8 disk)	n.a.	1
Clarification:		
Static thickener (100 ft dia.)	1	1
Solid-bowl centrifuges (36-in dia. × 72-in length)	n.a.	2
Refuse filter (10 ft 6 in dia.)	n.a.	1
Thickening cyclones (14-in dia.)	n.a.	2
Solids recovery system (4 × 8 ft)	n.a.	1
Drying:		
Thermal dryer (13 tons/hr)	n.a.	1
Magnetic recovery:		
Magnetic separators (10-ft length × 30-in dia.)	1	3

COAL PREPARATION

Very little coal is used directly as it comes from the mine. Most is "prepared" or beneficiated prior to consumption according to a variety of practices. The subject of coal preparation has been treated in two recent, comprehensive reports.[1] Detailed technical descriptions of the preparation process are available in these and other publications and will not be repeated here. Instead, this chapter concentrates on a discussion of the often obscure subject of coal preparation costs; extensive use is made of material originally developed by Phillips et al. in the material that follows.

The cost of coal preparation can vary greatly, depending on the level of work done on run-of-mine (ROM) coal. Phillips et al.[2] defined six "levels of preparation," as follows:

*Level A. A*bsence of preparation, indicating that coals are shipped as mined

*Level B. B*reaking for top-size control only and remqval of coarse refuse and trash

*Level C. C*oarse beneficiation through washing of $+\frac{3}{8}$ inch only; smaller material remains dry and is shipped without further treatment

*Level D. D*eliberate beneficiation through working of all material larger than 28 mesh; smaller material is either dewatered and shipped with coal or discarded as refuse

*Level E. E*laborate beneficiation through washing of all size fractions

*Level F. F*ull beneficiation of all coal to produce two or more products from one raw coal

Details of these preparation levels are presented in Table 1, taken from Phillips' report.

---

[1]P. J. Phillips et al., "Coal Preparation for Combustion and Conversion," prepared by Gibbs & Hill, Inc., for the Electric Power Research Institute, Report No. AF791, May 1978; and D. C. Nunenkamp, "Coal Preparation Environmental Manual," prepared by J. J. Davis Associates for the U.S. Environmental Protection Agency, EPA Report No. 600/2-76-138, May 1976.

[2]P. J. Phillips et al., *Op cit.*

Table 1 Levels of coal preparation

Level & brief designation	Scope	Yield weight, %	Recovery Btu, %	Reduction Potential		Work done on raw coal*	Typical circuits & equipment used	Refuse	Comments
				Ash	Sulfur				
A Absence	No Prep.	100	100	None	None	None—ship ROM coal	None	None	Not general practice
B Breaking	Top size control only	98–100	100	None to minor	None	Crushing to 3 in or less and removal of coarse refuse	Scalping screen, crusher, rotary breaker	Dry lumps and trash	General practice on all ROM coals
C Coarse	Coarse beneficiation	75–85	90–95	Fair to good	None to minor	Level B followed by: Dry screen @ ⅜ in & wet beneficiate @ +⅜ in only. Ship ⅜x0 as is.	Same as level B plus vibr. screens, jigs, heavy-media vessels or cyclone, dewatering, thickeners, filters	+⅜ in drained −28M ponded	Used where −⅜ in fraction fairly clean or much rock present in +⅜ in fraction.
D Deliberate	Fine beneficiation	60–80	80–90	Good	Fair	Level B followed by: Wet Screen @ ¼ in & wet beneficiate +28M. Discard 28Mx0.	Same as level C plus concentrating tables or hydrocyclones. Some thermal drying.	+¼ in drained +28M dewatered −28M ponded or filtered	Used with coals having good washability characteristics.
E Elaborate	Very fine beneficiation	60–80	80–90	Good to excellent	Fair to good	Level D plus wet beneficiate 28Mx0	Same as level D plus flotation circuits. Thermal drying prevalent.	Same as level D except more fines.	Used with coals having excellent washability characteristics.
F Full	Deep cleaning	60–80	85–95	Clean coal stream: excellent Middling stream: none to fair		Level E after greater than normal size reduction and separation into two streams: clean coal and middlings.	Same as level E plus additional size reduction.	Substantially same as level E	Two or more washed coal products of different qualities are obtained.

*Coal sizes shown are typical but will vary somewhat with each coal and process selected.
Source: Phillips, *op. cit.*

A further contribution to better understanding of coal preparation by Phillips' report is the derivation of a systematic methodology for calculating "relative costs of coal including preparation." The methodology is stated in the next section.

COSTS OF COAL PREPARATION

The methodology for calculating the major cost elements, which together determine the total cost of preparation, can be explained best by reference to Table 2, "Relative Coal Preparation Costs." The term *relative* precedes the title because the costs used were selected to demonstrate a method and may not necessarily reflect the actual costs in any particular situation. As a matter of fact, the total capital investments shown on line 12 against different levels of preparation could normally vary by plus or minus 50 percent and under unusual circumstances by more than that. There simply is no reliable way of estimating coal preparation costs unless careful analyses are made of each application. Even bidding to identical and carefully drawn specifications, different contracting engineers might quote prices in a ratio of 2:1 between high and low bidder, although ranges of 1.5:1 are more commonplace.

The tabulated costs should therefore be considered as illustrative of the methodology to assist readers in their own computations, which would then reflect their premises and purposes.

The costs shown on line 12 are updated costs extracted and adapted from similar data developed by the Commerce Technical Advisory Board for the U.S. Department of Commerce "Report on Sulfur Oxide Control Technology" (1975). They are considered representative of industry experience for the specific conditions which they reflect but should not be used as a basis for specific evaluations, especially when considering coal preparation and beneficiation in place of or as an adjunct to other technologies.

Because tabulated costs are presented as relative, and to facilitate comparisons, the following simplifying assumptions are made:

1. All raw coals contain 12,000 Btu per lb as mined, and cost $15 per ton ($0.625 per million Btu) delivered to the preparation plant.
2. A total of 1, 2, and 3 million tons of coal are produced annually by plants represented by Table 2, and enough ROM coal is delivered by the mines to permit these quantities to be produced.
3. The surface moisture of raw and clean coals is unchanged due to processing.
4. Local taxes and contributions to the UMWA, based on quantity of coal shipped, although they would partly offset the cost of preparation, are not considered substantial enough to warrant inclusion. They should however be reflected in more comprehensive estimates.
5. Various other premises are discussed on a line-by-line basis, with the line numbers in the first column of Table 2 serving as point of reference.

Table 2 Relative coal preparation costs*

1 Levels of preparation		A		B		C		D		E		F					
		Absence of preparation		Breaking only		Coarse beneficiation		Deliberate beneficiation		Elaborate beneficiation		Full Beneficiation					
2 Brief designations	Units											Average product		Clean coal		Middlings	
		$/ton	$/10^6 Btu	$/ton	$/10^6 Btu	$/ton	$/10^6 Btu	$/ton	$/10^6 Btu	$/ton	$/10^6 Btu	$/ton	$/10^6 Btu	$/ton	$/10^6 Btu	$/ton	$/10^6 Btu
3 Yield, weight	Percent	100%		95%		80%		75%		70%		80%		27%		53%	
4 Recover, Btu	Percent	100%		99%		95%		90%		87.5%		95%		35%		60%	
5 Btu content, raw coal	Btu/lb	11,000		11,000		11 000		11,000		11,000		11,000					
6 Btu content, clean coal	Btu/lb	11,000		11,460		13,060		13,200		13,750		13,060		14,260		12,450	
7 Processing rate, hourly	Tons/hr	667		700		834		889		953		834					
8 Production rate, hourly	Tons/hr	667		667		667		667		667		667		222		445	
9 Processing rate, yearly	Tons/yr	2,000,000		2,100,000		2,500,000		2,670,000		2,860,000		2,500,000					
10 Production rate, yearly	Tons/yr	2,000,000		2,000,000		2,000,000		2,000,000		2,000,000		2,000,000		667,000		1,333,000	
11 Plant capital cost	per ton/hr	0	0	3,500		10,000		20,000		25,000		18,000		18,000		0	0
12 Total capital required	$	0	0	2,500,000		8,340,000		17,780,000		23,825,000		15,012,000		15,012,000		0	0
13 Capital cost per ton per year of clean coal produced	$ per ton/yr	0	0	1.25	0.054	4.17	0.180	8.89	0.337	11.91	0.433	7.51	0.288	22.51	0.789	0	0
14 Fixed charges @ 25% pa	$/ton	0	0	0.31	0.013	1.04	0.040	2.22	0.084	2.98	0.108	1.88	0.072	5.63	0.198	0	0
15 Variable costs	$/ton	0	0	0.19	0.008	0.96	0.037	2.08	0.079	2.72	0.099	1.79	0.069	5.37	0.188	0	0
16 Processing costs	$/ton	0	0	0.50	0.021	2.00	0.077	4.30	0.163	5.70	0.207	3.67	0.141	11.00	0.386	0	0
17 Cost of Btu in rejects	$/ton	0	0	0.21	0.010	1.19	0.045	2.40	0.091	3.12	0.114	1.19	0.045	3.57	0.125	0	0
18 Total preparation costs	$/ton	0	0	0.71	0.031	3.19	0.122	6.70	0.254	8.82	0.321	4.86	0.186	14.57	0.521	0	0
19 Cost of raw coal in clean coal	$/ton	20.00	0.909	20.84	0.909	23.75	0.909	24.00	0.909	25.00	0.909	23.75	0.909	25.92	0.909	22.63	0.909
20 Cost of clean coal	$/ton	20.00	0.909	21.55	0.940	26.94	1.031	30.70	1.163	33.82	1.230	28.61	1.095	40.49	1.420	22.63	0.909
21 Total preparation cost	Mills/kWh	0	0	0.31		1.22		2.54		3.21		1.86		5.21		0	0
22 Annual owning and operating costs	$	0	0	1,420,000		6,380,000		13,400,000		17,640,000		9,720,000		9,720,000		0	0

Source: Phillips, *op. cit.*

*Coal data and costs on this table serve for illustration purposes only. Actual data and costs should be

Line-by-Line Discussion of Table 2

1. "Levels of preparation" are defined in Table 1 and the opening text of this chapter.
2. "Brief designations" are taken from Table 1.
3. The yield factor Y reflects the quantity of clean coal produced (output) from a given quantity of raw coal (input). It can be expressed in the following terms:

$$Y = \frac{\text{tons clean coal}}{\text{tons ROM coal}} \times 100 \qquad \text{or} \qquad Y = \frac{\text{tons/hr output}}{\text{tons/hr input}} \times 100$$

The yield factors selected here for different levels of preparation are typical of industry experience but are likely to vary considerably between installations and sometimes even from day to day at the same plant. Equipment selections normally anticipate such fluctuations through conservative sizing and provision for adjustments on the basis of operating experience.

4. The recovery factor R relates the total amount of Btu in the clean coal to the total amount in the raw coal processed. The missing Btu would be discarded with the rejected (refuse) material. The recovery factor can be expressed in the following terms:

$$R = \frac{\text{tons clean coal} \times \text{Btu per ton of clean coal}}{\text{tons raw coal} \times \text{Btu per ton of raw coal}} \times 100$$

The recovery factor, like the yield factor, will vary with each installation, reflecting coal characteristics and beneficiation processes selected.

The recovery factors selected here for the different levels of preparation are representative of a particular coal technology and end-product requirement. Actual recovery factors may be higher or lower, depending on process criteria. Generally, the finer the size consist of the coal, the lower the recovery factor but also the higher the quality of the clean coal produced.

5. B_R is the assumed calorific value of the ROM (raw) coals before preparation. Although shown here to be 11,000 Btu per pound, actual values will depend on specific coals, mining procedures, and many other factors.
6. B_C is the calculated calorific value in Btu per pound of the clean coal after preparation. It reflects both yield and recovery factors in accordance with the following equation:

$$B_C = B_R \frac{R}{Y} \tag{1}$$

where B_R is the calorific value of the raw coal in Btu per pound and R and Y are recovery and yield factors, respectively.

7. The hourly input of ROM coal in tons per hour has been calculated by dividing the hourly output of clean coal, line 8, by the plant yield factor Y, line 3. This assures that equal quantities of coal are produced regardless of preparation level considered and thus facilitates comparisons.
8. The hourly output of clean coal in tons per hour is calculated by dividing the annual capacity (2 million tons) by 3000 hours, representing two 7.25-hour

shifts per day, 230 days per year, less a 10 percent allowance for unscheduled stoppages.

When a plant is expected to operate a different schedule, such as 6 days per week or 3 shifts per day, the hourly capacity of the plant could either be reduced or the yearly output increased. The 10 shifts per week schedule has been chosen here because it allows a complete shift for maintenance and repairs. When plants are designed to operate around the clock, duplicate circuits and equipment would be required so that maintenance could be performed without interrupting production. The capital investment for such a plant would be somewhat higher than for a 2-shift plant, but overall costs may be lower.

9. The quantities of coal processed each year are calculated by multiplying the hourly processing capacity, line 7, by 3000 hours operating time.
10. The quantity of coal produced each year has been fixed at 2 million tons, a quantity typical of modern underground mining installations.
11. The costs on this line are based on cost estimates for similar plants proposed during 1977. They include minimal coal-handling and storage facilities valued at roughly $2 million, although actual costs will vary considerably between plants and could exceed the cost of preparation plants by a factor of 2.
12. The total capital investments are calculated by multiplying the unit costs on line 11 by the capacities on line 7.
13. The costs of clean coal expressed in dollars per ton per year are calculated by dividing capital costs on line 12 by the tons of clean coal produced annually, i.e., 2 million tons in these examples as shown on line 10.

    Two amounts are shown next to each other on lines 13 through 20. The first represents dollars per ton and the second dollars per million Btu. Both units can be used in such computations, provided that the Btu per pound values of the clean coals are shown. In each case here, the costs expressed in dollars per million Btu are the same as costs in dollars per ton of clean coal multiplied by 500 and divided by the Btu content on line 6 (see Equation 1).
14. The fixed charges in either dollars per ton or dollars per million Btu are calculated by multiplying the costs on line 13 by 0.25. This factor is representative of a 17.5 percent return on investment, a 10-year depreciation period, and a 50 percent tax on profits. Actual percentages should reflect applicable accounting practices.
15. The variable costs were taken from cost estimates prepared for such plants. They include an allowance of $1 per ton of rejects to cover their transportation and disposal. Fine rejects were dewatered by filter presses, and costs of such equipment are included in capital costs on line 12. Thermal dryers likewise are included, as are the costs of their operation.
16. Processing costs on lines 14 and 15 are totaled on line 16.
17. The costs of the Btu discarded with the rejects are shown on line 17. They can be computed by either of two methods:
    a. When expressed in dollars per ton of clean coal, the cost of the Btu in the rejects can be calculated by Equation (2):

$$\text{Cost of Btu in rejects} = \text{cost of raw coal (\$/ton)} \times 1\text{-}R/Y \qquad (2)$$

where Y and R are the factors from lines 3 and 4, respectively. In level D, for example,

Cost of Btu in rejects = $20/ton $\times$ 1-0.9/0.75 = $2.67/ton clean coal

b. When expressed in dollars per million Btu, the formula is shown by Equation (3):

Cost of Btu in rejects = cost of raw coal ($/million Btu) $\times$ $1/R$ - 1 (3)

For level D, for example,

Cost of Btu in rejects = $0.909/million Btu $\times$ 1/0.9-1 = $0.101/million Btu

The same conversion formula as explained for line 13 applies here as well.

18. Total preparation costs are the sum of lines 16 and 17.
19. The cost of the raw coal in the clean coal in dollars per ton is computed by multiplying the cost of the raw coal ($20 per ton) by the recovery R and dividing by the yield Y, as shown in Equation (4):

$$\text{Cost of raw coal in clean coal} = \text{cost of raw coal} \times \frac{\text{recovery } R}{\text{yield } Y} \qquad (4)$$

For level D, as example:

$$\text{Cost of raw coal in clean coal} = \$20 \times \frac{0.9}{0.75} = \$24/\text{ton}$$

The reason for this higher value is the increase in the Btu per pound content when raw coal is processed into clean coal.

When calculating the cost on a dollar per million Btu basis, the initial cost of $0.909 per million Btu remains unchanged, as illustrated by the alternate values on line 19.

20. The cost of clean coal is the sum of lines 18 and 19.
21. Total preparation cost, expressed in mills per kilowatt hour, is obtained from the costs on line 18, assuming that 10,000 Btu is required to generate 1 kilowatt hour. More or less efficient generating plants would have but a minor effect on these calculations.
22. The total owning and operating costs on line 22, expressed in dollars per year, were obtained by multiplying the costs on line 18 by the 2 million tons of coal produced in 1 year.

Comments on Level F Computations

As defined here, level F produces two products, clean coal and middlings. For cost estimating and comparison purposes, the data are presented in three columns. The first, called *average product,* is used for computation purposes because the same methods and equations used for levels A through E apply here as well. Although the average product exists only as a concept, it facilitates computations, especially the apportioning of costs between the clean coals and middlings. In the example used here, it was decided to assign both the processing costs and the cost of Btu in rejects to the clean coal exclusively, keeping the cost of the middlings at $0.909 per million Btu, same as the raw coal. The two columns under the heading *clean coal* thus represent the costs in the average product column multiplied by the ratio of total coal processed (665 tons per hour) divided by clean coal produced (222 tons per hour) or 3.0:1. This procedure is straightforward for the costs expressed in dollars per ton for lines 13 through 16 but must be modified for lines 17 through 20. The cost of Btu in rejects, line 17, expressed in dollars per ton is computed as before, but the cost in dollars per million Btu must be adjusted for the relative Btu content of the clean coal. The cost of $0.125 per million Btu (line 17) can thus be obtained by either of two methods:

$$\$0.048/\text{million Btu} \times {}^{667}\!/_{222} \times {}^{13060}\!/_{14260} = \$0.131/\text{million Btu}$$

$$\$1.25/\text{ton} \times {}^{667}\!/_{222} \times {}^{500}\!/_{14260} = \$0.131/\text{million Btu}$$

The costs of raw coal on line 19 expressed in dollars per ton for the clean coal and for the middlings is calculated either by multiplying the average $23.75 per ton by the ratio of Btu contents ($^{14260}\!/_{13060}$ and $^{12450}\!/_{13060}$) or by applying Equation (1) to the costs expressed in dollars per million Btu.

It may be noted that the plant capital cost per ton per hour capacity, line 11, is smaller for level F than for either levels D or E but higher than for level C. This is explainable by the fact that, for level F, only 222 tons per hour of clean coals are beneficiated intensely, whereas the 445 tons per hour middlings are processed to a lesser degree.

It cannot be overemphasized that the one-third to two-thirds split between clean coal and middlings and the decision to charge all costs of preparation only against the clean coal fraction was made for illustrative purposes only. In an actual case, results would reflect specific coal characteristics, costs, requirements, and commercial considerations.

EFFECT OF PLANT SIZE ON PREPARATION COSTS

The preparation cost elements found in Table 2 are indicative of those likely for typical plants. However, comparisons must be weighed against the simplifying assumptions by which the various costs were developed, and a comprehensive analysis attempting to gage the influence of plant size on capital and operating costs was prepared in 1966.[1] It concluded that one 800 ton per hour plant can beneficiate coal at a 30 percent lower cost than two 400 ton per hour plants. Comparing capital costs alone, one 800 ton per hour plant was estimated to cost 20 percent less than two 400 plants. More recent work suggests considerably smaller reductions, ranging from only 9 percent down to 3 percent, with the lower percentages applying to the more expensive plants. Other independent studies also reveal such

[1] E. T. McNally, R. C. Woodhead, J. L. Gamble, Gaging the Costs in Coal-Preparation Plant Selection, *Coal Age,* August 1966.

diverse cost-size scaling relationships that no simple pattern appears reliable enough to justify its use, except for very preliminary estimating purposes. Among the likely reasons why scaling factors have limited applicability to preparation plant costs are:

1. Most beneficiation circuit components cannot be readily scaled up (or down) in size. Additional capacity requires multiple units, with proportional acquisition, installation, and operating costs.
2. Even when larger-capacity equipment could be built at some initial savings, plant reliability and operational flexibility might be improved by use of multiple smaller units.
3. Provision for future expansion may reduce initial savings in favor of future benefits.
4. Certain major structures, such as silos, may be sized the same, regardless of plant capacity.

Whereas cost-size scaling factors may apply to capital and operating costs and therefore to cost of preparation C_P, the costs C_B, expressing Btu losses, would be unaffected. The table shows that costs reflecting C_B equal roughly one-half of preparation costs C_P, and thus amount to about one-third of the total cost of preparation C_T. Because C_B varies only as a function of recovery factor R and the cost of raw coal, this further reduces the sensitivity of preparation costs to cost-size scaling economies.

COAL-BLENDING TECHNOLOGY

Introduction

The mixing or blending of different raw materials to obtain a uniform feedstock possessing improved properties is an essential procedure in many industries. The metals industry could serve as a typical example, having practiced the blending of ores, as well as of coals for coke making, for many decades. Approximately 200 installations throughout the world are using bulk material blending on a large scale to improve iron, copper and nickel ores, cement kiln feeds, sinter feeds, chemicals, as well as coals for metallurgical, conversion, and combustion purposes. The increasingly stricter limits on the emission of sulfur dioxide have greatly intensified the search for low-sulfur coals. Because the supply of naturally occurring low-sulfur coals is limited, blending low-sulfur coals with higher-sulfur coals would extend available supplies and offer other benefits as well.

Power plants must comply with government-imposed limits on the emission of sulfur oxides and particulates. As stated elsewhere, emission standards vary substantially between states, within states, and for existing as compared to new plants. When, for example, Illinois allows emissions of up to 6 pounds SO_2 per million Btu from an existing plant, it offers coal-blending technology a far greater opportunity than other states which restrict their plants to 1.2 pounds SO_2 per million Btu or less.

Many factors favor or oppose blending as a coal preparation technology. This section explores the most significant ones, discusses typical systems and equipment in current use, and explains potential problems which should be avoided when considering the blending of steam coals. Coal-blending economics are briefly examined and current developments reviewed.

Basic Mathematical Relations of Coal Blending

The U.S. Environmental Protection Agency in its publications "Compilation of Air Pollution Emission Factors" (1973) uses an emission factor of 38 lb/ton times the percent sulfur to predict the emission of SO_2 (by weight) per tons of bituminous coal burned in external combustion sources without pollution control equipment.

$$SO_2 \text{ emission lb/ton} = 38\% \text{ S} \tag{5}$$

The factor of 38 reflects the fact that, while 1 pound of sulfur when burned forms 2 pounds of sulfur dioxide, 5 percent of the sulfur combines and remains with the ash.

Equation (5) can be rewritten in a more convenient form as

$$SO_2 \text{ lb/million Btu} = \frac{19,000\% \text{ S}}{B} \tag{6}$$

where % S = percent sulfur by weight

B = gross calorific value or gross heat content, Btu/lb

Equation (6) as Equation (7) expresses the maximum percent sulfur in a coal which would permit its combustion without flue-gas desulfurization (FGD).

$$\% \text{ S} = \frac{SO_2 \text{ lb/million Btu} \times \text{Btu/lb}}{19,000} \tag{7}$$

Taking as an example the EPA limit of 1.2 lb SO_2 per million Btu and assuming that a coal has a gross calorific (heat) value of 12,000 Btu per pound, its maximum allowable sulfur content would be

$$\frac{1.2 \times 12,000}{19,000} = 0.76\% \text{ S}$$

On the other hand, 6 lb SO_2 per million Btu allowed by law in some regions would permit use of a coal containing up to

$$\frac{6 \times 12,000}{19,000} = 3.79\% \text{ S}$$

whereas in Wyoming, where state laws restrict new sources to 0.2 lb SO_2 per million Btu, a 9370 Btu per pound subbituminous coal would have to contain less than $\frac{(0.2 \times 9370)}{19,000} = 0.10$ percent S, a practically impossible requirement.

When calculating the equivalent SO_2 from two blended coals, both their sulfur and BTU contents must be considered, as in

$$E = \frac{19,000\ S_1 W_1 + S_2 W_2}{B_1 \times W_1 + B_2 \times W_2}$$

where E = SO_2 emission, lb/million Btu

W_1 & W_2 = percentage by weight of coal no. 1 and no. 2, respectively

S_1 & S_2 = percentage by weight of sulfur in coal no. 1 and no. 2, respectively

B_1 & B_2 = Btu/lb value of coal no. 1 and no. 2, respectively

When the emission limit E is given, one can calculate the weight percentages of each coal by

$$\left(S_2 - \frac{E \times B_2}{19,000}\right)(100 - W_1) + \left(S_1 - \frac{E \times B_1}{19,000}\right)W_1 = 0$$

The following example illustrates this.

The allowable emission E in Michigan is 3 lb SO_2 per million Btu. Blending a medium-sulfur western Kentucky No. 9 coal (Table 3) containing

S_1 = 3.36% S

B_1 = 11,831 Btu/lb

with a low-sulfur eastern Kentucky No. 4 (Table 3) containing

S_2 = 0.78% S

B_2 = 13,445 Btu/lb

and substituting these values in Equation (8):

$$\left(0.78 - \frac{3.0 \times 13,445}{19,000}\right)(100 - W_1) + \left(3.36 - \frac{3.0 \times 11,831}{19,000}\right)W_1 = 0$$

where W_1 = 47% western Ky., No. 9 (medium-sulfur)

W_2 = 53% eastern Ky., No. 4 (low-sulfur)

If in place of the low-sulfur eastern Kentucky No. 4 coal a Montana subbituminous coal with 0.34 percent S but only 7500 Btu per pound were to be blended, the ratio would be

$$0.34 - \frac{3.0 \times 7,500}{19,000}(100 - W_1) + 3.36 - \frac{3.0 \times 11,831}{19,000}W_1 = 0$$

where W_1 = 36% western Ky., No. 9 (medium-sulfur)

W_2 = 64% Montana subbituminous (low-sulfur)

These examples illustrate the importance of Btu value and demonstrate that although the Montana subbituminous coal is lower in sulfur content by weight than the eastern Kentucky bituminous (0.34% S versus 0.78% S), its lower heating value more than offsets this advantage.

Therefore, a blend meeting the 3 pounds SO_2 per million Btu emission limits in the first example would use roughly equal proportions of both coals, while in the second example the ratio would be one-third high-sulfur and two-thirds low-sulfur coals. Only a careful examination of other important factors including delivered

Table 3 Analytical data of Kentucky coals

Type of analysis	Eastern Kentucky No. 4	Western Kentucky No. 9
Proximate analysis as Received:		
Moisture, wt. %	2.10	5.68
Ash, wt. %	8.87	12.52
Volatile, wt. %	38.45	37.40
Fixed carbon, wt. %	50.58	44.40
Heating value, Btu/lb	13,445	11,831
Total sulfur, wt. %	0.78	3.36
Ash-fusion temperature: Reducing atmosphere (height=width), #F	2,800	2,190
Ash slagging & fouling:		
Ash slagging factor Rs	0.078 (low)	1.02 (med)
Ash fouling factor Rf	0.096 (low)	0.087 (low)
Caking capacity: Free swelling index	4.5	4.0

Source: O. W. Stewart and J. K. Shou, "Clean Coal-Desulfurization and Blending," PD-9 Progress Report, University of Kentucky, Lexington, October 1975.

costs and combustion characteristics would permit a complete assessment of the relative advantages of either blend.

Coal-Blending Costs

Any discussion of costs attributable to coal blending is subject to so many assumptions, restrictions, and conditions that the mere citing of typical costs is likely to raise more questions than it answers.

A paper presented at the Second Symposium on Coal Utilization[1] included a graph showing the cost of mixing for various blending-facility ranges. According to that, an installation blending 4 million tons per year would add 75 cents to the cost of each ton of coal, while a similar but larger installation blending 8 million tons per year would add 65 cents per ton. It was subsequently learned[2] that the cited costs were based on 1973 estimates for a planned installation in Illinois and that they provide for a 20-year life and 10 percent cost of interest but not for taxes nor profit. When using the 1973 capital investments and operating costs escalated by 25 percent to 1976 and providing for a 15 percent return on investment after tax, in place of a 10 percent cost of interest, the simplified method for annualizing cost of capital (used in the first section) results in the following:

[1] M. L. Wilkey et al., "Coal Blending as a Means to Meet Air Emission Standards," Second Symposium on Coal Utilization, Louisville, Ky., October 1975.
[2] *Ibid.*

Return on investment	15.0%
Depreciation, 20-year	−5.0
Net profit	10.0%
Income tax	+10.0
Depreciation	+5.0
Fixed annual cost factor	25.0% of capital cost

	Yearly system capacity	
	4×10^6 tons	8×10^6 tons
Capital costs 1973	$15,750,000	$26,000,000
25% escalation	3,950,00	6,500,00
Capital costs 1975−1976	$19,700,000	$32,500,000
Fixed annual cost (25%)	$ 4,925,000	$ 8,125,000
O&M costs (escalated)	1,025,000	2,375,000
Total annual costs	$ 5,950,000	$10,500,000
Cost per ton handled	$ 1.50	$ 1.30

The per ton costs of 75 and 65 cents thus increase to $1.50 and $1.30, respectively, a 100 percent increase after allowing for escalation, profits, and taxes, but still a minor cost in relation to the benefits achievable. The fact that this projected installation did not pass the planning stage was reportedly due primarily to the inability of the prospective coal users to obtain assurance that the coal blends could be combusted after 1980 because of increasingly stricter emission regulations.

An example where a similar situation has resulted in firm contracts is represented by a transloading facility constructed for the Southern Railway in Pride, Alabama. This installation will include a coal-barge unloading, stacking-out, storage, reclaiming, and unit-train loading facility, capable of handling 10 to 12 million tons of coal per year.[1] Coals having different sulfur contents will be placed into separate storage piles. Simultaneous reclaiming from two or more piles will permit custom blending to satisfy the requirements of different electric generating plants being serviced by this installation. On the basis of a total budgeted cost of $13 million and a yearly capacity of 10 million tons, the cost per ton of coal handled may be as low as 60 cents.

Summary Assessment of Blending Technology

Coal blending is a readily available and very economical means of improving the quality of coals for combustion or for conversion to synthetic fuels. It can be useful both as an independent method for controlling the mineral contents of coals or in conjunction with coal beneficiation. Given certain feedstock requirements, blending can increase the homogeneity of coals or improve their ash characteristics. On

[1]*Coal Min. Process.,* November 1975.

the other hand, injudicious selection of coals for blending may cause deterioration of ash characteristics, with the possibility of combustion problems due to lowered ash-fusion temperatures.

The incremental costs attributable to blending can range from none to less than $1.50 per ton of coal processed. Lowest costs would result from the selective feeding from different bins, silos, or storage piles, either existing or required as part of a coal-handling and processing system. Highest costs would be incurred by the construction of a sophisticated single-purpose system using special equipment and procedures during both the placing into storage of individual coals and the reclaiming from storage of the blended coals.

Production, preparation, or blending commonly take place remote from coal utilization facilities. As a result, the coal must be transported to consumers. The next chapter reviews the subject of coal transportation.

TEN

TRANSPORTATION

Few coal-consuming facilities are located adjacent to mines, and therefore coal transportation is an essential part of the overall system of coal production and utilization. Actually, a mutual dependency exists, because coal represents a principal source of revenue for the transportation sector; for example, coal constituted about one-quarter of the revenue freight handled by Class I railroads in recent years and nearly one-quarter of the total handled by inland waterways.

Several modes of transportation are employed in coal delivery. Table 1 shows the breakdown of transportation methods for coal movement to electric utility plants in a recent year. Roughly half this coal was transported by rail, with another quarter of the total hauled by barge and the remainder by truck or other means. A brief discussion of some of the principal transportation modes is presented in this chapter.

COAL TRANSPORTATION BY RAIL

Coal moves by rail in four different ways: single-car movements, multiple-car movements, trainload movements, and unit-train movements. There is a potential fifth way: integral-train movements, which is a further development of the unit-train concept. These ways have distinct operational characteristics, primarily in equipment utilization, that result in cost differentials and are reflected in rates. As the terminology is not always uniformly used, the definitions given below, quoted from ICC *Ex parte 270,*[1] are adhered to in this section.

Single Car Rates. A single car rate is one that is published based on tonnage requiring the use of one (1) car only. This tonnage is usually 100 tons or less and is frequently based on the marked capacity of the car.

[1]U.S. Interstate Commerce Commission, "Investigation of Railroad Rate Structure—Coal," *Ex parte 270,* 1975.

297

Table 1 Transportation of coal for electric utility use, 1972

Method	Million tons	Percent
Rail	195	51
River barge	76.5	20
Great Lakes barge	17.6	5
Tidewater barge	2.4	1
Truck	48.4	13
Other	42.3	10
Total	382.2	100

Multiple Car Rates. Multiple car rates are based on a sufficient tonnage to require the use of two or more cars moving from one point of origin to one point of destination at one time. A frequently maintained condition for multiple car rates is 1,500 tons.

Trainload Rates. A trainload rate is a rate that is published based on sufficient tonnage to make up an entire train, usually 5,000 tons or more.

Unit Train Rates. A unit train rate is one that is published to apply to traffic moving in a sufficient set number of railroad cars and a given number of locomotives dedicated to one unit train, moving in continuously scheduled cycles between one point of loading and one point of unloading.

The basic differences between trainload and unit-train movements are:

1. Unit trains consist of dedicated sets of equipment operating on a fixed schedule. Trainloads may be a one-shot case and, in any event, are not scheduled.
2. Unit trains in most instances, but not always, are heavier than trainloads. Typical trainloads are in the 7000-ton (net) range, unit trains in the 9000- to 10,000-ton (net) range.

Shipper ownership of coal cars is increasing because of advantages associated with lower rates and better car control. At the close of 1974, electric utilities owned nearly 5000 cars. The concept of integral trains is usually associated with a 1961 report by the Kauffield Engineering Company, recommending trains consisting of dedicated equipment and carrying about 25,000 tons. Such trains would require specially strong couplers and draftgear, and certain numbers of cars would have to be permanently coupled by drawbars. Locomotives would be placed at the head and at one or two points within the train. Integral trains will probably come into being through shipper ownership, if at all, as there is a dislike by U.S. railroads (and banks providing financing) for anything that detracts from flexibility. All the features required for integral trains are, however, in current use, including draw-bars linking heavy ore cars in married pairs (Hammersley Iron Company, Western Australia).

The following discussion on *rate structures* is centered on unit trains as the vast majority of the projected increases of coal movements by rail to utilities will use that method. (The ICC estimates that 85 percent of all coal by rail will move in unit trains by 1985.) However, if the variety and complexity of coal rates are to be understood, a few introductory considerations may be helpful. For a detailed study of rate structures, one should consult ICC *Ex parte 270.*[1] Extensive use has been made of this reference in the preparation of this section.

Bituminous coal is rated class 17½ in the governing Uniform Freight Classification, although extremely little coal moves at class rates, which are based on carloads and reflect the times when railroads had little competition. Trainload and unit-train rates are more pertinent, as are rates based on annual volumes and on special conditions predicated on the movement of minimum tonnages over a specified time period. A frequent annual volume requirement is that 1 million tons of bituminous coal be transported during one calendar year. Annual volume rates exist for single-car, multiple-car, trainload, and unit-train shipments and vary because of geographic considerations, such as concentration rates, gathering rates, tidewater rates, etc. Unit-train rates, not only reflect these factors but also competitive conditions in the market place. ICC *Ex parte 270*[1] states:

Since mid-1964, the unit train concept has made considerable strides towards establishing itself as a major market pricing factor. A number of unit train rates have since been published in Eastern Territory. The level of each rate has been tailor-made on the basis of factors pertaining to the individual movement, and usually has applied from origin to one destination without observing the usual origin and destination relationships.

The Bureau of Mines[2] may be quoted on the same subject as follows:

Freight charges for unit train service are quite different from the traditional coal rate structures "made on an origin group and destination basis." *Rates for unit trains are individually negotiated and have no fixed relationship to those applicable to other origin or destination points.* When the rates were first negotiated, some relationship seems to have existed between single-car and multiple-car shipments. One example of this is the reference in 1959 to Lake Cargo rates from Illinois, Indiana and western Kentucky fields that range "from 80.1 to 87.8 percent of the corresponding single-car rate." But, as a general rule, no such relationship exists among the current unit train rates. In fact, unit train rates are now in effect for coal moving from the western mines to markets in the midwest over routes where no effective single-car rates has formerly existed. For such routes, the unit train rates were the first coal rates actually published. [Emphasis added.]

The productivity of unit trains is high. The combination of dedicated equipment, scheduled operations, absence of switching en route, and quick turnaround (loading and unloading time allowances are usually specified in unit-train contracts) significantly improve operational efficiency. In general, a car in unit-train service will carry over the course of 1 year from five to six times the amount of tons it would carry in any other type of service. This by itself explains the increasing importance of unit-train movements, particularly during times of shortage of capital and critical materials. High productivity is reflected in the unit-train rates, and these are, as might be expected, the lowest available. Figure 1 is an example of rates which have been available over a specific territory. These rates may not be available, however, for a particular case because unit-train rates, as stated before, are subject to bilateral agreements between the shipper and the carrier.

[1]*Ibid.*
[2]U.S. Bureau of Mines, "Transportation Costs of Fossil Fuels," 1971.

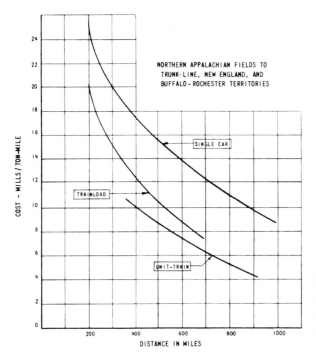

NORTHERN APPALACHIAN FIELDS TO
TRUNK-LINE, NEW ENGLAND, AND
BUFFALO - ROCHESTER TERRITORIES

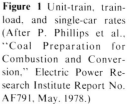

Figure 1 Unit-train, train-load, and single-car rates (After P. Phillips et al., "Coal Preparation for Combustion and Conversion," Electric Power Research Institute Report No. AF791, May. 1978.)

The preceding illustrates that coal transportation rates are indeed a complex matter, as has also been stated by the Interstate Commerce Commission[1] as follows:

> It is a fallacy to assume that the railroads have a single freight rate structure on coal or even a single rate structure within regions . . . . Although these [Rate] schedules are frequently constructed in conformity with a particular rate scheme, such as on a tapering mileage basis, in most instances the basis or bases for the rates are obscure and if known, that knowledge is limited to the rate-making railroad or to the most sophisticated tariff expert.

Cost-increase trends have, in the past, favored the large-volume coal shippers as railways have passed on only a fraction of the increases allowed by the ICC. This is understandable because:

1. It is a matter of survival for the railways to maintain or increase their share of coal traffic.
2. Inflationary trends in labor, materials, and fuel are to a certain degree offset by equipment productivity gains.

On a nationwide basis, from 1961 through 1974, coal rates have increased at the rate of 4.1 percent per year. Western trends are slightly higher, with increases over the last 7 years averaging just under 5 percent per year. There is no assurance

[1]ICC *loc. cit.*

however that future freight cost increases will follow this pattern, and at least a 7 percent yearly escalation may be realistic for the near to intermediate term. As a matter of fact, the WPI (Wholesale Price Index) for coal transportation increased by 10 percent between September 1975 and September 1976, and a further 4 percent increase was granted by the ICC effective January 7, 1977.

Unit-train Technology

The typical coal car built over the last 15 years for unit-train operation has a volume of 3600 to 4000 cubic feet and is rated at a nominal 100-ton net capacity. By AAR (Association of American Railroads) rules, a 100-ton car has a maximum weight, fully loaded, of 263,000 pounds on four axles. Because modern techniques and materials achieve a dead weight (empty) of approximately 60,000 pounds, the actual load-carrying capacity of such cars may be slightly in excess of the nominal 100 tons.

Coal cars are of two basic types, gondolas and hoppers. Gondolas are flat-bottom open cars (although coal cars with hinged covers were introduced recently) and must be unloaded by rotary dumpers which clasp and rotate the cars. Shortest dumping cycles are achieved when the cars are equipped with rotary couplers at both ends, so that they can be rotated and unloaded without time-consuming uncoupling. This calls also for the rotary-car dumper platen to be dimensioned exactly for the size (length) of the cars. Random-size dumpers are also available, as are tandem dumpers handling two coupled cars simultaneously.

Hopper cars are equipped with sloping plate bottoms and gates that open for a quick discharge. Triple-hopper cars are used most commonly but quadruple-hopper cars, with higher discharge rates, are gaining wider acceptance. For greatest rapidity in unloading, cars with longitudinal discharge gates opening a substantial fraction of the bottom are available. They offer remote and automatic operation of the gates and facilitate the simultaneous emptying of several cars over specially designed unloading trestles or hoppers.

The selection of a particular type of car for unit trains serving a large power station should be made only after careful analysis of all economic and operating factors. The features of the car selected will determine the type of unloading facility, and the combination of cars and unloading facilities determines the actual rate of unloading. Such an analysis should focus also on the ratio between trip time and loading-unloading times because they are an important part of any contract for unit-train transportation. Short distances (and therefore short-over-the road times) favor the use of high loading and unloading rates, while over long distances the influence of loading and unloading time decreases. Each case should be evaluated on its own and generalizations are inapplicable.

Typical car prices (mid-1976) may be of interest and are as follows:

100-ton gondolas	$30,000
100-ton triple hoppers	$32,000

Fast unloading cars with longitudinal gate hoppers, depending on the additional

Table 2 Railway motive power and cars required to move 1 million tons of coal per year in unit-train movements (including spares)

Average length of haul: 600 miles
Mid-1976 prices

Item	Number	Unit price, $	Total cost, $
3000-hp locomotives	5	550,000	2,750,000
100-ton cars	83	30,000	2,490,000
Total			5,240,000

equipment specified, may cost $35,000 − $40,000. A fully equipped rotary dumper facility (single-car dumper) may cost $1 million and more.

Current practice is for the railroads to own the locomotives, but consignee ownership of locomotives may become necessary in special cases because of the railroads' critical shortage of capital. In any case, the profile of the lines over which unit trains move and the weight of the trains determines the number and size of locomotives required. Typical locomotive requirements for a 10,000-ton coal unit train (one hundred 100-ton cars) range from three to five 3000-horsepower units and represent an investment of $1.65 to $2.75 million.

Table 2 shows equipment requirements for coal unit trains.

Although coal movements have to date averaged about 300 miles, the longer distances shown in Table 2 reflect the current trend.

Technological and Operational Trends

Technological and operational trends for the next decade have been studied because they bear on the availability of equipment to meet the projected coal traffic increase and on coal transportation costs. The following conclusions appear reasonable:

1. The locomotive and freight-car builders will have no problem meeting projected demands. Estimates at the most pessimistic level (Table 3) require only 30 percent of existing freight-car building capacity (including railway shops). Maximum demands on the locomotive industry would occur if all movements were to be made by trains; in that case the average demand over the next 10 years would be 470 locomotive units per year, or less than 25 percent of industry capacity at today's levels.
2. Rate increases are expected, therefore, to reflect inflationary trends and not to be influenced by equipment shortages.

In estimating the equipment required to handle the projected (1975 − 1985) increase to 820 million tons to be transported annually by rail, the following assumptions are reflected in Table 3.

1. Intermodal distribution for rail, river, and ex-river would remain essentially as in 1974.
2. Unit-train technology and operations would remain substantially the same as at present.
3. 100 percent of the existing fleet will be replaced. This is a conservative premise.

The assumptions made regarding modal distribution and technological changes are justified on the following grounds:

1. The intermodal distribution of coal transportation has not changed significantly in the last 15 years, and slurry pipelines, even if built in the numbers now suggested, would not affect this distribution to the point of influencing estimates of this kind.
2. Major technological changes are not likely to occur during the next decade.

The coal cars most frequently specified and purchased at this time are of 100-ton capacity. Fully loaded, they weigh 132 tons and have therefore an excellent capacity-to-total-weight ratio. As experience was gained with these cars, particularly under the high mileages accumulated in unit-train service, a number of weaknesses were detected but have been mostly corrected at this time. On the other hand, unit trains consisting of such cars were found to impose severe stresses on the rails and roadbeds at a time when much of the nation's rail mileage is suffering from the effects of years of deferred maintenance. Experience with 125-ton cars (157 tons fully loaded) has been very unfavorable from the standpoint of track maintenance, and the engineering departments of most railways are against their general use, particularly in unit-train service.

Most coal unit trains carry between 7000 and 10,000 tons (net), although lighter and heavier trains are operated. Consideration of coupling-gear strength and dynamics of long trains indicate that this range will remain unchanged. Where circumstances favor the operation of very heavy trains, in the range 10,000 to 15,000 tons and above, the insertion of remote-controlled "slave" locomotives, at some points within the train, has been used successfully in a number of instances.

Table 3 Coal-car requirements to handle 820 million tons of coal in 100-ton cars in 1985

Average distance: 600 miles
Estimates include 5 percent spares

	Case 1 (ICC projection)	Case 2 (1975 conditions)
Hypothesis	85% in unit trains	40% in unit trains
Cars required	115,000	243,000

Locomotive horsepower growth has slowed down from the pace of the sixties, and today the typical heavy-duty, six-axle locomotive is rated at 3000 horsepower net for traction, and weighs about 200 tons. This type of locomotive is well-adapted to the operating practices (loads and speeds) prevailing in this country, and no major changes are anticipated.

It has been stated above that U.S. freight-car builders can meet projected demands. While this is true on an intermediate-term basis, temporary shortages may occur, as they did in the recent past. Railroads, chronically short of capital, not only tend to postpone the purchase of equipment until a shortage begins to be felt but also cancel orders already placed when a momentary slack in demand occurs. The ownership of unit-train equipment by shippers or consignees may therefore be one of the most stabilizing factors in coal-car availability.

Another factor making even more undesirable the usual wide fluctuation in car-order levels is the supply of critical components such as wheels, certain castings, and special steel plates. Experience has shown that their supply cannot be readily expanded to levels much above industry's normal capacity because manufacturers are understandably reluctant to undertake expansions that may fall unused at relatively short notice and remain unused for substantial periods of time.

Finally, while most railway lines in the United States are underutilized, several major coal-carrying routes are being operated at high-capacity levels and may not be able to support much heavier traffic without rehabilitation, modernization of train-control systems, lengthening and relocation of passing sidings, rail renewals and, in some cases, electrification.

An evaluation of the capacity of the coal transportation system was prepared by Rifas and White.[1] Discussing the capacity of the rail system, they noted that "geographical features—mainly rivers and mountains—form barriers to the easy construction of rail links and the number of links crossing the barriers tends to become rather sparse." With respect to water transport, they noted that "there are four types of operating constraints limiting the arrival through part of the inland waterway systems—operating seasons, channel depth, channel width, and locks. There is no capacity limit on the open stretches of the waterway system. Congestion at certain locks, however, even now is causing cargo delays." Based on estimates of potential demand for transportation of coal and other commodities and estimates of the potential capability of the rail and water transportation systems to handle this demand, they concluded that "for many public utilities, which may be dependent on coal by 1985, there is legitimate cause for concern that the transportation system may not be able to carry the coal over the most direct, lowest cost routes."

The findings of their report were challenged by Briggs,[2] who stated emphatically that "under any reasonable set of assumptions, the railroads have, or can easily develop, the capacity to meet the nation's expanded demands for coal over the next decade. Moreover, the reasonableness of their rates will remain subject to close

[1]B. E. Rifas and S. J. White, "Coal Transportation Capability of the Existing Rail and Barge Network, 1985 and Beyond," Electric Power Research Institute Report EA-237, September 1976.

[2]R. E. Briggs, "The Coal-Hauling Potential of U.S. Railroads," presented at Seminar on Fuel Availability for Boiler Conversion, Texas Industrial Commission, Austin, Tex., Jan. 26, 1977.

Table 4 Comparison of U.S. FOB mine and railroad rates on bituminous coal for selected years, 1932—1974

Year	U.S. coal production million tons	Av. price FOB mine, $/ton	Av. rail rates, $/ton	Total, $/ton	% of destination value Coal	Rail rates
1932	309.7	1.31	2.26	3.57	36.7	63.3
1942	582.7	2.36	2.31	4.67	50.5	49.5
1952	466.8	4.90	3.35	8.25	59.4	40.6
1962	422.1	4.49	3.32	7.80	57.4	42.6
1972	595.0	7.57	3.67	11.20	67.2	32.8
1974	603.0	15.72	4.71	20.43	76.9	23.1

Source: ICC and NCA data.

regulatory scrutiny . . . ." Briggs went on to state that "the excess capacity of many rail tracks has long been one of the chief courses of weakness within the rail industry. It will be most enjoyable to see that surplus reduced."

It may be that both the report's authors and their critics may be right, and that the transportation system can handle prospective increases in coal traffic, with certain modifications over individual routes. Still, it will be important for electric utility companies (and other coal consumers) to become more involved in the transportation process to assure delivery of coal supplies at reasonable costs.

The cost of coal transportation by rail is determined by rates (Table 4). Between 1932 and 1942, average rail rates for coal shipment changed but little. A jump in rates took place between 1942 and 1952, after which rates remained reasonably steady until 1972. More recent rates have resumed the patterns of increases. Actually, rates have increased faster than the table shows because of changes in regulatory requirements. From 1890 to 1959, the Interstate Commerce Commission admitted only two types of coal rates: less-than-carload and carload (which was less). The ICC held that granting even lower rates for larger shipments was an "unjust discrimination against small shippers . . . ." Large-volume rates covering many carloads were permitted for the first time in 1959. However, these contributed to a high degree of inconsistency in coal transportation rates, because they varied widely for different origin-destination pairs, even within a relatively limited geographical area (Table 5).

Table 5 Selected rates and distances for Appalachian fields to trunk line, New England and Buffalo—Rochester territories

Rate base		Distance, miles	Rates $/ton	Mills/ton-mile
Annual volume	100,000 tons	524.5	6.55	12.5
	50,000 tons	519.5	6.07	11.7
Trainload:	7000 tons	482	5.20	10.8
	7000 tons	608	5.20	8.6

Source: ICC data.

By the very nature of rate making, it is next to impossible to come up with hard and fast rules that accurately predict transportation costs. Uncertainties in rail transportation costs are caused by the variety of rates in existence (not all of which may be available at any given point) and in barge transportation costs by the fact that barge companies are largely unregulated and may alter their rates seasonally (unless negotiated long-term contracts are in effect). Reliable transportation cost estimates are obtainable only after all parameters controlling the movements have been defined. Among these are, in the case of rail, the exact origin and destination, route, number of carriers involved, annual volume, type of movement and equipment ownership.

COAL TRANSPORTATION BY BARGES

Water transportation along the inland waterways, rivers, and the Great Lakes is the least expensive way to ship coal for the following reasons:

1. Water transportation has a low labor content when compared with rails, trucks, and even conveyors.
2. Water carriers do not have to supply or maintain their right-of-way, this being one of the reasons why they are less labor-intensive than railroads. At present, all safety and navigation aids, locks, dams, and channel maintenance are government provided and maintained by the Corps of Engineers at no cost to the users. Pressure for user fees to cover such costs is mounting, and might change present practices in the future.
3. Water carriers are largely nonregulated and enjoy a large degree of freedom in rate making.

In 1973, the average coal haul by barges was 350 miles, and 69 percent of the domestic inland water movements of coal originated in the following shipping areas:

Ohio River	31 percent
Monongahela River	24 percent
Green & Banen Rivers	14 percent
	69 percent

Table 6 shows the principal shipping areas for the inland waterways transportation of coal.

Barge transportation of dry bulk commodities is largely carried outside regulated rate structures because of provisions known as the *barge mixing rule*. These provisions and their effect on transportation have been the subject of a study by the U.S. Department of Transportation, reported to Congress under the title "The Barge Mixing Rule Problem" (March 1973), from which the following is extracted:

The "Barge Mixing Rule Problem" can be separated into four different elements:

1. *The Custom-of-the-Trade Provision.* All dry bulk commodities transported by water are exempt from economic regulations provided such commodities were moved in bulk by water on or prior to June 1, 1939.
2. *The Three-Commodity Restriction.* Dry bulk commodities transportation by water is exempt from economic regulation only if no more than three exempt dry bulk commodities are carried in one tow.
3. *The No-Mixing Rule.* Dry bulk commodity transportation by water is exempt from economic regulation only if no regulated commodities are moved in the same tow with exempt dry bulk commodities.
4. *Rate Publication.* Dry bulk exempt commodities may be carried for hire in interstate commerce without any publication of applicable rates either before or after the fact.

Clearly, there are important differences in regulations applying to the railway and the barge sectors of coal transportation. Rail and barge rates are arrived at by starting from different conditions and by applying different sets of rules. Thus rates should not be taken as a true measure of the relative cost of the services they cover.

Because most coal transported by barges in the United States moves downstream, there are no "grades" to overcome. Tow sizes are effectively limited by locks. Double locking is a time-consuming and expensive procedure which is avoided whenever possible. Partly as a result of the nearly homogeneous characteristics of coal barge traffic, barge rates are more nearly dependent on distance than rail rates (Figure 2). Figure 3 shows the range of the costs from which Figure 2 was derived.

A barge tow is a very good example of modern transportation technology akin to railroad unit trains, and major technological innovations are not expected to take place in the near or intermediate terms.

With barge capacities of 900 tons and over, there is no place in river coal traffic for the equivalent of single-car movement. The combination of sizes of barges and tows and the practice of entering into long-term transportation contracts (many

Table 6 Principal shipping areas for the inland waterways transportation of coal as of 1973

Shipping area	Tons	% of total
Ohio River	33,743,072	31.04
Monongahela River	26,281,271	24.14
Green & Banen Rivers	15,458,181	14.20
Mississippi River	8,084,640	7.42
Hanawha River	6,675,576	6.13
Tennessee River	6,436,607	5.91
Other areas	12,151,634	11.16
Totals	108,830,981	100.00

Source: ICC.

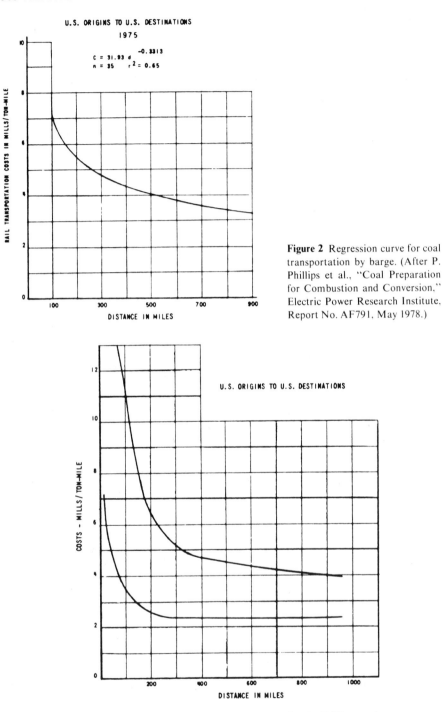

U.S. ORIGINS TO U.S. DESTINATIONS
1975

$C = 31.93 \, d^{-0.3313}$
$n = 35 \quad r^2 = 0.65$

RAIL TRANSPORTATION COSTS IN MILLS/TON-MILE

DISTANCE IN MILES

Figure 2 Regression curve for coal transportation by barge. (After P. Phillips et al., "Coal Preparation for Combustion and Conversion," Electric Power Research Institute, Report No. AF791, May 1978.)

U.S. ORIGINS TO U.S. DESTINATIONS

COSTS - MILLS/TON-MILE

DISTANCE IN MILES

Figure 3 Barge transportation costs range. (After P. Phillips et al., "Coal Preparation for Combustion and Conversion," Electric Power Research Institute, Report No. AF791, May 1978.)

from 5 to 20 years) make coal movements by barge very much like unit trains at annual volume rates.

As in the case of railways, the use of dedicated and shipper- or consignee-owned equipment is increasing. In 1973, about 580 towboats and 4000 barges were assigned to haul only coal.

Table 7 shows the number of pieces of equipment and their capital costs required to transport 1 million tons of coal per year 350 miles by barge tows. The capital costs are of the same order of magnitude as those shown for rail equipment when reduced to the same length of haul.

Continuing the parallel with railway transportation, the 1940s saw the final replacement of steam power by diesel engines in towboats. When eventually locomotive-type engines and other medium-speed diesel engines became available, considerable increases in towboat power were achieved, assisted by such technological improvements as double- and triple-screw installations; tunnel sterns, which mean large propellers; Kort nozzles, which produce large increases in thrust; and multiple-rudder installations, which result in more maneuverable towboats.

Although 10,500-horsepower towboats are currently in use, most coal traffic will probably continue to be handled by 5600-horsepower towboats pulling or pushing 1500-ton barges.

The advent of large tows and fixed configurations has brought about the introduction of intermediate barges with flat ends to increase propulsion efficiency while raked ends are preferred for the end barges. Another innovation is the bow-thruster, fitted to special vessels or even barges. By producing thrust, when required, at 90° to the direction of motion, it greatly increases the maneuverability of the tow and decreases docking and undocking time.

The probable limit to expansion of coal traffic in the inland waterways is lock capacity. Besides the insufficient capacity of individual locks, certain major "traffic jams" are already occurring at strategic spots such as the southern Illinois area where the Mississippi, Missouri, Illinois, Ohio, Cumberland, and Tennessee river traffic flows converge. Inadequate lock sizes are commonly causing delays of up to 16 hours and sometimes even days.

Traditionally, the Corps of Engineers has met with little opposition in obtaining legislation for the expansion or improvement of inland waterways. Resistance now seems to be increasing, led by environmentalists and railroads, and is causing more uncertainty as to whether and when some of the Ohio and Mississippi bottlenecks will be eliminated.

Table 7 Typical quantities and costs of towboats and barges to move 1 million tons of coal 350 miles as of 1975

Item	Number	Capital cost
5600-hp towboats	6	$14,000,000
1500-ton barges	107	18,000,000
Total		$32,000,000

Source: Gribbs and Hill.

MOTOR VEHICLES

Approximately 10 percent of all the coal produced in the United States each year is shipped by truck. For 1973, this represented over 68 million tons. Of this amount, over 48 million tons was shipped to electric utilities.[1]

The two primary advantages of truck transportation are not directly related to cost. The speed with which coal can be moved by truck can exceed that of railway transport depending on the circumstances. Another significant advantage of trucks is the high degree of route flexibility. In some instances, truck is the only method by which coal can be delivered to the final consumer.

Both the small user and small producer of coal may benefit from the use of trucks for the delivery of coal. This is especially true if additional railway lines would have to be constructed to serve the mine site or the consumer.

Off-road trucks are an important transporter of coal in surface mining operations, providing the most convenient method for coal movement from the pit to the next operating point. Depending on the situation, off-road haulers may move the coal to a processing plant, a railway siding or waterway loading dock, or to a mine-mouth generating plant. These large trucks, carrying from 30 to 240 tons of coal each trip, are important because of route flexibility which allows them to follow the source of the coal as it is mined. The most common distances for truck haulage appear to be on the order of 1 to 5 miles.

Recent developments in motor vehicles have led to a variety of coal haulers for off-road use, particularly from mine sites to a nearby storage and shipping location. The modern vehicles are characterized by larger load-carrying capacity, electric wheel drive powered by a diesel generator, and four-wheel drive and articulating vehicles for rugged terrain.

Capacity of the off-road trucks range from a 35-ton (475-horsepower) bottom dump hauler to a 240-ton (1200-horsepower) "big body" hauler. Tractor-trailer haulers have even higher capacities, as high as 390 tons.

Selection of a design for a particular application depends more on the specific needs of the situation rather than on simply choosing a desired capacity, however. Particular mines may require articulating bodies for maneuvering around rough terrain, a four-wheel or tandem drive for steep grades, or a combined scraper-hauler for strip mines.

The use of trucks to transport coal on the highways is economically advantageous under one or more of the following circumstances: (1) for the small producer of coal, (2) for relatively small amounts of coal moved over short or intermediate distances, or (3) for a small or irregular coal user not near a railway siding. The percentage of coal transported by truck has remained relatively constant at 10−13 percent of total production over the past 10 years, and there is no apparent evidence that this percentage is about to increase. One barrier to increased truck transport is the truckload factor of 60 percent compared with 80−90 percent in other modes of transport.[2]

[1] U.S. Bureau of Mines, *Miner. Yearb.*, 1973.
[2] National Coal Association, *Coal Traffic Ann.*, 1976.

PIPELINE-WATER SLURRY

Background

The use of pipelines to transport large volumes of solid materials in the form of a slurry is a relatively recent development. Some of the materials which have been transported in this manner are coal, iron concentrate, limestone and other cement raw materials, kaolin, and copper concentrate. The first coal pipeline in the United States was built between Cadiz and Cleveland, Ohio, and operated from 1958 to 1963. The low cost of transporting coal in this pipeline is cited as one of the prime reasons for the introduction of the unit-train concept and lower transport rates for coal by the railroads. A second coal-slurry pipeline has been built in Arizona to supply just under 6 million tons of coal per year to an electric generating plant.

In a slurry pipeline, the coal is reduced to a fine consistency before being mixed with water in the pipeline. The concentration of solids by weight is approximately 45 to 55 percent in a coal pipeline and the flowrate is on the order of 5 feet per second. Pumping stations are located every 30 to 60 miles along the pipeline. In general, the technology for long-distance transportation of solids in liquids is proven. The emphasis in technological development is now toward large systems and other solids to be transported.

The primary advantage of coal-slurry pipeline is the lower projected transportation cost per ton per mile. These lower costs result primarily from pronounced economies of scale as the annual throughput is increased and as the distance of transport is increased. Another significant advantage is that a new pipeline will usually be less expensive to construct than a new railroad, particularly in areas previously considered inaccessible. Thus the feasible locations for power plants or mines are increased in number.

Pipelines are highly reliable and thus are capable of high operating factors. In addition, since approximately 70 percent of the unit cost of transportation through a slurry pipeline is composed of capital related to fixed costs, the effects of inflation on annual transportation costs are minimal.[1]

Present Status

At present only one coal pipeline is in operation in the United States, the Black Mesa Pipeline in Arizona (273-mile, 18-inch pipeline). The Cadiz—Cleveland pipeline is in mothballs so that if rail rates rise enough to make its operation feasible, it can be reactivated with a minimum of expense.

The primary technical problems appear to be in the utilization of the slurry mixture rather than its transportation. Experiments have been performed using the slurry mixture without drying; however, this requires coals with special characteristics and is not a common practice. If the coal must be dried prior to use, then the method for this must be improved. Even with these problems, it appears that

[1] E. J. Wasp, Progress with Coal Slurry Pipelines, *Min. Congr. J.*, p. 27–32, April 1976.

the utilization costs of slurry coal are close to those of dry coal. The losses due to firing wetter material are offset by lower handling, storage, and crushing costs.[1]

Costs for the coal-slurry pipeline appear to be comparable to those projected for the integral train (1 to 2 cents per million Btu per 100 miles).[2] The most significant parameters in determining transportation costs are the annual tonnages and the distance transported. While slurry pipelines exhibit marked economies of scale (pipeline investment increased as the square root of the increase in capacity),[3] unit trains and integral trains do not exhibit this to nearly the same degree.

As mentioned before, the highest percentage of a pipeline's transportation cost is in relatively fixed capital costs; so the overall cost of transporting energy through a pipeline is relatively insensitive to inflation.

EFFECTS OF COAL PREPARATION ON TRANSPORTATION MODES AND COSTS

It was stated in Chapter 9 that coal beneficiation reduces the cost of coal transportation. Actually, this cause-and-effect relationship is a two-way street. A more appropriate statement would allow that coal preparation and beneficiation mutually influence the means and therefore the costs of handling and transporting coal. When coal preparation at its most elementary level provides for the control of the raw coal's top size to facilitate handling, almost any transportation mode can be considered and costs would fall within normal ranges. On the other hand, when raw coals must be crushed to ⅜-inch top size or smaller to optimize beneficiation, the clean coal may be unsuitable for shipment by conventional means. Because such finely crushed coal contains a high percentage of very fine particles, fugitive dust from handling and transportation may be unacceptable for ecological and economic reasons. When beneficiation of such fine coals is indicated, locating the washing plant close to the point of utilization should receive serious consideration as it might permit the use of fully enclosed transportation systems.

On the other hand, when coals are to be transported by slurry pipelines over long distances, they must first be reduced to a fine and closely controlled size consist for physical and economic reasons. At the pipeline discharge end, these fine coals typically must be dewatered and thermally dried prior to final pulverization and combustion. The combination of initial size reduction and eventual dewatering requires substantial capital and operating expenditures which, by themselves, represent a major cost element when beneficiating fine coals. If, therefore, coal-slurry transportation could be combined with beneficiation, substantial benefits, at little additional cost, may present themselves. Unfortunately, from that point of view, the subbituminous coals presently being considered for pipeline transportation are not

[1]*Ibid*, p. 27−32.

[2]M. Reiber and L. S. Soo, "Comparative Coal Transportation Costs: An Economic and Engineering Analysis of Truck, Belt, Rail, Barge, and Coal Slurry and Pneumatic Pipelines," University of Illinois, NTIS No. PB 274-379, August 1977.

[3]Wasp, *op. cit.,* p. 27−32.

very conducive to beneficiation as they are inherently low in ash and sulfur. As more is learned about beneficiating low-rank coals, this situation is likely to change. Actually, the current reluctance to wash low-rank coals is prompted largely by the expense and difficulties of drying these porous and moisture-absorbent coals. Thus, if slurry transportation proves to be more economical than rail movement it may overcome these considerations and encourage the beneficiation of low-rank coals.

Not all western coals are of low rank, however, and particularly Utah has important reserves of low-sulfur bituminous coals which are now being shipped East, some as far as Ohio. The following numerical example, summarized in Table 8, assesses the effects on transportation costs from beneficiating such coals. It compares transportation costs with beneficiation costs on the basis of the following assumed parameters:

Btu to be transported	30×10^{12} Btu/year ($\pm$million tons/year)
Levels of coal preparation	From Table 1, Chapter 9
Coal quality data	From Table 2, Chapter 9
Cost of coal preparation	From Table 2, Chapter 9
Mode of transportation	Trains plus barges
Transportation distance	2000 miles
Overall freight rate	$0.009 per ton-mile

The 2000-mile coal movement selected for this example results in a total transportation cost of $18 per ton. The same benefits would accrue however for any other coal movement where transportation costs are $18 per ton, regardless of the distance the coal travels.

Use of the $18 per ton rate for this example does not imply that transportation cost savings from coal beneficiation are insignificant in any but extreme cases. Just as transportation costs vary broadly for similar distances, so do preparation costs. Given a different set of circumstances, substantially the same results shown in Table 8 might be obtained also when freight costs are only $9 per ton and beneficiation costs half of those used in Table 2, Chapter 9, and in Table 8.

With these considerations in mind, Table 8 illustrates that:

1. The savings in freight costs more than offset the total cost of level C beneficiation as the incremental costs of preparation plus transportation are higher for level B (top-size control only) than for level C (coarse beneficiation).
2. With level D beneficiation, annual freight savings of $2,844,000 can be expected when compared to level B prepared coal. Actual preparation cost differential between levels D and B is $5,280,000. Thus 54 percent of the additional preparation costs have been offset by freight savings.
3. Preparation and transportation costs, when expressed on a dollar *per ton basis*, show a 10.5 percent increase between levels B and C, although on a *Btu basis* they decreased by 2.9 percent.
4. Shipping the Utah bituminous coal to the East without prior beneficiation would be wasteful both of money and energy. Not only is the delivered cost of

Table 8 Effects of coal preparation on transportation costs

	Level B preparation	Level C beneficiation	Level D beneficiation
Calorific contents of coal (from Table 2, Chap. 9)	12,505 Btu/lb	14,250 Btu/lb	14,400 Btu/lb
Tons/year equivalent to 30×10^{12} Btu	1,200,000 tons	1,053,000 tons	1,042,000 tons
Total cost of preparation including Btu Loss C_T, $/million Btu (Table 2, Chap. 9)	$0.027	$0.093	$0.203
Annual cost of preparation ($30 \times 10^6 \times C_T$)	$810,000	$2,790,000	$6,090,000
Annual cost of transportation (tons per year $\times$ $0.009 $\times$ 2000 miles)	$21,600,000	$18,954,000	$18,756,000
Annual cost of preparation plus freight	$22,410,000	$21,744,000	$24,846,000
Cost of preparation & transportation per ton of coal	$18.68	$20.65	$23.84
Cost of preparation & transportation per million Btu	$0.747	$0.725	$0.828

Note: Cost of raw coal not included above.

the washed coal lower than that of the same coal unwashed, but the total yearly tonnage transported would be about 12 percent smaller, v·'·h corresponding savings in diesel fuel consumed.

SUMMARY

Coal transportation and preparation are separate but closely interrelated technologies. Depending on specific circumstances, transportation may influence preparation, and vice versa. Some ROM coals are not conveniently transportable in their raw state, while the transportation of other coals may become far more difficult precisely because of their prior beneficiation. Between these extremes lie the vast majority of real situations where coal preparation and beneficiation improve a coal's handleability and lower its transportation costs. In some instances the costs of beneficiation are more than offset by freight savings, while in most other cases such savings are but one of the many benefits realized. Just as preparation costs vary widely in response to site and process-specific factors, so do transportation costs range between extremes in a complex pattern. When investigating coal availability it is therefore just as important to explore available transportation means and costs as it is to seek out suitable coals in required quantities and at the right price. Ideally, both investigations should be conducted concurrently, although some experts believe that economical and reliable transportation is more difficult to contract for than coal supplies. As average transportation distances increase with enlarged western coal production, transportation may indeed become a major bottleneck, although for the near term at least the costs of coal transportation are of primary concern.

Of further concern to coal utilization is the availability of water to support processing or facility requirements. This subject is discussed in the next chapter.

ELEVEN

WATER REQUIREMENTS FOR COAL DEVELOPMENT

Development and utilization of coal resources cannot be undertaken without the use of other natural resources. Activities throughout the coal fuel sequence are dependent on the continued availability of supplies of metallic and nonmetallic minerals, chemicals, and products manufactured from these and other materials, as noted by the U.S. Geological Survey.[1] It is important to bear in mind, however, that there is an additional resource which is essential to operations in the energy industry (and all other industries)—that resource is water. Each stage of the coal fuel sequence requires water in the performance of normal operating activities.

UNIT REQUIREMENTS

There have been several attempts to estimate the magnitude of water requirements for coal development and use. In the early 1960s, Kaufman and Nadler[2] included coal in an overall survey of water use in the mineral industry. Data for coal are summarized in Table 1 in original units of gallons per ton of raw coal; Table 2 recalculates these data into gallons per million Btu, assuming a constant heat rate. At the time of the survey, the total amounts of water used and conserved in coal mining and related activities were modest, regardless of mining method employed.

Present practices in mining and coal processes are different from those in vogue at the time of the survey. More water is used in underground mines in attempts to suppress dust, and more water is used in surface mining to suppress dust and to support reclamation activities that are much more extensive than those followed previously. An estimate of present magnitudes is given in Table 3. Also, more water is used for coal preparation in attempts to control sulfur content and remove

---

[1] Demand and Supply of Nonfuel Minerals and Materials for the United States Energy Industry, 1975–90—A Preliminary Report, *US Geol. Surv., Prof. Pap.* 1006A,B, 1976.

[2] A. Kaufman and M. Nadler, Water Use in the Mineral Industry, *US Bur. Mines Inf. Circ.* 8285, 1966.

Table 1 Water use for coal mining and related activities, 1962

Gallons per ton of raw coal

	Gross use	Consumed
Underground:		
Mining	15	15
Preparation	524	8
Other	13	13
Total	552	36
Surface:		
Mining	4	4
Preparation	524	8
Other	4	4
Total	532	16

Source: US Bur. Mines Inf. Circ. 8285, 1966.

other unwanted constituents. The present magnitude of water consumption for coal mining and related activities was estimated by calculations starting from factors representative of current operations; the calculations are shown in Table 4.

The tables show that water requirements for mining and reclamation are modest, amounting to only a few gallons per million Btu. Coal preparation requires more than 10 times as much water as does mining. Thus, while mechanized coal development may save effort in coal extraction, the fact that extensive coal cleaning is required to remove noncombustibles mixed in with coal leads to important water requirements.

Table 2 Water use for coal mining and related activities, 1962

Gallons per million Btu*

	Gross use	Consumed
Underground:		
Mining	0.75	0.75
Preparation	26.20	0.40
Other	0.20	0.65
Total	27.15	1.80
Surface:		
Mining	0.20	0.20
Preparation	26.20	0.40
Other	0.20	0.20
Total	26.60	0.80

*Assumed: 20 million Btu/ton.

Source: A. Kaufman and M. Nadler, Water Use in the Mineral Industry, *US Bur. Mines, Inf. Circ.* 8285, 1966.

Table 3 Estimated water use for coal mining and related activities, 1976

Gallons per million Btu*

	Gross use	Consumed
Underground:		
Mining	2	2
Preparation	30	1
Other	1	1
Total	33	4
Surface:		
Mining	0.5	0.5
Preparation	30.0	1.0
Other	1.0	1.0
Total	31.5	2.5

*Assumed: 20 million Btu/ton.

Table 4 Derivation of water requirements for present operations

Mining

$$\frac{100 \text{ acre-ft}}{\text{million tons}} \times \frac{325,851 \text{ gal}}{\text{acre-ft}} \times \frac{1 \text{ ton}}{20 \text{ million Btu}} = \textbf{2 gal/million Btu}$$

Preparation

1. $\frac{1000 \text{ tons}}{\text{hr}} \times \frac{24 \text{ hr}}{\text{day}} \times \frac{200 \text{ day}}{\text{yr}} \times 0.7 = \frac{3.4 \text{ million tons clean coal}}{\text{yr}}$

2. $\frac{7070 \text{ gal}}{\text{min}} \times \frac{60 \text{ min}}{\text{hr}} \times \frac{24 \text{ hr}}{\text{day}} \times \frac{200 \text{ days}}{\text{yr}} = \frac{2.0 \times 10^9 \text{ gal}}{\text{yr}}$

3. $3.4 \times 10^6 \text{ tons} \times \frac{20 \times 10^6 \text{ Btu}}{\text{ton}} = \frac{68 \times 10^{12} \text{ Btu}}{\text{ton}}$

4. $\frac{2 \times 10^9 \text{ gal}}{68 \times 10^6 \text{ Btu/ton}} = \textbf{30 gal/million Btu}$

Reclamation

1. $\frac{1800 \text{ tons coal}}{\text{acre-ft}} \times 7 \text{ ft} = \frac{12,600 \text{ tons}}{\text{acre}} \times 0.8 = \frac{10,080 \text{ tons}}{\text{acre}}$

2. $\frac{10,080 \text{ tons}}{\text{acre}} \times \frac{20 \times 10^6 \text{ Btu}}{\text{ton}} = \frac{2 \times 10^{11} \text{ Btu}}{\text{acre}}$

3. $\frac{0.75 \text{ acre-ft water}}{\text{acre}} \times \frac{325,851 \text{ gal}}{\text{acre-ft}} = \frac{244,388 \text{ gal}}{\text{acre}}$

4. $\frac{244,388 \text{ gal/acre}}{200,000 \text{ million Btu/acre}} = \textbf{1.2 gal/million Btu}$

Before estimating water requirements for thermal-electric power generation, it is useful to refer to recent trends. Water usage has increased steadily since World War II. Figure 1 shows withdrawal[1] of water for major usage categories. Although these national data do not reflect important regional differences, it is noteworthy that the largest category of water withdrawal is for thermal-electric power generation. Water withdrawal for irrigation is the second largest category. However, as shown in Figure 2, irrigation represents the largest category of water consumption, with thermal-electric power being rather small.

The quantities of water withdrawn for thermal-electric power generation have increased more than 200-fold since the end of World War II (Figure 3). While the trend shows evidence of beginning to level off as greater use of closed cooling systems is realized, this could prove difficult to achieve. The U.S. Geological Survey[2] pointed out that:

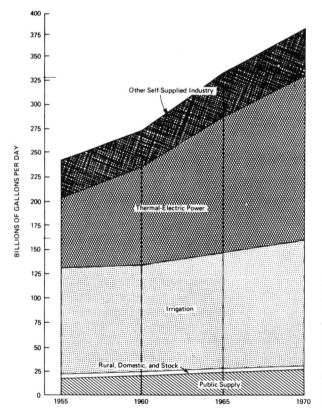

Figure 1 Withdrawal of water for major uses. (After Federal Energy Administration, Project Independence Blueprint, Water Requirements Task Force Report, "Water Requirements, Availabilities, Constraints, and Recommended Federal Actions," November 1974.)

---

[1] *US Geol. Surv. Prof. Pop., loc. cit.*

[2] *Withdrawal* of water refers to the total amount taken from a source. *Consumption* of water refers to the portion of withdrawn water that is not returned to the source.

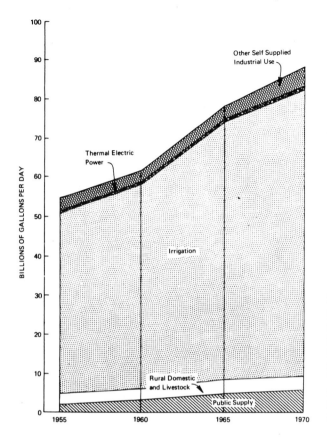

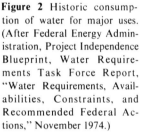

Figure 2 Historic consumption of water for major uses. (After Federal Energy Administration, Project Independence Blueprint, Water Requirements Task Force Report, "Water Requirements, Availabilities, Constraints, and Recommended Federal Actions," November 1974.)

Consumptive use by thermal electric generation will continue to grow and will increase relative to withdrawals. This seeming paradox is due to the fact that closed cooling systems have a greater evaporation loss relative to once-through systems as well as additional water consumption not applicable to once-through systems.

Accordingly, it seems reasonable to expect continued increases in water requirements for electric power generation throughout the remainder of the twentieth century, and possibly beyond. Water requirements for thermal-electric power generation may be determined readily from the above-cited published information (Table 5). The table shows that water *withdrawals* for this use amount to more than 15,000 gal per million Btu, while water *consumption* for power generation is only about 180 gal per million Btu (or about 1.2 percent of the total withdrawal). Even though the amount of water consumed in generating electric power is small in terms of the total withdrawal, the withdrawn-but-not-consumed water is still critical in the normal operation of power plants. Thus the larger amount of water withdrawn from sources for power plant use is the proper figure to use in planning or analysis.

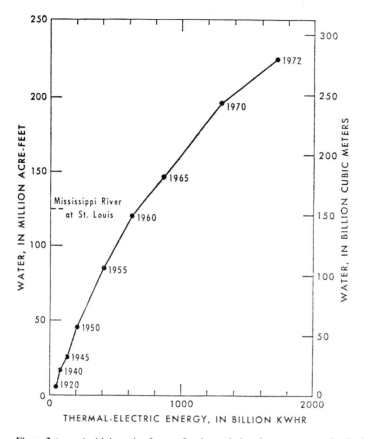

Figure 3 Annual withdrawals of water for thermal-electric power generation in the United States, 1920-1972. (After A. Kaufman and M. Nadler, Water Use in the Mineral Industry, *US Bur. Mines Inf. Circ.* 8285, 1966.)

INTEGRATED REQUIREMENTS

Table 6 summarizes the above-derived estimates of water requirements for key elements of the coal fuel sequence. The table shows that total water withdrawal for the sequence is nearly 16,000 gal per million Btu, of which 1.2 percent or 184 gal per million Btu is actually consumed.

Assuming that, for the immediate future, coal development and use will employ conventional technology, water requirements may be estimated. Table 6 indicates that as much as nearly 16,000 gallons per million Btu must be withdrawn from water sources to generate electricity from coal. This value can be translated into gallons per ton of coal by the following relationship:

16,000 gal/million Btu × 20 million Btu/ton = 320,000 gal/ton

The resulting amount expresses water requirements for the entire fuel sequence

Table 5 Estimated water withdrawals and consumption for thermal-electric power generation

Based on 1970 U.S. Geological Survey data

Withdrawal

1. $\dfrac{170 \times 10^9 \text{ gal}}{\text{day}} \times \dfrac{365 \text{ days}}{\text{yr}} = 6.2 \times 10^{13} \text{ gal/yr}$

2. $\dfrac{6.2 \times 10^{13} \text{ gal/yr}}{1.2 \times 10^{12} \text{ kWh/yr}} = \dfrac{51.7 \text{ gal}}{\text{kWh}}$

3. $\dfrac{51.7 \text{ gal}}{\text{kWh}} \times \dfrac{\text{kWh}}{3412 \text{ Btu}} =$ **15,200 gal/million Btu**

Consumption

1. $\dfrac{2 \times 10^9 \text{ gal}}{\text{day}} \times \dfrac{365 \text{ days}}{\text{yr}} = 7.3 \times 10^{11} \text{ gal/yr}$

2. $\dfrac{7.3 \times 10^{11} \text{ gal/yr}}{1.2 \times 10^{12} \text{ kWh/yr}} = \dfrac{0.61 \text{ gal}}{\text{kWh}}$

3. $\dfrac{0.61 \text{ gal}}{\text{kWh}} \times \dfrac{\text{kWh}}{3412 \text{ Btu}} =$ **180 gal/million Btu**

in terms of tons of coal equivalent. Applying this factor to electric utility coal projections[1] leads to an estimate of overall water needs for the coal-to-electricity process. These data are shown in Table 7. The table shows that water requirements in the East are projected to increase at a steady rate during the next decade, reaching more than 140×10^{12} gallons per year in 1985. According to projections of coal development and use in the West, water withdrawals are estimated to be quadrupled in this same time. It is important to bear in mind, as noted by the National Coal Association, that "rapid development forecast for Western coal will not be

Table 6 Estimated water requirements for conventional coal utilization activities, 1976

Gallons per million Btu

Activity	Withdrawal or gross use	Consumed
1. Coal mining	2	2
2. Coal preparation	30	1
3. Reclamation, etc.	1	1
4. Generation of electric power	15,200	180
Total	15,530	184

[1]National Coal Association, "A Study of Electric Utility Coal Requirements by Regions," manuscript, p. 9, November 1976.

Table 7 Estimated annual regional water withdrawals required for coal-based electric power generation (10^{12} gallons)

Year	East	West	Total
1975	99	30	129
1980	125	74	199
1985	141	123	264

the result of increased demands for low-sulfur Western coal by Eastern utilities. *By 1985, 86 percent of Western coal used by utilities will be burned in the West"* [Emphasis added.][1] Accordingly, the water required to support such operations will have to be found in the West (if such operations are to be feasible). This, as will be shown later, will be no easy task.

The discussion thus far concentrated on present or conventional water uses for coal development. In the future, it is possible that additional water may be required for processes that convert coal to gaseous or liquid fuels, although at rather early stages of development, it is possible to estimate the amount of water required for such processes. Table 8 presents two recent estimates of water consumption for coal gasification and liquefaction processes. The lower estimate by Probstein et al. refers to the process itself, whereas the Geological Survey estimate includes activities necessary to support the process. Although these estimates present water consumption only, it is possible to determine the total water withdrawal by analogy with conventional systems. Assuming that water consumed in coal conversion processes would represent only a fraction of the total withdrawal as in the case of conventional steam-electric power generation, then the water withdrawal requirements to support such processes could be as much as 2000 gal per million Btu. This point was emphasized by Probstein.[2]

Table 8 Comparison of total water consumption estimates for coal conversion processes

Gallons per million Btu

Process	Geological survey*	Probstein et al. †
1. Pipeline gas from coal, 250 million std. ft³/day	36-157	37
2. Coal liquefaction, 100 million bbl/day	32-200	30

*G. H. Davis and L. A. Wood, Water Demands for Expanding Energy Development, *US Geol. Surv. Circ.* 703, 1974.

†R. F. Probstein et al., "Water Needs for Fuel-to-Fuel Conversion Processes," presented at Symposium on Water Management for Energy Intensive Industries, AIChE 67th Annual Meeting, Washington, Dec. 3, 1974.

[1] *Ibid.*

[2] R. F. Probstein, et al., "Water Needs for Fuel-to-Fuel Conversion Processes," presented at Symposium on Water Management for Energy Intensive Industries, AIChE 67th Annual Meeting, Washington, Dec. 3, 1974.

1. Large amounts of water are required for various fuel-to-fuel conversion processes, much of which is required for cooling, mining, and other procedures not specifically composing the process.
2. Because of large water usage, it will be necessary to minimize cooling-water consumption if such processes are to be viable in water-short areas. Even then, it will probably be necessary to use brackish waters as plant feed in these areas.

Because of the present stage of process development, it is probably prudent to be conservative in estimating water requirements; for this reason, the upper limit of the range determined by the U.S. Geological Survey is used in the subsequent analysis. It is assumed that water requirements for consumption of substitute fuels would be roughly the same as for conventional steam-electric power plants. Table 9 presents total estimated water requirements for a coal fuel sequence including conversion processes. The table shows that water withdrawals and consumption are more than double that for conventional coal uses (compare Table 6). These large magnitudes of water requirements for coal conversion processes are hardly encouraging for their development (especially in the arid coalfields of the Western states).

PROSPECTIVE WATER SUPPLIES

Having arrived at estimates of total water requirements for coal-based systems, it is now appropriate to examine the prospective availability of water supplies to meet these and other demands.

The principal point to be made is that, regardless of approach, there is a strong interdependence of coal and water availability. Table 10 shows regional estimates of total water supply as of 1970 (regions are illustrated in Figure 4). The several regions are aggregated for purposes of comparison with the above East-West estimates of water requirements; for this report, it is assumed that the "Upper Mississippi" and "Lower Mississippi" water resource regions are part of the

Table 9 Total estimated water requirements for coal gasification and liquefaction processes (including consumption of product fuels)

Gallons per million Btu

Activity	Withdrawal	Consumed
1. Coal mining	2	2
2. Reclamation	1	1
3. Coal preparation	30	1
4. Coal conversion process	20,000	200
5. Consumption of substitute fuels	16,000	180
Total	36,033	384

Table 10 Estimates of the current supply condition as of 1970

10^{12} gallons per year

	Fresh surface water supply*	Fresh ground water use	Saline water use. ground & surface	Total gross supply
North Atlantic	11.6	1.2	8.	21.2
South Atlantic-Gulf	15.7	1.7	4.0	21.4
Great Lakes	3.0	0.5	0.1	3.7
Ohio	4.8	0.6	0.02	5.4
Tennessee	8.4	0.1		8.5
Upper Mississippi	4.4	0.8	0.01	5.2
Lower Mississippi	1.8	1.3	0.3	3 4
Souris-Red-Rainy	1.2	0.2	0.	1.5
Missouri	37.0	6.6	0. 2	14.3
Arkansas-White-Red	6.9	2.4		9.4
Texas-Gulf	2.4	2.2	2.	7.3
Rio Grande	1.0	0.9	0.1	1.9
Upper Colorado	11.2 (3.6)	0.03		11.3 (3.7)
Lower Colorado	1.9 (0.6)	1.6		6.9 (2.3)
Great Basin	0.9	1.5	0.01	2.4
Columbia-North	16.8	1.6	0.1	18.5
Pacific California	6.7	6.6	3.2	16.5
Total	101.6	25.5	19.4	146.5

Source: Federal Energy Administration, Project Independence Blueprint, Water Requirements Task Force Report, "Water Requirements, Availabilities, Constraints, and Recommended Federal Actions," November 1974.

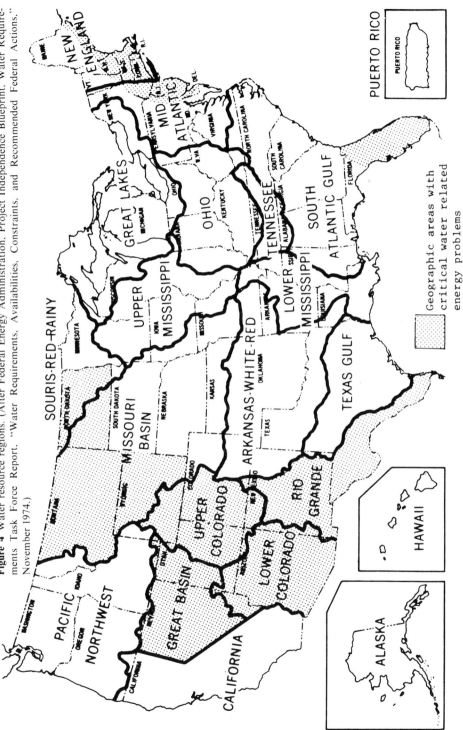

Figure 4 Water resource regions. (After Federal Energy Administration, Project Independence Blueprint, Water Requirements Task Force Report, "Water Requirements, Availabilities, Constraints, and Recommended Federal Actions," November 1974.)

Geographic areas with critical water related energy problems

Table 11 Estimated regional water supply

10^{12} gallons per year

Region	Gross water supply
East	68.8
West	77.7
Total	146.5

eastern coal-supply—use area. The estimated gross regional water supply is given (in comparable units to demand) in Table 11; the larger figure for the West is a reflection of the larger area covered.

Table 12 compares water demands for steam-electric power generation with indicated supplies. The table shows that eastern water demand for electric power already requires substantial reuse of water to meet power-generating requirements (i.e., the total supply is less than the water withdrawal requirements, so that return of nonconsumed water withdrawn from supplies is essential to serve other uses).

The western water demand, however, is projected to increase by more than four times in this decade, more than doubling every 5 years. Because of the magnitude of this projected increase, it is important to evaluate the consequences of such development in somewhat greater detail. As shown in Figure 4, certain areas of the West are likely to experience more intensive development than others, if the projected projects take place. Based on the locations of major coalfields, it seems apparent that the main activity will occur in the northern Missouri Basin and in the Upper Colorado Basin. These basins have the largest supplies of water, according to presently available data (Table 13).

Assuming that the total water supply for all western coal-based operations would come from these basins, it is possible to compare the available supply with projected demand. Table 14 shows that, regardless of the actual water supply, projected western coal developments would require by 1985 water withdrawals roughly five times the total estimated water supplies of the two main supply basins in the entire area. Clearly, substantial reuse would be required. It is also important to note that this estimate does *not* include the prospective coal conversion

Table 12 Comparison of projected regional water withdrawals for coal-based electric power generation to estimated regional water supplies

Withdrawal as percent of supplies

Year	Percent		
	East	West	Total
1975	144	39	88
1980	182	95	136
1985	205	158	180

Table 13 Water supplies in critical regions

10^{12} gallons per year

Region	Surface (runoff)	Groundwater (1970)	Total
Upper Colorado	3.6	0.03	3.63
Lower Colorado	0.6	1.6	2.2
Great Basin	0.9	1.5	2.4
Rio Grande	1.0	0.9	1.9
Missouri Basin	12.1	2.2	14.3
Total	18.2	6.23	24.43

Source: Federal Energy Administration, Project Independence Blueprint, Water Requirements Task Force Report, "Water Requirements, Availabilities, Constraints, and Recommended Federal Actions," November 1974.

projects mentioned for this same area. It hardly seems likely that such dramatic shifts in patterns of water usage could be accomplished (especially in such a short time) without far-reaching implications within the western coal area and beyond its borders. As never before, it will be essential to evaluate prospects for water availability in relation to coal development to ensure that undue stress is not placed on known supplies and that there are sufficient supplies available to meet standing requirements as well as prospective new projects.

Table 14 Comparison of projected western water withdrawals for coal-based electric power generation to estimated supplies in the Missouri Basin and Upper Colorado Basin

Year	Supply, 10^{12} gal	Demand, 10^{12} gal	Demand as % of supplies
1975	24.3	30	123
1980		74	303
1985		123	503

THREE

UTILIZATION

Just as coal production is simple in concept but complex in practice, so is coal utilization more intricate than it appears. Facilities and equipment for coal utilization also evolved through trial and error, and this pattern seems likely to continue. Thus, knowledge of present practices and trends of coal utilization can serve as a guide for projection and analysis of possible futures.

Trends in bituminous coal production for the last 100 years are shown in Figure 1. Production increased steadily from 1870 to about 1920, but since that time, coal

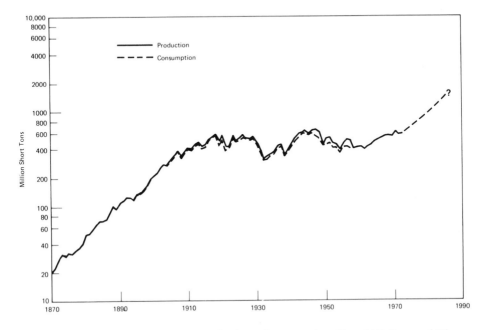

Figure 1 U.S. trends in bituminous coal production and consumption. (From U.S. Bureau of Mines, *Miner. Yearb.*, various years.)

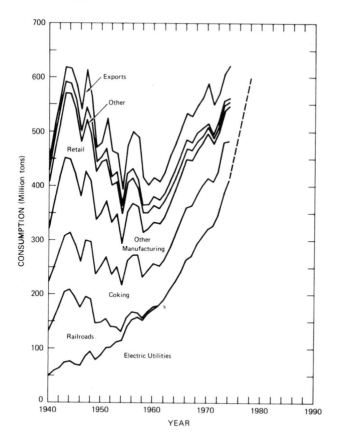

Figure 2 Patterns of coal consumption in the United States. (From U.S. Bureau of Mines, *Miner. Yearb.*, various years.)

production has fluctuated in a relatively narrow range (except during the Depression). This suggests that the industry capacity has been geared to about 400 to 600 million tons annually for roughly 50 years. Clearly, the projected increases in coal production requirements to levels at 1 or 1.5 billion tons annually before the end of the century would represent significant departures from long-established trends. It seems apparent that these changes would have to include both technological improvements and altered institutional structures to take best advantage of new technical capabilities. Without such a coordinated approach to the problem of providing estimated levels of case production, it is not at all certain that the necessary coal will be available to meet demands.

The history of coal consumption in the United States over the last 30 years is one of shifting consumer patterns (Figure 2). In the early 1940s, coal use was scattered relatively evenly among retail, manufacturing, coking, railroad, and electric utilities. This diversity in coal use was changed substantially during the late 1940s through the 1960s. At these times, the railroad market for coal virtually disappeared, the retail market was significantly reduced, and less coal was used by manufacturing and coking customers because of improvements in technological efficiency.

Following a period of adjustment within the coal industry, the lost markets were replaced by the rapid growth of coal use by electric utilities. In less than 40 years, utility use of coal increased 10-fold from about 50 million tons in 1940 to nearly 500 million tons in 1977. As a result, the electric utility industry now consumes more than two-thirds of the present total national coal production. If projections of future developments are realized, electric utility coal consumption could reach about three-quarters of total production by the end of the twentieth century.

Most of the coal used by electric utilities will be burned to generate power. An emerging use for coal is as a feedstock for producing gaseous and liquid fuels, although formidable technical and economic obstacles must be overcome before such processes can be relied upon for routine service.

The economics of coal utilization are likely to be influenced strongly by the demands of the electric utilities, the largest coal consumer. Furthermore, historical controls of coal characteristics upon patterns of utilization seem likely to continue, and traditional factors which influence coal development are likely to persist in the future.

TWELVE

COAL-FIRED POWER PLANTS

The main use of coal is in combustion for generating electricity. This is accomplished by a series of three conversion stages. First, the chemical energy of coal is converted to heat energy in a boiler and the heat is transferred to a working fluid, usually water and/or steam. Second, the heat energy of the working fluid is converted to mechanical energy, typically by a turbine. Third, the mechanical energy is converted to electrical energy by a generator. Detailed technical descriptions of power-generating facilities are available in numerous reference works and will not be repeated here.[1] Instead, a brief review of the principal features of coal-fired power plants will be presented as an introduction to discussion of present and forecast patterns of coal use by electric utilities.

There is a wide variation in the properties of coal (Chapter 2). Thus detailed information of the particular coals to be used in an individual unit is essential to guide the unit's design and ensure optimum performance. Actually, the final selection of a burning method and boiler type is based on a combination of technical factors, engineering judgment, economics, and experience.

The combustion of hydrogen is achieved quite readily when coal is burned in boiler furnaces, but combustion of carbon to carbon dioxide requires a continuous supply of oxygen in contact with coal particles. Furthermore, there must be intimate mixing of coal particles and air, and sufficient turbulence to remove combustion products from the fuel surface while maintaining fresh air for continued combustion. Less time is required for combustion with greater turbulence.

Steady improvements in methods of firing boiler furnaces have been made during the last half century. Two principal methods are stokers and pulverized-coal.

---

[1] See, for example, "Steam: Its Generation and Use," Babcock & Wilcox Company, New York, 1972; "The Efficient Use of Fuel," United Kingdom Ministry of Technology, London, 1958; Power from Coal, *Power Magazine,* pp. S−25 to S−48, March 1974.

STOKERS

Stokers were among the early developments in steam boilers. Basically, stokers are designed to feed coal onto a grate within the furnace, where combustion takes place. The grate also accounts for removal of ash. There are four main types of stokers: spreaders, underfeed, water-cooled vibrating-grate, and chain-grate—traveling-grate.

Spreader stokers feed coal from a hopper onto a rotary place which has ribs for distributing the coal into the furnace and over the area of the fuel bed. Fine coal particles are burned while suspended above the fuel bed, whereas heavier coal particles are combusted on the bed, which lies on a grate.

Underfeed stokers are supplied with coal from beneath the fuel bed by either rotary screws or pushers. Coal rises in the bed, and volatile gases are distilled and mixed with air. This mixture is combusted as the coal moves upward in the furnace, and ignites the coal itself. Combustion continues as coal is displaced outward by incoming supplies of new coal. Ash is discharged over side grates and removed. Underfeed stokers are used only in small applications.

Water-cooled vibrating-grate and *chain-grate—traveling-grate stokers* supply coal directly from a hopper to grates that oscillate to move. This permits more effective ash disposal from the furnace. These stokers are being displaced by spreader stokers.

Generally, stokers are no longer used in new power generation applications, although they still see limited service in some older installations. As shown in Figure 1 stokers require about 1.5 pounds of coal per kilowatthour and are less efficient than units handling pulverized coal.

PULVERIZED-COAL SYSTEMS

Pulverized-coal systems represented an advance over stokers, because mechanical systems for coal feeding were greatly streamlined. A continuous process is employed. Coal is pulverized to the consistency of fine talcum powder, delivered to the furnace as an intimate mixture with combustion air, and burned in a continuous operation. Pulverized-coal furnaces must be large enough for oxygen to reach coal particles by diffusion, and temperatures must be high enough to accomplish complete combustion. Ash particles remaining after combustion are much smaller than the initial pulverized-coal particles and are carried along with flue gases and later trapped electrostatically by filters.

Most pulverized-coal systems are direct-firing, in which coal is fed directly to pulverizers and furnaces in one continuous operation. Formerly, coal was pulverized and placed in a bin from which it was then fed to the furnace. That system is used infrequently today in older units that are not in regular service.

Powerful fans are commonly used to force air through the pulverizer, where the air picks up pulverized coal and delivers it to the furnace. The air-to-coal ratio is monitored to maintain optimum combustion conditions. It is possible to adjust either the coal fed or the primary airflow in proportion to operating-load requirements.

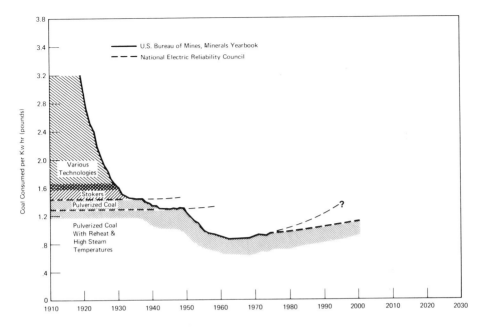

Figure 1 Trends in coal utilization for power generation. (From U.S. Bureau of Mines, *Miner. Yearb.*, various years.)

Pulverized-coal firing is a highly efficient system and, as Figure 1 shows, represents a distinct improvement over prior systems, using less than 1 pound of coal per kilowatthour. It is reasonable to expect that pulverized-coal firing will continue to be used extensively in the electric utility industry.

Trends in coal utilization for power generation are shown in Figure 1. The amount of coal required to generate a kilowatthour of electricity was cut in half during the 1920s and further reduced during the 1930s with the introduction of stoker-fired systems. The coal requirements per kilowatthour remained essentially constant until the late 1930s, when pulverized-coal systems enabled somewhat lower amounts of coal to be used; these systems prevailed throughout the 1940s. Beginning in 1950, pulverized-coal systems with reheat and high steam temperatures made their appearance and resulted in a one-third reduction of coal requirements per kilowatthour. After the mid-1960s, a return to somewhat lower steam temperatures and adjustments to power plants for pollution control resulted in a slight increase in the amount of coal required per kilowatthour. Projections by the National Electric Reliability Council indicate that there will be a continued increase in coal requirements per unit of power generation; it is estimated that, by 1985, we will have returned to the level of coal use which prevailed in 1955 (about 1 pound per kilowatthour). If present trends continue throughout the rest of this century, there will be continued increases in the quantity of coal necessary to produce a unit of electricity. It is even possible that higher rates of coal utilization may occur. With projected increases in electricity demand, increased rates of coal usage to generate electricity would add to the quantity of coal production required to supply essential fuels. Increased coal production over presently estimated levels (especially that stemming from lower efficiency in utilization) would accelerate the rate of depletion of known coal deposits. It seems clear that at a minimum it is important to perform the necessary work to contain any increases in coal required for power generation and, ideally, return to lower rates of coal usage.

A review of existing coal-fired generating capacity, together with projected additions and requirements, is given next.

EXISTING GENERATING CAPACITY, ADDITIONS, AND RETIREMENTS, 1975 TO 2000

Data on existing power-generating capacity as well as planned additions and retirements are compiled each year by the nine Electric Reliability Council regions and reported to the Federal Power Commission under FPC Order 383.[1] The regions are located and identified in Figure 2.

These data are the collected best estimates and projections of the nation's electric utility companies, and as such are perhaps the most authoritative accounting of present and future power systems. It must be recognized, however, that the data reflect the objectives and approaches of individual utility companies as to the mix of generating capacity required (or desired) by them in meeting electric energy requirements in their service area. No attempt has been made in this section to manipulate the data or to impose value judgments upon it. Rather, the data are presented for the sole purpose of providing a base for achieving an overview of power-generating capacity during the remainder of the century.

Existing Capacity

A summary of these data for the interval 1975−1984 (inclusive) is presented for each power plant type by region in Table 1. The table shows for example, that existing generating capacity in the East Central Area Reliability Coordinating Agreement (ECAR) is 74,316 megawatts. Planned additions during the next 10 years are for 40,745 megawatts, and retirements of 1,657 megawatts, bringing the total in the ECAR region at the end of 1984 to 116,708 megawatts. Coal-fired steam turbines constitute nearly four-fifths of the total generating capacity at present, and it is planned to increase this capacity by one-third in the next 10 years. However, the proportion of total ECAR generating capacity represented by coal will be reduced to about 70 percent in 1984 because of the planned addition of 17,815 megawatts of nuclear-powered capacity during this time. However, recent deferrals and cancellations of nuclear plants could reduce this planned capacity (discussed in greater detail in a later section). In response to shortfalls in meeting nuclear capacity targets, any or all of the following approaches could be taken: (1) lower electricity demand through conservation, etc., (2) expand generating ca-

---

[1] Submitted on April 1 of each year.

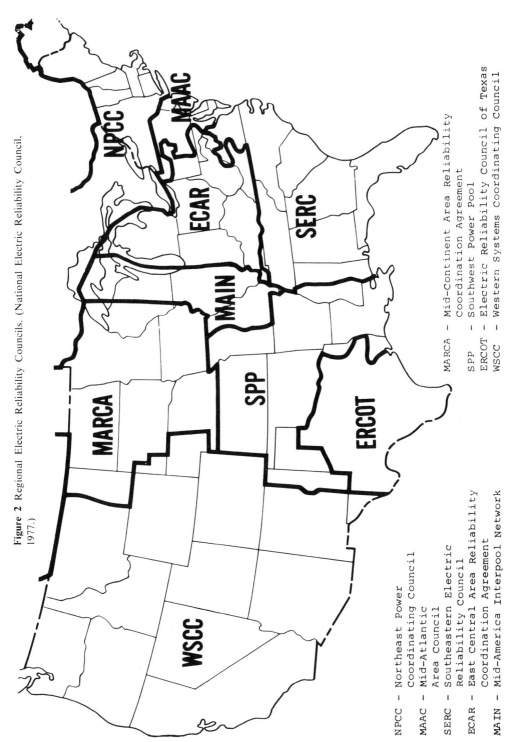

Figure 2 Regional Electric Reliability Councils. (National Electric Reliability Council. 1977.)

NPCC – Northeast Power
        Coordinating Council
MAAC – Mid-Atlantic
        Area Council
SERC – Southeastern Electric
        Reliability Council
ECAR – East Central Area Reliability
        Coordination Agreement
MAIN – Mid-America Interpool Network

MARCA – Mid-Continent Area Reliability
         Coordination Agreement
SPP   – Southwest Power Pool
ERCOT – Electric Reliability Council of Texas
WSCC – Western Systems Coordinating Council

Table 1 Existing generating capacity, additions, retirements to 1984 (Megawatts)

Power plant	Region										
	ECAR	ERCOT	MAAC	MAIN	MARCA	NPCC	SERC	SWPP	WSCC	Total
Steam turbine:										
Coal										
Existing	61,821	1,785	14,229	23,445	8,245	5,189	49,650	3,980	13,070	181,414
Additional	20,607	10,728	4,800	9,619	10,209	3,750	11,089	21,128	21,267	113,197
Retired	516		5,027	20		18		50	36	5,667
Total	81,912	12,513	14,002	33,044	18,454	8,957	60,739	25,058	34,301	288,944
Oil										
Existing	3,406	3,568	12,333	1,870	609	23,716	16,716	3,934	23,763	89,915
Additional	2,183	761	4,030	2,550	127	3,429	11,664			24,617
Retired	523		485			428	120	9	286	1,978
Total	5,066	4,329	15,878	4,420	736	27,573	28,260	3,923	23,477	112,554
Gas										
Existing	330	25,398		680	543		239	27,098	2,427	56,715
Additional		1,452					440	973		2,865
Retired	220	169			164		37	299	12	881
Total	130	26,681		680	707		642	27,772	2,415	58,699
Combustion turbine:										
Existing	4,111	639	8,058	2,717	2,551	5,686	10,108	1,887	4,706	40,462
Additional		1,215	1,490	1,517	866	814	5,311	1,453	818	13,484
Retired	328									328
Total	3,783	1,853	10,548	4,234	3,417	6,500	15,419	3,340	5,524	53,618
Combined cycle:										
Existing	270	774	35			110	432	842	607	3,070
Additional			126			330	968	645	8,310	10,379
Retired										
Total	270	774	161			440	1,400	1,487	8,907	13,439

										Total
Nuclear:										
Existing	1,547		4,338	6,195	3,760	6,997	10,972	830	2,873	37,512
Additional	17,815	2,350	17,981	15,060	4,651	17,433	53,057	11,605	16,516	156,468
Retired	90								840	930
Total	19,272	2,350	22,319	21,255	8,411	24,430	64,029	12,435	18,549	193,050
Hydro:										
Existing	564	283	941	468	2,955	5,316	9,533	2,356	35,336	57,752
Additional	40						779	27	10,981	11,827
Retired									14	14
Total	604	283	944	468	2,955	5,316	10,312	2,383	46,303	69,565
Pump storage:										
Existing	2,267		1,286	924		2,632	660	258	1,106	9,133
Additional	100		3,060		1,000	3,000	2,580	191	2,925	12,856
Retired										
Total	2,367		4,346	924	1,000	5,632	3,240	449	4,031	21,989
Other:										
Existing				85					502	587
Additional	20		38	6	38	130	13,310		1,396	14,900
Retired									20	58
Total	20		38	91	38	130	13,310		1,918	15,429
Total:										
Existing	74,316	32,446	41,220	36,384	18,663	49,646	98,310	41,185	84,390	476,560
Additional	40,745	16,526	31,525	28,752	16,726	28,886	99,198	36,022	62,213	360,593
Retired	1,657	169	5,512	20	329	446	157	358	1,218	9,866
Total	113,404	48,803	67,233	65,116	35,060	78,066	197,351	76,849	145,385	827,287

Source: National Electric Reliability Council, FPC Order 383-3.

pacity and other types, (3) defer retirement of existing generating units, (4) reduce reserve capacity, and (5) increase power imports from other regions. For the ECAR region, already dependent as it is on coal, it would appear that expanded coal use would be a logical response to curtailed nuclear development. Table 1 presents comparable data for the other regions, permitting similar evaluations of potential situations to be undertaken.

Table 2 presents data on the percentage distribution of generating capacity in 1984, taken from the detailed statistics given in Table 1. This table reveals the following:

1. Coal-fired steam turbines are projected to account for more than one-fifth of generating capacity in every region but NPCC. Coal is the majority power system in three regions (ECAR, MAIN, and MARCA) and is generally between one-fifth and one-third of the total in the other regions.
2. Oil-fired steam turbines are projected to account for more than one-fifth of total generating capacity only in two regions (MAAC and NPCC). Other regions have less than this amount.
3. Gas-fired steam turbines are negligible or small proportions of the capacity in every region but two (ERCOT and SWPP), where they represent more than half and one-third, respectively, of the total.
4. Combustion turbines constitute less than 10 percent of the total capacity in every region but MAAC (where they account for only 15 percent).
5. Combined-cycle systems are negligible in their contribution to total capacity, reaching a maximum of 6 percent of the total in WSCC.
6. Nuclear systems are projected to be about one-quarter of total capacity in five regions (MAAC, MAIN, NPCC, SERC, and MARCA). The other regions are estimated to be less than one-fifth of total capacity by 1984.
7. Hydroelectric systems are less than 10 percent of the total capacity in every region but WSCC, where about one-third of the total is from this type.
8. Pump-storage systems are less than 10 percent in each region, reaching a maximum of 7 percent in NPCC.
9. Other power systems are seen to be negligible contributors to overall capacity, with a maximum of 7 percent of the total foreseen for SERC.

These regional data are aggregated into overall national figures in Table 3, which presents a comparison of projected 1984 capacities with the actual situation of 1975. The table shows that coal units are expected to continue to account for more than one-third of the total capacity, although their share is seen to decline slightly. Similar declines are foreseen for oil and gas systems and for combustion turbines and hydro. The most dramatic changes in the mix of generating technologies during the next 10 years is the projected threefold increase in nuclear power. Further discussion of this point is contained in a later section.

Additions and Retirements

Table 1 presented detailed data on the capacity in megawatts to be added or retired during the interval 1974–1984. These data are expressed for the nation as a whole

Table 2 Distribution of generating capacity in 1984 (percent)

Power plant	ECAR	ERCOT	MAAC	MAIN	MARCA	NPCC	SERC	SWPP	WSCC	Total
					Region					
Steam turbine:										
Coal	72	26	21	51	52	11	31	33	23	35
Oil	4	9	24	7	2	35	14	5	16	14
Gas	neg.	55		1	2	neg.	neg.	36	2	7
Combustion turbine	3	4	15	6	9	8	8	4	4	6
Combined cycle	neg.	1	neg.			neg.	1	2	6	2
Nuclear	17	5	33	33	24	31	32	16	13	23
Hydro	1	neg.	1	1	8	7	5	3	32	8
Pump storage	2		6	1	3	7	2	neg.	3	3
Other	neg.	neg.	neg.	neg.	neg.	neg.	7	7	1	2
Total	99	100	100	100	100	99	100	99	100	100

Source: Table 1.

Table 3 Comparison of generating capacity types

Percentage of total United States

Power plant type	1975	1984
Steam turbine:		
Coal	38	35
Oil	19	14
Gas	12	7
Combustion turbine	8	6
Combined cycle	1	2
Nuclear	8	23
Hydro	12	8
Pump storage	2	3
Other	neg.	2
Total	100	100

Source: Table 1.

as a percentage of existing capacity by fuel in Table 4. This table shows that:

1. Existing coal power systems which constitute important generating capacities will be augmented at a high rate, nearly two-thirds of existing capacity.
2. Existing oil, gas, combustion turbine, and hydro systems will be augmented at a relatively slow rate, less than one-third of existing capacity.
3. The largest additions to generating capacity are for nuclear, combined-cycle, and "other" systems.
4. Retirements represent a very small portion of existing capacity, averaging about 2 percent for all fuel types. The largest retirement rate (9.9 percent) is for "other" systems, with the smallest for hydro and pump-storage systems. *The significance of these very small retirement rates is that there will be continued use of existing power-generating systems at least until the middle of the next decade and probably beyond.*

Table 4 U.S. power plant additions/retirements (1975–1984) as percentage existing capacity (by fuel)

Fuel	Additions	Retirements
Coal	62.4	3.1
Oil	27.4	2.2
Gas	5.1	1.6
Combustion turbine	33.3	0.8
Combined cycle	338.1	0.3
Nuclear	417.1	2.5
Hydro	20.4	neg.
Pump storage	140.8	neg.
Other	394.0	9.9
Overall	75.7	2.1

Table 5 presents power plant additions and retirements to 1984 for all types of systems by region. The table shows that:

1. Additions will double present generating capacity in ECAR and SERC.
2. Additions will increase present capacity by more than three-quarters in MAAC, MAIN, MARCA, SWPP, and WSCC.
3. Additions will increase present capacity by more than half in ERCOT and NPCC.
4. Retirements in MAAC will be more than one-tenth of present capacity.
5. Retirements are of the order of 2 percent of present capacity in ECAR, MARCA, and WSCC.
6. Retirements in other regions are less than 1 percent of present capacity and can probably be considered negligible.

The data in Tables 4 and 5 indicate that existing power-generating systems will continue to form the backbone of the electric utility industry for the immediate future. Retirements of present systems are small, and even sizable additions to existing capacity will not replace present plants in most regions. Therefore it seems likely that the several regions will have an array of several power plants of different types and ages throughout the next 10 years. This situation will require that new additions be compatible with the existing systems, a potential constraint upon the amount of innovation or improvement in facilities that could be achieved.

The magnitude of the projected additions to generating capacity may be examined by dividing the total capacity to be added from 1974 to 1984 by the capacity of a typical sized unit (Table 6). The table shows that nearly 500 individual units are estimated to be installed during this next decade. Stated another way, roughly four new power-generating facilities would have to go into service every month for this entire period to accomplish the apparent utility industry plans. Without any doubt, this would be an undertaking of unprecedented magnitude. If

Table 5 Power plant additions/retirements (1975–1984) as percentage existing capacity (by region)

Region	Additions	Retirements
ECAR	108.7	2.2
ERCOT	50.9	0.5
MAAC	76.5	13.4
MAIN	79.0	neg.
MARCA	89.6	1.8
NPCC	58.2	0.8
SERC	100.9	0.2
SWPP	87.5	0.9
WSCC	73.7	1.4
Overall	75.7	2.1

Table 6 Estimated number of new power plants to be added from 1974 to 1984

Fuel	Total capacity to be added, MW	Typical size unit, MW	Number of units
Coal	113,197	800	142
Oil	24,617	600	41
Gas	2,865	400	7
Oil/gas	23,863	500	48
Nuclear	156,468	1,000	157
Hydro	11,827	4,000	3
Pump storage	12,856	600	21
Other	14,900	200	75
Total	360,593		494

Source: Fed. Power Comm. (now Fed. Energy Reg. Comm.).

costs were of the order of about $1 billion per 1000 megawatts,[1] the total cost for these additions would be in the neighborhood of $360 billion.

Projected Capacity

The several regions also report projected total generating capacity for the period 1985−1994 (Table 7). The table shows that overall capacity is expected to be nearly doubled in this period. However, this projection does not subdivide total capacity by power-plant-system type.

It is possible to estimate the generating mix in the mid-1990s to the end of the century by reference to the above data for the near term. It was shown that the retirement rate for present power plants during the next decade is small. With this as a base, it is possible to estimate the retirement rate for the remainder of the century. The following assumptions were employed:

Coal. Retirement rate from 1984 to 2000 is estimated at double the 1974−1984 rate owing to the age of existing units, length of service, reliability of operation, and cost.

Oil. Retirement rate from 1984 to 2000 is estimated at four times the previous rate owing to the age of units and oil shortages.

Gas. Retirement rate from 1984 to 2000 is estimated at nearly 10 times the previous rate owing to fuel shortages and high cost.

Combined oil/gas. Retirement rate is estimated at double the previous rate owing to age of units.

Nuclear. Retirement is estimated at equivalent to previous rate owing to delays, operating problems.

Hydro. Retirement rate is assumed to be negligible.

Pump storage. Retirement rate is assumed to be negligible.

Other. Retirement rate is estimated as same as present.

[1] From recent experience, reported by FEA.

Table 7 Projected capacity (thousand megawatts)

Region	1985	1986	1987	1988	1989	1990	1991	1992	1993	1994
ECAR	123.7	132.4	141.9	151.6	160.7	168.5	180.0	191.1	203.8	216.6
ERCOT	63.3	68.4	72.8	77.7	82.6	89.1	94.8	99.9	105.3	111.5
MAIN	71.6	76.5	81.4	85.6	91.1	96.0	103.0	108.1	113.3	121.2
MAAC	66.5	68.1	74.4	75.8	78.3	81.9	86.7	90.9	94.3	99.0
MARCA	27.6	29.2	30.8	32.6	34.4	36.3	38.0	40.6	42.9	45.3
NPCC	44.5	46.4	49.5	50.5	52.8	55.1	55.8	57.0	59.2	60.9
SERC	206.3	220.3	236.4	254.0	273.1	292.2	310.3	331.8	354.0	376.1
SWPP	87.4	94.1	101.5	110.0	118.8	128.6	138.1	150.4	159.6	171.9
WSCC	154.0	162.0	169.0	176.0	183.0	190.0	202.0	211.0	222.0	233.0
Total	844.9	897.4	957.7	1013.8	1074.8	1146.7	1208.7	1280.8	1354.4	1435.9

Source: Fed. Power Comm. (now Fed. Energy Reg. Comm.).

Table 8 Estimated power plant retirement, 1984−2000, as percentage of 1984 capacity (by fuel)

Fuel	Retirement rate 1974−1984, % of 1974	Estimated retirement rate 1984−2000, % of 1984
Coal	3.1	6.0
Oil	2.2	8.0
Gas	1.6	10.0
Oil/gas	0.8	1.6
Nuclear	2.5	2.5
Hydro	neg.	neg.
Pump storage	neg.	neg.
Other	9.9	10.0

Source: Fed. Power Comm. (now Fed. Energy Reg. Comm.).

The resulting estimated retirement rates for the several power systems from 1984 to 2000 are shown in Table 8 (as percentage of 1984 capacity for each system). When these retirement rates are applied to the 1984 generating capacity, the remaining capacity in continued service by 2000 is obtained (Table 9). This table shows that more than 779,000 megawatts of generating capacity in theyear 2000 will be from power systems installed prior to 1984. Recalling that Table 7 indicated projected generating capacity by 1994 of about 1,435,000 megawatts, it is apparent that roughly half the end-of-century capacity will be installed in the next 10 years.

The question remains as to what the detailed types of additions to capacity will be in the period 1984−2000. Employing an approach similar to that for projecting retirements, it is possible to estimate the addition rate for different power systems. The following assumptions were made:

Coal. Addition rate at three times the pre-1984 rate owing to phase out of oil and gas and national policy for domestic resource development

Table 9 Estimated generating capacity in 2000 after retirements (by fuel)

Fuel	1984 capacity, MW	Retirement rate 1984−2000		Remaining 2000 capacity, MW
Coal	323,725	6.0	−19,424	304,301
Oil	107,082	8.0	−8,567	98,515
Gas	52,968	10.0	−5,297	47,671
Oil/gas	62,012	1.6	−992	61,020
Nuclear	177,743	2.5	−4,444	173,299
Hydro	66,988	neg.	0	66,988
Pump storage	20.441	neg.	0	20,441
Other	7,620	10.0	−762	6,858
				779,093

Source: Fed. Power Comm. (now Fed. Energy Reg. Comm.).

Table 10 Estimated power plant additions, 1984–2000, as percentage of 1984 capacity (by fuel)

Fuel	Addition rate 1974–1984, % of 1974	Estimated addition rate 1984–2000, % of 1984
Coal	62.4	180
Oil	27.4	10
Gas	5.1	2
Oil/gas	33.3	3
Nuclear	417.1	200
Hydro	20.4	20
Pump storage	140.8	70
Other	394.0	200

Source: Fed. Power Comm. (now Fed. Energy Reg. Comm.).

Oil. Addition rate at one-third of pre-1984 rate owing to resource shortages, high prices, dedication of oil to other uses

Gas. Addition rate at half the pre-1984 rate

Combined oil/gas. Addition rate at one-tenth the pre-1984 rate because of resource shortages, high prices

Nuclear. Addition rate at half the pre-1984 rate owing to fuel availability, high capital charges, public resistance

Hydro. Addition rate the same as pre-1984 rate

Pump storage. Addition rate at half the pre-1984 rate

Other. Addition rate at half the pre-1984 rate

The resulting estimated addition rates for the several power systems from 1984 to 2000 are shown in Table 10 (as a percentage of 1984 capacity for each system). When these addition rates are applied to the 1984 generating capacity, the resulting addition for each is obtained (Table 11). Nearly 1 billion megawatts of new additions is projected between 1984 and 2000. The bulk of these additions are esti-

Table 11 Estimated capacity, 1984–2000 (by fuel)

Fuel	1984 capacity, MW	Addition rate 1984–2000, % of 1984	New 2000 capacity, MW
Coal	323,725	180	582,705
Oil	107,082	10	10,708
Gas	52,968	2	1,059
Oil/gas	62,012	3	1,860
Nuclear	177,743	200	355,486
Hydro	66,988	20	13,397
Pump storage	20,441	70	14,309
Other	7,620	200	15,240
			994,764

Source: Fed. Power Comm. (now Fed. Energy Reg. Comm.).

Table 12   Estimated generating capacity in 2000 by fuel (megawatts)

Fuel	Pre-1984 capacity after retirements	Post-1984 additions	Total
Coal	304,301	582,705	887,006
Oil	98,575	10,708	109,223
Gas	47,671	1,059	48,730
Oil/gas	61,020	1,860	62,880
Nuclear	173,299	355,486	528,785
Hydro	66,988	13,397	80,385
Pump storage	20,441	14,309	34,750
Other	6,858	15,240	22,098
Total	779,093	994,764	1,773,857

Source: Fed. Power Comm. (now Fed. Energy Reg. Comm.).

mated to be coal (59 percent) and nuclear (36 percent) power systems, with small contributions from other systems.

The total estimated generating capacity in 2000 is the sum of (1) that installed prior to 1984 after retirements and (2) new additions subsequent to 1984; these data are presented in Table 12. The table shows that, under the stated assumptions employed in this analysis, half the generating capacity in 2000 will be fired by coal. Nuclear systems are forecast to contribute less than one-third of the total. It is important to note that a continued role for oil and gas systems is foreseen, all together representing more than one-tenth of the total capacity. Most oil and gas systems will be old by that time, and it is likely that their efficiency would be low and operating costs high. This could place further burdens on other systems, or lead to requirements for additions to capacities over and above those estimated.

The magnitude of the projected additions to generating capacity from 1984 to 2000 may be estimated by considering typical size units in relation to totals (Table 13). The table shows that more than 1200 units are projected to be installed during this 15-year interval. In other words, roughly seven new power-generating facilities

Table 13   Estimated number of new power plants to be added from 1984 to 2000

Fuel	Total capacity to be added, MW	Typical size unit, MW	Number of units
Coal	582,705	800	728
Oil	10,708	600	18
Gas	1,059	400	3
Oil/gas	1,860	500	4
Nuclear	355,486	1000	356
Hydro	13,397	4000	3
Pump storage	14,309	600	24
Other	15,240	200	76
Total	994,764		1212

Source: Fed. Power Comm. (now Fed. Energy Reg. Comm.).

would have to go into service every month for a decade and a half if the projection were to be realized. This is nearly double the rate of plant addition determined above for 1974 to 1984. The dimensions of these projected endeavors to expand power-generating capacity can truly be described as stupendous or colossal. So is their cost; at a base of $1 billion per 1000 megawatts, the price tag for those facilities added between 1984 and 2000 would be at least $1 trillion.

The magnitude of generating capacity remaining in service over long times, as well as the enormity of estimated additions, suggests that it will be essential to give close attention to power-plant reserve capacities, availability, and productivity so as to make optimum use of installed facilities. These subjects are examined in the next section.

RESERVE CAPACITY, OPERATING AVAILABILITY, AND PRODUCTIVITY

Reserve Capacity

The Regional Electric Reliability Council reports also contain data on reserve generating capacity expressed as a percentage of noncoincident peak load. These data are compiled for each region by year from 1975 to 1994 (Table 14). The table shows that:

1. Reserve capacities in 1975 range from a high of 40.7 percent (NPCC), doubtless an effect of the earlier Northeast power blackout, to a low of 21.3 percent (SERC), with most regions in the relatively narrow range of 20 to 28 percent.
2. The reserve capacities projected for 1974 range from a high of 32.5 percent (NPCC) to a low of 12 percent (SWPP), with most regions in the relatively narrow range of 13 to 21 percent.
3. The average national reserve capacity is projected to decline nearly continuously during this 20-year period, from 26.3 percent in 1975 to 17.6 percent in 1994.

The projected average national reserve capacities are plotted (together with historical data) in Figure 3. The figure shows that reserve capacity decreased from its high point of nearly 90 percent during the Depression of the 1930s to its low point of about 10 percent in the late 1940s following World War II. Reserve capacity increased through the 1950s, then declined again during the 1960s, and began to rise again during the early 1970s. If this trend continues (as indicated), there could be a return to substantial excess reserve capacity prior to the end of the century. However, the projected reserve capacities reported in Table 12 show a relatively steady decline throughout the remainder of the century.

Also shown on the figure is an estimate of reserve capacity in the year 2000 at between 8 and 12 percent.[1] If this lower reserve capacity were to be realized, then

[1] E. N. Bomke, "A Forecast of Power Developments, 1975–2000," ASME paper, June 17, 1975.

Table 14 Reserve capacity (percent)

Region	1975	1976	1977	1978	1979	1980	1981	1982	1983	1984	1985	1986	1987	1988	1989	1990	1991	1992	1993	1994
ECAR	25.0	26.3	22.9	20.0	19.4	19.4	18.8	16.8	14.0	14.8	15.0	15.8	16.7	17.4	17.4	16.5	17.2	17.3	17.8	18.0
ERCOT	25.1	21.8	20.4	16.9	13.6	16.5	14.0	16.5	15.7	14.7	15.2	15.8	15.6	13.3	15.7	15.5	15.3	14.4	13.6	13.4
MAIN	22.1	21.1	16.9	15.2	17.2	14.3	15.0	16.2	15.4	18.0	13.0	13.8	14.1	13.3	13.6	13.0	14.0	13.1	12.2	13.1
MAAC	28.3	22.9	24.0	20.7	18.7	16.7	18.7	24.1	20.3	20.9	19.0	17.0	20.4	18.1	17.0	17.1	18.0	18.2	18.0	17.9
MARCA	27.0	28.0	28.0	21.0	27.0	30.0	27.0	27.0	23.0	24.0	21.0	16.0	15.0	15.0	15.0	15.0	15.0	15.0	15.0	15.0
NPCC	40.7	39.6	40.1	33.3	31.9	27.8	28.5	30.7	31.2	30.5	32.6	33.2	34.4	33.6	33.8	33.7	33.0	31.8	32.0	32.5
SERC	21.3	21.4	19.7	19.2	17.9	15.2	17.2	17.6	16.1	16.2	14.7	14.4	14.6	15.1	15.5	15.8	15.5	15.5	15.5	15.4
SWPP	22.9	20.4	15.2	17.5	16.6	18.9	16.3	19.9	19.4	17.9	13.0	13.0	13.0	13.0	13.0	14.0	13.0	14.0	12.0	12.0
WSCC	23.9	21.9	25.0	26.4	24.6	25.4	26.0	24.4	25.5	26.2	25.0	25.0	25.0	23.0	22.0	21.0	21.0	21.0	21.0	21.0
	26.3	24.8	23.6	21.1	20.8	20.5	20.2	21.5	20.1	20.4	18.7	18.1	18.8	18.2	18.1	18.0	18.0	17.8	17.5	17.6

Source: Fed. Power Comm. (now Fed. Energy Reg. Comm.).

Table 15 Estimated generating capacity in 2000 (megawatts)

Pre-1984 capacity after retirements	Post-1984 additions at reduced reserve capacity	Total
779,093	915,183	1,694,276

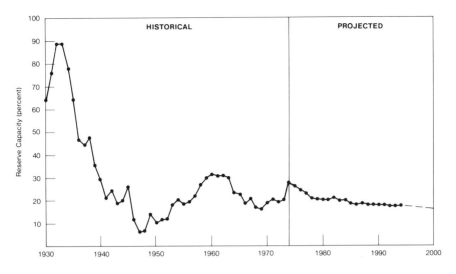

Figure 3 Trends in reserve capacity. (From Edison Electric Institute. *"Statistical Yearbook,"* 1976.)

the pattern would probably have to begin to change in the early 1980s (as sketched). This would tend to lower the estimated requirements for generating-capacity additions that were described in the previous section. For example, the estimated post-1984 additions assume a reserve capacity double that forecast by Bomke; if the lower reserve capacity were employed, it may be possible to reduce the additions to generating capacity shown in Table 14 by as much as 6 to 8 percent, as indicated in Table 15. Clearly, the lower reserve capacities would significantly reduce the magnitude of required addition, resulting in substantial savings of capital. If lower reserve capacities are to be realized without jeopardizing overall electric service, the availability and performance of existing power plants become critical. These subjects are considered next.

Availability

Coal-fired power plants were forecast in the previous section to constitute about half the generating capacity by the end of the century. This analysis therefore concentrates on the availability of these units. The Edison Electric Institute collects statistics on power plant operations and availability and publishes periodic reports.[1] Data on coal-fired power plants from a recent report were plotted, resulting in the graphs of Figures 4 and 5.

Figure 4 shows the relationship of unit-equipment operating availability to unit size during the period from 1964 to 1973. The data show that each size category experienced declining availabilities over a range during the 10 years. The median

[1]Edison Electric Institute, "Report on Equipment Availability for the Ten-Year Period, 1964–1973," Publication No. 74-57, December 1974.

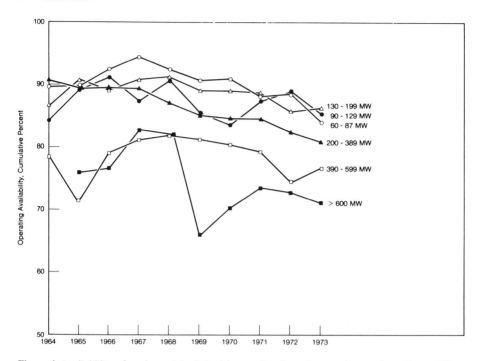

Figure 4 Availability of equipment (unit basis) as a function of year of operation. (From Edison Electric Institute, *"Statistical Yearbook,"* 1976.)

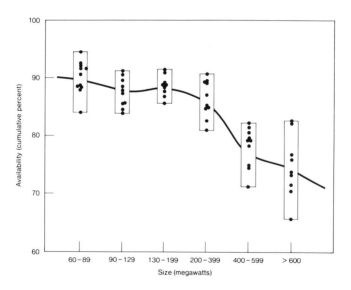

Figure 5 Relationship of unit-equipment operating availability to unit size. (From Edison Electric Institute, *"Statistical Yearbook,"* 1976.)

of each range was connected with a smooth curve. Examination of the curve indicates that power plant availability generally declines with increasing generating capacity. The rate of decline is relatively slow for power plants less than 389 megawatts; in addition, smaller units have median availabilities greater than 85 percent. In contrast, larger units have median availabilities of only about 74 to 76 percent.

Figure 5 shows operating availability in several unit-capacity intervals as a function of year of operation. The figure shows that the availability of all units declined from 1964 to 1973. Smaller units have the highest availability and generally experienced lesser declines. In contrast, largest units had the lowest availabilities and had wide fluctuations in availability.

At least one reason for declining availability of coal-fired power plants in recent years is the quality of coal being burned. A further reason is in the reductions in design margins of newer, larger power plants in the interests of achieving lower capital costs.

To improve the availability of coal-fired power plants in the future, it seems clear that greater attention to fuel quality is required, as well as the reinstitution of adequate margins of operating design.

Productivity

An index of capital productivity is given by the ratio of output to capacity. Figure 6 shows a plot of historical data for electrical generation with respect to installed

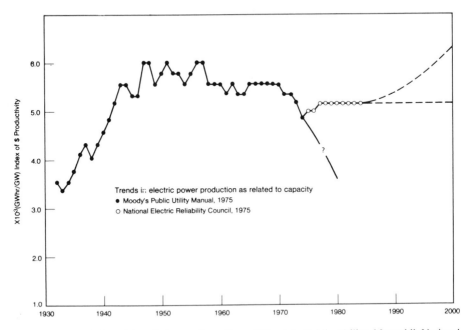

Figure 6 Productivity of installed capacity. (From "Moody's Public Utility Manual," National Electric Reliability Council, 1976.)

capacity, as well as projections drawn from Regional Electric Reliability Council data. There were steady increases in productivity during the 1930s and 1940s, followed by an uneven but real decline during the 1950s and 1960s. This decline accelerated during the early 1970s, probably in response to the imposition of increasingly stringent environmental control requirements. If this recent trend is continued, it would appear that the industry would be returning to situations comparable to that which existed during the 1930s. It is projected, however, that the recent decline will be arrested and that productivity will stabilize at a new lower level and perhaps renew its upward climb toward the end of the century.

CONCLUSIONS AND IMPLICATIONS

An overview of power-generating capacity from 1975 to the year 2000 was presented, based on data for existing capacity, planned addition plus retirements, and reserve capacity reported by electric utility companies to the Federal Power Commission. The following conclusions and implications are derived from this analysis:

1. Existing generating capacity in 1974 was 476,560 megawatts from all types of systems.
2. Planned additions to existing capacity less planned retirements were projected to result in 1984 generating capacity of 827,287 megawatts. Achievement of this planned capacity would require roughly four new power-generating facilities to go into service every month during the decade.
3. Estimated additions to generating capacity from 1984 to 2000 would be 994,764 megawatts, or roughly seven new generating units per month during this interval.
4. The total estimated generating capacity by fuels in 1984 and 2000 is shown in Table 16; by the end of the century, 1,773,857 megawatts of installed capacity is projected.
5. The estimated generating capacity would be reduced to 1,644,276 megawatts if lower amounts of reserve capacity were to be realized.
6. The contribution of existing technology for power generation throughout the remainder of the century suggests that greater opportunity for new technology appears to occur late in the century, but only if this technology can be perfected early enough to allow concrete plans to be formulated and implemented.
7. Uncertainty exists over the supply of coal and uranium to meet power-generating needs in the 1980s and beyond. Shortfalls in these critical fuels would probably lead to even greater reliance upon imported petroleum, on the order of about 5 million barrels per day by the mid-1980s.

The data indicate that substantial expansion of generating capacity in the electric utility industry will be possible in the next 10 to 15 years only by reliance upon the same technology that sustains the industry at present; only evolutionary

Table 16 Summary of estimated power-generating capacity in 1984 and 2000 (megawatts)

	1984	2000
Coal	288,944	887,006
Oil	112,554	109,223
Gas	58,699	48,730
Combustion turbine	53,618 ⎫ 67,057	62,880
Combined cycle	13,439 ⎭	
Nuclear	193,050	528,785
Hydro	69,565	80,385
Pump storage	21,989	34,750
Other	15,429	22,098
Total	827,287	1,773,857

Source: Fed. Power Comm. (now Fed. Energy Reg. Comm.).

change is likely in this short time. Moreover, continued use of this technology seems certain throughout the balance of the twentieth century and even beyond. The fossil fuels (coal, oil, and gas) will continue to be used in power generation. Oil and gas will be a declining part of the total, but they will continue to be employed because of (1) the need to protect investments in existing power plants, (2) environmental constraints in certain areas, and (3) the inability or unwillingness to bear costs of reconverting power systems to alternative fuels.

In view of the indicated importance of present-day technologies for power generation (and the empirical engineering/operational expertise necessary for their utilization), it would be prudent to devote increasing attention to a better understanding of these technologies. Only with sound knowledge of what the electric utility industry actually employs (or is likely to dependent upon) in providing customer service can realistic and effective R&D efforts be conceived and implemented to aid the industry.

Still, a considerable effort is directed toward perfection of advanced coal utilization technology, especially in gasification and liquefaction. This subject is reviewed in the following chapter.

COAL CONVERSION PROCESSES

Although direct burning of coal will continue to be the principal utilization method, increasing attention is being given to processes that "convert" coal into various solid, liquid, and gaseous products. The processes alter the chemical character of coal. Basically, because coal has a low hydrogen-to-carbon ratio, conversion processes require the addition of hydrogen or the removal of carbon to arrive at the desired products. The hydrogen-to-carbon ratio of products can be increased either by skimming off the volatile components of coal (as in pyrolysis) or by direct addition of hydrogen (as in hydrogenation).

Coal conversion processes have been known for nearly two centuries. Gas manufactured from coal was first produced during the late eighteenth century by heating coal in the absence of air. "City gas," a mixture of coke-oven gas, coal, and water gas, was a common source of fuel for residential and municipal uses in metropolitan centers for 150 years until replaced by natural gas and electricity. Liquids from coal were first produced in the early 1900s. The most extensive effort in production of coal-derived liquid fuels was that of Germany in World War II.

A substantial and growing body of literature exists on coal conversion processes.[1] Rather than duplicate such information, this chapter will summarize the principal features of coal conversion processes; the reader is referred to the cited references for detailed technical data. This chapter discusses conventional conversion processes requiring mining and treatment of coal in specialized facilities while Chapter 14 examines underground (*in situ*) processes.

---

[1]"Chemistry of Coal Utilization, Supplementary Volume," H. H. Lowry (ed.). See, for example, Wiley, New York, 1963; National Academy of Engineering, "Evaluation of Coal Gasification Technology," Washington, 1974; McRae, Dudas, and Rowland (eds.), "The Energy Source Book," Aspen Publications, Germantown, Md., 1977.

CONVENTIONAL PROCESSES

Conventional coal conversion processes are carried out in facilities akin to petroleum refineries or power plants. Coal is extracted from reserves through mining and then is typically prepared and transported to the conversion plant. Conversion plants may be of two different types, gasification or liquefaction.

Gasification

Chemical synthesis of gas from coal requires three essential ingredients. Coal provides carbon, steam provides hydrogen, and air provides oxygen. Heat for the process may be supplied directly by combustion of coal or externally. Direct heat is thermally more efficient and is less complicated operationally than indirect-heating methods.

Three combustible gases are produced by coal gasification processes—hydrogen, carbon monoxide, and methane. Methane is the primary component of natural gas and has a heating value of about 1000 Btu per cubic foot. The heating values of carbon monoxide and hydrogen are about one-third that for methane. Also, several noncombustible gases are produced, including carbon dioxide, hydrogen sulfide, and nitrogen.

Gasification products are determined mainly by the methods of introducing hydrogen, oxygen, and heat into the reactor vessel. For example, if air is used as the source of oxygen, nitrogen is produced as a by-product, and the heating value of the resulting gas is reduced. The use of oxygen is more costly than air but eliminates the nitrogen problem and increases the heating value of the produced gas. The types and properties of gases are controlled by the design of each gasification process. There are many alternatives to reactor types, coal-bed configurations, and operating temperatures and pressures.

Reactor types. Three general categories of reactor vessels are undergoing experimentation: gasifiers, hydrogasifiers, and devolitilizers. . Gasifiers employ reactions of coal and water at elevated temperature to produce gases. Hydrogasifiers produce methane by reacting hydrogen with coal under pressure. Devolitilizers decompose large coal molecules through reactions with hydrogen.

Bed configurations. Three basic types of bed configurations are employed in gasification systems: fixed-bed, fluidized-bed, and entrained. Fixed-bed systems use a grate to support coal, through which steam or hydrogen is passed. Conventional fixed-bed systems are incompatible with caking coals, unless modified to rotate or stir the bed to avoid agglomeration of the coal. The fluidized-bed system employs finely sized coal that is agitated by gas flowing through the coal to produce a lifting or fluidlike effect. The result is an expanded coal-surface area which promotes reaction efficiency. Entrained systems also use finely sized coal, which is transported in steam or oxygen to the reactor.

One of three classes of product gas can be produced in coal gasification systems,

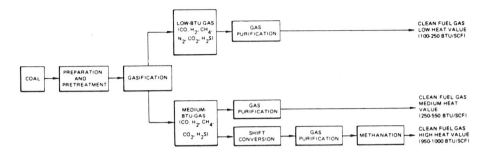

Figure 1 Fuel gas from coal. (From *Oil Gas J.*, Aug. 26, 1974.)

determined by the selection of options for process characteristics. These are (Figure 1):

1. Low-heating-value gas (100−250 Btu per standard cubic foot)
2. Intermediate-heating-value gas (250−550 Btu per standard cubic foot)
3. High-heating-value gas (950−1000 Btu per standard cubic foot)

As the figure shows, most gases resulting from coal gasification processes require purification and/or upgrading prior to utilization. Generally, the higher-heating-value gases are more costly than those of lower heating value because of process characteristics and subsequent gas treatments.

Liquefaction

The production of liquids from coal is similar in concept to gasification. Either hydrogen must be added or carbon removed from the compounds in coal, altering the hydrogen-to-carbon ratio. However, liquefaction methods differ sharply from gasification in their use of recycled gas and liquid products for a number of purposes. Liquefaction includes four major approaches to coal conversion: hydrogenation, pyrolysis, catalytic conversion, and solvent refining (Figure 2).

Hydrogenation. In this reaction, hydrogen is introduced (either as a gas or as a hydrogen-rich solvent) to react with coal. Gaseous hydrogen results in products including gases, liquids, and solids. Hydrogen-containing solvents carry with them ash and inorganic sulfur contained in coal, following the reaction.

Pyrolysis. Heat is applied in the absence of an oxidizing agent to break chemical bonds between clusters of coal molecules, resulting in decomposition of coal to a liquid hydrocarbon, gases, and char. The char is primarily carbon withdrawn from the coal, bringing the remaining hydrogen-to-carbon ratio into the liquefaction range.

Catalytic conversion. Catalytic conversion is a two-stage approach to coal liquefaction. The coal is partially oxidized to produce a synthesis gas of carbon monoxide and hydrogen. This gas is then passed over an appropriate catalyst at proper temperature and pressure to form a liquid product. The products are

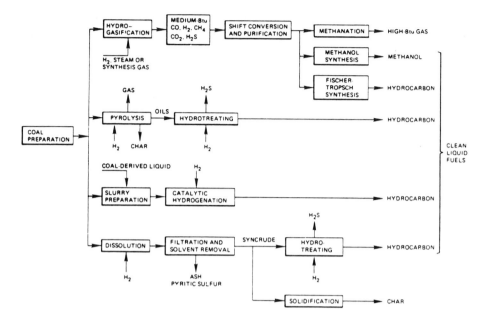

Figure 2 Liquid fuels from coal. (From Energy from Coal, A State-of-the-Art Review, U.S. Energy Research and Development Administration, ERDA 76-67.)

strongly influenced by the carbon monoxide-to-hydrogen ratio in the synthesis gas, the catalyst, and the operating pressures and temperatures.

Solvent refining. This is essentially pyrolysis in the presence of a solvent to obtain a liquefied product. Under these conditions, coal dissolves into the solvent and picks up hydrogen. The solution is filtered, removing most of the ash and some undissolved coal. The remainder is a liquid containing solvent, dissolved coal, and a light oil from the reaction of coal with hydrogen. Rapid reduction in pressure drives off the solvent, leaving a solid product. This solid has considerably less ash and sulfur content than the original coal. In addition, a variety of other products may occur, including fuel oils and high-Btu gas. By an additional hydrogenation step, a predominately liquid product can be manufactured.

From the brief description given above, it should be apparent that conventional processes for coal gasification and liquefaction are quite complex. A number of approaches may be available, each with its own advantages and disadvantages. Regardless of approach, each is limited by knowledge about the detailed chemical composition of coal, as well as by experience in long-term, large-scale process operations. In an attempt to gain such knowledge and experience, a major effort in coal conversion research and development is being undertaken in the United States. An important part of that effort pertains to the demonstration that coal conversion processes can be employed in routine commercial operations. Still, such efforts require time. Even with the outlay of sizable funds for research and development, it is projected by government and private research organizations alike that conventional coal gasification and liquefaction facilities will not be ready to enter commercial service until the 1990s at the earliest. Clearly, if these projections prove to be accurate, little coal will be used in conventional conversion processes during the twentieth century.

An estimate of the number of potential coal gasification and liquefaction plants that appear to be supportable by most favorable coal reserves is given in the next section.

ESTIMATE OF NUMBER OF POTENTIAL GASIFICATION AND LIQUEFACTION PLANTS IN THE UNITED STATES

Introduction

Gasification and liquefaction of coal is being researched by government agencies and private organizations in an attempt to perfect processes to yield economical substitutes for declining supplies of domestic natural gas and crude oil. The technology and economics of coal gasification and liquefaction processes have been examined in many publications in recent years. Also, the projected demands for gaseous and liquid fuels and projected possible levels of development of coal conversion processes and financial aspects of such undertakings have received considerable attention. Relatively lesser emphasis has been given to the analysis of coal and water reserves for conversion projects. This deficiency has been largely remedied by a recent report of the U.S. Bureau of Mines that delineates areas where sufficient coal is available to support gasification operations.[1] Because liquefaction processes will probably have similar requirements for coal reserves and water resources, it appears reasonable to conclude that the areas identified by the Bureau of Mines include coal reserves that could be developed for processing by either approach. Because it focuses on "those areas having the highest potential," the Bureau of Mines report is of special interest; all other areas of coal reserves would appear to be of lesser potential. Therefore, analysis of the data assembled by the Bureau of Mines for the most favorable areas should yield a reasonable estimate of the number of coal conversion plants that may be constructed in the United States.

Methodology

The Bureau of Mines employed a systematic methodology in the report, considering the history of coal gasification, a review of gasification processes, environmental considerations, and operating and economic factors. A set of basic criteria was presented for selecting areas with coal and water reserves capable of support-

[1]A. E. Lindquist, Siting Potential for Coal Gasification Plants in the United States, *US Bur. Mines Inf. Circ.* 8735, p. 43, 1977.

ing exclusive gasification plant development, and county-level analyses were made for several states in major coal-bearing regions. The principal assumptions are summarized below:

1. "Basic" substitute natural gas (SNG) plants of 250 million standard cubic feet per day were assumed.
2. Basic SNG plants, at 55 percent thermal efficiency, were assumed to require coal in amounts equivalent to 4.76×10^{15} Btu over a 35-year plant life.
3. Recoverable coal reserves were assumed to be 57 percent of the deep reserve base and 85 percent of the shippable reserve base. (Note that these recoverability factors are those of typical individual mines. As shown in Chapter 3, recoverability from the reserve base is actually about half the above percentages. Therefore, the coal reserve data employed by the Bureau of Mines represent an *upper limit* to the amount of coal which could be developed for gasification or liquefaction.)
4. Only coal with greater than 1.9 percent sulfur was considered for eastern deposits; lower-sulfur coal deposits are assumed to be dedicated to electric utility, steel, or export uses. No distinction in sulfur content was made for western coals.
5. Only strippable coal deposits were considered as likely for western development in the near future.
6. The reserve base figures for each county were employed to calculate reserves by applying the above recoverability percentages. Using the average heating value for coals in a given county, the annual coal requirements for SNG processing were estimated and the minimum coal reserve required for 35 years operation was calculated. Counties having coal reserves above the 35-year minimum were tabulated.
7. Areas having sufficient water reserves to support SNG plant operations were then identified and compared with the coal areas.
8. Assuming that "presently planned or projected SNG developments propose ultimate expansion to 1000 million standard cubic feet per day," and using the above-derived data on coal reserves and water availability, eight areas of "high potential for gasification development" were identified; these are listed in Table 1 and illustrated in Figure 3. (Note that the allowance for expansion in gasification development also covers the use of coal or water reserves for some other coal conversion use, such as liquefaction.)

Analysis

The eight areas of high potential for gasification development listed in Table 1 may be analyzed in greater detail using information presented by the Bureau of Mines in the appendix to its report.[1] There, data were presented on heating content, estimated recoverable reserves for deep and strip mining (using the above recoverability percentages), and the number of beds targeted for development by each

[1]Lindquist, *op cit.*, pp. 38–43.

Table 1 Areas of high potential for gasification development

Area no.	State and county	Type of reserve base
1	Ohio (Jefferson, Harrison, Belmont) Pa. (Washington, Greene) W. Va. (Marshall, Marion, Monongalia)	Deep
2	Ky. (Hopkins, Muhlenberg, Webster, Union, Henderson) Ill. (Hamilton, Williamson, Saline, Gallatin)	Strip-deep
3	Ill. (St. Clair, Washington, Perry, Madison, Sangamon, Christian, Macoupin, Montgomery, Bond)	Deep-strip
4	Ill. (Vermilion, Edgar)	Strip-deep
5	Ill. (Knox, Fulton, Peoria)	Strip
6	N. Mex. (San Juan)	Strip
7	Mont. (Big Horn, Rosebud, Powder River, Custer) Wyo. (Campbell, Johnson)	Strip
8	N. Dak. (Dunn, Mercer)	Strip

Thus, despite the complex of factors involved in picking particular sites, SNG plants located within these areas should be in viable coal-supply positions.

mining method. These data are summarized for the areas of high potential in Table 2. Also shown in Table 2 is an estimate of the average reserves per seam, calculated by dividing the estimated recoverable reserves for each mining method by the number of seams in that county amenable to that method. This was done in recognition that coal production, especially in deep mining, is carried out on a

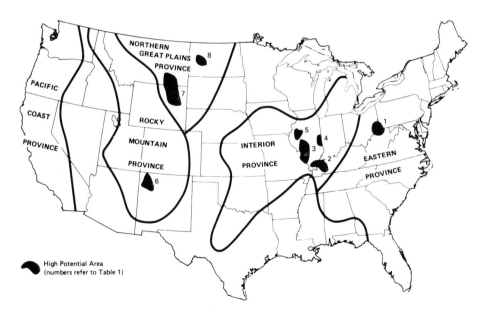

Figure 3 Areas of high potential for gasification development. (From A. E. Lindquist, Siting Potential for Coal Gasification Plants in the United States, *US Bur. Mines Inf. Circ.* 8735, 1977.)

Table 2 Summary of data on coal reserves for areas of high potential

USBM area	State	County	Aug. btu (as rec'd)	Recoverable reserves, millions tons*			No. coal seams	Average reserves per seam	
				Deep	Strip	Total		Deep	Strip
1	Ohio	Jefferson	12,650	729.34	253.68	983.02	6D, 6S	121.56	42.28
		Harrison	12,590	865.69		865.69	6	144.28	
		Belmont	12,500	2,227.34	246.50	2,473.84	5D, 2S	445.47	123.25
	Pa.	Washington	12,840	1,434.87		1,473.84	5	286.97	
		Greene	13,160	3,029.66		3,029.66	4	757.42	
	W. Va.	Marshall	12,900	1,734.95		1,734.95	4	433.74	
		Marion	13,590	1,089.02		1,089.02	8	136.13	
		Monongalia	13,220	1,490.91		1,490.91	8	186.36	
				12,601.78	500.18	13,101.96			
2	Ky.	Hopkins	12,190	1,029.23	651.75	1,680.98	9D, 10S	114.36	65.18
		Muhlenberg	11,890	511.99	926.65	1,438.64	7D, 9S	73.14	102.96
		Webster	12,570	818.77		818.77	5	163.75	
		Union	12,650	1,097.99		1,097.99	7	156.86	
	Ill.	Henderson	11,120	857.06	425.81	1,282.87	4D, 4S	214.27	106.45
		Hamilton	11,260	1,390.89		1,390.89	2	695.45	
		Williamson	11,940	755.69	309.58	1,065.27	8D, 6S	94.46	51.60
		Saline	12,370	1,384.84	354.69	1,739.53	7D, 5S	197.83	70.94
		Gallatin	12,590	1,003.67		1,003.67	5	200.73	
				8,850.13	2668.48	11,518.61			
3	Ill.	St. Clair	11,030	542.27	988.34	1,530.61	2D, 1S	271.14	988.34
		Washington	10,910	886.47		886.47	2	443.24	
		Perry	11,240	647.18	784.43	1,431.61	2D, 2S	323.59	391.72
		Madison	10,760	778.88	432.84	1,211.72	2D, 2S	389.44	216.42
		Sangamon	10,490	2,017.82		2,017.82	4	504.46	
		Christian	10,600	1,908.41		1,908.41	5	381.68	
		Macoupin	10,650	1,950.04		1,950.04	7	278.58	
		Montgomery	10,660	2,226.79		2,226.79	7	318.11	
		Bond	10,780	1,043.93		1,043.93	2	521.97	

4	Ill.	Vermillion	10,930	12,001.79	2204.61	14,206.40	3D, 2S	282.51	143.98
		Edgar	11,480	847.52	287.95	1,135.47	4	249.36	
				997.44		997.44			
5	Ill.	Knox	10,730	1,844.96	287.95	2,132.91	3		171.43
		Fulton	10,790		514.28	514.28	5		302.25
		Peoria	10,540		1,511.27	1,511.27	4		302.22
					1,208.89	1,208.89			
6	N. Mex.	San Juan	11,620	0	3,234.44	3,234.44	5‡	341.40	
					1,707	1,707			
7	Mont.	Big Horn	9,480	17,200	6,975	24,175	10‡	1,720	698
		Rosebud	8,820	11,780	4,775	16,555	10‡	1,178	478
		Powder River	7,730	10,180	7,425	17,605	10‡	1,018	743
		Custer	7,470	419	1,515	1,934	10‡	42	152
	Wyo.	Campbell	8,000	8,182	14,572	22,754	11	818	1,457
		Johnson	7,940	756	1,700	2,456	10	76	170
				48,517	36,962	85,479			
8	N. Dak.	Dunn	6,310		1,700	1,700	2‡		850
		Mercer	7,200		1,688	1,688	2‡		844
				0	3,388	3,388			
U.S. total				83,815	50,664	134,479			

*Reserves estimated by U.S. Bureau of Mines at recovery rates of 57 percent (deep) and 85 percent (strip) from the demonstrated coal reserve base.
†Only strippable coal in the West has been considered for SNG development in the near future. Source below, p. 15.
‡Western coals assumed to occur in the number of seams estimated.
Source: A. E. Lindquist, Siting Potential for Coal Gasification Plants in the United States, US Bur. Mines, Inf. Circ. 8735, p. 43, 1977.

seam-by-seam basis. To get a realistic picture of potentials for coal reserve development, it is essential to have some information on the amount of reserves in a given seam. (While it is recognized that the calculated data on reserves per seam are only averages, this is considered adequate for purposes of this preliminary analysis.) The results of this calculation suggest that, for many counties, the total coal reserves are present in many seams, few of which appear to have truly sizable reserves.

The data for total coal recoverable reserves in a given county and the average recoverable reserve per seam can be employed to arrive at estimates of the numbers of coal gasification plants that could be supported in each area. Table 3 shows, for each area of high potential, the Bureau of Mines' value for total coal requirement of an SNG plant over a 35-year lifetime. The maximum number of SNG plants in each county was calculated by dividing the total SNG plant coal requirements into the total recoverable coal reseves (assuming that *all* reserves would be developed). Nationally, this assumption suggests that as many as 353 SNG plants (or their equivalent) could be supported by the areas of high potential.

However, it does not seem realistic to expect that *every* coal seam in every county will be developed. Geologic factors may preclude this. Even if the geology of the coalfields might permit complete development of all seams, patterns of prior mining could present restrictions that would eliminate reserves. Furthermore, it seems likely, in view of current directions in regulation of coal development activities, that governmental bodies at various levels will pursue regulatory practices that effectively preclude attainment of the maximum development condition. Thus the estimates of the maximum number of SNG plants calculated and shown in Table 3 are regarded as merely an *upper limit* which is rather unlikely of being reached (or even approached).

What, then, is a more reasonable estimate of the number of SNG plants (or comparable facilities) that could be supported in the selected areas? An estimate of a "possible" number of SNG plants in each area was prepared by assuming that only one coal seam (or its equivalent) would be developed by each type of mining method in each county. The average reserve per seam (Table 2) was divided by the total coal requirements for SNG plant lifetime to determine the possible number of plants. Where the average reserves per seam were less than the total coal requirements, it was assumed that no SNG plant could be operated in that county; for simplicity, mine-mouth operations in a given county were considered as the only operating mode, and no intercounty coal movements were taken into account The resulting estimate of the possible number of SNG plants, totaling only 51 nationally, thus represents a value toward the lower limit of the scale. Consideration of intercounty coal movements in the area of high potential may tend to increase this estimate, but a very detailed analysis beyond the scope of this section would be required to investigate the possible contribution from such an approach. However, it is the writer's opinion that differences in coal quality may restrict the degree to which intercounty coal movements may be acceptable in meeting process requirements. By the same token, no interarea coal movements were considered as likely.

The data presented in Table 3 are illustrated in Figures 4 and 5. Figure 4 shows the maximum number of gasification plants, while Figure 5 shows the lower possible number. In each case, development would be concentrated in the Illinois Basin sector of the Interior Province. It is noteworthy that this region is already rather extensively developed for agriculture (and other activities), so that the maximum SNG development figures are judged by the writer to be hardly likely.

It is also important to note that in many areas (especially those of the East and Midwest where major SNG development could occur at either level) coal reserves would require underground mining for their development. In recent years, the costs of underground mining have escalated rapidly and productivity has plummeted, making this activity, at best, a costly enterprise. Note, also, that the costs given in the Bureau of Mines report are "based on January 1975 indexes."[1] Present estimated capital investment requirements for coal mine development are approximately three times the values shown.[2] Clearly, this may be expected to have a significant impact on the potentials for coal development for SNG (or any other) plants. Finally, it was noted above that the estimated recoverability percentages used by the Bureau of Mines were appropriate to individual mines, and that recoverability from the reserve base should be *roughly half* the values used. With half the coal reserves, it follows that the estimated number of coal gasification plants should be reduced by half also. Table 4 shows that, using a recoverability factor which reflects conditions leading to incomplete recovery from the reserve base (as well as losses in mining operations themselves), the estimated number of coal gasification plants that could be supported by the eight areas of high potential ranges between 25 and 174 facilities. For the same reasons indicated above, the maximum number is regarded as an upper limit and unobtainable. However, the lower possible number is probably too conservative. Development of more than one seam by each mining method in each county would probably take place in several locations, and this could lead to a substantial increase in available coal reserves to support plant operations. Coupled with some relatively minor movements of coal from one site to another, the additional coal could support greater numbers of plants; the exact numbers of plants is unknown. However, it is considered possible that the actual number of conversion plants which could be supported by these areas of high potential may occur around the midpoint of the range indicated by the lower recoverability factor; *namely, about 100 SNG plants (or their equivalent) appear to be feasible from a coal reserve standpoint.* This number is probably uncertain by roughly 10 to 15 percent.

Outlook and Implications

The U.S. Bureau of Mines has identified eight areas of high potential for coal gasification development. It is reasonable to expect that these same areas would be preferred for other coal process development such as liquefaction. Areas not included in the high-potential category are, by definition, deficient in one way or another that makes them less attractive for coal conversion operations.

---

[1]Lindquist, *op cit.*, pp. 12,13.

[2]G. W. Land, "Capital Requirements For New Mine Development," Proceedings Third Conference on Mine Productivity, Pennsylvania State University, Apr. 5–8, 1976, pp. 104–118.

Table 3 Estimated numbers of coal gasification plants

USBM Area	State	County	Total coal requirement for 35-year SNG plant, million tons	Maximum number of SNG plants*			Possible number of SNG plants†			Present projects
				Deep	Strip	Total	Deep‡	Strip	Total	
1	Ohio	Jefferson		4	1	5	0	0	0	
		Harrison		5		5	0		0	
		Belmont		13	1	14	2	0	2	
	Pa.	Washington	165	8		8	1		1	
		Greene		18		18	4		4	
	W. Va.	Marshall		10		10	2		2	
		Marion		6		6	0		0	
		Monongalia		9		9	1		1	
2	Ky.	Hopkins		73	2	75	10	0	10	
		Muhlenberg		4	3	7	0	0	0	
		Webster		2	4	6	0	0	0	
		Union	5	3		3	0		0	
	Ill.	Henderson	207	4	2	6	1	0	1	
		Hamilton		6		6	3		3	
		Williamson		3	1	4	0		0	
		Saline		6	1	7	0		0	
		Gallatin		4		4	0		0	
3	Ill.	St. Clair		37	11	48	4	0	4	
		Washington		2	4	6	1	4	5	
		Perry		3	3	6	2	1	2	
		Madison		3	2	5	1	1	2	
		Sangamon	207	9		9	2		2	
		Christian		9		9	1		1	
		Macoupin		9		9	1		1	
		Montgomery		10		10	1		1	
		Bond		5		5	2		2	
				54	9	63	12	6	18	

		County	Reserves							
4	Ill.	Vermillion	207		4	1	5	1	0	1
5	Ill.	Edgar			8	1	9	2	0	2
		Knox				2	2		0	0
		Fulton	207			7	7		1	1
6	N. Mex.	Peoria			0	14	14	0	2	2
		San Juan	189			9	9		1	1		1
7	Mont.	Big Horn			n.a.	24	24	n.a.	2	1
		Rosebud			n.a.	16	16	n.a.	1	2
		Powder River	290		n.a.	25	25	n.a.	2	1
		Custer			n.a.	5	5	n.a.	0	2
		Campbell			n.a.	50	50	n.a.	5	0
		Johnson			n.a.	5	5	n.a.	0	5
	Wyo.				0	125	125	0	10	10
					n.a.	5	5	n.a.	2	2
					n.a.	5	5	n.a.	2	2
8	N. Dak.	Dunn	335		n.a.	5	5	n.a.	2	2		1
		Mercer			n.a.	5	5	n.a.	2	2		1
	U.S. total				0 / 172	10 / 181	10 / 353	0 / 28	4 / 23	4 / 51	3

‡ Only strippable coal in the West is considered for SNG development in the near future. *US Bur. Mines Inf. Circ.* 8735, p. 15, 1977.

* Maximum number of SNG plants calculated by assuming *all* recoverable reserves for a given county were developed to supply SNG plants (from Table 2).

† Possible number of SNG plants calculated by assuming that *only one* seam (equivalent) will be developed by each type of mining method in any one county.

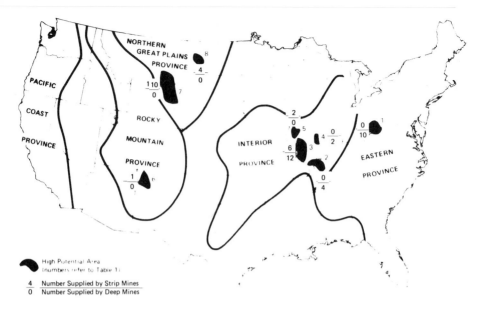

Figure 4 Areas of high potential for gasification development, showing maximum number of gasification plants. (From A. E. Lindquist, Siting Potential for Coal Gasification Plants in the United States, *US Bur. Mines Inf. circ.* 8735, 1977.)

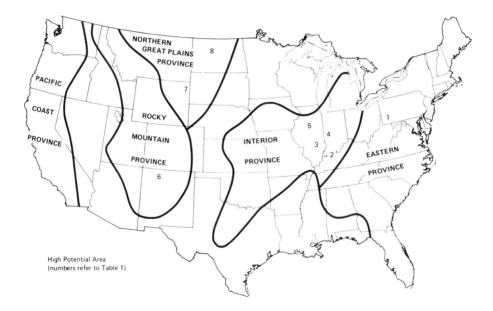

Figure 5 Areas of high potential for gasification development, showing "possible" number of gasification plants. (From A. E. Lindquist, Siting Potential for Coal Gasification Plants in the United States, *US Bur. Mines Inf. Circ.* 8735, 1977.)

Table 4 Estimated number of possible coal gasification plants

USBM area		USBM recoverability factor*		Recoverability factor derived in Chapter 3	
		Maximum	Possible	Maximum	Possible
1.	Ohio, Pa., W. Va.	75	10	37	5
2.	Ky., Ill.	48	4	24	2
3.	Ill.	63	18	31	9
4.	Ill.	9	2	4	1
5.	Ill.	14	2	7	1
6.	N. Mex.	9	1	4	0
7.	Mont., Wyo.	125	10	62	5
8.	N. Dak.	10	4	5	2
	U.S. Total	353	51	174	25

*US Bur. Mines Inf. Cir. 8735, 1977.

A review of coal reserves in the areas for high potential indicates that costly underground mining would be required in many areas of the East and Midwest. This seems certain to have a negative impact on the overall economics of coal conversion processes.

Estimates of the numbers of potential coal gasification plants were derived under alternative assumptions of coal recoverability and degree of development. It was concluded that about 100 SNG plants (or their equivalent) could be supported by the areas of high potential. Assuming that all these plants were built to produce pipeline-quality substitute natural gas, then each plant at 250 million standard cubic feet per day capacity operating 330 days per year would produce 82,500 million standard cubic feet annually. One hundred such plants operating for 35 years would produce a total of 289 trillion cubic feet of gas. This, clearly is a substantial amount of gas, just slightly greater than present estimated reserves of natural gas. However, it probably will not be possible to build or operate more than a few SNG plants at any given time, and the cumulative impact and output from these plants upon the overall gas supply picture would appear to be small.

Also, it is important to bear in mind that the areas of high potential will probably become targets for other coal-using facilities, especially liquefaction. *Thus, the total number of coal conversion plants of all kinds may be about 100,* to be divided among gasification and liquefaction (or any other candidate technologies) in yet-to-be-determined fashion. Because any such plant will require long-term commitments of coal reserves, water resources, and capital, it would be prudent to carry out detailed cost-benefit studies of each option for each area.

Establishment of refinerylike facilities for coal gasification is not the only approach being investigated. Also under consideration are methods for underground coal gasification, as described in the following chapter.

FOURTEEN
UNDERGROUND COAL GASIFICATION: TECHNICAL REVIEW

A brief description of underground coal gasification (UCG) is presented in this chapter, together with a discussion of the principal advantages and disadvantages of this approach to development of coal resources. Chapter 3 presented an analysis of coal resources to identify those which appear to have the greatest potential for application of this technique.

APPROACH

Underground coal gasification is defined by the U.S. Bureau of Mines[1] as "a method of burning the coal in place to produce a combustible gas which can be burned to generate power or processed into chemicals and fuels. Air and/or steam is blown underground to support the controlled combustion in the coal seam." Such gasification is difficult because, unlike ordinary plant operations, the operator must accept conditions imposed by nature which cannot be altered (such as coal quality, direction of flow, shape of "reactors," heat loss, and rate of "feed"). Thus it is not surprising that underground gasification technology has evolved slowly, with doubtful results to date.

Underground coal gasification processes may be classified, according to the method employed in achieving access to the coal seam, as either *shaft* or *shaftless* systems.[1]

Shaft systems require extensive underground mining in preparation for actual gasification. Although experiments with shaft systems have been conducted

---

[1]U.S. Bureau of Mines, "A Dictionary of Mining, Minerals, and Related Terms," p. 1183, 1968.

[2]J. L. Elder, Underground Gasification of Coal, in H. H. Lowry (ed.), "Chemistry of Coal Utilization," pp. 1023–1041, Wiley, New York, 1963.

abroad (notably in the Soviet Union), they have not been attempted in the United States.

Shaftless systems in this country are employed exclusively in tests of possible UCG systems. Access openings to a target coal bed are developed by drilling boreholes for inlet of air, steam, or oxygen and gathering of produced gas. The major requirement with shaftless systems is in establishing satisfactory gasification paths between system inlets and outlets.

PROCESS PHASES

The UCG process comprises two main phases:

1. Permeability enhancement or "linkage," in which narrow (3-4 feet wide), roughly cylindrical channels are established in the coal seam between boreholes intended for reactant inlet and gas outlet. The character and extent of natural fractures in the coal strongly influence the direction and degree of permeability enhancement. Linkage may be accomplished by at least five methods:

   a. *Directional drilling,* in which boreholes are drilled into the coal seam. This technique was used in the Soviet Union where steeply dipping seams occur. The longwall generator concept of the Morgantown Energy Research Center (to be described later) also employs this technique.

   b. *Countercurrent ("reverse") combustion,* in which partial utilization of carbon in the coal occurs along pathways defined largely by the natural permeability of the coal. A flame front is established over a narrow region and moves in the opposite direction to gas flow between boreholes, with the flame-front velocity determined by the rate of airflow. The result of this technique is narrow, fixed channels that are not subject to plugging caused by coal swelling or the presence of condensing tars (to be illustrated later in the discussion of the Laramie Energy Research Center experiments).

   c. *Electrolinking,* in which an electric current is used to carbonize coal. This technique is highly sensitive to coal properties and is quite difficult to control.

   d. *Hydrofracking,* in which pumped water under pressure is used to fracture the coal, employing admixed sand to maintain the openings.

   e. *Explosive fracturing,* in which chemical (or even, conceivably, nuclear) explosives are employed to establish permeability in the seam. This technique was proposed by the Lawrence Livermore Laboratory (and will be described later).

The purpose of linkage is to increase the permeability of the coal seam and provide a channel to allow for the flow of sufficient quantities of reactant fluids to permit gasification reactions to proceed efficiently. The reactions proceed outward into the coal away from the permeability channels, with the product gases being released into the channels. It is desirable to locate the channels "as close to the bottom of the coal seam as possible" to prevent the combustion zone from "overriding" to the top of the seam and covering potentially gasifiable coal with ash or slag.[1]

2. Gasification is accomplished by a combustion process and "in a variety of chemical reactions . . . in which, as the temperature rises, chemical bonds of increasing strength are broken. The actual chemical reactions occur very rapidly, but diffusion through the solid slows the evolution of volatiles."[2] Furthermore, Gregg and Olness point out that:

> The underground gasification of coal is a complex physical-chemical process and is difficult to study because it occurs well below the ground surface. The course of the process is influenced by many different factors. These factors can be divided into two basic categories; the chemical process of the formation of the fuel gas and the four-dimensional hydrodynamic interaction between the reactant product gas phase and the solid coal seam. The interaction of these factors is only imperfectly known and thus it is difficult to arrive at rigorous scientific or engineering interpretation of the results of gasification.

Recent engineering progress in the linked vertical well process (to be described later) suggests that many of the above concerns may have been alleviated, and much is now known about the process.

A particularly important problem is water influx into the reaction zone. Gregg and Olness[3] point out that:

> Water is added unavoidably into the reaction zone by leakage from the surrounding formations. In fact, the Soviet experience in the use of air for underground gasification has revealed that *the natural water intrusion rate can easily* exceed the optimum rate and *result in reduced efficiency of the process due to excessive cooling of the reaction zone.* [Emphasis added.]

In consequence, "optimum ratios of operating temperature and oxygen/steam must be determined for each system with its particular set of operating parameters."

As noted above, the natural variability of coal seams manifests as both horizontal and vertical changes in properties, especially moisture content. Gregg and Olness note that "gas composition changes with decreased temperature . . . as temperature decreases the reaction rates slow so that the equilibrium compositions are not reached and the final product gas composition is determined primarily by the rates of reaction, not the equilibrium composition."

The rate of groundwater influx into the gasification zone thus has an important influence on the reactions and the product gas. With higher levels of water influx, the heating value of the product gas decreases (by increasing the carbon dioxide concentration at the expense of carbon monoxide and hydrogen). Generally speaking, thicker coal seams have larger water inflow rates (and in certain localities,

---

[1] L. A. Schrider et al., "The Outlook for Underground Coal Gasification," 1975 Lignite Symposium, Grand Forks, N. Dak., May, 1975.

[2] D. W. Gregg and D. V. Olness, "Basic Principles of Underground Coal Gasification," Lawrence Livermore Laboratory, UCRL-52107, Aug. 18, 1976.

[3] *Ibid.*

many thick coal seams are aquifers); "therefore if everything else is constant, thicker coal seams are likely to have more water than thinner ones."[1] However, it appears to be possible to use air injection pressure to achieve a measure of control over water influx (and, to a certain extent, gas leakage as well). Therefore, it would be necessary to gasify a thick seam at a faster rate to control water influx.

A further problem is that:[2]

> No quantitative field data on the performance of an underground coal gasification system as a function of the plastic properties of coal are available.
>
> The primary plastic property of concern is the degree to which the coal swells as it is heated and the potential for plugging the bed to gas flow. This could adversely affect the potential for the hooked vertical well process in eastern bituminous coals.

ENGINEERING INSIGHTS FROM SOVIET TESTS

Based on several decades of trial and error, the following engineering methods derived from Soviet tests of UCG systems are noteworthy (summarized by Gregg and Olness):

1. Operate at low pressure and use high-permeability approaches in coal (to avoid leakage of product gas).
2. Use high gas-flow rates to compensate for water intrusion and to maximize channel widths.
3. Establish directional control of gas flow along permeable linkage paths.
4. Achieve high-permeability linkages.
5. Form linkage channels at the seam bottom.
6. Operate in thick seams to minimize heat losses.
7. Maximize borehole survivability to reduce costs; protect against subsidence.
8. Sequentially gasify multiple seams from the top down.
9. Maintain a continuous-sweep gasification system.
10. Minimize process sensitivity to coal swelling.

It would appear that the prospects for success in UCG operations require the achievement of most or all of the above conditions.

Regardless of the means of establishing gasification paths, underground coal gasification is essentially a batch process (although it would be possible to design installations for continuous gas output). As gasification progresses, more and more coal is consumed and removed from the reaction zone, making it difficult to maintain contact between the reactants and ultimately resulting in reduced product volumes and in lower product quality. When this occurs, it becomes necessary to move to a new reaction path and start again.

The quality of gas is dependent upon many factors, especially whether combus-

[1]*Ibid.*
[2]*Ibid.*

tion is accomplished with air-blown or oxygen-blown systems. Although oxygen-blown systems can lead to a higher-quality product, they tend to be more complex and costly, so that their application to large-scale operations is not at all assured.

Maintenance of combustion can prove difficult should there be substantial water inflow into the reaction zone or high-water content of adjacent strata. This can lead to heat losses because of water vaporization and condensation. Water entering the reaction zone in smaller quantities can influence the quality of product gas. A further problem is in gas leakage through the containing strata, lowering the amount of recovered products.

PRESENT U.S. UNDERGROUND COAL GASIFICATION CONCEPTS

Three UCG concepts are being explored in the United States at the present time. These are:

1. The linked vertical well (LVW) process being investigated by the ERDA Laramie Energy Research Center (LERC) and, independently, by Texas Utilities.
2. The longwall generator (LWG) process being examined by the ERDA Morgantown Energy Research Center (MERC).
3. The packed-bed process being experimented with by the University of California's Lawrence Livermore Laboratory (LLL).

Each of these processes will be described briefly.

Linked Vertical Well (LVW) Process

This process is closely related to the UCG tests conducted in the Soviet Union. The following description is taken from a recent review prepared by ERDA.[1]
Figure 1A. The coal seam is then ignited at the bottom of one well (B) using a downhole electric heater. Air is injected at an adjacent well. The injected air percolates through the coal seam to the ignition well, supplying oxygen to sustain the fire. The fire moves from the ignition well toward the injection well, i.e., toward the source of oxygen (part C). As the fire proceeds toward the source of oxygen, a highly permeable pathway is formed between wells because of carbonization of the coal along the pathway. This carbonization process removes the volatile matter from the coal, leaving a highly porous char behind. When the fire reaches the bottom of the injection well, the system is ready for gasification, as shown in part D.

This preparation process is known as *reverse combustion linking*. It is necessary

[1]Energy Research and Development Administration, "The Laramie Energy Research Center's Underground Coal Gasification Program," manuscript, 1976.

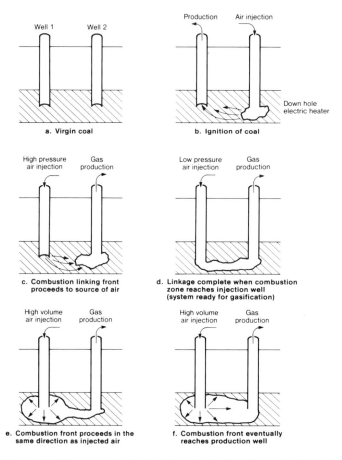

Figure 1 LVW process description. (From L. A. Schrider and J. W. Jennings, "An Underground Coal Gasification Experiment, Hanna, Wyoming," AIME Paper No. SPE 4993, Oct. 6-9, 1974.)

because coal in its natural state does not have sufficient permeability to allow air injection at the rates needed to achieve efficient gasification. After the reverse combustion linking is completed, a path between wells has been prepared which does allow high air-injection rates. Linking at the Hanna site involves injection of low volumes of air (approximately 100 to 200 cubic feet per minute) at high pressure. The injection pressure used is 1 pound per square inch per foot of depth to the coal seam, e.g., 250 pounds per square inch if the coal is 250 feet below ground surface.

Upon completion of linking, high volumes of air are injected at low injection pressures (part E). During this period of high-volume injection, which begins immediately after linking is completed, the fire expands from the injection well back toward the well where the coal was ignited. All gases produced during both the linking and gasification periods are removed at the well where the coal seam was ignited.

This expansion begins generally with a spherical geometry with some distortion toward the production well owing to the presence of the linkage pathway. Based on temperature measurements at different levels in the coal seam, the reaction front during this early stage expands vertically until it encompasses a full 30-foot thickness of the seam. Then this reaction front proceeds at a rate of 1 to 2 feet per day over the full thickness of the seam toward the well where the coal was ignited, consuming all the coal over a distance of 40 to 50 feet wide until the fire breaks through to the production well. In this manner, nearly the whole coal seam thickness between wells is utilized, as shown in part F.

The low-Btu gas produced at Hanna consists of 4 to 6 percent methane, 45 to 50 percent nitrogen because air rather than pure oxygen is injected, 12 to 18 percent carbon monoxide, 15 to 20 percent hydrogen, 10 to 15 percent carbon dioxide, small amounts (less than 1 percent) of ethane and propane, and approximately 0.1 percent hydrogen sulfide. The combustible gases contained in this mixture are hydrogen, methane, carbon monoxide, ethane, and propane. Nitrogen and carbon dioxide have no heating value and simply dilute the gases produced from underground coal gasification, thereby yielding the low-Btu gas. A method for achieving a higher-Btu gas would be to inject oxygen rather than air. No nitrogen would then be produced. Plans to do this at Hanna have been made, but the first-generation process is to develop the system using air because oxygen injection requires stringent safety precautions and preparation not necessary during air injection. If the process can be demonstrated using air injection, progress on to oxygen injection should be possible.

Longwall Generator (LWG) Process

This process is at a very early stage of experimentation. The concept is illustrated in Figure 2. Basically, parallel 6-inch boreholes are directionally drilled from the

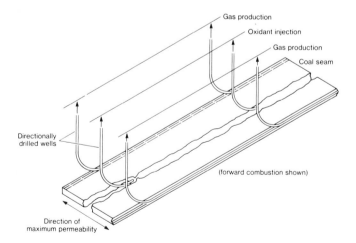

Figure 2 Longwall generator concept, cutaway diagram. (From Z. L. Shuck and J. Pasini, III, "A Report on Progress in Underground Coal Gasification," International Energy Engineering Congress, Chicago, Nov. 4-5, 1975.)

surface at separations of 100 feet to enter an undeveloped coal seam and follow it horizontally for a distance of up to 500 feet. Combustion proceeds in an areal sweep pattern from one borehole toward the adjacent parallel well. Initial drilling problems have delayed the commencement of this experiment.

Packed-bed Process

This process is a relatively new development. The following description is taken from a recent review.[1]

The basic procedure consists of using chemical explosives to fracture a coal deposit and create a well-defined, permeable reaction zone. The coal is then burned in place, using oxygen, rather than air, to produce gases that can be upgraded to pipeline quality in a surface gas-treatment facility.

A model of the process, based on a coal deposit in the Powder River Basin of Wyoming, is shown in Figure 3. A simplified block diagram is shown in Figure 4.

In this process, chemical explosives emplaced in an array of drilled holes are used to fracture a coal-and-shale sequence at depths ranging from 500 to 3000 feet below the surface. Gas-collection wells are then drilled to the bottom of the fractured-coal zone. Some of the charge-emplacement holes may be reentered to regain access to the top of the zone. These wells and injection holes are cased to prevent water entry and gas loss. In the next step, oxygen is injected and combustion is started at the top of the fractured zone. After good combustion has been established, oxygen injection is replaced with an oxygen-water or oxygen-steam mix-

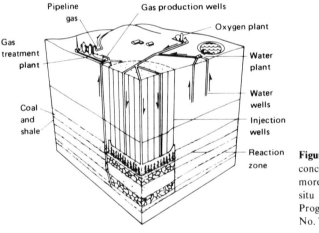

Figure 3 In situ coal gasification concept. (From Lawrence Livermore Laboratory, "The LLL in situ Coal Gasification Research Program in Perspective," Report No. TID 26825, June 10, 1975.)

[1]Lawrence Livermore Laboratory, "An In-Depth Evaluation of LLL's R&D Program for the *In-Situ* Gasification of Deep Coal Seams," TID-27008, Feb. 24, 1976. (Hereinafter cited as "LLL Report.")

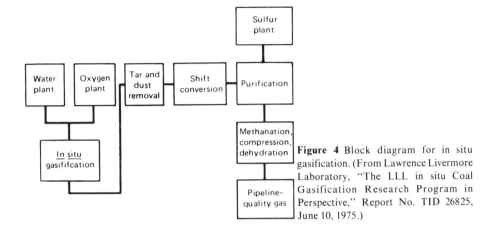

Figure 4 Block diagram for in situ gasification. (From Lawrence Livermore Laboratory, "The LLL in situ Coal Gasification Research Program in Perspective," Report No. TID 26825, June 10, 1975.)

ture. The oxygen is used to burn some of the coal to generate the large quantities of heat required for the endothermic gasification reaction of steam and carbon to produce carbon monoxide and hydrogen. In essence, the process operates much like an aboveground packed-bed reactor: The shattered coal is gasified with steam and oxygen just as in a conventional high-Btu, coal gasification plant.

ADVANTAGES AND DISADVANTAGES OF UNDERGROUND COAL GASIFICATION

The UCG process is not as far advanced as the more conventional processes. However, engineers have recognized for some time that the underground process has both advantages and disadvantages when compared with gasification in surface installations. A much better understanding of the mechanisms of underground coal gasification will be required in the future so that, for a specific power generation project, a selection can be made between underground and surface methods based on sound economic principles. Nevertheless, even at the present time, underground gasification appears to have potential advantages under certain circumstances because much of the subbituminous coal resources of the Western states cannot be mined by conventional methods (to be described in the following section).

Some principal disadvantages and advantages of underground coal gasification are next discussed briefly.

Disadvantages

1. Extensive surface subsidence possible. Subsidence, however, has occurred extensively in many mined areas and is not unique to in situ processing.

2. Variable Btu content of the produced gas. A better understanding of the in situ process may lead to alleviation of this problem. Injection of oxygen and removal of carbon dioxide from the product gas could also produce a gas with a nearly constant Btu content.

3. Unpredictability. In surface gasification, optimum conditions of temperature, pressure, and injection gas compositions are known within reasonable limits. The effect of such variables on underground gasification is becoming understood on the basis of current work. Remaining uncertainties are economic and environmental (hydrology, subsistence, etc.).

4. Leakage of product gases out of the gasification region or leakage of water into it. Both these possibilities may be eliminated through careful pressure control; for example, the coal stratum gasified in the first Hanna field test is an aquifer. Injected-air pressures, however, were higher than hydrostatic pressures, and quenching of the combustion front did not occur.

5. Adverse effects upon groundwater quantity and quality. Disruption in drainage patterns through aquifers could result from underground coal gasification and subsidence. The quality of groundwaters could be adversely affected by dissolved salts, organic matter, or leaching of minerals from the reaction zones upon completion of gasification, with no option for alternate disposal as exists with surface facilities.

6. Low efficiency of resource use.

Advantages

1. Lower labor requirements, greater safety. Coal mining remains one of the most hazardous occupations. Although the demand for coal is rapidly increasing, the potential work force of experienced miners remains roughly constant. Historically, new labor contracts negotiated with the United Mine Workers Union are reported to have increased labor costs of coal mining significantly over the duration of the contract. The increasing demand for coal and the history of the labor market seem to dictate that this trend will continue. Because of its great simplicity, underground coal gasification requires a smaller work force than conventional mining coupled with a surface gasification plant. This is a very important consideration in sparsely populated areas of the West. Many undesirable side effects are known to be associated with too-rapid population growth. Water resources are very limited, and the cost is high for the construction of entire communities with all services where none now exist.

2. Only prospective method for recovering energy from very deep or otherwise unminable coal deposits.

3. Capital requirements greatly reduced. Coal gasification plants are capital-intensive. A plant to be constructed in Converse County, Wyoming, is estimated to cost $500 million (in terms of 1974 dollars) for a capacity of 2,350,000 therms per day. The Eastern Panhandle Pipeline Company supplies a number of large utilities with fuel. This single company estimates a deficit in

available natural gas supply of 1.085 million cubic feet per day of 10,500,000 therms per day by 1983. Coal gasification to meet this deficit would require an investment of several billion dollars over the next 7 or 8 years. It is unclear whether such massive amounts of capital can be obtained.

Underground coal gasification requires far less materials, construction time, and capital because of the simplicity of the method. Still further savings are accomplished where on-site power generation is practicable. Gas turbines operate efficiently with low-Btu gas, and at the same time less equipment (and less construction time) is required for power generation from gas turbines as compared to steam turbines.

4. No ash-disposal problem. If gasification is carried out on the surface, then a considerable amount of ash must be disposed of in some way. If the gasification plant is located near the mine, then the mine itself may serve as the disposal site. For gasification plants distant from the coal source, a serious problem arises because several thousand tons of ash must be discarded daily.

5. Brackish water may be used in the in situ process, whereas high-quality process water is required in aboveground gasification. All gasification processes require at least 0.6 pound of water per pound of coal. It is already apparent that the lack of an adequate supply of high-quality water will seriously impede aboveground gasification. There are substantial quantities of underground brackish water available in the West which could be used for underground gasification.

Although the technology for underground coal gasification is clearly important, the critical factor in its application may be the array of unanswered questions being researched at present. This topic is analyzed in the following section.

STATUS OF RESEARCH AND DEVELOPMENT

The preceding section outlined several major reasons why underground coal gasification may be considered as a possible means to recover energy values from certain coal deposits. However, in any potential application, a large number of questions arise which cannot be answered at the present time because of a lack of fundamental understanding of the process. Some important *geological* questions are:

1. What geological conditions and what operating conditions are required for a UCG project to be economically competitive with other means for coal development?

2. What geological conditions will permit optimum energy recovery from a given coal seam?

3. Under the most favorable conditions, can underground gasification achieve resource recovery comparable or superior to conventional mining methods?

4. Is fluctuation in the Btu content of gas caused by inherent variability in the coal seam?

5. Will the Btu content of the gas be affected if the air-injection rate varies widely (either because of geological or operational considerations)? If so, what are the ranges of values anticipated?
6. What are the dynamic interrelationships between seam thickness, ash content, heating value, reactivity, and other properties of the coal and how do these affect the performance of an underground gasification project?
7. How do pressure, gas-injection rate, injection-gas composition, well spacing, and other variables interact with seam conditions to affect underground gasification?

Essential Engineering Information Required for Successful UCG Projects

1. The relationship between well spacing and the irretrievable loss of sensible heat to the overburden and underburden (cap rock and base rock).
2. The effect of well spacing upon the on-site utilization of sensible heat of the produced gases.
3. Combustion-front sweep efficiencies in relation to the geometric placement of wells.
4. Vertical sweep efficiencies for thick coal strata.
5. The effect of air-injection rate and pressure control upon the produced-air Btu content.

In an attempt to investigate geological and process questions to obtain information essential for design and appraisal of UCG processes, a program of research and development has been implemented by the federal government. Texas Utilities Company is supporting private work on underground coal gasification, but this is proprietary and therefore outside the present review. The federal program[1] comprises experimentation and field tests with four process concepts; budget levels are approximately $8 million annually. Two of the concepts (longwall generator/deviated wells; steeply dipping bed process) employ borehole drilling to provide permeability enhancement, while the other two concepts employ combustion (linked vertical well concept) or explosive fracturing (packed-bed process) for this purpose.[2] Each of the processes is at present in a preliminary design unit or pilot plant stage, and this work is scheduled to continue through the end of 1982 (refer to Figure 5). If the development of underground coal gasification follows the pattern established by the nuclear light-water reactor, then some 15 years would be required between the initial pilot plant experience and large-scale commercial operation.[3] This period of time could be optimistic, because it is not at all apparent that underground coal gasification would receive priorities and assured funding com-

---

[1] Energy Research and Development Administration, "A National Plan for Energy Research, Development, and Demonstration: Critical Energy Choices for the Future," ERDA 76-1. Vol. 1, The Plan, Apr. 15, 1976; Vol. 2, Program Implementation, June 30, 1976. (Hereinafter cited as "ERDA 76.")

[2] Refer to ERDA 76, vol. 2, pp. 51 et seq. for further details.

[3] ERDA 76, vol. 1, p. 31.

parable to that devoted to nuclear power; it is conceivable that the time period could be extended an additional 10 to 15 years. Should this additional time be required, the onset of large-scale commercial UCG projects would be after the year 2000 (Figure 5). While it is possible to begin the commercial planning stage earlier than estimated, it seems most likely that most prospective developers will wish to have as much data as possible prior to making such decisions, and an early start is not considered to be likely.

According to the National Plan,[1] one objective of the R&D program is "to assist in technology transfer to encourage an in-situ coal-conversion industry with a *production potential of three to four quads by 2000.*" [Emphasis added.] For these levels of production to be realized, it would seem to be necessary for commercial development to commence immediately upon completion of the pilot plant stage. It hardly seems possible for such production levels to be attained in a short time, owing to the array of natural and technical uncertainties to be overcome. For the reasons cited above, this seems highly unlikely. Therefore, it is difficult to have much confidence that the estimated production potential will be realized.

OUTLOOK AND IMPLICATIONS

The outlook for underground coal gasification may be assessed by discussion of four factors that strongly affect its commercial potential: technology, environ-

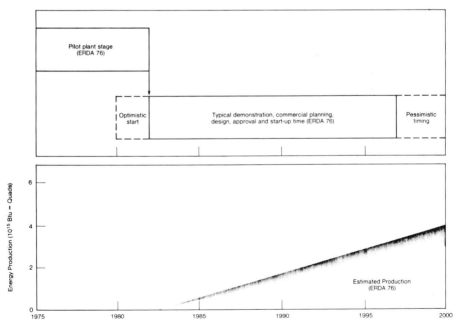

Figure 5 Typical UCG schedule.

[1]ERDA 76, vol. 2, p. 51.

ment, product quality, and economics. Each will be discussed briefly below.

Technology

Originally conceived in the Soviet Union as an alternative to mining, present plans in the United States are to use underground coal gasification as a supplement to mining. This change in basic concept represents an admission that, despite numerous experiments and field tests, the technology of underground coal gasification is not sufficiently advanced to contribute to fuel supplies in the coming decade or so. As a result, for the foreseeable future, those who are dependent on coal as an energy source will have to rely upon mining for coal recovery. A factor contributing to the relatively undeveloped state of underground coal gasification has been an associated imperfect understanding of coal, its deposits, and associated geological features and phenomena. As a result of recent work, such technical data as are required for evaluation of the potential of successful UCG projects can be specified and obtained in field exploration. Without such data, it is likely that underground coal gasification will remain as an engineering curiosity, limited to special cases or sites where considerable technical talent is concentrated on making the process work, somehow. Even with such data, it is not at all apparent that the technology can be perfected without a time-consuming and costly development phase whose outcome can only be described as uncertain. In the technical sense, therefore, underground coal gasification represents a considerable risk, and it is doubtful that many firms would be willing to pursue it based on the present outlook.

Environment

Numerous articles have been written about the "little environmental impact"[1] associated with underground coal gasification. However, most of these articles seek to compare underground coal gasification against conventional mining and subsequent processing. The reason for such an approach, of course, is that underground coal gasification is at such an early stage of development that environmental impacts remain essentially unknown. It is possible that there could be substantial, wide-ranging, and long-lasting adverse environmental effects of underground coal gasification, principally through its potential influence on groundwater quantity and quality. In a manner not unlike surface mining, underground coal gasification could disrupt aquifers and thereby interfere with the quantity of water available over considerable distances. Postcombustion products, burned adjacent rocks (substitute "red dog"?),[2] and subsided overlying strata may combine to interfere with the flow of groundwater and divert it from normal pathways. This could lead to water shortages in some areas; hardships would be the result in water-poor regions for those dependent upon such supplies.

---

[1]LLL Report, *op. cit.,* and others.

[2]Red dog is rock material of a reddish color resulting from combustion of rocks adjacent to coal seams, and occurs in substantial quantities in the western coalfields.

Perhaps even more significant, however, is the potential impact of underground coal gasification on groundwater quality. It is reasonable to expect that it will not be possible to control coal combustion in such a way as to exclude groundwater from the reaction zone. Thus at least a portion of the groundwater will be vaporized and removed with the product gas. This will leave a smaller amount of groundwater remaining in the coal seam (or other aquifer) to carry the normal load of dissolved salts. The salt concentration of groundwaters would therefore increase. Dispersal of these salt-laden groundwaters (assuming that their flow would not be impeded entirely) could lead to unknown but possibly devastating effects upon the fragile balance of nature in semiarid regions of the West. Dissolved organic matter resulting from combustion products could also adversely affect water quality.

While the dimensions of such effects are presently unknown, it is not necessary to wait for the results of new UCG developments to investigate these phenomena. It should be possible to obtain the essential information required for evaluation of groundwater effects by study of the naturally burned coal and surrounding rocks, as well as the flow patterns and quality of water that they contain. Such work could be performed by the U.S. Geological Survey (or the equivalent bodies of the several states) while the pilot plant programs are in progress. This would provide another essential element of information vital to the responsible assessment of the prospects for underground coal gasification. Without such information, the risks of irreversibly damaging groundwater quantity and quality would appear to be quite great in many areas, and this outlook is far from promising.

Product Quality

When coal is gasified underground in the presence of air, a low-Btu gas results ($\leqq 175$ Btu per standard cubic foot); when the reaction occurs in the presence of oxygen, a medium-Btu gas is produced (~ 300 Btu per standard cubic foot). Because of the higher cost of oxygen-blown systems, it seems most likely that most UCG projects would product low-Btu gas. It is too expensive to transport such low-heating-value gas over long distances, and therefore the gas must be utilized at its source. It is not clear whether postproduction gas processing will be required prior to its use.

> No special cleanup problems are indicated . . . if the low-Btu gas is used for steam raising but the requirements for expansion through a turbine may require special treatment, especially for the alkali metals, *although these requirements are not well established at the present time.* [Emphasis added.][1]

There may also be problems in using product gas from underground coal gasification in turbines or combined-cycle power plants. Product gas has 0.35 grains of particulate matter smaller than 2 microns diameter per standard cubic foot, and it does not appear possible for such gas to be used in turbines unless serious erosion

---

[1] C. F. Brandenburg, D. D. Fischer, A. E. Humphrey, and L. A. Schrider, "In-Situ Coal Gasification—Prospects as a Source of Utility Fuel," manuscript, 1976.

could be tolerated. This is quite unlikely, and it would appear that highly efficient particulate removal systems (not presently available commercially) would have to be developed to use product gases in such systems, irrespective of the alkali metal problem cited above (much like surface gasification systems).

In view of these factors regarding the quality of gas produced from underground coal gasification, the outlook for its use in electric utility systems is at best clouded. Considerable work would have to be done to ensure that any gases resulting from a successful production system could actually be employed efficiently. At present it appears that this problem is not sufficiently well-defined to enable formulation of sound approaches to deal with it.

Economics

As a consequence of the array of uncertainties in process characteristics, environmental impacts, and product quality cited above, it is difficult to arrive at estimated process economics having much precision. To be sure, there have been many recent attempts to estimate potential costs of various types of gas produced by underground coal gasification.[1] While differing in the estimated commercial price of product gas, the several studies are in general agreement on a number of factors that constitute any economic evaluation of underground coal gasification, as follows:

1. Costs of product gas are inversely proportional to (*a*) seam thickness, (*b*) coal heating value, (*c*) well spacing. In other words, costs will increase with thinner seams, lower-heating-value coals, and closer-spaced wells.
2. Costs of product gas are directly proportional to seam depth, (i.e., costs are higher with deeper seams).
3. At a given depth and well spacing, costs of product gas are inversely proportional to seam thickness (e.g., costs are higher for thinner seams under comparable conditions).
4. At a given depth, seam thickness, and well spacing, costs of product gas are inversely proportional to production rate (e.g., costs will be higher for slower production rates).
5. Costs of product gas are inversely proportional to resource recovery factor (e.g., costs will be higher with less efficient gasification of in-place coal).

Each of these factors is subject to considerable variation, depending on local conditions, and it is therefore difficult to arrive at definitive economic estimates of the cost of gas from underground coal gasification at this time. The studies cited indicate costs that range from an optimistic figure of about $1 per million Btu

---

[1]See, for example, LLL Report, *op. cit.;* J. W. Jennings, "Some Economic Considerations of Underground Coal Gasification," presented at SPE-AIME Northern Plains Section Regional Meeting, Omaha, Neb., May 15–17, 1975; M. K. Buden et al., "Factors Influencing the Economics of Large-Scale In-Situ Coal Gasification Operations," prepared for Office of Energy R&D Policy, National Science Foundation, Washington, by Bechtel Corporation, November 1975.

to a more conservative figure of nearly $5 per million Btu. This wide range reflects the several technical and operational uncertainties cited above. At present, in view of the speculative nature of costs for underground coal gasification, it seems only prudent to adopt a conservative approach toward the economics of this yet-to-be-proven technique. While R&D in progress may lead to more favorable, lower costs, it would be quite risky to plan new power-generating developments based on such costs.

Implications

The outlook for underground coal gasification as reviewed above is at best uncertain. The implication of this situation is not favorable to the adoption of such technology by the electric utility industry. Faced with the legal requirement to provide electric service upon demand, utilities require proven, reliable technologies of known (and viable) cost. Also, the lag time in developing a new fuel supply and/ or generating capability necessitates having such basic knowledge about technical performance and costs roughly a decade in advance of actual operations. As indicated in a previous section, it does not seem likely that such information on underground coal gasification can be available much before the end of the century. Accordingly, it seems hardly likely that this approach to recovery of energy values from coal would represent an option for electric utility industry planners in the remainder of the twentieth century.

Conventional and developing methods for coal utilization were reviewed in the preceding chapters. This material provides the background for a discussion of the economics of coal utilization in the following chapter.

FIFTEEN

ECONOMICS OF COAL UTILIZATION

REPORTING AND IMPLICATIONS

It is essential to understand how coal production data are compiled and reported as an introduction to the data themselves. At one time, practically all bituminous coal was placed on the market as run-of-mine.[1] Increasingly, bituminous coal is processed and cleaned or washed to improve its quality by removing waste material and other impurities introduced in mining and to reduce the sulfur and ash content. "It must be borne in mind that washing reduces the tonnage that goes on the market."[2] As with most minerals, coal production is traditionally reported by the amount of salable material shipped from the mines. At present, therefore, production figures commonly reflect the smaller amount of cleaned coal rather than the total material mined.[3] Accordingly, coal production statistics understate the actual amount of material mined. On a national basis, the U.S. Bureau of Mines estimates that 15 to 20 percent of the total material mined is waste or refuse and therefore only 80 to 85 percent is salable coal.

Consumers specify coal from which impurities have been removed by cleaning to facilitate its use. Some facilities or uses of coal would be adversely affected by coal having excessive amounts of ash, sulfur, or other impurities; this is not seen to be a serious problem for coal conversion processes. Also, specifying coal by its properties enables consumers to acquire their supplies from more than one locality (other things being equal) to offer wider opportunity for a second and reliable coal supply in the event of production problems.

The history of the coal industry is one of intensive price competition.[4] Accordingly, those who are able to produce a higher-quality product are able to command

---

[1] E. S. Moore, "Coal," 2d ed., Wiley, New York, 1940.

[2] *Ibid.*

[3] U.S. Bureau of Mines, *Minerals Yearbook,* various issues.

[4] E. R. Phelps, testimony before Subcommittee on Minerals, Materials, and Fuels, U.S. Senate Committee on Interior and Insular Affairs, Nov. 17, 1971.

a higher price. If other things such as operating costs are relatively equal, or if added costs for cleaning are more than offset by higher prices, this means that the higher-quality product will result in higher profits. It is essential to bear this fact in mind when reviewing coal production data and productivity statistics. The following discussion focuses on West Virginia, historically a principal coal-producing state of the nation.

CLEAN COAL

Statistics contained in the U.S. Bureau of Mines' *Minerals Yearbook* series provide a basis for estimating the amount of coal that is cleaned. At present, roughly half the total production is cleaned. Roughly two-thirds or more of underground production is cleaned, while only about one-third of surface mine output is cleaned. Therefore, the technology employed in coal extraction has an important bearing on the character of the product and the need for subsequent processing.

The high proportion of reject material from deep mining varies with mining method, volume of production, and size of mine. Continuous miners are highly efficient machines capable of excavating large volumes of material in a relatively short time. However, they do not discriminate between coal, slate, or roof and bottom materials, and even slight variances in coal seam thickness and character or operator action can lead to removal of significant amounts of waste materials. These waste materials are brought to the surface with coal, but must be removed there in the preparation or cleaning process.

STRUCTURE OF COAL MARKETS

In a convenient oversimplification, coal production is often ascribed to the "coal industry" as if this were a homogeneous and monolithic entity which performed its operations according to uniform practices and procedures. This viewpoint is both inaccurate and unrealistic. Organizations engaged in coal commerce are just as varied in their makeup and conduct as those in any other enterprise, if not more so because they deal regularly with the uncertainties of nature and her deposits of coal that they labor to exploit. The coal industry comprises firms of widely varying size (as measured in tons of coal produced) and diversity of markets where production is sold and consumed. The size of coal firms is largely determined by the reserves of coal that they control, with the largest firms holding the greatest and best-quality reserves.[1] However, firms with smaller reserves can secure viable positions so long as their coal is of high quality and of particular value in some special application or consumer requirement. Still, according to the yardstick of production, larger firms dominate what is popularly described as the coal industry.

Coal markets are subdivided into two main classes, commercial and captive.

[1]E. C. Christensen, "Economic Redevelopment in Bituminous Coal," Harvard, Cambridge, Mass., 1962.

1. The *commercial* coal market comprises firms separately engaged in coal production and utilization (i.e., coal producers typically do not use their product, and coal consumers typically do not produce it). There are two principal types of transactions in the commercial coal market, term contracts and spot sales.

   a. *Term contracts* covering roughly four-fifths of total production are established between producer and consumer to specify amounts of coal of identified quality to be delivered at agreed-upon prices for an increment of time. These agreements vary widely in their specificity, coverage, and enforceability. Some contracts are quite informal, being little more than a gentleman's agreement that producers will "take care of" consumers' needs at prices to be determined by market conditions. Other contracts are rather encompassing in their attempt to include pertinent aspects of production, quality, prices, and other conditions of purchase, but these are frequently so qualified or subject to modification that they amount to little more than informal agreements themselves.

   b. *Spot sales* represent about one-fifth of total production. These are individual transactions between producers (or coal brokers) and consumers for one-time purchases of given quantities of coal. Although large producers tend to employ term contracts, they also engage in the spot market. Mainly, however, the spot market is employed by smaller producers, or brokers acting on their behalf; note that large producers frequently serve as brokers for smaller producers, either to supplement contracted production or in spot market dealings directly. The spot market is important in overall commercial coal transactions, because it establishes the effective upper limit toward which term contract prices may rise.[1]

2. The *captive* coal market, as the name implies, is one in which coal consumers carry out their own production operations to satisfy their needs. In other words, these firms are vertically integrated with respect to coal supplies. While some captive coal production may find its way into the spot market from time to time, its principal use is to serve internal consumption requirements.

The portion of coal consumption which is commercial or captive varies with the consuming industry. In the steel industry, captive coal production predominates, accounting for roughly two-thirds of total coal use, with the remainder from commercial sources (Table 1). In contrast, the electric utility industry and "other" industries rely on commercial coal production for roughly nine-tenths of their requirements, with the remainder from captive operations (Tables 2 and 3). The tables show, moreover, that the proportions of commercial and captive production have not been constant over time but have varied in these industries during the past quarter century.

Because the electric utility industry is the largest present coal consumer, and is projected to more than double its consumption by the end of the century, it is im-

---

[1]Council on Wage and Price Stability, "A Study of Coal Prices," March 1976.

Table 1 Captive coal production—steel industry (thousand tons)

Year	Total steel industry coal use	Steel industry captive coal production	Captive coal production as % of total
1950	114,722	62,000	54.0
1955	114,730	65,282	56.9
1960	86,393	52,515	60.8
1965	102,245	62,006	60.6
1970	101,419	65,372	64.5
1973	99,990	58,512	58.5
1974	97,000	52,012	54.0
1975	88,000	56,209	64.0
1976	94,000		

Table 2 Captive coal production—electric utilities (thousand tons)

Year	Total electric utility coal use	Electric utility captive coal production	Captive coal production as % of total
1950	88,262	10,000	11.3
1955	140,550	11,129	7.9
1960	173,882	9,314	5.4
1965	242,729	13,433	5.5
1970	318,921	15,105	4.8
1973	386,879	19,082	4.9
1974	391,000	29,893	8.0
1975	402,000	44,789	11.0
1976	430,000		

Table 3 Captive coal production—other industries (thousand tons)

Year	Total other industries coal use	Other industries captive coal production	Captive coal production as % of total
1950	249,176	9,200	3.7
1955	166,633	7,185	4.3
1960	117,209	6,044	5.2
1965	113,535	7,894	7.0
1970	94,981	8,149	8.6
1973	69,037	7,291	10.6
1974	73,000	6,537	9.0
1975	69,000	6,733	10.0
1976	75,000		

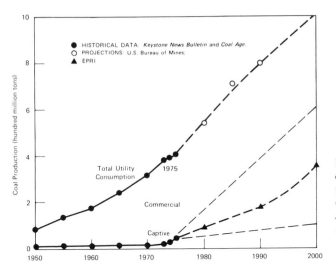

Figure 1 Relationship of captive electric utility coal production to utility consumption. (From *Keystone News Bull., Coal Age,* and U.S. Bureau of Mines, *Miner. Yearb.,* various years.)

portant to examine the outlook for coal markets for this mainstay industry. Figure 1 shows historical electric utility coal consumption, largely from the commercial market with minor amounts of captive production.

Also shown are three alternative projections of possible future market shares.

1. A lower limit of captive coal operations may be estimated by assuming that if historical patterns of markets continue in the electric utility industry and captive coal production represents only about one-tenth of total consumption, then about 100 million tons of coal will be produced by utilities for their own use in the year 2000. This would be a small part of the total but would still represent a doubling of electric utility coal operations.

2. An upper limit of captive coal production for electric utility use may be estimated by assuming that the size of the commercial coal market is maintained at about 400 million tons for the next 25 years. This would mean that the captive coal market would need to expand to about 600 million tons in the year 2000; in this event, electric utility operations would be greater than those of the "coal industry" itself. Clearly, this upper limit does not appear to be realistic.

3. A more plausible estimate of the division of the electric utility coal market throughout the end of the century may be derived by assuming that captive coal operations by utilities doubles by 1980 and each decade thereafter. This would result in an increase in the captive market share to about one-third of the total in the year 2000. Under this "modest" assumption the magnitude of captive coal production at the end of the century would be nearly as great as commercial coal production today. It is noteworthy that many electric utility companies not presently engaged in coal production have important coal hold-

ings (some acquired only recently). The likelihood that these reserves would experience development in the next 25 years appears strong.

No matter which of the lower estimates is realized, it seems apparent that there will be a greater involvement by electric utility companies in the production of coal as well as in its consumption.

U.S. SUPPLY-DEMAND RELATIONSHIPS FOR COAL

Annual supply-demand relationships of U.S. bituminous coal for the period 1950 to 1975 are shown in Table 4, derived from data reported by the U.S. Bureau of Mines.[1] Stocks on hand at the beginning of a year are added to that year's production and imports to yield the total supply; total demand is represented by the sum of reported consumption and exports. Total demand is subtracted from total supply to determine the stock available at the end of the year (equivalent to that present at the start of the following year).

During 1975 U.S. coal production was about 640 million tons, an increase of more than 30 million tons over the 1974 level.[2] Domestic coal consumption in 1975 increased by about 10 million tons, at least part of which was from stocks that declined during the year. Exports of coal were at about 66 million tons, an increase of more than 7 million tons over 1975. The U.S. Bureau of Mines notes that about 75 percent of total U.S. exports were from West Virginia, equivalent to about 53 million tons.

Exported coal is commonly higher-quality, metallurgical-grade coal and thereby commands a premium price. The increased amount of exported coal doubtless made a positive contribution to the national balance of payments. However, the higher prices for export coal could have spurred the industry to seek new production, and could have led to an increase in strip mining for either a part of export production or to provide for domestic needs, or as blending material for deep-mined coal for either purpose.

If exports of coal continue at their 1975 level or increase, then present or increased levels of surface mining may be necessary to meet these requirements as well as to satisfy domestic fuel requirements. Without surface-mined coal the nation would face a domestic and export fuel shortage that could lead to increased dependence on foreign fuel supplies which could adversely affect the balance of payments and national security. It is not clear, however, that the present export levels will continue. Recent coal developments in Australia could have an influence on U.S. coal exports,[3] especially in the Pacific. Moreover, there are significant coal reserves in mainland China which "can no longer be ignored as a considerable force on the world energy scene."[4] It is possible that these developments

[1] U.S. Bureau of Mines, *Miner. Yearb.*

[2] Westerstrom, *loc. cit.*

[3] See, for example, U.S. Bureau of Mines, *Minerals Yearbook,* various years.

[4] M. Seet, Coal in China is Bursting at the Seams, *Mining Eng.,* pp. 68–71, September 1971.

Table 4 Computed stock and total U.S. supply of coal (thousand tons)

Year	Stock as of Jan. 1	+ Production	+ Imports	− Consumption	= Exports	Calculated stock as of year end	Difference calculated stock and USBM report = "losses or unaccounted for"	"Losses or unaccounted for," % of total production
1950	45,111	516,311	346	454,202	25,468	82,098	9,582	1.9
1951	72,516	533,665	292	468,904	56,722	80,847	4,211	0.8
1952	76,636	466,841	262	418,757	47,643	77,339	594	0.1
1953	76,745	457,290	227	426,798	33,760	73,704	−6,910	1.5
1954	80,614	391,706	198	363,060	31,011	78,417	9,216	2.3
1955	69,201	464,633	337	423,412	51,277	58,808	−9,615	2.1
1956	68,423	500,874	356	432,858	68,553	67,530	−10,478	2.1
1957	78,008	492,704	367	413,668	76,342	80,335	−444	0.1
1958	80,779	410,446	307	366,703	50,293	73,922	−2,363	0.5
1959	76,285	412,028	375	366,256	37,227	84,455	8,523	2.1
1960	76,202	415,512	261	380,429	36,491	74,533	1,289	0.3
1961	73,244	402,977	164	374,405	34,970	66,682	−4,736	1.2
1962	71,418	422,149	232	387,774	38,413	67,148	−2,543	0.6
1963	69,691	458,928	267	409,225	47,078	72,049	1,966	0.4
1964	70,083	486,998	293	431,116	47,969	77,703	2,361	0.5
1965	75,342	512,088	184	459,164	50,181	77,901	508	0.1
1966	77,393	533,881	178	486,266	49,302	75,528	1,002	0.2
1967	74,466	552,626	227	480,416	49,528	96,921	3,793	0.7
1968	93,128	545,245	224	498,830	50,637	88,682	3,157	0.6
1969	85,525	560,505	109	507,275	56,234	82,412	1,930	0.3
1970	80,482	602,932	36	517,158	70,908	95,312	3,037	0.5
1971	92,275	550,000	100 (est.)	494,873	56,654	97,648	3,448	0.6
1972	89,985	595,386	47	516,776	55,997	112,645	3,855	
1973	116,500	591,000	127	556,022	52,870	98,735	3,465	
1974	102,200	603,406	2,080	552,709	59,926	95,051	1,478	
1975	96,529	640,000	1,150	562,000	66,000	109,679	6,321	
1976	116,000							

Source: U.S. Bureau of Mines, *Minerals Yearbook* series.

could lead to a decrease in the level of U.S. exports to this region.

Table 4 shows that the calculated year-end stocks are not necessarily consistent with those reported by the U.S. Bureau of Mines for the start of the following year. For example, we calculate the 1955 year-end stock as about 58.8 million tons, but the stock as of January 1, 1956, is reported as about 68.4 million tons, or a difference of more than 9.6 million tons (about 2.1 percent of total 1955 production).

The difference in calculated annual coal stocks from actual reported stocks is shown in Figure 2. Differences were greatest during the 1950s, attaining levels (positive or negative) approximately 10 million tons excess or deficit compared to reported stocks. There were also wide fluctuations in differences during the 1950s, with the total difference between data for 1954 and 1955 being nearly 20 million tons. The reason for these wide fluctuations is unknown, not being commented upon by major reference sources such as *Minerals Yearbook*. Also unknown is why there are peaks and valleys in the difference functions, or why they occur at particular times. It is true that the 1950s were a time of turmoil in the coal industry in which production was at a relatively low level and the numbers of workers were being reduced as greater mechanization took place, and this may be the principal explanation (refer to Chapter 7 and discussion of work force and productivity). Still, we can find no technical reason why coal production, handling, processing, transportation, consumption, or reporting should be subject to such fluctuations over such short times.

In contrast, the 1960s present a relatively uniform pattern in which the differences in calculated and reported stocks are consistently smaller and generally indicate calculated stocks greater than reported stocks. Although the recent past has seen less fluctuation in differences, the rising trend is a matter of concern and should be carefully watched.

Calculated stocks greater than reported stocks may be interpreted to reflect "losses and unaccounted for production."[1] Coal losses include material lost from rail cars during transportation between mine and consumer, as well as materials subjected to spontaneous combustion in mine or consumer storage. This coal would be reported as having been produced but would not be reported as having been consumed (consumption is nominally on an "as-burned" basis). Unac-

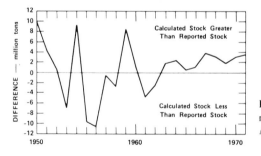

Figure 2 Calculated annual coal stock minus reported stock. (From U.S. Bureau of Mines, *Miner. Yearb.*, various years.)

[1]Thomas W. Hunter, Bituminous Coal and Lignite, "Minerals Facts and Problems," *US Bur. Mines Bull.* 650, pp. 35–61, especially fig. 1, p. 43, 1970.

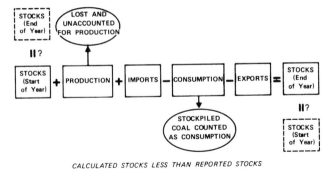

Figure 3 Schematic of coal supply-demand relationships.

counted-for production is coal in transit between mine and consumer. Although production has been recorded, officials of the U.S. Bureau of Mines comment that it is often difficult to balance production and consumption owing to the amount of coal in the transportation system. Calculated stocks less than reported stocks imply that coal reported to have been consumed may have merely entered stockpiles and was not actually consumed. Actually, there is an element of uncertainty in each item of data employed in calculating stocks, but the production and consumption categories constitute the largest tonnages of coal and even slight errors in these figures would have a disproportionate effect on the net balance. Figure 3 is a schematic showing the supply-demand relationships described above. A moderate amount of uncertainty in coal statistics is probably to be expected, owing to the wide geographic scope of the industry, the diversity of participating companies, the variety of operational stages, and the character of consumer use.

The recent (1960s) trend toward an increase in the amount that calculated stocks are greater than reported stocks suggests that there is an increase in lost and unaccounted-for production. Part of the reasons for the increase in lost production might be the production of greater amounts of fines by more mechanized equipment. At the same time as lost or unaccounted-for production was increasing, there was also an increase in surface mining. The significance of these factors is not clear, and could be entirely coincidental. Alternatively, it could be interpreted to mean that surface mining of coal is employed (at least in part) to compensate for coal losses. However, the force of this argument is diminished by the unexplained, much larger losses or unaccounted-for production in the 1950s, a time when surface mining was a relatively small factor in production.

Influencing Factors

As a first step, it is useful to examine factors that may influence production and consumption statistics.

Production is reported by coal mining companies in terms of coal loaded on rail cars (FOB mine). This represents coal ready to enter the market, implying that the coal to be cleaned has already been processed and wastes removed, and that the remainder is reported as run-of-mine. Run-of-mine coal produced by mechanized mining equipment will have greater amounts of fines.[1]

There is little coal storage at most coal mines, but it is possible that some coal is lost to spontaneous combustion in mine storage; this would also make the delivered total less than the production total. In sum, the end effect of coal losses upon the total annual coal production figure would appear to be small. Unless compensated for by other factors, the effects of coal losses would be to make the reported production figure higher than the actual coal entering the market, and could lead to calculated stocks being greater than reported stocks. Still, it does not seem likely that losses alone could lead to the magnitude of the differences between calculated and reported stocks.

Unaccounted-for production could, unless compensated for, influence the balance calculations in opposite ways:

1. If counted as production but not as entering into consumption, calculated stocks greater than reported stocks would result.
2. If counted as production and entered into consumer stockpiles that were treated as consumption, calculated stocks would be less than reported stocks.

Actually, both alternatives probably exist in varying degrees in the coal industry. In addition, the timing of coal shipment and receipt relative to reporting periods is important in determining the amount of coal in transit. It is difficult to estimate the amount of coal that might at some time be considered in this category. Generally, the total appears to be less than 2 percent of total annual supply.[2] This would be consistent with the data calculated in Table 4. In spite of this apparent consistency, the fact that there are wide fluctuations in calculated stocks relative to reported stocks over short intervals of time leads to an element of uncertainty that these influences on coal production, handling, processing, transportation, consumption, or reporting could be attributable to technical or operational factors alone.

ANALYSIS OF COAL USE TRENDS BY ELECTRIC UTILITIES

Although the total coal consumption by electric utilities has never been greater (over 400 million tons in 1975), the heating value has never been lower (roughly

---

[1] R. L. Schmidt, W. H. Engelman, and R. R. Fumanti, A Comparison of Borer, Ripper, and Conventional Mining Products in Illinois No. 6 Seam Coal, *US Bur. Mines Rep. Invest.* 7687, 1972. "The conventional product had the least fines of the three production methods. The borer product had more fines than did the ripper product, but it also had a greater amount of large pieces. Any change in mining method that results in a coarser product at the coal face has at least three potential advantages: First, the decreased surface area retards methane diffusion; second, the quantities of dust in the respirable range are lowered; and third, the reduction in energy consumed leads to more efficient extraction." This implies that the recent trend toward continuous mining is adverse to the stated advantages, as it leads to small particles, has great amounts of dust, and requires greater energy in extraction.

[2] Hunter, *loc. cit.*

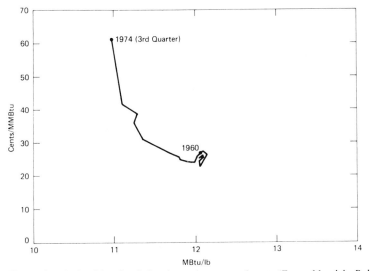

Figure 4 Relationship of unit heating values to coal cost. (From *Moody's Public Utility Manual*, 1974.)

11,000 Btu per pound in 1974) (Figure 4). At the same time heating value was decreasing, delivered prices (including transportation) were escalating, reaching more than 60 cents per million Btu in 1974. This means, of course, that to maintain a given heat rate, utilities have had to buy more coal of lower quality—at the higher price.

The present coal quality and cost situation comes after nearly two decades of increasing efficiency in coal utilization (Figure 5). The lower part of the L-shaped

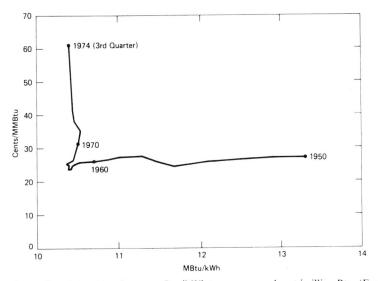

Figure 5 Relationship of average Btu/kWh to average coal cost/million Btu. (From *Moody's Public Utility Manual*, 1974.)

curve shows that improvements in coal use lowered the Btu requirement from 13,500 to 10,400 Btu per kilowatt hour. This was accomplished while coal costs were relatively stable at around 25 to 27 cents per million Btu. A marked change occurred at the end of the 1960s. Coal cost more than doubled over previous levels, while the generating requirements (million Btu per kilowatt hour) remained relatively constant. The rapid rise in cost may be attributed to a combination of inflation, decreased production, increased operating costs, and more restrictive coal-quality requirements. Note that the costs shown here are for long-term contracts; spot market levels are generally greater.

Of the several factors contributing to this rapid rise, a decline in coal mine productivity experienced in the early 1970s is particularly noteworthy. Average productivity declined from its high of nearly 20 tons per miner-day in 1969 to about 17 tons per miner-day in 1974. Figure 6 is a plot of coal mine productivity and heating value of coal consumed by electric utilities. Until the late 1960s, electric utility coal was greater than 23.5 million Btu per ton and coal mine productivities were steadily increasing. During the early 1970s, both coal mine productivity and heating value of the product steadily declined. The figure suggests that a more useful measure of coal productivity for electric utility purposes may be the number of Btu produced per miner-day. This value can be more directly related to electric utility costs and thereby may facilitate analysis by expressing coal production in terms of end-use requirements.

The figure also suggests that the latest coal mine productivity level may be tolerable so long as the quality of the coal is maintained. For example, in 1974 average coal mine productivity was 17.25 tons per miner-day. If the heating value of coal were about 23.2 million Btu per ton, the effective productivity would have been 400 million Btu per miner-day. However, the actual average heating value in 1974 was only about 22 million Btu per ton; at the 1974 coal mine productivity level, this is only 380 million Btu per miner-day. To achieve 400 million Btu per

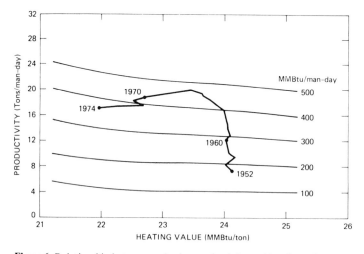

Figure 6 Relationship between coal mine productivity and heating value consumed by electric utilities. (From *Moody's Public Utility Manual,* 1974, and National Coal Association)

miner-day at the lower heating value, coal mine productivity would have to be increased to about 18.5 tons per miner-day. Achievement of the higher coal mine productivity would require a substantial investment in R&D, as well as time, to demonstrate and install new mining equipment.

PATTERNS OF COAL PURCHASES BY ELECTRIC UTILITIES

The Federal Power Commission compiles monthly information from each electric utility on the cost and quality of fuels used in the steam electric plants, through FPC Form 423.[1] Key information from these reports is summarized below.

Figure 7 shows that roughly four-fifths of steam-coal deliveries to electric utilities in 1975 were contract purchases, with the remainder being spot purchases. Approximately two-thirds of utility coal was produced by surface mining. Figure 8 shows that roughly half of utility coal in 1975 was greater than 2 percent sulfur content.

Trends in steam-coal purchases are shown for the last several years in Figure 9. The figure shows that, while both spot and contract purchases were relatively level before the coal miners' strike of 1974, purchases have increased since that time. The increase of contract purchases has been particularly noteworthy, rising from about 24 million tons to nearly 36 million tons monthly. Spot market purchases shrunk in the first half of 1976 to about 5 million tons per month in mid-1976. It will be important to monitor trends in utility purchases to determine if the spot market will continue to shrink. As many small producers are involved in spot market transactions, any curtailment or reduction in magnitude could have

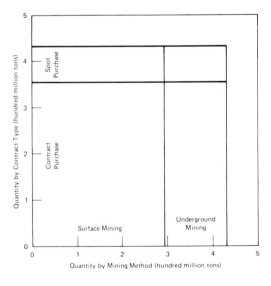

Figure 7 Comparison of steam-coal deliveries to electric utilities by contract type and mining method (1975). (From Federal Power Commision, Form 423.)

[1]See also "Annual Summary of Cost and Quality of Steam-Electric Plant Fuels," Staff Report by the Bureau of Power, Federal Power Commission, May 1975, May 1976 (with supplements).

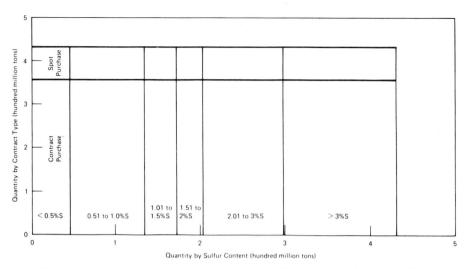

Figure 8 Comparison of steam-coal deliveries to electric utilities by contract type and sulfur content (1975). (From Federal Power Commission, Form 423.)

potentially severe impacts upon certain companies or localities.

Data on electric utility coal consumption and stocks is given in Table 5 and shown in Figure 10. The figure shows that coal stocks on hand at electric utilities increased from about 80 million tons in early 1975 to more than 120 million tons in mid-1976. Because the electric utility industry's general practice has been to build up coal stocks in anticipation of a possible strike upon contract expiration, growth in stocks that occurred in late 1977 could be foreseen.

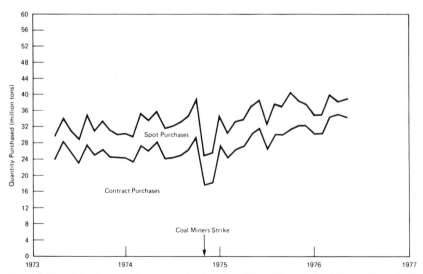

Figure 9 Trends in steam-coal purchases by electric utilities. (From Federal Power Commission, Form 423.)

Table 5 Electric utility coal consumption and stocks (thousand tons)

Month	(1) Stocks at beginning of month	(2) Deliveries during month	(3) Consumption during month	(4) Calculated stocks at end of month	(5) Reported stocks at end of month	(6) Difference (calculated from reported)	(7) Deliveries as % of: Consumption	Stocks
				1975				
Jan.	81,429	34,580	35,238	79,456	81,429	−1,608	94	38
Feb.	81,064	30,560	32,533	81,619	81,064	− 253	102	41
Mar.	81,872	33,339	32,784	85,262	81,872	−1,394	111	41
Apr.	86,656	33,842	30,452	93,303	86,656	+ 276	122	43
May	93,027	37,057	30,410	98,458	93,027	+ 624	116	41
June	97,834	38,489	33,058	93,999	97,834	− 38	89	33
July	94,067	32,532	36,367	93,719	94,067	− 388	99	40
Aug.	94,107	37,491	37,839	98,406	94,107	+ 616	113	39
Sept.	97,790	36,787	32,488	105,227	97,790	+ 451	123	41
Oct.	104,776	40,248	32,811	109,832	104,776	+ 767	115	36
Nov.	109,065	38,241	33,185	109,452	109,065	−1,236	101	35
Dec.		37,911	37,524		110,688			
				1976				
Jan.	110,688	35,111	39,887	105,912	105,301	+ 611	88	32
Feb.	105,301	34,953	34,950	105,304	104,770	+ 534	100	33
Mar.	104,770	39,836	36,082	108,524	108,435	+ 89	110	38
Apr.	108,435	38,147	33,841	112,741	113,096	− 355	113	35
May	113,096	39,261	34,067	118,290	119,409	−1,119	115	35
June	119,409		36,183		122,331			
July	122,331							
Aug.								
Sept.								
Oct.								
Nov.								
Dec.								

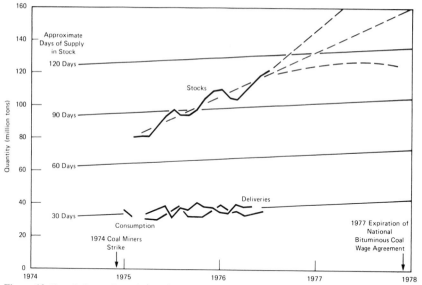

Figure 10 Trends in coal stocks held by electric utilities. (From Federal Power Commission, Form 423.)

Very large stocks of coal on hand at electric utilities could have a dramatic effect on coal industry patterns, among which are (1) potential return to a buyer's market, (2) depress coal price (or at least, dampen out fluctuations), (3) delay the pace and reduce the scale of new mine development (why rush to open new mines or purchase new equipment when the largest consumer has ample inventories of coal on hand?), (4) tie up electric utility capital in coal (at $20 per ton, 200 million tons of coal stocks would represent $4 billion). (This latter point is critical because inflated coal prices designed to capture "economic rent" could place effective limits on the extent of buyer control over coal markets. Probably, *real* control would consistently lie just beyond the reach of the utility industry's financial stamina.)

Finally, the presence of very large coal stocks at electric utilities would appear to encourage them to be selective in their purchases. While this may appear to offer opportunities for new entrants, the tradition is to remain loyal to tried and proven suppliers whose effective control over prices, performance, and product is known. Thus the prospect for new entrants would appear to be limited as utilities seek to protect relationships with existing suppliers.

PATTERNS OF COAL SHIPMENTS AND USE BY ELECTRIC UTILITIES

The Federal Power Commission[1] collects data on the origin and destination of coal shipments to electric utilities each month and provides both monthly and annual reports. Table 6 presents data for 1975 domestic coal shipments. The table shows

---

[1]Federal Power Commission (now, Federal Energy Regulatory Commission), *op. cit.*

Table 6 Origin and destination of coal* deliveries to electric utilities in 1975 (thousand tons)

Destination	Ala.	Ariz.	Ark.	Colo.	Ill.	Ind.	Iowa	Kan.	Ky.	Md.	Mo.	Mont.	N.Dak.	N.Mex.	Ohio	Okla.	Pa.	Tenn.	Tex.	Utah	Va.	Wash.	W.Va.	Wyo.	Total
Ala.	11638.6				367.2	25.4			6860.2									432.3							19323.7
Ariz.		3398.2												579.6						169.8					4147.6
Colo.				4118.5																				2272.5	6391.0
Del.																	971.0								971.0
D.C.									60.0												30.0		3.0		93.0
Fla.	282.1				913.2				4231.2																5426.5
Ga.	1455.0				11.0	482.0			10918.0									1479.0			157.0				14502.0
Ill.				10.3	21218.1	379.3			1182.1			9310.5			9.1					20.0			0.3	1866.3	33999.3
Ind.				1.6	3134.6	18896.4			5045.5			819.0			0.9					130.3	23.4		75.0	2841.4	30968.1
Iowa				134.8	2518.5	6.7	601.3		22.2		174.3	267.8								12.7				1701.0	5508.7
Kan.			10.4					1683.0								292.4								1244.2	3230.0
Ky.					1969.0				21664.2									102.3			0.3				25482.7
Md.									17.0	533.3							2240.5				5.0		891.3		3687.1
Mass.									288.0																288.0
Mich.					274.5	82.2			5778.7			1056.0			8362.3		691.0				0.5		5116.6		21361.8
Minn.					1717.3			319.2	98.3			6205.1			0.4	26.8				60.9			3.0	2.2	8797.4
Mo.					10661.1				315.0		3776.4		680.4			1363.3				1.6				997.7	17826.2
Miss.					893.4				637.6											2.0					1531.0
Mont.												1196.9													1196.9
Neb.				136.9				56.2																1316.3	1509.4
Nev.		3820.0																		655.8					4475.8
N.H.																	46.4						930.4		977.2
N.J.									98.2								468.4				391.2		1373.9		2331.7
N.Mex.														7184.9											7184.9
N.Y.				5.0					524.0								4591.6	467.2							5970.8
N.C.									7151.9												8075.7		2161.9		19740.8
N.Dak.												166.4	4610.7												4777.1
Ohio									9036.8						29113.6		2168.2						6540.6		46860.3
Pa.									1080.4	25.5					20.3		30070.3				36.2		4216.2		35448.9
S.C.	9.2								4147.9									72.7			249.0		0.4		4479.2
S.Dak.												24.0	1609.3			7.0								182.0	1822.3
Tenn.					715.5	290.2			16078.7						1683.1			4850.0			872.3		3.6		24493.4
Tex.																			9146.0						9146.0
Utah																				1955.0					1955.0
Vt.																							8.4		8.4
Va.									1065.8								1.0	48.0			2373.7		533.8		4022.3
Wash.																						4200.0			4200.0
W.Va.									2567.1	802.6					390.2		182.4						21220.6		26293.1
Wis.				20.2	4856.9				2072.7			2161.2			26.6		572.4	0.1			1130.1		4.6	1052.8	11552.5
Wyo.																								7235.4	7235.4
U.S. total	13384.9	7218.2	10.4	4437.1	49250.3	22940.0	601.3	2060.0	100941.1	1371.9	3950.7	21376.8	6900.4	7764.5	39606.5	1813.8	42003.2	7484.8	9146.0	3370.5	13869.1	4200.0	43923.7	21591.3	429216.5

* Does not include anthracite and imported coal.

Table 7 Origin and destination of imported coal delivered to U.S. electric utilities in 1975 (thousand tons)

Destination	Origin				Total
	Australia	South Africa	Poland	Canada	
Alabama	36.7				36.7
Florida	33.0	259.1		39.0	331.1
Massachusetts	29.0	36.0	139.7		204.5
Total	98.7	295.1	139.7	39.0	572.3

that Kentucky is the largest single supplier of coal to electric utilities, with over 100 million tons, with the next largest states (Illinois and West Virginia) combined still being less than the Kentucky total. In addition to domestic coal, U.S. utilities imported more than 500,000 tons of coal from abroad, as shown in Table 7.

The data on coal shipments may be employed in analyzing patterns of coal use by electric utilities. Table 8 shows that:

1. Nearly half the coal produced for electric utilities is used in the state where it was mined (roughly 211 million tons out of 429 million tons).
2. Slightly more than half the coal produced for electric utility use is exported for consumption outside the state where it was mined (roughly 219 million tons). However, approximately half this exported coal (about 112 million tons) is shipped to other coal-producing states for consumption there. As a result, the grand total amount of coal consumed by electric utilities in coal-producing states is more than 323 million tons (three-quarters of total annual consumption).
3. Approximately one-quarter of coal produced for electric utility use (about 106 million tons) is shipped to coal-consuming states having no coal production. Three of these states supplement domestic production with minor amounts of imported coal.

In summary, present patterns of coal shipment to electric utilities may be represented as shown in Table 9. The table shows that present electric utility coal use is concentrated in states that already have a strong prior history of coal production and utilization. It will be difficult to alter the proportions of coal use because of established patterns of transactions, coal production, transportation, and utilization equipment in being and because of applicable regulations. It would not be unreasonable to expect that the costs of coal utilization would tend to increase in inverse proportion to the magnitude of the established infrastructure (e.g., states with most extensive coal use would experience lowest costs, and conversely). This could become an important factor in attempts to convert power plants to coal use. For example, of the 37 power plant units recently certified by EPA for coal utilization,[1] 25 are located in coal-producing states and only 12 are in non-coal-producing states.

[1] EPA Certifies 37 Power Units for Coal, *Keystone News Bull.*, p. 3, September 1976.

PRICES OF COAL SUPPLIES TO ELECTRIC UTILITIES

Prices of coal have increased greatly in recent years.[1] This increase has been most pronounced in the spot market where only small amounts of coal are sold, but it is also reflected in the larger markets covered by long-term production contracts. (This subject was covered in detail in the earlier section on the "Structure of Coal Markets.") As noted above, many of the major coal users employ long-range contracts (3 to 15 years) in an attempt to secure dependable long-range fuel supplies.[2] Long-term contracts have the effect of removing coal production from the commercial market and represent at least a "dedicated" market, if not a captive one.

It was suggested[3] that the short-term or spot market has decreased in recent years and that there have been sharp increases in coal prices for this limited market. As a result, it was suggested that the coal shortage in the short-term market resulted from an understanding among the large coal companies or their parents, "so that the resulting increased prices in this thin market can be used to justify artificial upward adjustments in prices charged under long-term contracts."[4]

This matter may be examined further by noting that coal mines vary greatly in capacity. A total of nearly two-thirds of national production comes from large mines. These larger mines are highly mechanized. Mechanization requires a significant investment in equipment:

The capital investment required for mechanization which makes possible comparatively high productivity rates, also represents fixed charges which often raise unit costs when recession [or any other cause] brings about curtailment in the operating periods. This is what may be called the Achilles Heel of mechanization .... The competitive pressure [of those *smaller operators*] who remain [in operation during periods of stress] is like a bite at the heels of the larger mechanized units, if it contributes to reduction in their operating time. Moreover, it is like two bites if the tentative terms of large contracts held by the mechanized units of the industry are threatened with shifts in unit realization prices as well as in income.[5]

In the period since passage of the Federal Coal Mine Health and Safety Act of 1969, a reduction in productivity of about 20 to 25 percent was noted[5] as operators changed their practices to comply with the act. As the foregoing quote illustrates, this reduction in operating time hits especially hard at mechanized mines with high fixed costs. One way to cover these increased costs relative to desirable earnings is to raise prices. The spot market (coal sold FOB at the mine directly to consumers) is generally used by coal producers as a basis for establishing contract prices under new or renegotiated short-term and long-term contract sales.

[1]See, for example, Soft Coal Prices Soared 118.5% in 3 months; Marginally Efficient Mines are Reopening, *Wall St. J.*, p. 2, Feb. 8, 1974.

[2]R. Moyer, "Competition in the Midwestern Coal Industry," Harvard, Cambridge, Mass., 1964.

[3]W. Rowley, testimony before U.S. Senate Subcommittee on Special Small Business Problems on the Select Committee on Small Business, July 13, 1971.

[4]C. L. Christensen, "Economic Redevelopment in Bituminous Coal," Harvard, Cambridge, Mass., 1962.

[5]J. W. Straton, "Productivity and Cost Changes 1969−1971 resulting from P. L. 91−173," AIME Meeting, San Francisco, Feb. 21, 1972.

Table 8 Patterns of coal shipment and use

State	(1) Total coal produced for electric utilities	(2) Indigenous coal used in state of production	(3) Exported coal to other states (1)−(2)	(4) Total electric utility coal use	(5) Imports from other states (4)−(2)	(6) Imports from other countries	(7) Total imports (5)+(6)
			Coal-producing states				
Ala.	13,385	11,639	1,746	19,324	7,685	37	7,722
Ariz.	7,218	3,398	3,820	4,148	750		
Ark.	10		10				
Colo.	4,437	4,119	318	6,391	2,272		
Ill.	49,250	21,218	28,032	33,999	12,781		
Ind.	22,940	18,896	4,044	30,968	12,072		
Iowa	601	601		5,509	4,908		
Kan.	2,060	1,683	377	3,230	1,547		
Ky.	100,941	21,664	79,277	25,483	3,819		
Md.	1,372	533	839	3,687	3,154		
Mo.	3,951	3,776	175	17,826	14,050		
Mont.	21,377	1,197	20,180	1,197			
N. Dak.	6,900	4,611	2,289	4,777	166		
N. Mex.	7,765	7,185	580	7,185			
Ohio	39,607	29,114	10,493	46,860	17,746		
Okla.	1,814		1,814				
Pa.	42,003	30,070	11,933				
Tenn.	7,485	4,850	2,635	24,493	19,643		
Tex.	9,146	9,146		9,146			
Utah	3,371	1,955	1,416	1,955			
Va.	13,869	2,374	11,495	4,022	1,648		
Wash.	4,200	4,200		4,200			
W. Va.	43,924	21,221	22,703	26,293	5,072		
Wyo.	21,591	7,235	14,356	7,235			
Total	429,217	210,685	218,532	323,376	111,692	37	7,722

	Coal-consuming states			
Del.	971	971		
D.C.	93	93		
Fla.	5,427	5,427	331	5,758
Ga.	14,502	14,502	205	493
Mass.	288	288		
Mich.	21,361	21,361		
Minn.	8,767	8,767		
Miss.	1,531	1,531		
Neb.	1,509	1,509		
Nev.	4,476	4,476		
N.H.	977	977		
N.J.	2,332	2,332		
N.Y.	5,971	5,971		
N.C.	19,741	19,741		
S.C.	4,479	4,479		
S. Dak.	1,822	1,822		
Vt.	8	8		
Wis.	11,553	11,553		
Total	105,808	105,808	573	6,251

Table 9 Summary of patterns of coal shipment for electric utility use (1975)

	Million tons
1. Coal consumed in the state where it was produced	211
2. Coal exported from one coal-producing state but consumed in another coal-producing state	112
3. Total coal consumed in coal-producing states	323
4. Coal consumed in non-coal-producing states (including imports from abroad)	106
5. Total electric utility industry coal shipments	429

The coal price situation may be further illustrated by the following quotation:[1]

It quickly became apparent that compliance with the provisions of the [Federal Coal Mine Health and Safety Act of 1969] entailed markedly higher operating costs, the degree of increase depending on the mining circumstances. The inability or unwillingness of many mine operators to comply fully with the new provisions, moreover, led to the closing of many mines for various periods of time until compliance was achieved. At the same time, the industry was plagued by a rash of critically-timed wildcat strikes that cut back output. On top of all this, there occurred a sudden surge in Japanese demand for Eastern metallurgical coal. *We are told by electric utility buyers that this involved what can fairly be described as panic buying, in which price and quality were almost irrelevant,* not only diverting a significant portion of steam coal production to the export market, but tying up hopper cars which otherwise would have moved domestic shipments. The result was an extremely sharp increase in spot coal prices and many instances of nondelivery under long-term contracts, until their price, too, underwent adjustment. [Emphasis added.]

The shrinkage of the spot market in recent years has led to increased prices, and this was accentuated during the early 1970s, leading to higher prices in an attempt to cover the costs associated with decreased productivity. However, the increase in coal prices during the early 1970s was "phenomenal"; February 1974 prices were more than 118 percent higher than November 1973 prices.

The increase in coal prices may have been in anticipation of further costs to comply with new legislation, as well as to increase profits. "If you think the price of coal is high now, wait until the mines are forced to buy all the expensive mining equipment to replace the present nonpermissible equipment."[2]

The overall coal price situation was examined by the American Public Power Association, and their conclusion was as follows:

When full consideration is given to the unusual trends that have recently taken place in the coal industry

The takeover of large independent coal companies by large oil and other powerful industrial concerns,

The insistence by these companies that long-term contracts be signed with the questionable explanation that this is necessary to satisfy the money lenders,

The resulting removal of coal supplies from the spot and short-term market, and

The sharp price increases that would be expected to occur in a more limited market,

it is quite likely that there could be some agreement or understanding to create a coal shortage in the spot or short-term market so that the resulting increased prices in this thin market can be used to justify an artificial upward adjustment in prices charged under long-term contracts. This would be a convenient mechanism for raising prices, since long-term contracts are normally based in part upon prevailing and prospective prices in the spot market at the time the long-term contract is negotiated. Thus, these recent developments suggest the possible existence of conspiratorial activities which were undertaken for the purpose of increasing the profit of the coal companies for the benefit of their new parents.

[1] C. D. McDowell, statement before the Subcommittee on Special Small Business Problems of the Select Committee on Small Business, U.S. House of Representatives, October 1970.
[2] National Economic Research Associates, "Fuels for the Electric Utility Industry, 1971–1985," 173p, 1972.

Clearly, the above quotation represents an opinion that remains to be substantiated or refuted through analytical processes. Unfortunately, it appears to be widespread, even without proof. Without such proof, it is probably counterproductive to ascribe conspiratorial actions to coal producers. It is more likely that these events represent the normal response of tough-minded business executives to the prevailing market and institutional conditions in ordinary pursuit of a satisfactory return. Although it is rather easy to imagine all sorts of nefarious schemes leading to enormous profits—and the history of the coal industry is not without its share of unscrupulous operators—there does not appear to be, at present, firm evidence to sustain the suggestions alluded to above. It is included here only to illustrate commonly voiced concerns about coal industry operations, not to imply endorsement, because facts for an objective evaluation are lacking. This conclusion is consistent with the results of a more recent study of coal prices,[1] which found that:

> Utilities committed to burning coal by past investment decisions had little alternative in 1974 but to purchase coal in a market in which the price was soaring, regardless of whether they had a fuel adjustment clause.

Further, it was found that:

> The recent price behavior in [the coal] industry was consistent with what would be expected in a competitive natural resource market that had experienced sudden increases in demand.
>
> In a natural-resource market where short-run supply elasticity is low, it is reasonable to expect sudden increases in demand to produce rapid increases in price.

Figure 11 shows the pattern of electric utility coal prices for 1973 to 1975. The spot market price, higher than the contract price, experienced a threefold jump in

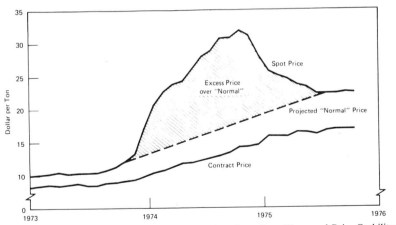

Figure 11 Electric utility steam-coal prices. (After Council on Wage and Price Stability, "A Study of Coal Prices," March 1976.)

[1]"A Study of Coal Prices," Council on Wage and Price Stability, Staff Report, 97 pages, March 1976.

1974 following the Arab oil embargo and the anticipated UMWA strike. While the spot market price declined in late 1975, it still was more than double the early 1973 levels.

Contract prices also increased in this interval of time, approaching a doubling also. It appears that contract prices tend to rise toward the ceiling represented by spot market prices, as suggested earlier. As a result of these events, both the spot price and the contract price are now greatly increased.

Historically, spot prices and contract prices have moved, roughly, together. To be sure, spot market prices are subject to wider fluctuations than contract prices. However, if it is assumed that the "normal" situation would be for trends of both prices to be parallel, then it is possible to measure the magnitude of the difference between actual and normal prices (which is realized as profit by coal producers selling in the spot market). Actually, this is an oversimplified analysis; it probably represents minimum profits, because it is not at all apparent that the projected normal spot price would rise at the rate indicated under more stable conditions.

Figure 12 presents monthly patterns in steam-coal purchase quantities and price by type of purchase. The figure shows that the largest quantities (on the order of 25 to 35 million tons per month) are purchased through contracts of varying types and duration. The average price of contract purchases ranged between 30 and 80 cents per million Btu during the period sampled. In contrast, much smaller quantities were sold through spot purchases (from 4 to 10 million tons per month). The average price of spot market purchases ranged from 40 and 150 cents per million Btu during the same time.

In an attempt to analyze the difference between contract and spot purchase prices, the average monthly price per million Btu was divided by the monthly tonnage to obtain an index value relating price, quality, and quantity. The index value

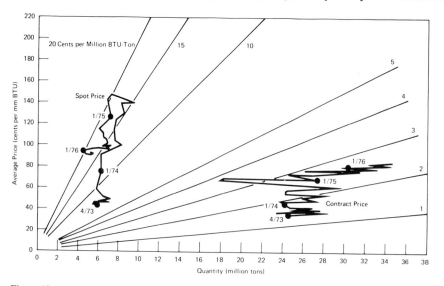

Figure 12 Monthly patterns in steam-coal purchase quantities and prices. (From Federal Power Commission, Form 423.)

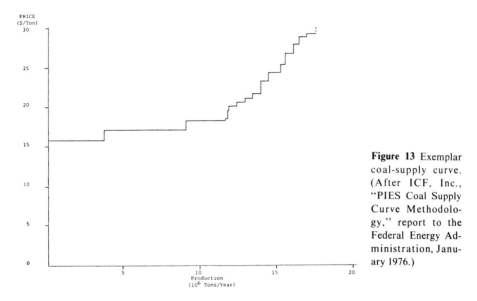

Figure 13 Exemplar coal-supply curve. (After ICF, Inc., "PIES Coal Supply Curve Methodology," report to the Federal Energy Administration, January 1976.)

is in derived units of "cents per million Btu-ton," employed for comparison only (as shown by diagonal lines on the figure). The presence of tons in the denominator indicates that the quantity of coal production has a major influence on cost, essentially independent of quality. The figure shows that, using this index value, contract prices in the last 2 years ranged from 2 to 3 cents per million Btu-ton. In contrast, spot prices were from 5 to 10 times greater, ranging from 15 to 20 cents per million Btu-ton. Thus, while electric utilities may well be justified in purchasing one-fifth of their coal supplies on the spot market, they may expect to pay from 5 to 10 times as much as contract prices for this privilege. In looking toward the future, it hardly seems reasonable to expect that many utilities would wish to expose themselves to such large price differentials for any but a very small portion of their coal supplies (and then only when absolutely necessary). As a result, it appears reasonable to conclude that the recently observed shrinkage of the spot market (Figure 10) may well continue, perhaps down to one-tenth of the total purchases or even less.

Coal-supply curves (relating quantities of coal producible at indicated prices) were derived for several different coal types and regions.[1] These data provide a systematic basis for translating coal reserve estimates into potential production amounts at increasing price levels. An illustrative supply curve for low-sulfur coal from the northern Appalachian region is presented as Figure 13. The figure shows that quantities are small, and that prices are relatively steady until about three-quarters of the reserves are exhausted, whereupon a rather marked increase in prices takes place. Similar curves are available for other coal types and other regions.

[1]ICF, Incorporated, "PIES Coal Supply Curve Methodology," final report to Federal Energy Administration, January 1976.

Table 10 Summary of sensitivity-analysis results

Scenarios	Percentage change from base case price		
	High	Average*	Low
Cost factors:			
20% increase in capital costs	9.9	7.0	4.7
20% increase in labor costs	7.9	6.0	4.0
20% increase in power & supplies cost	5.9	3.7	2.0
20% decline in productivity	16.7	8.4	1.7
20% increase in required rate of return	7.5	4.9	2.7
5% factor cost inflation with 13.4% rate of return	5.6	3.6	1.6
6% labor inflation; 5% capital power and supplies inflation; 13.4% rate of return	9.6	8.3	7.1
Reserve factors:			
20% lower demonstrated reserves	11.6†	3.8	0.0
20% higher committed reserves	45.6†	6.9	0.0
20% lower recovery factors	14.6†	3.5	0.0
20% of uncommitted surface reserves illegal to mine	6.2	2.4	0.0
20% higher marginal overburden ratio and 20% thinner marginal seam thickness	26.4‡	5.5	0.0
Smaller allowable deep mines	23.9‡	8.6	0.0

*Simple average of percentage increases over the cases analyzed.
†Result for central Appalachia low-sulfur coal.
‡Result for northern Appalachia high-sulfur coal.

The coal-supply curves are rather insensitive to any particular factor.[1] Table 10 shows that varying *cost factors* by as much as 20 percent rarely leads to changes in price by more than 10 percent. The lone exception is for deep mines with low output per miner-day which show a significant price increase to a productivity decline. *Reserve factors* have a potentially greater impact on prices, especially within a given region or coal type. Clearly, uncertainty in reserve magnitude or character can have a major impact on resulting coal prices. (Note that reserve factors uniformly influence prices on the high side. It would not be unreasonable to suggest that reserve owners could employ uncertainty about reserve magnitude, degree of development or commitment, recoverability, and mining conditions to set their prices toward the upper limit of the indicated range over the base price. This, of course, could lead to returns that are significantly in excess of costs, greatly complicating the task of analyzing coal prices.)

Figures 14 and 15 present estimated minimum acceptable selling prices per ton from surface and deep mines, respectively, as reported by ICF, Incorporated. The figures show that:

[1]ICF, Incorporated, "Coal Supply Curve Sensitivity Analysis," draft report to EPRI, September 1976.

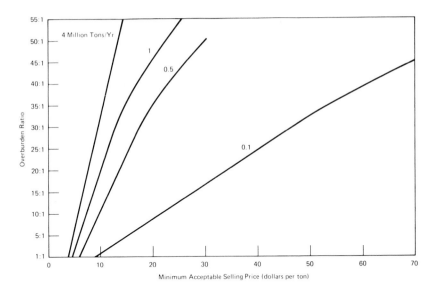

Figure 14 Estimated minimum acceptable selling price for raw coal from strip mines (1975 dollars per ton, FOB mine). (From ICF, Inc., "PIES Coal Supply Curve Methodology," report to the Federal Energy Administration, January 1976.)

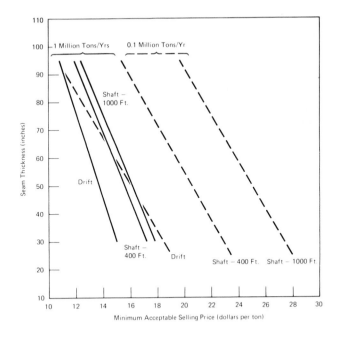

Figure 15 Estimated minimum acceptable selling price for raw coal from deep mines (1975 dollars per ton, FOB mine). (From ICF, Inc., "PIES Coal Supply Curve Methodology," report to the Federal Energy Administration, January 1976.)

1. Surface mining prices for larger mines (0.5 million tons per year and greater) are less than $20 per ton for overburden ratios up to 30:1. However, the smallest surface mines have prices more than double those of larger mines at the same overburden ratios. Therefore great care is required in analyzing prospective prices; the minimum acceptable selling prices of smaller mines could well serve as the ceiling toward which the prices of larger mines may rise. Any prices above the minimum acceptable would result in enhanced profits for operators of the larger properties (further accentuated because these profits would be applied to a higher volume of output). While it does not seem likely that prices of 4 million ton per year mines could rise toward those of a 0.1 million ton per year mine, it is plausible to consider prices rising to the level of a 1 million ton per year mine (a difference of one-fifth to one-quarter, depending on overburden level). If the 4 million ton per year mine were able to obtain the price of a 1 million ton per year operation, the excess price over its minimum acceptable would be retained as profit. Owing to uncertainties as to mining conditions and reserves, the buyer would have no effective means of independently verifying that the negotiated price was, in fact, not excessive.

2. A similar situation appears to be present for deep mines. Figure 15 shows estimated minimum acceptable selling prices for two illustrative sizes of deep mines with a range of entry types. The deep mines have somewhat higher prices than surface mines (except for the smallest surface mines). As with surface mines, smaller deep mines have higher minimum acceptable selling prices than larger mines. In this case, however, higher prices are found for thinner seams and for those seams of all thicknesses at greater depth. Again, it is possible to postulate that the higher prices of smaller deep mines could serve as a ceiling toward which the prices of larger deep mines may rise. In practice, however, it is reasonable to expect that prices among mines with the same thickness but different depth could be used to achieve greater prices than the minimum acceptable. For example, if a mine in a 72-inch seam at a 400-foot depth were to charge prices equivalent to one in the same thickness of seam at a 1000-foot depth, the price would be roughly 50 cents per ton greater. If prices were charged on the basis of a slightly smaller mine at the same depth (not shown), the price would be more than $1 greater.

In view of the above, it is of obvious importance for the electric utility industry to have its own means of evaluating the validity of prospective coal price agreements to avoid the potential for being overcharged.

Figure 16 shows trends in fuel cost to utilities for electric generation over the past quarter coal prices. Coal's increase is not as great as that for oil (or as it would be for natural gas in the absence of regulations for price controls). Rising fuel prices have had an important impact on total electric utility finances. Figure 17 shows trends in fuel prices as a percentage of total operating revenues. Stable for about 20 years, fuel prices have increased by about 50 percent in recent years, and now constitute approximately one-quarter of total revenues, on the average. However, as shown in Figure 18, the situation is even worse in some power systems, where fuel costs are one-third or more of total operating revenues.

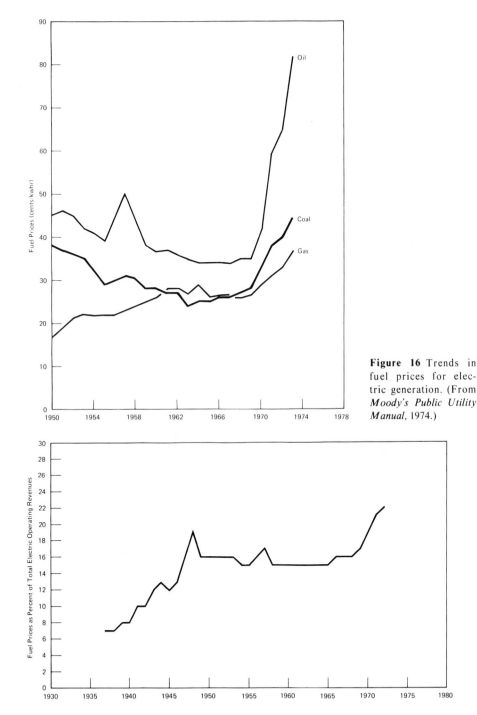

Figure 16 Trends in fuel prices for electric generation. (From *Moody's Public Utility Manual,* 1974.)

Figure 17 Trends in fuel prices as percentage of total electric operating revenues. (From *Moody's Public Utility Manual,* 1974.)

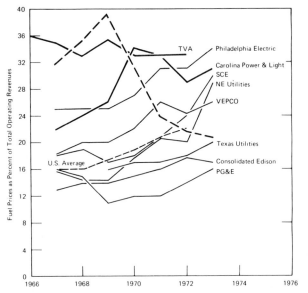

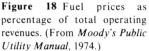

Figure 18 Fuel prices as percentage of total operating revenues. (From *Moody's Public Utility Manual*, 1974.)

The impact of increased fuel prices upon electric utilities operating costs has been severe. A rash of requests for rate increases related, at least in large part, to higher fuels prices has resulted, with rates charged by the nation's 50 largest utilities increased by an average of 55.4 percent during the first six months of 1974.[1] In part, this increase in rates is required to maintain utility revenues to ensure ability to meet foreseeable generating needs.[2]

OUTLOOK FOR COAL PRODUCTION AND USE
Present Conditions

Figure 19 displays the patterns of coal production and utilization for an exemplar year (1973), as evidenced in published statistics of the National Coal Association. Raw coal production from all mining methods in that year totaled 725 million tons. Roughly half the total was used directly without beneficiation; almost all this coal was used by electric utilities. This means that electric utility facilities were largely designed to handle the characteristics of raw coal. In view of the fact that coal preparation has as its purpose the enhancement of coal properties and removal of certain mineral constituents, the preparation process actually yields a different coal from the raw feed. It is not at all apparent that the prepared coal could be employed with comparable operating efficiency in power plants designed and operated on certain raw coals.

The beneficiation process results in the rejection of approximately 25 percent of

[1] Nation's Utility Rates Up 55.4 Percent, *San Jose Mercury*, p. 57, September 1974.
[2] Utilities Ask Rate Rises to Maintain Revenue as Customers Head Urgings to Save Energy, *Wall St. J.*, Jan. 7, 1974.

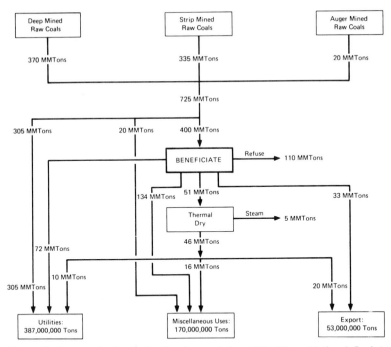

Figure 19 Coal production and utilization statistics, 1973. (From National Coal Association, *Coal Data,* 1974.)

the raw coal feed as refuse. Only about one-quarter of beneficiated coal is used by electric utilities. Nearly two-thirds of beneficiated coal goes to other industrial uses. The remaining one-fifth of beneficiated coal is exported.

The largest magnitudes of coal are (1) raw coals used directly by electric utilities without beneficiation, (2) beneficiated but not thermally dried coals, used in other industries, and (3) refuse resulting from the beneficiation process. Coals in the first two categories are consumed, but refuse is nominally discarded near coal beneficiation plants.

Outlook

Under commonly projected conditions, great increases in coal production will be required to satisfy future energy demands. It was estimated in several recent studies that coal output must be double or triple its magnitude by the early 1990s (Figure 20). Most recent plans call for lower rates of growth than portions of earlier analyses, but the increase in indicated coal production is nevertheless substantial in comparison to present levels of production. Such prospective growth contains the seed of a principal historical concern of the coal industry—overcapacity.[1]

[1]See, for example, S. A. Schweitzer, "The Limits to Kentucky Coal Output—A Short Term Analysis," University of Kentucky Institute for Mining and Minerals Research, TR 81-74-IMMRZ, March 1974.

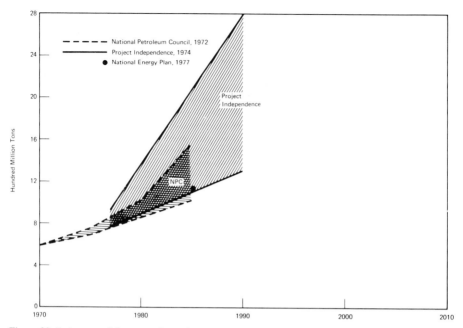

Figure 20 Estimates of future coal requirements. (From National Petroleum Council, 1972; Project Independence Blueprint, 1974; National Energy Plan, 1977.)

Trends in coal industry production as a percentage of capacity from 1890 to the present are shown in Figure 21. The older data clearly demonstrate the cyclic (boom or bust) nature of the coal industry. However, following World War II, the cycles have largely been damped out, and more effective use of production capacity has been realized.

Careful planning will be required to avoid future overcapacity, especially in view of the projected expansion of coal production to meet forecast energy requirements.

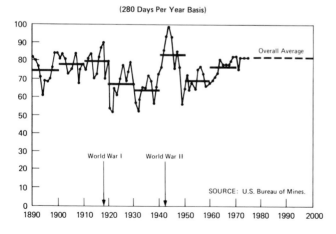

Figure 21 Trends in coal production as percentage of capacity. (From U.S. Bureau of Mines, *Miner. Yearb.*, various years.)

Expanding future coal production capacity over the short term will not be without problems. For example, an official of the National Coal Association listed the following conditions for rapid increase in coal production and use:[1] "if wildcat strikes and absenteeism ceased, if [the industry] had adequate transportation and mine supplies, air pollution control variances, price control exemption, strict but non-harassing enforcement of health and safety laws, and the continued right to produce coal from surface mines with adequate reclamation."

The nature of the assumptions stated as prerequisites for expanding coal production are such that they cannot all be realized. The conclusion therefore, seems inescapable that the coal industry foresees real difficulty in accomplishing any significant increase in output over the short term.

This conclusion is consistent with the findings of Schweitzer,[2] who noted the following problem areas in the expansion of output in the near term.

1. Effects of current and proposed government regulations.
2. Availability of productive resources, such as equipment, labor, and materials.

Further, he noted that:

The problems created by these factors include limits on industry willingness and ability both to maximize production with existing resources and to acquire additional coal-producing resources. The instability of government regulation, in fact, is probably the most burdensome of the difficulties the industry faces.

It seems clear that resolution of uncertainties about governmental regulations — or assurance that regulations will not be used as a means to harass the industry as it seeks both to comply and to carry out operations economically — is required to make progress in advancing the productive capacity of coal to meet future requirements.

This concern appears to be well-founded, if a projection by the Federal Energy Administration proves to be correct.[3] These data, shown in Figure 22, suggest that estimated production potential is greatly in excess of estimated coal demand. Using FEA data on estimated uncommitted coal production, the portions of total production potential that are committed were calculated (shown as the lowest region in Figure 22). Committed coal production is forecast to account for roughly two-thirds or more of production potential through the early 1980s. However, by the mid-1980s, roughly half the total is forecast to be uncommitted. Given the coal industry's historical concern over the prospect of overcapacity, this magnitude of projected uncommitted coal production can only be unsettling, at best. At worst, the specter of such an enormous amount of uncommitted coal production could so

[1] E. R. Phelps, testimony before Subcommittee on Minerals, Materials, and Fuels, U.S. Senate Committee on Interior and Insular Affairs, Nov. 17, 1971.

[2] A recent (and related) concern has been about the ability of the coal industry to expand coal output. See, for example, Schweitzer, *loc. cit.*

[3] Federal Energy Administration, Energy Supply and Environmental Coordination Act, Prohibition Orders; Intention to Issue to Certain Installations, *Fed. Regist.,* pt. III, pp. 22486–24519, Friday May 13, 1977.

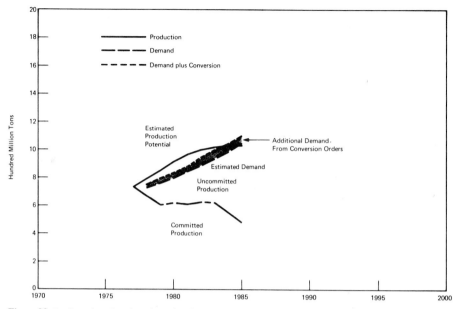

Figure 22 Projected national coal production. (From Federal Energy Administration, *Fed. Regist.*, pt. III, pp. 22486-24519, Friday May 13, 1977.)

disrupt the coal industry as to paralyze needed actions for an orderly expansion of output in service of projected demands.

The situation at electric power plants does not seem to be as uncertain as estimated by the FEA. The Federal Power Commission estimated the status of coal-supply contracts at new power plants over the next decade.[1] It was found that more than four-fifths of the total demand in 1980 at new power plants was covered with coal-supply contracts, and that two-thirds of the 1985 demand was covered. Applying these same percentages to requirements for existing plants leads to the overall picture for the electric utility industry shown in Figure 23. Less than one-sixth of total coal requirements in 1980 are not presently committed, according to these data, while only about one-fourth the total 1985 demand remains to be covered. In view of the time available to meet these demands, it seems reasonable to expect that the coal industry would be able to satisfy them in an orderly fashion. This analysis underscores the importance of detailed analyses of projected coal utilization patterns by sector. The following section presents one such analysis.

Detailed analysis. It was estimated by *Coal Mining and Processing*[2] that with doubled coal demand in 1985 there would be a substantial amount of uncleaned coal (1009 million tons). These data were employed to construct a projection of coal utilization patterns in 1985 (Figure 24). The figure shows that the electric utility industry is again the largest user of coal, with most of the coal not cleaned. While the

[1] Federal Power Commission, "Status of Coal Supply Contracts For New Electric Generating Units, 1976–1985," January 1977.
[2] P. 76, September 1975.

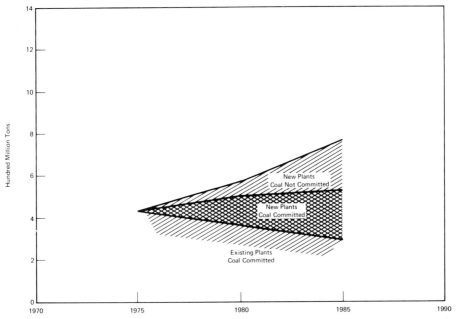

Figure 23 Status of coal-supply commitments for electric utility plants. (From Federal Power Commission)

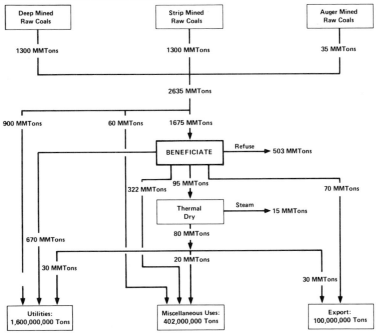

Figure 24 Projected coal production and utilization statistics—1985. (Adapted from National Coal Association, *Coal Data,* 1974; projections by writer.)

amount of coal cleaned is nearly double that cleaned in 1973, production of refuse is proportionally increased as well. Although the amount of clean coal provided to utilities is more than doubled, this is still only about one-fifth of the total estimated 1985 utility coal consumption. These data suggest that utilities will continue primarily to use raw coal, doubtless because of its lower cost and the existence of facilities designed to handle raw coal in this time period.

Figure 25 shows projected coal utilization patterns in 2000. It was assumed that by this time 55 percent of all coal would be cleaned (with 30 percent rejects, an increase over present levels), and 45 percent would not be cleaned. As before, the largest amount of uncleaned coal would continue to be used by electric utilities. However, the amount of cleaned coal for utility use is projected to increase by nearly an order of magnitude, in an attempt to meet air quality requirements. The increased amount of beneficiated coal leads to annual production of refuse in amounts nearly as much as present-day coal production itself!

Projections such as those given above are always subject to uncertainty, given the diversity and dimensions of the industries involved. Also, projections become much more "iffy" the farther one attempts to look into the future. Therefore, the statistics given should be regarded as illustrative; whatever their actual magnitude, it seems apparent that there will be substantial increases over present levels that are bound to present problems to the electric utility industry. Some of these problems are addressed in the following section.

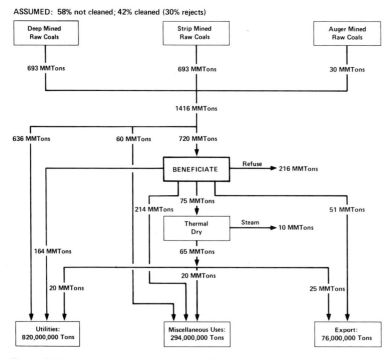

Figure 25 Projected coal production and utilization statistics—2000. (Adapted from National Coal Association, *Coal Data,* 1974; projections by writer.)

Comparison of projected coal supply and demand for electric utility use. This section presents a comparison of two recent projections of coal supply and demand for electric utility use.

Estimated future coal requirements for electric utilities in the contiguous United States were taken from data published by the National Electric Reliability Council (NERC).[1] These data give estimated total coal requirements and western coal requirements by year to 1985; eastern coal requirements were calculated by the writer (Table 11).

Estimated future coal production for electric utility use was derived from data published by the National Coal Association (NCA).[2] These data give estimated total coal production in addition to current production. Discussions with NCA personnel indicated that the end uses of this new production are expected to be similar to current production; about two-thirds of eastern coal will be dedicated to steam uses and about one-third to metallurgical uses, while essentially all western coal will be for steam. To derive estimated coal production for electric utility requirements, these factors were employed in recalculating the totals published by NCA.

The following assumptions were used in estimating future coal supply:

1. The supply base of eastern steam coal (established production) was assumed to be 352 million tons. To allow for depletion of established production operations, this amount was reduced by 3 percent per year (the average historical depletion rate). See Table 12.
2. The supply base of western steam coal was assumed to be 77 million tons. This amount was not reduced for depletion, because it is "new" production and depletion is not anticipated in the next 10 years.
3. Planned or additional tonnages compiled by the NCA must be reduced by 20 percent to allow for actual capacity utilization (refer to Figure 21). Because of labor, maintenance, transportation, or other problems, an 80 percent capacity utilization factor is experienced.

The resulting estimates of new coal production were added to the supply base to obtain the total estimated coal supply for electric utilities in the next decade. Table 13 shows estimated electric utility coal requirements. The data are illustrated in Figure 26. The figure shows that coal supply and demand for electric utility use is projected to be in a delicate balance for the next decade.

To be sure, it is important to note NCA's caution that estimated coal-supply additions are rather uncertain past 1981. Note further that the situation indicated by the data in Figure 26 is conservative: the projected coal supply from the East is expected to remain at its present level, with additions to production merely

[1] National Electric Reliability Council, "Fossil and Nuclear Fuel for Electric Utility Generation: Requirements and Constraints, 1976–1985," p. 27, June 1976.

[2] National Coal Association, "A Study of New Mine Additions and Major Expansion Plans of the Coal Industry," manuscript, August 1976.

Table 11 Estimated coal supply by region (million tons)

Region	1976	1977	1978	1979	1980	1981	1982	1983	1984	1985	1986
East (supply):											
Base	352	341	331	321	311	302	293	284	276	267	259
Additions	19	20	19	16	13	13	18	10	9	6	5
Total*	371	380	389	395	398	402	411	412	413	410	407
West (supply):											
Base	77	77	77	77	77	77	77	77	77	77	77
Additions	27	35	39	46	31	33	23	20	15	6	3
Total*	104	139	178	224	255	288	311	331	346	352	355
Total utility coal supply	475	519	567	619	653	690	722	743	759	762	762

*Totals = base supply − depletion where applicable + cumulative additions.

Table 12 Coal mine expansions planned, announced, or under construction (million tons)

Year	Reported new production capacity (gross)			Estimated net new capacity after allowance for replacement*		
	East	West	Total	East	West	Total
1976	18.88	26.66	45.54	3.38	26.66	30.04
1977	19.61	34.81	54.42	4.61	34.81	39.42
1978	19.10	38.50	57.60	4.10	38.50	42.60
1979	15.51	46.30	61.81	0.51	46.30	46.81
1980	13.13	31.30	44.43	0	31.30	31.30
1981	13.30	32.70	46.00	0	32.70	32.70
1982	17.71	22.50	40.21	2.71	22.50	25.21
1983	9.95	19.60	29.55	0	19.60	19.60
1984	8.45	15.20	23.65	0	15.20	15.20
1985	6.35	5.60	11.95	0	5.60	5.60
1986	4.90	3.10	8.00	0	3.10	8.00
Total	146.88	276.27	423.15	15.31	276.27	291.58

*"Eastern additions must be discounted by approximately 15 to 17 million tons annually to allow for replacement of existing mining capacity." The lower figure (15 million tons) is used in this table. Where reported new capacity in the East is less than 15 million tons, it is assumed that *all* such capacity is replacement.

Source: National Coal Association, "A Study of New Mine Additions and Major Expansion Plans of the Coal Industry," manuscript, August 1976.

Table 13 Estimated electric utility coal requirements (thousand tons)

Year	(1) Estimated coal requirements*	(2) Projected coal consumption†	(3) Excess requirements over consumption (added to stocks) (1)−(2)	(4) ICF alternative consumption projection	(5) Excess requirements over consumption (1)−(4)	(6) Excess requirements as % consumption (3)−(2) × 100
1975	404,093					
1976	447,259	438,200	9,059	438,200	9,059	2
1977	481,969	466,500	15,469	464,700	17,269	3
1978	535,536	499,600	35,936	495,000	40,536	7
1979	575,906	538,900	37,006	531,100	44,806	7
1980	623,853	585,900	37,953	577,400	46,453	6
1981	665,966	627,500	38,466			6
1982	704,953	664,200	40,753			6
1983	737,815	701,300	36,515			5
1984	780,069	735,900	44,169			6
1985	826,680	771,800	54,880			7

*National Electric Reliability Council, "Fossil and Nuclear Fuel for Electric Utility Generation, Requirements and Constraints, 1976−1985, P. 27, June 1976.

†ICF, Inc., "Electric Utility Coal Consumption and Generation Trends, 1976−1985," final report to Federal Energy Administration, p. 42, August 1976.

compensating for depletion of present mines. It may be expected that expanded development of eastern coal would take place in the event that flue gas desulfurization units are required on all coal-using facilities. Located in the midst of the primary coal market, eastern coal would have a substantial advantage over western coal under such conditions. Assuming that total projected coal demand was unchanged, then expanded eastern coal production would tend to reduce the magnitude of western coal development. In short, Figure 26 represents the *minimum* amount of eastern coal production in the next decade, and the *maximum* amount of western coal development. The actual production will probably fall somewhere between these estimates.

Although the above data (especially Figure 26) shows overall production in excess of consumption, there are important regional differences, particularly in the East.

ICF also points out that:

Excess production capacity occurs when planned production is in excess of projected consumption and represents any potential production without a buyer. It does not mean that any of this excess will actually be mined. . . . If consumption and stocks cannot absorb planned production, then production cutbacks will occur. Cutbacks could take several forms, including low spot market prices, early mine closings, delays and/or cancellations of new mine capacity, and cutbacks at existing mines.[1]

These effects of excess production capacity are all too well-known by the coal industry, which has a long history of boom and bust conditions brought on by just such a situation. Consequently, it does not seem reasonable for coal producers to knowingly expose themselves to the risk that overcapacity may occur, bringing with it the traditional adverse impacts upon coal company operations and viability. Clearly, this issue is of central importance to coal producers and consumers.

Recent purchases by electric utilities of relatively low-rank subbituminous coal indicate that [environmental] constraints are already limiting production of higher-rank bituminous coal . . . it is possible to conclude that "price leadership" has, in effect, shifted to the producers of the low-rank subbituminous coal. The relative abundance of the low-rank coal insures that for the foreseeable future, price will be determined by the costs and constraints affecting the production and transport of

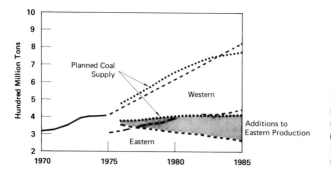

Figure 26 Comparison of projected coal supply and demand for electric utility use. (From National Electric Reliability Council and National Coal Association.)

[1]ICF, Inc., "Production and Consumption of Coal, 1976–1980," report to the Federal Energy Administration, May 1976.

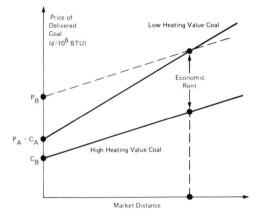

Figure 27 Relationship between economic rent and market distance. (After J.G. Asbury and K.W. Costello, "Price and Availability of Western Coal in the Midwestern Market," American Society of Mechanical Engineers, Preprint No. 76-IPC-PWR—7, 1976.)

this coal. *Although production of higher rank [lower cost] coal will continue, the owners and producers of this coal can be expected to maximize their "economic rents" by raising their mine prices to levels that bring the price of their delivered coal into line with the price of delivered low-rank coal.* As Figure [27] illustrates, because the economic rent increases with market distance, it is in the interest of the holders of higher [heating value] coal to seek out the more distant markets. [Emphasis added.][1]

It would appear, therefore, that producers of eastern coal may be able to compensate for the slow rate of growth relative to western coal by using expanded western production as a means to capture their economic rent, principally from the electric utility industry. It would be also reasonable to conclude that eastern coal producers have the capability to eliminate the indicated supply deficit of eastern coal (probably at the inflated "economic rent" price levels, so they could win out either way).

In view of this situation, it is difficult to escape the conclusion that there are a number of diverse factors that exert important influences over coal development. These factors are examined in the next chapter.

[1]J. G. Asbury and K. W. Costello, "Price and Availability of Western Coal in the Midwestern Market," presented at Power Division of American Society of Mechanical Engineers, Industrial Power Conference, Memphis, Tenn., May 16-19, 1976. Preprint 76-IPC-PWR-7.

SIXTEEN

FACTORS INFLUENCING COAL DEVELOPMENT

Principal factors influencing coal development may be categorized as follows:

1. Reserve quantity and quality
2. Mining, production, and transportation
3. Availability of critical resources
4. Appropriate labor participation
5. Access to capital
6. Research and development

It is common to encounter discussion of these factors under the general heading of "constraints" to coal production. Actually, however, as pointed out in Chapter 8, the coal industry is dynamic and situations may be reversed (or at least greatly altered) in a short time; what may appear to be a constraint at one period may no longer be one later. Each of these factors merely represents an element of a complex, interlocking system which must function in a coordinated fashion to accomplish coal production. None of them is inherently a constraint upon operations; neither is any factor necessarily an incentive for coal development. Successful ventures require a balanced linkage of these several factors, which are briefly described in this chapter.

RESERVE QUANTITY AND QUALITY

Coal reserves required to support large-capacity modern mines are substantial. To be minable with efficient, mechanized equipment by either deep or surface mining methods, the reserves must be in a contiguous block and of sufficient magnitude to support the mining operations (and/or the facilities which consume the coal) for at least 20 years. For example, with a 5-foot-thick seam in the eastern coalfields, and a requirement for about 15,000 tons per day to supply a plant, the total reserve over a 20-year lifetime would be about 1800 million tons; in terms of area, this would cover roughly 45 square miles. The greater thicknesses of western coal deposits would require proportionally smaller areas.

It seems clear that it would be no simple task to assemble such large blocks of reserves if one had to start from scratch. This is especially true in the East where there are a large number of small reserve blocks owned by different persons. Still, even in the East there are sizable, contiguous areas of coal reserves held or controlled by coal mining companies as a result of acquisitions or leases dating back to the early part of this century or before. These reserves could possibly be targets for development to supply coal to existing or projected coal-processing units in the future. An important question that clouds the potential use of eastern coal reserves is the extent to which they may be committed to special-purpose uses for which there is no effective substitute at present.

In the West, the land-ownership pattern is far different. Large blocks of coal-bearing lands are owned by the federal government. These public lands are typically interspersed with lands held by private organizations in a "checkerboard" pattern according to alternate sections of the township and range system of surveying. Although the problem for the coal developers who seek to work western coal deposits is simplified in that they have only a few coal-owning organizations to deal with, the fact that the largest acreages are publicly owned means that major questions of public policy must be decided before rights to develop the reserves can be conveyed and operations begun. While obvious targets for future development, it remains to be seen if the questions regarding access to public coal lands in the West will be resolved in a fashion and at a time to permit orderly development to proceed.

Market conditions also exert an important influence on the manner of coal reserve development, especially for less readily mined deposits.[1]

> The vigor in which the less accessible reserves are recovered by the mining industry depends largely on the condition of the coal market at the time of mining. Hence, during a buyer's market, the commercially-oriented mining industry is compelled to mine the easier and less costly reserves. Conversely, during a seller's market, the need to rapidly expand production results in more difficult mining and higher cost coal as few obstacles are encountered in finding markets. Hence, a seller's market tends to enhance the recovery of reserves while a buyer's market does not.

Christensen further noted that there is:

> . . . a need for a more realistic estimate of those reserves of coal that are likely to be mined in the future. Such estimates should not be limited to the compilation of the amount of reserves in the ground; but, where possible, should also include information concerning the ability for producing these reserves.

So far, the discussion has concentrated on the ownership of lands and the relative quantity of coal that may be developed. It is also vital to examine coal quality

---

[1]C. L. Christensen, "Economic Redevelopment in Bituminous Coal," Harvard, Cambridge, Mass., 1962.

in this regard. For example, Leonard[1] noted that "in close parallel with the reserve problem is the need to develop better methods for the characterization of coal seams and associated lithotypes, based on drill core data, once an area is selected for mining."

Details on the sulfur content of coal reserves are either very generalized according to major area (East versus West) or very specific according to seam or mine.[2] There appears to be a need for better data on a regional or local area basis. As Chapter 3 shows, a more precise public definition of coal reserves appears to be essential as a means to guide future efforts in coal development and use. In this context, what is required is further data or physical as well as chemical characteristics. The emphasis on sulfur content should not ignore other coal constituents which could influence its efficienty or cost of use. As noted by the Bureau of Mines,[3]

> To a great degree, increased knowledge of the inherent coal characteristics allows boiler designers to capitalize on those characteristics and to design units specifically to take advantage of heretofore undesirable coals.

Still, the degree of coal substitution that can be achieved is limited.[4]

> Replacement of coal supplies, currently being moved preferentially to wet-bottom furnaces, with coal of low sulfur content is not a simple coal substitution. While some of the lower sulfur coals could be expected to possess ash fusion temperatures compatible to wet-bottom furnaces, the *bulk of those quality coals would have ash-fusion temperature well above the 2600° F limit and be totally unsuited to continuous boiler operation.* [*Emphasis added.*]

These remarks are especially directed at the problems of using western coal in eastern facilities that were designed and built for coal of different characteristics.

Although the Bureau of Mines attempted to relate broad coal properties to types of combustion systems,[5] the amounts and locations of coal reserves having these properties remains to be established with the necessary prevision. As a result, it is possible that future engineering efforts could succeed in developing an efficient process or apparatus which could not operate to its optimum design conditions because of a lack of coal having the requisite properties. In some respects, this appears to have occurred in the past, contributing in part to the present situation. Clearly, the availability of coal reserves with specific properties and characteristics needs to be determined with considerable precision to make most effective use of coal in the future. The present state of knowledge about the quality of coal reserves thus also represents an important influence on expansion of coal production in the future.

[1] J. W. Leonard and D. R. Mitchell, "Coal Preparation," chap. 7, AIME, New York, 1968.
[2] National Petroleum Council, "U.S. Energy Outlook", December 1972.
[3] U.S. Bureau of Mines, "Restrictions on the Uses of Coal," manuscript, 57 pages, June 1971.
[4] *Ibid.*
[5] *Ibid.*

MINING, PRODUCTION, AND TRANSPORTATION

After coal reserves have been discovered, delineated, and evaluated, "the next step is to select a mining method that is physically, economically, and environmentally adaptable to recovering [the coal] from the deposit. . .the spatial characteristics of the [coal] and surrounding rock limit the methods that can be employed to mine it."[1] With regard to coal mining methods, it is noted that:[2]

> A popular thesis suggests that the proper approach to selecting the method of mining should be rooted in the inverse solution, whereby the limitations of various methods in use serve as criteria to eliminate most of these methods from consideration in the specific case. . . . Although such a negative approach unquestionably is valid in discarding obviously inapplicable mining systems from consideration, it falls short in defining the best system, which in practice quite often turns out to be a variation of a textbook standard, or a combination of two or more such standards.

In the first instance, then, the geological features of the coal deposits represent an important influence upon the application of mining methods; for example; it was noted earlier that deep mining methods developed to work the thin seams of the East are not applicable to the thick seams of western deposits. This represents a potential constraint to their development, requiring R&D for development of new technology to allow these deposits to be recovered. Still, as a part of the examination of the feasibility of undertaking such R&D, it will be essential to determine the magnitude of recoverable reserves in western thick seams and the relative benefits to be expected from an investment in new technology.

The use of existing technology in coal extraction is subject to a different type of constraint. These constraints were analyzed recently for the situation in Kentucky, exemplar of the nation at large: "[the] capacity of the Kentucky Coal industry to increase its output is seriously limited in the near term."[3] Two main problems were cited:

1. Effects of current and proposed government regulations
2. Availability of productive resources, such as equipment, labor and materials, and rail cars

These problems, of course, cover the production operations from beginning to end. It was noted that "the problems created by these factors include limits on industry willingness and ability both to minimize production with existing resources and to acquire additional coal producing resources."[4]

---

[1] R. G. K. Morrison, and P. L. Russell, Selecting a Mining Method —Rock Mechanics, Other Factors, in Cummins and Given (eds.), "SME Mining Engineering Handbook," vol. I, section 9, American Institute of Mining, Metallurgical, and Petroleum Engineers, New York, 1973.
[2] S. H. Boshkov, and F. D. Wright, Underground Mining Systems and Equipment, in *ibid.*, sec. 12.
[3] S. A. Schweitzer, "The Limits to Kentucky Coal Output: A Short-Term Analysis," University of Kentucky Institute for Mining and Minerals Research, TR 81-74-IMMR2, March 1974.
[4] *Ibid.*

The principal operational problems are discussed briefly below as cited by Schweitzer:

Recent government regulations of coal mining operations:[1]
1. Reduce the volume of output capacity below that which existing capital equipment and labor would be able to produce in the absence of regulation

2. Reduce the willingness of coal-mining firms to employ their equipment and labor in ways that optimize coal production

3. Reduce the ability of the industry to attract additional financial capital with which to expand its mining capacity

Although the recent legislation relative to the coal industry has been prompted by external conditions in the industry that are matters of intense public concern, the above industry reactions suggest that such changes to established patterns of operations are resisted "because all these things make mining more costly."

Most operators will endeavor to comply with the laws and regulations: "Indications are that compliance has slowed the mine owners only slightly and that workers at the face are still productive. The decline in employee productivity is almost entirely due to the fact that non-producing workers have had to be hired . . . these workers reduce the computed average tonnage per employee."[2] The principal concern over such compliance is in the added cost to operations, which of course, is a major constraint to profit.

AVAILABILITY OF CRITICAL RESOURCES

Coal development operations require assured supplies of essential equipment and materials. The magnitudes of these quantities were reviewed by the National Academy of Engineering and the Federal Energy Administration for doubled coal production by the mid-1980s.[3] Some of the main actions required to realize doubled production include (regardless of when the actions may be taken):

1. Develop 140 new 2 million ton per year eastern underground mines.
2. Develop 30 new 2 million ton per year eastern surface mines.
3. Develop 100 new 5 million ton per year western surface mines.
4. Recruit and train 80,000 new eastern coal miners.
5. Recruit and train 45,000 new western coal miners.
6. Manufacture 140 new 100 cubic yard shovels and draglines.

---

[1] Especially in deep mining as a consequence of the Federal Coal Mine Health and Safety Act of 1969, but also in surface mining as a consequence of state-level environmental protection legislation.

[2] Schweitzer, *loc. cit.*

[3] National Academy of Engineering, "U.S. Energy Prospects: An Engineering Viewpoint," 1974; also Federal Energy Administration, "Project Independence Blueprint," November 1974.

7. Manufacture 2400 continuous mining machines.
8. Manufacture 8000 railroad locomotive units.
9. Manufacture 150,000 rail cars of 100-ton capacity.

Although the magnitudes of future equipment and supply requirements for expanded coal output are great, the basic conclusion of the Project Independence Report was that the capability of manufacturers to satisfy these needs was generally "adequate" in all but the fastest growth case. Indeed, as noted in Chapter 8, many producers of mining-related equipment are experiencing overcapacity, rather than being constrained by inadequate means to meet customer demands. Similar situations appear to exist in other key aspects of the coal industry.

Attaining the projected levels of output of essential equipment and materials will require the commitment of many critical resources. To obtain a complete understanding of the effort involved in coal development, it is necessary to evaluate the commodity requirements for each stage of the conventional coal-to-electric power fuel sequence.

Estimates of the nonfuel mineral raw-material requirements for stages in the process of energy production by systems based on fossil fuels and geothermal, hydroelectric, nuclear, and solar energy were prepared recently by the U.S. Geological Survey.[1] These estimates present the magnitudes of commodities necessary to realize energy demand as forecast by the Federal Energy Administration in their Project Independence Report.[2] While useful in providing "some concept of the total amount of materials that may be required by expanded energy production in the United States," these estimates are based on a series of assumption and specifically defined "modular units," designed to support "various production scenarios" but complicating the task of evaluating commodity needs for an entire fuel sequence. Also, in their present form it is not easy to recognize patterns of commodity use across several stages of fuel utilization so that potential areas for conservation may be identified.

In an attempt to place the commodity estimates on a common basis for analysis, data presented by the U.S. Geological Survey were recalculated to express magnitudes as *tons of a commodity per million tons of coal* (*or coal equivalent*); these data are shown in Table 1 (notes to the table describe the derivation of the data). The table shows that the greatest variety of commodities is in coal mining, the least in barge transportation systems and processing plants. Total commodities required for the entire fuel sequence per million tons of coal are shown, the largest amount being for iron (steel).with the next largest being concrete and/or cement. Iron is the principal commodity in every stage of the fuel sequence but the consumption of coal in power plants (where concrete predominates per million tons of coal).

---

[1] J. P. Albers et al., Demand for Nonfuel Minerals and Materials by the United States Energy Industry, 1975−90, *US Geol. Surv. Prof. Pap.* 1006−A, 1976, and G. H. Goudarzi et al., Supply of Nonfuel Minerals and Materials for the United States Energy Industry, 1975−90, *US Geol. Surv. Prof. Pap.* 1006−B, 1976.

[2] Federal Energy Administration, Project Independence Report, November 1974. The "business-as-usual" case was employed as the basis for estimating.

Table 1 Overview of critical resources for the conventional electric utility coal-to-power fuel sequence.

Tons per million ton of coal

Commodity	Surface mine[a]	Underground mine[b]	Barges[c]	Towboats[c]	Unit trains[d]	Coal-processing plants[e]	Pulverized coal steam-electric power plants[f]	Total	Energy requirements for commodity production[g] tons coal equiv.	Total energy requirements to product commodities for coal fuel cycle, tons coal equiv/million tons coal
Aluminum	1.29	1.37		0.49	3.56			6.71	13.45	90.25
Antimony	1.47	0.63						2.10	n.a.	n.a.
Asbestos	0.20	0.06					0.14	0.40	0.38	0.15
Boron	0.07	0.01						0.08	0.48	0.04
Cadmium	0.15	0.02						0.17	n.a.	n.a.
Chromium	3.72	17.91		0.06	2.68	9.34	33.71	45.52	n.a.	152.37
Cobalt	0.05	0.02					0.83	0.90	n.a.	n.a.
Concrete	255.55	425.93				34,956.35	35,637	71,274.83	n.a.	14,967.54
Copper	47.05	30.57		1.49	38.31	1.55	166.70	285.67	6.18	1,765.44
Iron	956.97	1753.87	26,269	2,332	4,020	514.57	8,479.03	45,325	1.88	85,211.00
Lead	0.83	3.20			2.64		0.61	6.67	1.49	9.94
Magnesia							0.61	0.61	1.49	0.91
Manganese	15.15	15.02	211.86	18.80	27.29	4.13	68.41	360.66	2.73	984.60
Mica (scrap)	1.42	0.63					0.45	0.45	0.91	0.41
Molybdenum	5.67	4.35		0.03	1.06		0.45	2.50	7.99	19.98
Nickel	0.05	0.02					4.19	15.30	21.83	334.0
Nidbiom	0.02	0.01						0.07	n.a.	n.a.
Silver	0.01	0.09			0.18			0.03	n.a.	n.a.
Tin	0.05	0.02						0.28	n.a.	n.a.
Vanadium	0.05	0.02						0.18	n.a.	n.a.
Zinc	0.14	0.37					0.11	0.51	3.59	1.83
										103,537.14

a U.S.G.S. data for commodities required for a surface coal mine producing 4.5 million ton per year were divided by 4.5 to yield commodities per million ton.

b U.S.G.S. data for commodities required for a 2.7 million ton per year underground mine were divided by 2.7 to yield commodities per million ton.

c One million tons of coal transported 350 miles by barge is estimated to require 6 towboats and 107 barges. (Gibbs & Hill, Inc., "Coal Preparation for Combustion and Conversion," pp. 5–25, 1977).

d One million tons of coal transported 600 miles by unit train is estimated to require five locomotives and eighty-three 100-ton cars. (*Ibid.*, pp. 5–18).

e Coal-processing plants assumed to be equivalent to "low-Btu fuel gas, fixed-bed, atmospheric pressure" plants. (*US Geol. Surv. Prof. Paper* 1006A, p. A–7, 1976).

(1) 1600 x 10^6 std. ft^3/day x 1000 Btu/std. ft^3 = 1600 x 10^9 Btu/day

(2) 1600 x 10^9 Btu/day x 330/yr = 528 x 10^{15} Btu/yr.

(3) 528 x 10^{15} Btu/yr x ton/20 x 10^6 Btu = 26.4 x 10^6 tons coal.

f Coal-using power plants estimated to require roughly 3 million tons per 1000 megawatts. Using data from *US Geol. Surv. Prof. Paper* 1006A, 1976, the magnitude of new generating capacity assumed is equivalent to about 1 billion tons.

g Energy requirements for commodity production are taken from *US Geol. Surv. Prof. Paper* 1006B, p. B–9, 1976. Original values in MMBtu/ton were converted to tons of coal equivalent as follows:

$$\frac{10^6 \text{ Btu}}{\text{ton}} \times \frac{\text{tons coal equivalent}}{20 \times 10^6 \text{ Btu}} = \frac{\text{tons coal equivalent}}{\text{ton}}$$

Table 1 also shows estimated energy requirement (in tons of coal equivalent) to produce the several commodities. These data are employed in estimating the total energy requirements to produce commodities for the coal fuel cycle (in terms of tons of coal equivalent per million tons of coal). The calculations are explained in the notes to the table. Results show that roughly 100,000 tons of coal per million tons of production is required to produce the necessary commodities for the entire coal fuel sequence. Thus, approximately *one-tenth* of the total energy in coal must be committed to the production of essential commodities that directly support coal production and utilization operations. Clearly, the magnitudes and prospective availabilities of vital nonfuel commodities are of great importance to electric utility activities.

APPROPRIATE LABOR PARTICIPATION

No matter what technology is employed in coal production, the availability of workers with sufficient ability to be trained as miners and with a willingness to pursue mining occupations will be a determining factor in the level of production realized. Moreover, the total work force picture must include the workers in supporting industries who provide goods and services used by miners in their jobs. Thus, even the large numbers of new miners estimated to be required by the NAE report cited earlier are probably an understatement because the work force requirements of supporting industries are not included. Important as the need for new miners and new personnel may be, "even more crucial is the shortage of professionally-trained people."[1] Mining engineers are particularly in short supply, and positive actions will be required to alleviate potential adverse effects on production from shortages in technical personnel. It was noted that "recruiting young men for work in the coal mines may become increasingly more difficult because of poor public image of the industry, the hazardous nature of the work, and adverse publicity stemming from mine disasters, and the remote location of mines from readily accessible urban areas."[2]

Each of these problem areas has been recognized by the leaders of the coal industry. Thoughtful discussions of the "public image" problem have been offered. "There are indications that the problem is not so much one of a bad public image, but a lack of public understanding."[3] Major efforts have been made in recent years to inform the public about the importance of coal development as well as the responsible manner in which this development is carried out by most operators with respect to environmental quality and safety of workers. Yet, such positive efforts are too frequently blunted or countered by heavy-handed coal industry actions in other areas.

Unless present patterns are altered, it would appear that the coal industry's "image" problem will persist, leading to perpetuation of work force and other problems of an institutional nature.

[1] National Petroleum Council, *op. cit.*
[2] U.S. Bureau of Mines, *op. cit.*
[3] F. Buckner, The Coal Industry and Its Public Image, *Min. Congr. J.*, pp. 44—47, July 1970.

Technology can be employed in dealing with work force problems, at least up to a certain point. Although mechanized production equipment is highly complex, requiring very skilled personnel for its maintenance and repair, it is nevertheless true that its operation can be performed by relatively unskilled labor; "based on actual experience, another main advantage [of longwall mining] is that men with little or no mining experience can be trained much more quickly than is possible with the other types of coal mining. If the current shortage of skilled miners continues, this can be vitally important."[1] This suggests that the skill of miners required for operations is inversely proportional to the degree of mechanization represented by mining technology. Longwall mining is highly mechanized, permitting the use of relatively unskilled labor (or labor which can be trained to perform relatively simple tasks). Conventional mining, at the other extreme, is less highly mechanized, demanding highly skilled and/or experienced workers to achieve production operations. The work force problem facing the coal industry, in short, is critically related to the technologies employed in operations.

The work force required for coal production, often regarded as a "constraint" or a "problem" to expanded output, is clearly not a simple matter. As the above remarks suggest, the situation is not so much a numbers question but a concern that a sufficient work force possessing essential skills or experience (or, at least, willing to be trained in such skills) will pursue regular jobs in coal production operations. This is a far different issue than estimates of numbers of workers alone, involving both management and labor organizations as well as the individuals who seek only rewarding occupations. Clearly, such relationships are quite complex, requiring careful and detailed analyses. Probably, given sufficient reason to justify the endeavor, there will be adequate numbers of workers to operate coal production entities and assure meeting future levels of output.

ACCESS TO CAPITAL

Expansion of coal production capacity will require large capital investments. This situation "has resulted in an extremely serious problem with respect to securing adequate financing, whether for the expansion of existing facilities or the opening of new mines . . . . It is important that the coal industry recognizes that it is going to be competing in the financial markets with every other borrower."[2] This point was also made by E. B. Leisenring, Jr., of Westmoreland Coal Company,[3] who pointed out that assumption of risks by utilities would make bankers more willing to put up equity loans for mine construction. However, J. L. Williams, Jr., of TVA, maintained that while the coal purchaser should share some risks with the producer, coal companies are making unreasonable demands.

---

[1] N. Robinson, "Financing Energy Needs," presented at 1973 Mining Convention/Environmental Show of the American Mining Congress, Denver, Colo., Sept. 9–12, 1974.

[2] Cited by J. G. Phillips, Coal Industry Problems Hamper Production Goals, *Natl J. Rep.*, pp. 951–961, June 29, 1974.

[3] *Ibid.*

Escalation provisions, designed to cover every possible facet of increased cost, are being insisted upon . . . In some instances, suppliers want clauses designed to guarantee that return on investment will never go below 20 percent. Some suppliers want to renegotiate prices periodically, in order to keep the contract in line with current market prices, regardless of whether the cost of producing the coal has changed.[1]

It is interesting that coal producers would seek to establish a *floor* of 20 percent return on investment as the above quote indicates. This suggests that their present rate of return is, in fact, equal to or greater than 20 percent. Clearly, this conclusion is at variance with the conventional wisdom about the relative profitability of coal producing companies. Nevertheless, it is consistent with a recent analysis of profits in mining industries[2] which found that the return on shareholders' investment for a limited sample of coal-producing companies was about 30 percent, or roughly three times that of the typical producer of other mineral commodities. It seems reasonable that most business executives would seek to establish arrangements whereby they could continue to enjoy such a return; those that are expected to provide such profits can be expected to be most reluctant to impoverish themselves to enrich others.

The coal industry's position is that the electric utilities, which are generally allowed by state regulatory bodies to pass increased fuel costs on to consumers without a new rate hearing, are in a better position to bear the risk of loss than is the coal industry, which has experienced depressed earnings for much of the period since World War II.

Coal industry officials maintain that higher prices for coal are necessary to generate the necessary capital for its expansion. Especially during conditions of inflation as experienced at present, the capital problems facing both coal producers and consumers must be analyzed carefully and thoroughly before arriving at decisions for such major undertakings if capital is not to become a constraint upon developments.

RESEARCH AND DEVELOPMENT

Research and development activities are nominally addressed at solving technical or economic problems and are not themselves commonly regarded as a constraint. Yet, Schweitzer[3] found that with respect to coal production, "industry representatives felt that near-term problems might be obscured by the great emphasis being placed on research and development . . . ." Therefore, R&D could itself be a constraint to growth in coal production mainly because, "the prospects for new technologies defy conclusive analysis; research is risky because we cannot be sure what it will produce."[4]

---

[1] *Ibid.*

[2] E. Just, Metal Mining Profits Are Inadequate, *Min. Congr. J.,* December 1973.

[3] Schweitzer, *loc. cit.*

[4] R. L. Gordon, "Coal's Role in the Age of Environmental Concern," presented at MIT Energy Conference, January, 1973.

Coal production as an enterprise is replete with uncertainties in fundamental factors such as deposit characteristics, mining situations, worker attitudes, market economics, equipment performance, transportation availability, financing, and government regulations. Each of these factors could pose an important constraint upon coal operations, to the detriment of both producers and consumers (not to mention other groups dependent on coal for their well-being). With all these risk-producing uncertainties, it could be asked with some logic why coal developers should add a further risk through support of R&D when the outcome of that work would be in itself uncertain.

In an attempt to minimize their risk, coal producers have relied upon evolutionary growth in mining technology, mainly through trial and error. New developments in equipment such as the mobile loader and the continuous mining machine were undertaken largely by equipment manufacturers, not coal producers. Successful new developments that proved themselves through test and performance demonstrations were slowly adopted by the coal producers and employed in their routine operations through a gradual process that resulted in further trials and errors.

Historically, coal producers have devoted little effort to formal R&D programs.[1] To be sure, the trial-and-error engineering work resulted in advancements in the state of mining technology, but it is not accurate to describe such work as R&D. A possible explanation for the coal producer's limited involvement in R&D is that such activities represented a compounding of uncertainties and an introduction of a completely avoidable risk.

Under normal circumstances of moderate coal demand such risks would remain beyond the calculus of coal producers who were, logically, preoccupied with the array of problems and natural uncertainties associated with "winning" coal from deposits that nature created.[2] However, the situation is completely changed under extraordinary circumstances where society in general and coal consumers in particular are preoccupied with achieving and maintaining a secure domestic supply of coal to meet present or projected energy requirements. Under such conditions of strong societal demand for coal supplies, a willingness may be needed on the part of producers, consumers, and the public which they serve to perform R&D leading to greater assurance of coal supply or realization of moderation of costs for this fuel. The guidance of coal producers would be sought in formulating such public R&D programs to make them most relevant to actual coal production problems.[3] The coal producers, who are quite knowledgeable about the technical prob-

[1] See *Coal Age,* p. 78, May 1964.

[2] It is important to recognize that, in many circumstances, coal production was described as *winning.* Indeed, this term persists today. The U.S. Bureau of Mines, "Dictionary on Mining, Mineral and Related Terms," p. 1240, 1968, defines *winning* as "the excavation, loading, and removal of coal or ore from the ground." It reflects the struggle of the coal producers against the imperfectly understood processes of nature that created the deposits which they labored to exploit.

[3] See, for example, S. W. Gouse, and E. S. Rubin, "A Program of Research, Development and Demonstration for Enhancing Coal Utilization to Meet National Energy Needs," Report of the CMU/NSF-RANN Workshop on Advanced Coal Technology, Carnegie-Mellon University, Pittsburgh, Pa., October, 1973.

lems they face, are principal sources of information about the R&D needs of their industry, and their expertise is essential to formulation of a rational program. Moreover, as taxpayers, they are also entitled to such benefits as may derive from efforts in R&D on coal production as may be carried out with the support of public funds. In effect, the coal producers have transferred the risk of unsuccessful R&D to other bodies and have retained the right of choice regarding the operational application of such successes as may be realized from R&D efforts. For the coal producer, therefore, the present situation where sizable public expenditures for coal extraction R&D are anticipated[1] presents a number of difficult choices.

The nature of the coal industry is such that adoption of new technologies must be carried out with great care and over an extended period of time to avoid severe economic and structural dislocations. Large coal mines have been increasingly developed in recent years, and constitute more than half of total production today. Every indication is that large mines will represent an even larger share of total production in the future. These mines are established only under long-term contracts that cover supplies to particular consumers for 20 to 30 years. Thus coal producers have entered into investments in available, existing coal extraction technologies for existing and new mines which they have firm plans for employing at least for the period of their contracts, i.e., throughout the remainder of the present century. To responsibly meet their obligations under established contractual agreements, the producers probably have no other choice but to rely upon available technology. In a real sense, therefore, a breakthrough in R&D could render existing (or worse, planned) operations economically obsolete, thereby jeopardizing substantial investments in time and money as well as continued production to supply consumer needs.

In short, the coal industry's structure and practice appears to limit its ability to implement technological change, unless the new technology is available at the inception of a given operation. Although it is possible to estimate schedules for performance of R&D,[2] it is probably unrealistic to attempt to plan on successful results of such work at any particular time. As a result, the coal industry is forced to rely on existing technology (or incremental optimization changes to that technology) in planning for future operations. The consequence of this situation is to limit the flexibility of the coal producers to benefit from technological change. The extent and manner to which the industry's freedom of action in this regard is restricted should be assessed in comparison to other industries; it would appear that the coal industry is somewhat unique in respect to its implementation of new technologies than are other industries.

Coal consumers, moreover, are faced with an equally difficult situation. They bear the risk that the R&D expenditures undertaken on their behalf could prove

---

[1] See U.S. Department of Interior Program Plan for Coal Extraction Research and Development.

[2] See, for example, U.S. Environmental Protection Agency, R&D Energy Task Force Program, Standard Timelines, manuscript, 1974. It is probably unrealistic to plan as did EPA, for "major decisions on total coal production increases" in mid-1980. Those decisions have probably already been made. The only question to be decided is the timing of such developments and the implications of timing on possible technologies.

imperfectly successful, and despite expenditure of substantial sums, their coal-supply condition may change but little either because of failure in the R&D itself or in the limited application of the R&D results by the coal-producing organizations and supporting industries. Successful efforts will be realized only through understanding of all aspects of coal development and use.

Index